D0907413

The Foundations of Ethnic Politics

Despite implicating ethnicity in everything from civil war to economic failure, researchers seldom consult psychological research when addressing the most basic question: What is ethnicity? The result is a radical scholarly divide generating contradictory recommendations for solving ethnic conflict. Research into how the human brain actually works demands a revision of existing schools of thought. At its foundation, ethnic identity is a cognitive uncertainty-reduction device with special capacity to exacerbate, but not cause, collective action problems. This insight leads to a new general theory of ethnic conflict and nationalism that can improve both understanding and practice. Supporting this claim is a wide-ranging discussion of patterns in secessionism, international integration, state collapse, race relations, and deadly ethnic violence found across the globe. Special attention is paid to an in-depth case study of national separatism in Eurasia, which produces a major reinterpretation of nationalism's role in the USSR's breakup and interstate relations in the Commonwealth of Independent States.

Henry E. Hale (Ph.D. Harvard 1998) is Assistant Professor of Political Science and International Affairs at George Washington University. His work on ethnic politics, regional integration, democratization, and federalism has appeared in numerous journals, ranging from *Comparative Political Studies* to *Europe-Asia Studies* to *Orbis*. His first book, *Why Not Parties in Russia? Democracy, Federalism, and the State* (Cambridge University Press, 2006), received the Leon D. Epstein Outstanding Book Award from the Political Organizations and Parties section of the American Political Science Association (APSA). His "Divided We Stand: Institutional Sources of Ethnofederal State Survival and Collapse" (*World Politics*, 2004) won the APSA Qualitative Methods section's Alexander L. George Award. The National Science Foundation, the Carnegie Corporation of New York, and the National Council for Eurasian and East European Research have funded his research. He has also been the recipient of a Fulbright research scholarship, a postdoctoral fellowship at Harvard's Davis Center for Russian and Eurasian Studies, and a Peace Scholarship from the U.S. Institute of Peace.

Cambridge Studies in Comparative Politics

General Editor
Margaret Levi *University of Washington, Seattle*

Assistant General Editor
Stephen Hanson *University of Washington, Seattle*

Associate Editors
Robert H. Bates *Harvard University*
Torben Iversen *Harvard University*
Stathis Kalyvas *Yale University*
Peter Lange *Duke University*
Helen Milner *Princeton University*
Frances Rosenbluth *Yale University*
Susan Stokes *Yale University*
Sidney Tarrow *Cornell University*
Kathleen Thelen *Northwestern University*
Erik Wibbels *Duke University*

Other Books in the Series

Lisa Baldez, *Why Women Protest: Women's Movements in Chile*
Stefano Bartolini, *The Political Mobilization of the European Left, 1860–1980: The Class Cleavage*
Robert H. Bates, *When Things Fell Apart: State Failure in Late-Century Africa*
Mark Beissinger, *Nationalist Mobilization and the Collapse of the Soviet State*
Nancy Bermeo, ed., *Unemployment in the New Europe*
Carles Boix, *Democracy and Redistribution*
Carles Boix, *Political Parties, Growth, and Equality: Conservative and Social Democratic Economic Strategies in the World Economy*
Catherine Boone, *Merchant Capital and the Roots of State Power in Senegal, 1930–1985*
Catherine Boone, *Political Topographies of the African State: Territorial Authority and Institutional Change*
Michael Bratton and Nicolas van de Walle, *Democratic Experiments in Africa: Regime Transitions in Comparative Perspective*
Michael Bratton, Robert Mattes, and E. Gyimah-Boadi, *Public Opinion, Democracy, and Market Reform in Africa*
Valerie Bunce, *Leaving Socialism and Leaving the State: The End of Yugoslavia, the Soviet Union, and Czechoslovakia*

Continued after the index

The Foundations of Ethnic Politics

SEPARATISM OF STATES AND
NATIONS IN EURASIA
AND THE WORLD

HENRY E. HALE
George Washington University

CAMBRIDGE
UNIVERSITY PRESS

CAMBRIDGE UNIVERSITY PRESS
Cambridge, New York, Melbourne, Madrid, Cape Town, Singapore, São Paulo, Delhi

Cambridge University Press
32 Avenue of the Americas, New York, NY 10013-2473, USA

www.cambridge.org
Information on this title: www.cambridge.org/9780521719209

First published 2008

Printed in the United States of America

A catalog record for this publication is available from the British Library.

Library of Congress Cataloging in Publication Data

Hale, Henry E., 1966–
   The foundations of ethnic politics : separatism of states and nations in Eurasia and the world /
Henry E. Hale.
   p.   cm. – (Cambridge studies in comparative politics)
Includes bibliographical references and index.
ISBN 978-0-521-89494-4 (hardback) – ISBN 978-0-521-71920-9 (pbk.)
1. Ethnic relations – Political aspects.   2. Ethnicity – Political aspects.   3. Ethnic violence.
I. Title.   II. Series.
GN496.H33   2008
305.8–dc22   2007044190

ISBN   978-0-521-89494-4 hardback
ISBN   978-0-521-71920-9 paperback

Contents

Acknowledgments

In conducting research and writing this book, I have benefited enormously from the generous support of others, support that came in the form of funding provided, time spent, ideas contributed, encouragement proffered, or all of this combined. Among institutions, I must begin with Harvard's Government Department, where the core of this project was born and subjected to the tough love of my dissertation committee, which included Timothy Colton (my chair, to whom I owe an unparalleled debt), Robert Bates, and Celeste Wallander. Deserving of special mention is Mark Saroyan, who as a junior professor at Harvard guided me through my first forays into theories of ethnic politics before he passed away far too young. His influence on my thinking (whether or not he would have ultimately agreed with it!) has been enormous. Even before this, though, it was Harvard's Lubomyr Hajda who encouraged me to study Soviet nationalities while earning my AM in what was during 1988–90 called the "Regional Studies: Soviet Union" program. Thanks to him, I began studying Turkic languages, ultimately settling on Uzbek. Colton, Jerry Hough, Jeffrey Hahn, and Blair Ruble also provided me with the invaluable opportunity to conduct fieldwork during 1992–4 while serving as the graduate student representative in the former Soviet Union for their project on transitional legislatures. These days, for a graduate student living in Moscow, a monthly stipend of $100 per month would sound like a cruel joke. But in the early postcommunist period, that was more than enough to conduct fieldwork and even eat out once in a while.

I am grateful to numerous other institutions and their leaderships for providing me with financial support for various aspects of this general research project, including The United States Institute of Peace (for a Peace Scholarship); Harvard's Government Department (for a Mellon Dissertation Completion Fellowship); Harvard's Davis Center for Russian and Eurasian Studies (for a postdoctoral fellowship); the Harvard Ukrainian Research Institute (for a fellowship in Ukrainian studies); Harvard's Center for International Affairs (for office space and a lively intellectual environment); George Washington University's Department of Political Science, Elliott School of International Affairs, Institute for Global and International Studies, and Institute for European, Russian, and Eurasian Studies (for research assistance, research funding, and a conference on my book manuscript); Indiana University's Department of Political Science and Russian and East European Institute (for employment and research funding); Columbia University's Harriman Institute (for visiting scholar status during two summers spent in New York); and others that provided me with various opportunities to gain feedback on my ideas.

As for individuals, along with those already mentioned, I am especially grateful to those who read entire drafts of various book-length products that materialized at different stages of this project, including Eric McGlinchey and participants in a "book incubator" conference organized by Deborah Avant and Hope Harrison at George Washington University, where readers were Muriel Atkin, Zsuzsa Csergo, James Goldgeier, Michael Hechter, Gina Lambright, and Celeste Wallander. Others who devoted time to providing helpful feedback on ideas that went into this project or other forms of intellectual assistance include, but are not limited to, Josephine Andrews, Ken Benoit, Paul Brass, Jerome Chertkoff, Stephen Hanson, Joel Hellman, Michael Hiscox, Debra Javeline, Stathis Kalyvas, Steven Kelts, Mark Kramer, David Laitin, Eric Lawrence, Pauline Jones Luong, Kimberly Morgan, Mark Nagel, Brad Palmquist, David Park, Daniel Posner, Jane Prokop, Robert Putnam, Sarah Queller, Anya Peterson Royce, John Sides, Curt Signorino, Naunihol Singh, Emmanuel Teitelbaum, Daniel Treisman, Erik Voeten, Steve Voss, Steven Wilkinson, Robert Young, and participants in various seminars or talks where some of these ideas or their predecessors were discussed, including especially members of the Post-Communist Politics Seminar at Harvard's Davis Center and of the Program on New Approaches to Russian Security, based first at Harvard and later at the Center for Strategic and International Studies. I am also indebted to far more people than I can mention here, including in the United States and abroad, for assistance with the logistics of my research, but I acknowledge them in general terms here. The research assistance of Jake Berg and Sergiu Manic on parts of this project was also much appreciated.

I owe an immense debt of gratitude to Lewis Bateman and Margaret Levi at Cambridge University Press, as well as to their able team, for guiding this manuscript to publication and helping me improve its quality along the way. I am also thankful for the input of all of the anonymous reviewers of the manuscript or of those parts of it that were sent to journals earlier.

Naturally, when one works on a manuscript for as long as I have on this one, those closest to the author are essential to its production and quality. Here I first and foremost have in mind my wife, Isabelle Kaplan, who not only helped me develop and "weed out" my ideas through discussions that are too many to count, but kept me focused on the more important aspects of life while still helping me find time to do the vast amount of work I needed to do to see this project through to fruition. My parents and grandparents, too, played a major part in this production, especially in supporting me through the lean years of graduate school when the research project was just getting off the ground.

Of course, the views expressed in this book are those solely of the author and do not necessarily reflect the views of the Institute of Peace or any other source of funding or support for the book.

I am also grateful to the following publishers, thanks to whom parts of three of my previously published articles are reprinted with permission in this book:

- *Comparative Politics*, for: Henry E. Hale, "The Double-Edged Sword of Ethnofederalism: Ukraine and the USSR in Comparative Perspective," *Comparative Politics*, v.40, no.3, April 2008, pp. 293–312.
- Sage Publications, for: Henry E. Hale, "Explaining Ethnicity," *Comparative Political Studies*, v.37, no.4, May 2004, pp. 458–85.
- Cambridge University Press, for: Henry E. Hale, "The Parade of Sovereignties: Testing Theories of Secession in the Soviet Setting," *British Journal of Political Science*, v.30, no.1, January 2000, pp. 31–56.

Note on Transliteration

Russian, Ukrainian, and Uzbek language material is transliterated here using the Library of Congress system with the following exceptions:

General exceptions:

- Y is used at the beginning of soft vowels (ya, ye, yu) that are the first letters in words
- Soft signs are omitted at the end of proper names of people, places, companies (e.g., Perm not Perm')
- Common spellings are employed for words or names that widely appear in English-language media (e.g., Chechnya not Chechnia)

Exceptions made for people's names:

- Soft signs are omitted from people's names (e.g., Yeltsin not Yel'tsin) except where used by a person him- or herself in Western publications (e.g., Marat Gelman but Vladimir Gel'man)
- The letter y is used at the end of names that would otherwise end in ii or iy
- The letters ie are substituted for 'e (e.g., Glaziev not Glaz'ev or Glazev)

I

Introduction

Next to almost every "ethnic hotspot" is another "ethnic spot" that remains conspicuously cool. While Ukrainians and the Baltic republics mobilized in 1991 for independence from the USSR, the Central Asian republics remained bastions of unionism. When Hindu–Muslim riots exploded in the Indian state of Gujarat in 2002, intercommunal peace was the norm in next-door Maharashtra. As Nigeria's Igbo and Hausa-Fulani regions became embroiled in the 1967–70 Biafran civil war, the adjacent Yoruba territory remained relatively calm. And in the international arena, Norway stubbornly kept its distance from the European Union as its neighbor Sweden joined the integrative project in 1995. Even within the hotspots themselves, the heat is not uniform. Some Iraqi villages descend into interconfessional strife while others are more successful at escaping it, and some individuals in Chechnya back independence from Russia while others oppose it. Nor is there consistency over time. The supposedly "age-old enemies" of Yugoslavia, Serbia, and Croatia have been at peace far more often than at war and the same is true with the Hutu and the Tutsi, the groups involved in the tragic Rwandan genocide. Variation such as this constitutes the great puzzle of ethnic politics.

All agree that uncovering the source of such variation is important. The worst ethnic conflicts have killed hundreds of thousands at a time, as has been the case in Yugoslavia, Rwanda, and Nigeria in the last half century. Large numbers have also perished in ethnically charged international conflicts, including World War II and the current "war on terror." Ethnicity is also widely held capable of bringing down states, with the USSR – one of the two great superpowers that structured the whole of international relations for much of the last century – being a particularly prominent victim.[1] Still others see ethnic conflict as a fundamental obstacle to democracy, perhaps the greatest political achievement of

---

[1] For example, Mark R. Beissinger, *Nationalist Mobilization and the Collapse of the Soviet State* (New York: Cambridge University Press, 2002).

humankind.[2] Ethnic politics is also frequently blamed for corruption and a whole host of economic ills, including what two leading economists call "Africa's growth tragedy."[3]

The sharpest disagreement comes over how to explain these puzzles. And this disagreement is fundamental. Some see ethnicity itself as the problem, understanding it as a realm inherently conducive to conflict that cannot be stopped, only contained. Others see ethnicity as entirely epiphenomenal, as a mere "spin" that politicians put on events so as to mask their true motives, usually alleged to be greed or political ambition. Each approach, like the variety of theories that fall between the extremes, contributes certain useful insights. But as will be shown, each also leaves a great deal unexplained.

The present volume seeks to put theories of ethnic politics on firmer theoretical ground by starting at the ground level, developing a theory of identity and ethnicity that is based solidly on research in human psychology. It is striking how few existing works – be they in political science, sociology, history, anthropology, or economics – actually engage the psychological literature, even as some of them make reference to the "psychology" of ethnicity. The few to engage such research have made significant strides, but the following pages will argue that many of them rely too heavily on one particular psychological theory that newer research has partially discredited. The difference is crucial: Where works citing the older psychological theory tend to conclude ethnicity is inherently fraught with conflictual tendencies, the present study contends that "ethnicity" does not produce any behavioral motivation at all, be it conflictual or cooperative. Does this study then agree with those treating ethnicity as entirely epiphenomenal or irrelevant? Not at all. Ethnicity represents a kind of crucial "first step" that people must take before engaging in any sort of action: It is one means of making sense of an impossibly complex social world so that they can then successfully navigate it. Thus, although ethnicity provides no motivation for behavior, it is a powerful determinant of the strategies that people use to pursue the things that do motivate them, including wealth, power, security, self-esteem, status, or, more generally, what are called here "life chances." This perspective, when properly developed, displays surprising capacity to explain not only why ethnic politics is often associated with the pursuit of material ends, but why it is frequently fraught with emotion and passion. And it does so in a way that facilitates theory building, paving the way for more rapid advances in our understanding of ethnic politics.

At the most general level, then, this volume makes two fundamental claims. First, it contends that theories of ethnic politics must be better grounded, more solidly rooted in an understanding of *what* ethnicity actually is and *why* it is what

[2] For example, Donald L. Horowitz, "Democracy In Divided Societies," *Journal of Democracy*, v.4, no.4, October 1993, pp. 18–37; John Stuart Mill, *Considerations on Representative Government* (1861), Chapter 16, "Of Nationality as Connected with Representative Government," *http://www.la.utexas.edu/research/poltheory/mill/repgov/repgov.c16.html*.

[3] William Easterly and Ross Levine, "Africa's Growth Tragedy: Policies and Ethnic Divisions," *Quarterly Journal of Economics*, v.112, no.4, November 1997, pp. 1203–50.

it is. Scholars have certainly made advances without such a theory by simply assuming ethnicity is one thing or other. But the social sciences will surely make more, faster progress by coming to agreement on a sounder set of assumptions.

Second, this volume argues that *ethnicity* is primarily about uncertainty reduction while *ethnic politics* is primarily about interests. Ethnicity is a result of humans' cognitive drive to reduce the uncertainty they face in the world, whereas what people do with their less uncertain worlds depends on their particular interests. The most fundamental human interest, it is argued, is the maximization of life chances, from which flow the instrumental pursuits of wealth, security, and power as well as seemingly irrational desires for status and self-esteem. Explanations of ethnic politics, then, must divorce ethnicity from the realm of motives (desires, preferences, values) at the same time that they introduce it into the realm of strategy, the choice of actions designed to maximize life chances through interaction with the social world. Consistent application of these principles, which might be called a *relational* approach to ethnicity, tends to produce more fecund theory that is better at explaining why ethnic conflict and other patterns of ethnic behavior occur in some instances but not others.

All this is demonstrated through "case comparisons within a case study." This book's most fundamental arguments concern ethnic politics in general; however, it would clearly be impossible to provide a convincing comprehensive test of such a broad theory in a single volume. The utility of the relational approach is thus illustrated by training attention on one particular type of ethnic politics, the case of *national separatism*. National separatism is important because it is widely held to be the culmination of national development, the peak manifestation of nationalism, reflecting a nation's collective desire to establish or protect its own state in the international arena, one that is equal or superior in status to all other states. It has inspired myriad politicians to extol its virtues and authors to expose its vices. Many hold it among the most important driving forces of the last two centuries of human history, motivating revolutions in 1848 and laying international integration efforts low in the twenty-first century.

A note on terminology helps specify what exactly is in focus here. This volume follows Hechter in defining "nationalism" as "collective action designed to render the boundaries of the nation congruent with those of its governance unit." A "nation," in turn, is an ethnic group associated with a particular territory.[4] "National separatism" is thus a form of nationalism whereby congruence is promoted or defended through one of two means: (1) splitting a smaller territorial governance unit off from a larger one or (2) opposing the integration of one territorial governance unit into a broader one. That is, "national separatism" includes both an ethnic region's secessionism and a nation-state's opposition to joining an international integration project. "Separatism" pure and simple need not involve distinct nations, but for convenience's sake the present volume assumes ethnic

---

[4] Michael Hechter, *Containing Nationalism* (New York: Oxford University Press, 2000), pp. 7–14. A governance unit, as Hechter defines it, is not necessarily an independent country but can also be an autonomous region formally recognized to be within a larger state.

content when using the shorter terms "secessionism" and "separatism" unless explicitly stated otherwise. The term "ethnic group" requires more discussion and will be defined precisely only in Chapter 3. For now, however, it can be understood to refer simply to any culturally distinct group. All this underpins the following claim: If we can show that a new theory sheds light even on such a thoroughly researched and crucially important "case" as national separatism, we can establish cause for that theory to be considered in other realms of ethnic politics as well.

Because separatism is itself a broad topic, having global scope, it is useful to engage in a set of case comparisons within this study of the case of separatism. That is, this volume focuses in particular on patterns of separatism in a single part of the world so as to make a maximally concrete argument for the usefulness of the theory. This part of the world is "Eurasia," a term understood here as corresponding to the territory of the former USSR. This region constitutes an excellent source of case comparisons for several reasons. Perhaps most obviously, it is substantively important, covering nearly one-sixth of the world's land mass, containing thousands of nuclear warheads, and boasting some of the world's largest hydrocarbon reserves. And indeed it was here that national separatism is said by many leading scholars to have had its historically greatest impact, bringing down the seemingly invincible superpower that was the Soviet Union. Given how extensively this topic has been researched, it will be a particularly impressive feat for a theory to generate new insight here.

For the social scientist, however, another feature of Eurasia is even more important: Its range of ethnic groups and its history make it an unusually useful "natural laboratory" in which different causal theories can be ruled out or supported through both interpretive and quantitative comparative analysis. In particular, the USSR by 1991 contained fifty-three ethnically defined regions, more than any other ethnofederation. Since these regions varied significantly and visibly in manifesting separatist attitudes, and since all kinds of data are available on factors potentially related to separatism, it is probably safe to claim that no single country could provide more leverage in weighing competing theories of official regional separatism than could the former USSR. Moreover, it has been possible to visit and conduct research in Eurasia, interviewing key decision makers, surveying public opinion, gathering important documents, reading influential publications, and obtaining the vast array of relevant data that are available. This study seeks to take advantage of these opportunities, employing everything from regression analysis to deep, on-the-ground qualitative interpretation involving original materials in three local languages (Russian, Ukrainian, and some Uzbek) and close to a total of two years spent in Eurasia between 1992 and 2007.

While as many as forty-five of the USSR's ethnic regions are considered in the statistical analyses and many of these are discussed in the qualitative study, it proves useful to focus in special depth on two ethnic regions that pose a particularly stark puzzle: Ukraine and Uzbekistan. These cases are puzzling because leading experts writing before 1990 had argued the greater challenge to Soviet rule would come from the Uzbeks, not the Ukrainians. Indeed, Uzbeks possessed many attributes that existing theory often argues promote secession: They were among the poorest groups in the union, were growing rapidly in population, faced discrimination in other parts of the union, displayed reluctance to move away from their region, and were culturally very distant from Russians due to their Islamic tradition and Turkic tongue. The Ukrainians, on the other hand, spoke a language highly similar to Russian, had more upward mobility in the union, and were among occupied one of the more-developed regions in the country. But by the end of 1991, it was clear that the older predictions had it backwards: Ukraine's secession dealt the death blow to the USSR, while Uzbekistan consistently pushed for the union to be preserved.

At this point it is crucial to note what this book is and is not about. It is not primarily a book about the Soviet Union's demise. Nor is it mainly about Ukraine and Uzbekistan. Instead, it is a book making two larger theoretical points germane to the study of ethnic politics more generally: first, that we need to put theories of ethnic politics on firmer ground; and second, that a starting point can be the proposition that ethnicity is about uncertainty reduction, while ethnic politics is about interests. These are the core elements of the relational theory of ethnicity noted previously. The next two chapters of this book (Chapters 2 and 3) are therefore devoted to making the case for these propositions in general terms, relying on logic and extensive reference to research (especially psychological research) conducted in different parts of the globe. The subsequent chapter (Chapter 4) is also unrestricted geographically, demonstrating how the relational theory of ethnicity can make possible a theory of national separatism that has logical and empirical advantages over existing alternatives. This is the relational theory of separatism. Chapters 2–4 thus constitute Part I of this volume, the part devoted primarily to general theory applicable to multiple areas of the world. The chapters in Part II (Chapters 5–10) weigh various implications of the relational theory of separatism against alternative theories through deep qualitative and quantitative analysis of the Eurasian cases. The conclusion (Chapter 11) returns to the geographically general discussion, considering how the relational theory can help us understand different varieties of ethnic politics (not just separatism) in different parts of the world (not just Eurasia). The case comparisons involving Ukraine and Uzbekistan, therefore, are not meant to document a complete history of either of these republics, and the book does not intend to tell the full story of how the USSR collapsed. Readers interested in such full and complete histories might consult a variety of textbooks and historians' accounts that are now available. The material presented on Ukraine and Uzbekistan here, then, is just that which is needed to clearly establish the relative advantages of the relational theory of separatism in explaining Ukraine's and Uzbekistan's divergent and changing relationships to the union between the time when Gorbachev started liberalizing the USSR and the year 2007.

Despite this firm focus on the larger theory, the larger theory does inform a new and compelling interpretation of a landmark episode in Eurasian history. Thus, there is an important story in this volume. Readers who are interested in this story and less interested in the logic that undergirds it are invited to skim or skip Part I (Chapters 2–4), proceeding straight to the empirical discussion of Part II (especially Chapters 5–9). These latter chapters have been written in such a way that they should be comprehensible on their own and interesting for their substantive content as well as their value in testing the relational theory. They are not, however, written chronologically. Instead, they are structured much like an onion is, with each chapter peeling off one layer as a necessary step for advancing to a deeper part of the argument. This structure was chosen to maximize the chapters' value for demonstrating the power of this book's theory while still providing an interpretation of Eurasian separatism that is interesting in its own right.

This new interpretation greatly illuminates the role of ethnicity in Ukraine's secession, the union's collapse, Uzbekistan's struggles to manage autonomy, and the troubled development of the Commonwealth of Independent States (CIS), the international organization that formally supplanted the USSR. For one thing, we find that the driving force behind Soviet-era separatism, the motivation behind the separatist activity that was so visible between 1988 and 1991, was not really "ethnic" or "national" at all. Soviet republics sought autonomy not as an expression of national identity but as a way to escape a collective action problem in the union, a fear that the union government would one day use its power to a given republic's detriment rather than to its benefit. In fact, it is argued that the top preference of republic masses (including Ukrainian ones) was consistently for a cooperative *union*, not for national independence. The problem was whether any union was actually likely to *be* cooperative rather than exploitative. At the same time, ethnicity was far from irrelevant: Consciousness of a significant ethnic divide between a republic and the union made republic representatives more likely to see significant dangers of exploitation in the union since it lent a sense of separation from control over events in the union and, at times, called attention to historical precedents for these dangers. Ethnicity thus did not provide a motive for secessionism, but it accentuated the collective action problem that did provide this motive. Ethnicity did not provide the values that people sought through secession, but it did influence what strategies they thought would best give them what they valued. This part of the story starts to emerge in Chapter 5.

Accordingly, the final years of the USSR were not a period of steadily growing separatism, not a period where increasingly nationally conscious groups took greater and greater advantage of Soviet decay to fight for the independence they supposedly sought. Instead, they were a period of give-and-take between the union and republic governments, a time when Soviet leader Mikhail Gorbachev pragmatically shifted strategies multiple times in an effort to convince republic leaders and masses that secessionist strategies were not to their advantage, that a reformed union was not likely to be exploitative. Indeed, we find strong evidence that Gorbachev very nearly succeeded. By launching a qualitatively new approach, an approach whose value is revealed by relational theory, he had successfully turned back the tide, reversing the trend of growing separatism in key republics like Ukraine and Uzbekistan. Indeed, because Ukraine's secession more than anything else prompted Russia to give up on the Soviet Union and seal its demise, we can even conjecture that the union most likely would have been saved (with only minimal losses) had an avoidable series of events not taken place in the form of the August 1991 coup attempt, which undermined Gorbachev's new approach. This part of the story is found in Chapter 6.

The theory also reveals how there was at least some potential to have saved the union even after the August putsch. Even though some 90 percent of Ukrainian citizens voted for secession and ratified their national independence in a December 1991 referendum, relational theory helps us see how a majority vote could *also* have supported saving the union had this been proposed to them ("framed") in the right way, a way addressing their ethnically charged strategic concerns – even during the fateful fall of 1991. In short, the union-breaking outcome of Ukrainian secession could have been flipped had republic leaders adopted a different way of framing the choices people had for solving the collective action problem at the heart of the union. All this is shown in Chapter 7.

But the story is not quite so simple as to boil down to leaders' manipulation of voting behavior. The analysis also suggests that the unionist outcome in Uzbekistan could have been reversed as well, that Uzbeks could have been led to support independence as well as integration. This raises the key question of exactly why it was that the Uzbek and Ukrainian leaders adopted different framing strategies. The answer, it is argued, returns us to the second core argument of this volume. If ethnicity is about uncertainty reduction, then ethnic politics is about *interests*. And material interests turn out to be crucial here. Leaders in both Ukraine and Uzbekistan, it is shown, had reason to be responsive to their populations' economic interests in the union. Moreover, their own personal material interests actually coincided with these mass interests in the most general sense. And these mass material interests depended crucially on levels of development: The more-developed Ukraine had less to gain from the union than the less-developed Uzbekistan. Thus, as the dangers of exploitation in the union rose, Ukraine was the first to "abandon ship," with both masses and leaders seeing their own material prospects as better outside the union than inside. Overall, then, ethnicity provided a crucial lens through which people assessed the dangers in the Soviet Union and the credibility of Gorbachev's various promises, influencing the calculations of material interest that played the major role in determining whether a given republic opted out. Chapter 8 makes this argument.

We strikingly find these same forces driving Eurasian states' policies regarding reintegration in the CIS straight through 2007. Those successor states with the least ethnic material distinguishing them from control of the former union (Russia and Belarus) remained the two leading unionists, and the least developed among the other republics (such as Uzbekistan and Kyrgyzstan) have also showed remarkable consistency in backing more integrationist measures despite some fluctuation. Ukraine, more economically developed than Uzbekistan, has charted a consistently more separatist course despite being led by a reputedly "pro-Russian" president for the decade of 1994–2004. This case is made in Chapter 9, which also considers the other new Eurasian states. Chapter 10 confirms the relational theory against its rivals through a rigorous quantitative analysis of patterns in actual republic behavior and public opinion in as many as twelve non-Russian republics in the Gorbachev era.

In terms of the big picture of separatism and the Soviet breakup, perhaps the most striking revelation of this volume's relational theory is just how contingent the whole process was. There was no inexorable ethnically inspired separatist march, either causing or responding to the weakening of the Soviet state. Ethnic groups were not trapped by their histories, seeking desperately and consistently to get out if they had suffered grievous wrongs in the union in the past. Nor did Soviet institutions doom the state to collapse by leading avaricious elites, under the cover of national slogans, to eat away at it from within. Instead, there were multiple moments where different outcomes were possible. Ukrainian separatism had been rising in 1990 and early 1991, but it had also been halted by mid-1991. The coup undermined Gorbachev's strategy, but surely this coup could have been averted or carried out differently. Ukrainians voted for independence, but they might also have supported unionist alternatives to the status quo had these alternatives been proposed to them instead. Ukraine's president framed his compatriots' options in a secession-inducing way, but his choice may have been entirely different had Ukraine shared Uzbekistan's lower levels of development. The proper way to understand such contingency is not to write ethnicity off as being irrelevant or epiphenomenal, but to better understand how it accentuates the kind of collective action problems that in fact set this whole process in motion. Indeed, had the USSR involved no significant ethnic distinctions among republics, the union probably still would have been reformed and decentralized, but it probably also would still exist.

In the most general terms, the Eurasian case comparisons within the case study of separatism serve the crucial purpose of demonstrating the power of the broader relational approach to ethnic politics. They show how a theory that is based on sound microlevel theory, on propositions consistent with psychological research on human behavior, can generate a story that makes new and better overall sense of very important manifestations of ethnic politics. We learn more about what ethnicity is and how it is likely to be involved in politics. And we also gain some hope for new understandings of what had previously been seen as intractable conflicts. Indeed, if ethnicity is not primarily a set of inherently conflictual values or motives, then it would seem possible to avoid or minimize ethnically charged conflict. At the same time, we risk making conflicts worse if we base solutions on the notion that ethnicity is irrelevant or epiphenomenal. Instead, ethnicity is relational. Thus, even though solutions to ethnic conflicts must not treat ethnicity as a motive, they should address the reasons why people tend to interpret particular situations with reference to ethnic divides. If this sort of ethnic interpretation can be obviated, we might find that we can reduce the intensity of or propensity for conflict. If ethnic interpretations cannot be obviated in a given situation, then the best solutions are likely to be those that accommodate ethnic difference.

This brings us back to this volume's two core propositions. We do need a theory of ethnicity grounded solidly in psychological research on human behavior. And the relational theory advances us in that direction: Ethnicity is driven by uncertainty reduction, while ethnic politics is driven by interests.

PART I

THEORY WITH WORLDWIDE EXAMPLES

2

The Need for a Microfoundational
Theory of Ethnicity

The first core argument of this book is: If we are ever to come to agreement on the sources of ethnic politics and the solutions to its ills, we must come to agreement on the nature of ethnicity itself. Some may question whether this is true.[1] Surely the discipline of physics has generated enormous insights even though its two most powerful theories, relativity and quantum mechanics, are not based on or derivable from each other. In this light, some rational choice theorists would argue all that matters is finding working assumptions that, when plugged into theory, regularly produce outcomes that correspond to observed events regardless of whether they actually reflect true motivations.[2] Although this is a reasonable pragmatic approach for periods when agreement on fundamentals is lacking, this does not mean it will not be fruitful to strive for a better understanding of the basic principles of ethnicity. Surely physics made numerous advances thanks to the theory of relativity even though significant progress had still been made on the basis of the older Newtonian physics. And just as surely, a "grand unification theory" of physics is widely sought because of expectations that it will generate new, sounder insights.

The fact that ethnicity falls into the realm of the social sciences rather than the natural sciences is not grounds for abandoning the quest for a fundamental theory of ethnicity. The social sciences, of course, are not "hard" sciences largely because human beings have so much room for choice, because the choices they make can involve so many different variables, and because social behavior is fundamentally strategic in that what one person decides to do frequently depends upon what other people are expected to do.[3] This does not mean general claims about human behavior are impossible. What it does mean, though, is that social science theory

---

[1] See Chaim Kaufman, "Possible and Impossible Solutions to Ethnic Wars," *International Security*, v.20, no.4, spring 1996, pp. 136–75.

[2] For example, Alvin Rabushka and Kenneth Shepsle, *Politics in Plural Societies* (Columbus: Merrill, 1972).

[3] Gabriel A. Almond and Stephen J. Genco, "Clocks, Clouds, and the Study of Politics," *World Politics*, v.29, no.4, July 1977, pp. 489–522.

is necessarily probabilistic. The best we can hope for is to develop theory that correctly anticipates or explains behavior more often than not, that identifies a core logic that usually holds true but that may nonetheless be overwhelmed by the complex array of other factors in any particular situation. Sometimes generalizations can be quite strong: For example, all other things equal, most people would prefer to have $100 than to have $1. This sort of insight forms the basis for both economic theory and business planning. The point is not that materialism should be the basis for a theory of ethnicity, but that meaningful generalizations about social behavior are possible and that theory (albeit probabilistic theory) will benefit by being based on more accurate and more generalizable assumptions regarding human behavior.

What we want, then, is an answer to what might be dubbed the fundamental question of ethnicity: *Why and when do individuals think and act in terms of macrolevel categories, particularly in terms of ethnic groups and nations?* Unfortunately, very few scholars studying ethnic politics today have devoted much attention to this question in their publications. The vast bulk of work on ethnic politics either simply assumes an answer or implies one without actually stating it. Some studies do not even go this far, leaving scholars to wonder just what is being described. The discipline that has most extensively and systematically explored microlevel human motivations and behavior is psychology, so it makes sense that the most fecund theories in the long run are likely to be those that are consistent with broad findings in this field. Yet psychologists themselves hardly ever generalize their results to explain patterns of ethnic politics, and other social scientists only rarely cite pertinent psychological research. This failure to adequately justify or sometimes even specify what is often the most fundamental element of one's theory has some very negative consequences for scholarship. Not only can it hinder theory verification, but it often obscures the real sources of theoretical divergence and thus leaves them unaddressed.

This would not be a big problem if scholars essentially agreed on the fundamentals and if this agreement was generally in line with what psychological research has to tell us, yet neither of these conditions holds. Perhaps most alarmingly, the most influential current theories of ethnic politics imply radically different answers to the question of why individuals might think and act in terms of ethnicity. One side claims that ethnic identification and behavior are driven by conflictual motives that are inherent to ethnicity itself. The other side asserts that ethnicity is essentially epiphenomenal, that ethnic identification and behavior are driven almost entirely by other motives, such as the desire for material gain, security, and power. Moreover, these differences on the fundamentals generate profoundly different explanations for everything from ethnic wars to national separatism to ethnic voting. And by implication, they also produce entirely different proposals as to how "ethnic conflict" might best be resolved or prevented. It also does not appear to be the case that one side has the correct answer, and the other does not. Significant problems surround the foundational assumptions of most existing works on ethnic politics that posit any. This is not to dismiss these works as useless or bad: Many are absolutely brilliant in explaining the particular types of ethnic behavior on which their sights are set. The problem often arises only when it comes to generalizability: The core assumptions frequently do not hold up well when applied to other forms of ethnic behavior. In fact, it will be argued that many such theories can essentially be refounded on new assumptions and thereby greatly strengthened: This usually requires some reinterpretation of past findings, but it generally leaves many seminal insights intact. Just as the theory of relativity did not invalidate all previous discoveries in physics, so there is no reason why a new foundational theory of ethnicity must invalidate all works on ethnic politics that came before it. The rest of this chapter identifies the range of existing answers to the fundamental question of ethnicity, making the case that a new one is warranted.

What follows, however, differs from the most common way of characterizing the ethnic politics literature, which is usually presented as a debate between "primordialism" and "constructivism" (versions of which are sometimes also called "circumstantialism" or "instrumentalism").[4] Primordialists, as suggested by the term itself, are widely held to believe that ethnic identities are age-old and enduring. Constructivism, on the other hand, has essentially become a blanket term capturing all other theories, all accounts that do not actually believe that ethnic identities are literally age-old or permanent. As it happens, even those who have applied the term "primordialist" to themselves are actually constructivists by these criteria. One self-avowed primordialist, Van Evera, succinctly puts it: "The constructivist claim that ethnic identities are socially constructed is clearly correct. After all, our social identities are not stamped on our genes, so they must be socially constructed."[5] Chandra defines constructivism more narrowly as the dual belief that people have "multiple, not single, ethnic identities" and that identification can shift.[6] She astutely narrows in on an important divide in the literature, but it is only one of degree: Leading primordialist theorists do write about identity evolution and cultural change and at the same time would likely not deny that people have multiple identity dimensions that are differentially relevant or important in different situations. They merely emphasize the tendencies to group stability and constraints on situational manipulation that are prevalent in many contexts after identities are constructed – but so do many theorists who are universally considered to be leading constructivists, such as Anderson and Gellner.[7] It indeed seems that even primordialists are constructivists. It also seems that this

---

[4] For a slightly different (though related) critique of this characterization, see Henry E. Hale, "Explaining Ethnicity," *Comparative Political Studies*, v.37, no.4, May 2004, pp. 458–85.

[5] Stephen Van Evera, "Primordialism Lives!" *APSA-CP*, v.12, no.1, winter 2001, pp. 20–2.

[6] Kanchan Chandra, "Introduction: Constructivist Findings and Their Non-Incorporation," *APSA-CP*, v.12, no.1, winter 2001, pp. 7–11.

[7] Benedict Anderson, *Imagined Communities*, revised edition (New York: Verso, 1991); Clifford Geertz, "The Integrative Revolution: Primordial Sentiments and Civil Politics in the New States," in Geertz, ed., *Old Societies and New States*, 3rd edition (New York: The Free Press, 1967), pp. 105–28; Ernest Gellner, *Nations and Nationalism* (Ithaca, NY: Cornell University Press, 1983); Edward Shils, "Primordial, Personal, Sacred, and Civil Ties," *British Journal of Sociology*, v.8, June 1957, pp. 130–45.

particular way of categorizing the literature does not really elucidate the most fundamental cleavages in the field, to which we now turn.

One large body of theory is built on the assumption that ethnicity inherently reflects motivations that tend to put groups in conflict. Two important caveats are crucial for understanding this point. First, the key words are "tend to": Few would argue all groups are always in active states of conflict with all other groups. Instead, the core tenet of this set of theories is that ethnicity arises out of motivations that naturally put groups potentially at odds. People may not necessarily be aware of their ethnicity (as with isolated hunter-gatherer tribes) and even when they are aware of it, they may face constraints that suppress or override these conflictual tendencies. Nevertheless, to introduce an ethnic difference between two otherwise identical and entirely peaceful groups is to introduce a tension between them that raises the likelihood of conflict. Second, "conflict" is defined broadly: It can be both violent (as in ethnic riots) and nonviolent (as in competition among ethnic parties in a democracy). While grouping theories under broad labels risks oversimplifying some highly sophisticated works, the pages that follow will refer to such theories as *ethnicity-as-conflictual* theories because this will help make the following discussion more readable despite the somewhat infelicitous terminology. Because ethnicity-as-conflictual theories come in many forms, it is instructive to break them down further into three categories: hard, soft, and ultrasoft.

Hard Ethnicity-as-Conflictual Theories: Relative Values

Two tenets distinguish the "hard" perspective: that ethnic identity is rooted in fundamental human desires for dignity, self-esteem, and/or belonging, and, crucially, that these values are intrinsically *relative*, that they are realized through distinguishing one's own group from that of another. That is, people derive dignity, self-esteem, and/or belonging from being part of an ethnic group that is considered somehow better than another group or set of groups. The key reason why people identify so strongly with ethnic groups – even to the point of being willing to kill or die for their groups – is that they are inherently linked with people's deepest feelings, the things that stir the blood, core needs for dignity, self-esteem, and/or belonging. When one's group is threatened, cheated, or denigrated, one's own self is threatened, cheated, or denigrated. Such theories typically note that people see their own ethnic groups as birth-based and hence, to some degree, an extension of the family, which is the social unit most intimately tied to these core human values.[8] Strongly related to this idea is the general view that group identity itself has intense value for individuals and that

---

[8] These theorists almost all recognize that the belief in "ethnicity as extended kinship" may be empirically false. The key is only that people tend to believe it is true.

threats to one's group identity are seen as threats to the self. Ethnicity thus tends to generate intergroup violence, separatism, nationalist mobilization, ethnic voting, and other forms of divisive behavior, with variation mainly arising when different groups are "balanced" or constrained in some way from asserting or resisting dominance.[9] Many of these theories stress the importance of nonmaterial struggles for ethnic symbols, which are said to evoke highly emotional responses because they either indicate the degree to which their group's identity is under threat or connote groups' relative status and hence become crucial sources of personal dignity and self-esteem.[10]

Several of these hard studies are quite sophisticated, explicitly grounding themselves in research on human psychology at the same time that they seek to explain macrolevel ethnic conflict.[11] Among these, two traditions of psychological research tend to be discussed. The first is the famous work of Erikson, whose writing is cited to claim that individuals have an inherent drive to "find" their own identity and that identity can be a value in and of itself. The second body of psychological work has been even more influential on the field of ethnic politics: the tradition pioneered by Tajfel and commonly known as Social Identity Theory (SIT) or the Bristol school of thought. The core idea, at least as interpreted in hard ethnicity-as-conflictual theories, is that people think and act in terms of groups so that they can then ascribe positive traits to their own group and negative traits to other groups, thereby raising their own self-esteem. The core propositions of this theory might be summarized as follows: People are driven by a fundamental need for self-esteem; people can gain self-esteem through belonging to a group they believe is superior to another group; this sense of superiority can be achieved by denigrating another group as well as by adding value to one's own group; people will opt to maximize their group's advantage over another group even when this means sacrificing material gains for their own group;

---

[9] This category includes not only most self-avowed primordialists but also many who explicitly reject primordialism. Among the former are: Walker Connor, "Beyond Reason: The Nature of the Ethnonational Bond," *Ethnic and Racial Studies*, v.16, no.3, pp. 373–89; Geertz, "The Integrative Revolution"; Harold R. Isaacs, *Idols of the Tribe: Group Identity and Political Change* (New York: Harper & Row, 1975); Shils, "Primordial, Personal"; Rabushka and Shepsle, *Politics in Plural Societies*. Nonprimordialists whose work rests on "hard" assumptions include: Anthony Smith, *Myths and Memories of the Nation* (New York: Oxford University Press, 1999), pp. 57–96; Charles Taylor, "The Politics of Recognition," in Amy Gutmann, ed., *Multiculturalism: Examining the Politics of Recognition* (Princeton, NJ: Princeton University Press, 1994), pp. 25–73; Ashutosh Varshney, "Nationalism, Ethnic Conflict, and Rationality," *Perspectives on Politics*, v.1, no.1, March 2003, pp. 85–99. Some international relations theories appear based on hard ethnicity-as-conflictual assumptions: Samuel P. Huntington, *The Clash of Civilizations and the Remaking of World Order* (New York: Simon & Schuster, 1996); Stephen M. Saideman, *The Ties that Divide: Ethnic Politics, Foreign Policy, and International Conflict* (New York: Columbia University Press, 2000).
[10] Donald L. Horowitz, *Ethnic Groups in Conflict* (Berkeley: University of California Press, 1985); Stuart J. Kaufman, *Modern Hatreds* (Ithaca, NY: Cornell University Press, 2001); Roger Petersen, *Understanding Ethnic Violence* (New York: Cambridge University Press, 2002); Anthony D. Smith, *The Nation in History: Historiographical Debates about Ethnicity and Nationalism* (Hanover, NH: University Press of New England, 2000).
[11] For example. Donald L. Horowitz, *The Deadly Ethnic Riot* (Berkeley: University of California Press, 2001); Kaufman, *Modern Hatreds*; Petersen, *Understanding Ethnic Violence*.

people think in terms of groups, invest meaning in them, and act in terms of them largely to gain self-esteem in this way. This theory is based on research in a wide variety of cultures and the tendency to discriminate and sacrifice well-being for the sake of maximizing intergroup difference is found to hold even when people are assigned to groups completely arbitrarily in a laboratory setting.[12] All this is held to mean that ethnic groups are inherently conflictual because the motives behind their formation are competitive and zero-sum by their very nature.[13]

The hard approach has several shortcomings, at least insofar as it is a candidate for a fundamental theory of ethnicity. Empirically, to suppose that the motives behind ethnic groups are inherently conflictual would seem to predict far more ethnic conflict than in fact occurs. As Fearon and Laitin have shown, when one actually considers all the possible intergroup lines along which conflict could break out worldwide, the norm by far is ethnic peace.[14] The most sophisticated hard theorists might reply that the prevalence of ethnic peace is not surprising because constraints on violent proclivities tend to be strong and widespread, but these same theorists have trouble explaining what was noted in the first paragraph of this book: Even where constraints have collapsed enough to allow conflict, it is not even close to universal. Next to almost every ethnic hotspot lie multiple zones of ethnic peace.

Perhaps the biggest problem for the hard theories, though, is that their microlevel foundation has been rendered dubious by more recent research. A key psychological underpinning of these theories is Tajfel's finding that people, when given a chance to choose between maximizing group difference and maximizing their own group's welfare, prefer to maximize group difference as a means of enhancing their own self-esteem. But since the 1970s and 1980s, when most of the seminal research cited by the hard theorists was published, new findings have undermined the basis for the claim that ethnic groups inherently reflect a discriminatory or conflictual urge to gain self-esteem. For one thing, this form of discriminatory behavior was found to have depended on as many as two conditions that Tajfel did not recognize were present in his study's laboratory environment.

---

[12] Henri Tajfel, "Social Psychology of Intergroup Relations," *Annual Review of Psychology*, v.33, 1982, pp. 1–39.

[13] Pierre Van den Berghe (*The Ethnic Phenomenon*, New York: Elsevier, 1981) goes further than most by arguing people have a biologically evolved tendency, which underlies ethnic tensions, to prefer relatives over strangers. Dunbar, though, has countered that nepotism's long-run effect on reproduction rates may be quite weak or even indeterminate given that, as van den Berghe himself notes, the tendency to ethnocentrism is subject to a great deal of cultural manipulation and suppression. Moreover, in environments where cooperation is imperative, nepotism may have negative adaptive value. Dunbar also notes that the long-run genetic consequences of a supposedly inherited nepotism gene can in principle be indistinguishable from the long-run genetic consequences of a much more flexible general capacity for developing "rules of thumb" and employing a feedback mechanism, something that the present book will argue is closer to the truth. See Robin I. M. Dunbar, "Sociobiological Explanations and the Evolution of Ethnocentrism," in Vernon Reynolds, Vincent Falger, and Ian Vine, eds., *The Sociobiology of Ethnocentrism* (Athens: University of Georgia Press, 1987), pp. 48–59.

[14] James D. Fearon and David D. Laitin, "Explaining Interethnic Cooperation," *American Political Science Review*, v.90, no.4, December 1996, pp. 715–35.

First, some research has pegged the discriminatory behavior in these experiments to a sense of the appropriateness of competition conveyed in the experimental setting, resembling a kind of game.[15] Second, because the experiment's participants' own rewards depended upon how *other* experiment participants allocated rewards, other work has found that the discriminatory behavior Tajfel reported resulted not from the mere fact of grouping but from an *expectation of ingroup reciprocity* in reward allocation. When the grounds for expecting reciprocity are removed from such experiments by detaching participants' own rewards from others' allocation decisions (i.e., people are simply divided into groups and asked to allocate between one ingroup member and one outgroup member), the discrimination-preferring behavior disappears. People *are* still found to have more positive feelings toward ingroup members than toward outgroup representatives. In other words, group-oriented behavior still results even when these groups have minimal meaning. But these "minimally grouped" people are not found to act in discriminatory ways that sacrifice their own well-being.[16]

Additionally, the broader notion that self-esteem is the driving motive behind group formation and group behavior has also been called into question. For one thing, the degree to which one's group is stigmatized has been shown to have no effect on the self-esteem of those in it.[17] Furthermore, it is well established that people can derive self-esteem not only through associating with groups but sometimes by distinguishing themselves from groups, as well as through many other avenues. It is thus unclear why self-esteem would derive more from group membership than from self-individuation.[18] Self-esteem-based theories of group formation also cannot explain the widespread finding that minority status groups sometimes show favoritism toward other groups.[19] Empirical research has also failed to find a consistent correlation between denigrating outgroups and increasing one's own self-esteem.[20] Methodologically, investigators have called into question the particular instruments used to measure self-esteem in Tajfel's experiments, arguing that they sometimes capture such constructs as "impression

---

[15] Rogers Brubaker, Mara Loveman, and Peter Stamatov, "Ethnicity as Cognition," *Theory and Society*, v.33, no.1, 2004, pp. 31–64, fn.52.

[16] Toshio Yamagishi, "The Group Heuristic: A Psychological Mechanism That Creates a Self-Sustaining System of Generalized Exchanges," paper prepared for workshop on "The Co-evolution of Institutions and Behavior," Santa Fe Institute, January 10–12, 2003; Toshio Yamagishi and Toko Kiyonari, "The Group as the Container of Generalized Reciprocity," *Social Psychology Quarterly*, v.63, no.2, June 2000, pp. 116–32.

[17] Shelly D. Farnham, Anthony G. Greenwald, and Mahzarin R. Banaji, "Implicit Self-Esteem," in Dominic Abrams and Michael A. Hogg, eds., *Social Identity and Social Cognition* (Malden, MA: Blackwell Publishers, 1999), pp. 230–48, 230; Donelson Forsyth, *Group Dynamics*, 3rd edition (Belmont, CA: Brooks/Cole Wadsworth, 1999), p. 80.

[18] Michael A. Hogg and Barbara A. Mullin, "Joining Groups to Reduce Uncertainty: Subjective Uncertainty Reduction and Group Identification," in Dominic Abrams and Michael A. Hogg, eds., *Social Identity and Social Cognition* (Malden, MA: Blackwell Publishers, 1999), pp. 249–79, 251.

[19] Hogg and Mullin, "Joining Groups," p. 268.

[20] Forsyth, *Group Dynamics*, p. 394.

management" and "self-deception" rather than true self-esteem.[21] Finally, the fact that different frames of reference are found to produce different evaluations of the same categories also casts doubt on the notion that ethnic identification is primarily and inherently a way of attaining self-esteem at the expense of other groups.[22]

Soft Ethnicity-as-Conflictual Theories: Absolute Values

A more moderate view shares the notion that ethnicity is based on inherently conflictual tendencies but sees these tendencies as being rooted in value differences that are defined in absolute more than relative terms. In other words, ethnic differences reflect values that are simply divergent, not the creations of a desire for favorable comparisons with other groups. By these lights, ethnicity and nationality are constituted by cultural attributes that frequently involve particular beliefs and desires that are likely to differ from those of other groups. For example, speakers of Language A might not feel any better about themselves by knowing that speakers of Language B are downtrodden, but they may prefer to live in a country where Language A is the sole government language to one where Language B is the sole government language. Similarly, inhabitants of a particular territory are likely to share socioeconomic ways of life that give them shared interests differing from those of groups residing elsewhere. It may be, then, that ethnic groups simply reflect distinctive cultural values, a supposition that would lead one to expect intergroup conflict (violent or otherwise) to be a normal occurrence.

Hechter has provided the most solid theoretical and psychological grounding for this approach. The basic drive to form groups is neither self-esteem nor any values intrinsic to the mere fact of being in a group. Instead, ethnic groups arise out of the desire for culturally distinctive collective goods (such as state institutions), which are valued due to the shared practices and ways of life (religion, language, modes of production) that culture represents. Hechter makes two crucial points here. First, there is a problem of aggregation: Only individuals in the very smallest social units (e.g., family, village) are likely to *fully* share a culture, which means that for larger and more complex groups, ethnic activity must involve some process of determining which aspects of all the microlevel cultures become defining features of the larger "national" culture. Second, if ethnic groups reflect a desire for culturally distinctive public goods, they face the same collective action problems as any other group that may desire a public good: People must be somehow convinced to contribute to the provision of the good instead of attempting to get a "free ride," taking the benefit while letting others

---

[21] Farnham, Greenwald, and Banaji, "Implicit Self-Esteem," p. 230.

[22] Dominic Abrams, "Social Identity, Social Cognition, and the Self: The Flexibility and Stability of Self-Categorization," in Abrams and Michael A. Hogg, eds., *Social Identity and Social Cognition* (Malden, MA: Blackwell Publishers, 1999), pp. 196–229, 202.

bear the costs of production. The resulting insight is that successfully mobilizing ethnic groups typically have developed a crucial ability to sanction members who do not uphold their ethnic duties, such as exclusion from ethnic mutual support networks or more personal punishments like shaming. These sanctioning mechanisms define and sustain group boundaries, which become the reference points around which culture develops and becomes more homogeneous. The result for the successful groups is high "group solidarity," by which individuals contribute a large share of their own resources toward group ends. This can account for strong ethnic loyalty and conflictual tendencies without assuming that these always exist due to a supposedly innate drive for self-esteem at the expense of other groups.

Hechter also shows that this view is consistent with relevant psychological research. Appearing to accept Tajfel's hypothesis that individuals maximize self-esteem, Hechter cites findings that people identify most strongly with those aspects of identity that have the greatest implications for their social status and material well-being. People are most concerned about reordering group status rankings when they cannot escape their own groups. For this reason, ethnic solidarity tends to be very strong where there is a cultural division of labor, where cultural markers largely determine one's place in the economy. Self-esteem considerations, then, do not generate distinct group values but instead help determine which among many group memberships become most salient to an individual.[23]

Other than Hechter's account, most soft ethnicity-as-conflictual theories are not really theories of ethnicity but theories of other phenomena that ethnicity happens to explain. Brief arguments are typically given as to why ethnicity might reflect distinctive and conflict-facilitating values, but this claim is rarely seen to be in need of much elaboration. One well-known theory in this tradition is Lijphart's argument for "consociational democracy," an institutional system designed to maximally accommodate the divergent cultural values of major ethnic groups that he, along with many others, considers to be a major challenge to democracy.[24] The soft approach also underpins a large literature by economists, much of which concludes that ethnic pluralism reflects inherently different values and thus damages economic well-being by generating social conflict.[25]

The soft approach leaves several important questions unanswered, however. For one thing, if ethnic groups arise from common values and overcome the

---

[23] Michael Hechter, *Containing Nationalism* (New York: Oxford University Press, 2000); Hechter, *Principles of Group Solidarity* (Berkeley: University of California Press, 1987).

[24] Arend Lijphart, "Self-Determination Versus Pre-Determination of Ethnic Minorities in Power-Sharing Systems," in Will Kymlicka, *The Rights of Minority Cultures* (New York: Oxford University Press, 1995), pp. 275–87. On ethnic cleavages (broadly defined) and democracy, see Mill, *Considerations*; Seymour M. Lipset and Stein Rokkan, "Cleavage Structures, Party Systems, and Voter Alignments: An Introduction," in Lipset and Rokkan, eds., *Party Systems and Voter Alignments: Cross-National Perspectives* (New York: Free Press, 1967).

[25] For example, Alberto Alesina, Reza Baquir, and William Easterly, "Public Goods and Ethnic Divisions," *Quarterly Journal of Economics*, v.114, no.4, November 1999, pp. 1243–84. Similar assumptions are made by works on the scale of nations; for example, Alberto Alesina and Enrico Spolaore, *The Size of Nations* (Cambridge, MA: MIT Press, 2005).

collective action problem through a system of monitoring and sanctions, how can we explain group behavior when no system of monitoring or sanctions is in place or when no culturally specific collective goods are in fact at stake? Indeed, this aspect of Tajfel's "minimal group" experiments remains unchallenged: Even though expectations of reciprocity embedded in the experimental setting are found to have generated the "self-sacrificing" intergroup discrimination cited by hard theories of ethnicity, people still displayed group-oriented behavior (just not pure denigration) when the grounds for expecting reciprocity were removed.[26] Theories boiling ethnicity down to shared desires for culturally specific public goods also do not answer the following question in a completely satisfying way: Why should the values attached to ethnicity be any different from the values attached to other lines that impact people's lives? Hechter is convincing that a powerful nationalism can arise when distinct values are produced by a cultural division of labor, in which people's group status and socioeconomic prospects are all in alignment, but why do so many people see ethnicity as usually trumping other lines of cleavage involving class, urbanization, talents, ideology, and so on when they do not align? One answer might be that there is actually no difference, but the very fact that so many people and scholars *believe* ethnicity is somehow special begs an answer in its own right. Thus, even though ethnicity and values are clearly related, it would appear that the exact relationship remains to be specified.

Ultrasoft Ethnicity-as-Conflictual Theories: Constructed Values

A third body of work positing that ethnic identity involves conflictual tendencies might be labeled an "ultrasoft" approach. It is ultrasoft in the sense that identity in general, and the values attached to ethnicity in particular, are seen as almost purely a matter of consciousness. People belong to an ethnic group when they believe they belong to an ethnic group. Ethnic groups are associated with conflictual drives when people link their ethnic identity to desires that put them at odds with other ethnic groups. This is not purely tautological since most such accounts hold that consciousness is produced through complex but specific historical experiences that shape people's beliefs about what their place in the world is and should be. Moreover, most of these theories hold that these specific historical experiences have constructed people's senses of ethnic identity in such a way that ethnic groups have a tendency to be in conflict, at least in "modern" times.

Many of the most prominent works in this tradition stress the crucial roles of industrialization and the state in generating nationalism. Marx and Engels were among the earliest such theorists, arguing that the idea of national loyalty was essentially generated by ruling capitalists so as to distract the working class from its "true" identity as the proletariat, a distraction temporarily made possible by the

---

[26] Yamagishi, "The Group Heuristic"; Yamagishi and Kiyonari, "The Group as the Container."

realities of the capitalist stage of development.[27] Many non-Marxist works stressing industrialization or "modernization" also treat ethnic politics and nationalism as a temporary phase in history: Industrialization brings previously isolated communities into contact with each other and generates modern states that promote domestic unity by fostering loyalty to a national culture. This produces conflict because state-sponsored nationalism is defined against outside groups and because local groups whose cultures are left out of the nationalization project tend to define their own ethnic consciousness in opposition to the dominant culture.[28] In other cases, the state actually institutionalizes distinctions between local and dominant ethnic identities.[29] One of the most famous arguments in the ultrasoft tradition is Weber's account of how the national government in Paris turned "peasants into Frenchmen" over the course of the nineteenth century through homogenizing, consciousness-inculcating state policies like education and conscription.[30] Theorists differ as to just how enduring is the historically contingent development of conflict-prone national consciousness. Whereas Weber treats nations as highly stable once created, others like Haas write that national consciousness and its conflictual tendencies are bound to fade as soon as the historical contingencies that produced them depart the global scene (e.g., as international integration becomes the norm).[31]

Of course, the key problems with Marxist and modernization theories are that ethnic politics is frequently strong in places industrialization and mass literacy have hardly touched (e.g., Rwanda) and that ethnic tensions have hardly disappeared in the most "advanced" economies (e.g., Quebec). Thus, a number of theories put greater stress on historical contingency, shedding the deterministic baggage of Marxism and modernization theory.[32] This sort of approach now has a strong foothold even in the theory of international relations.[33] Others focus less on particular historical paths and more on the general argument that nationalism and ethnicity are social constructs built on the notion of opposition to an "other." For these theories, the essential historical question is not so much how people

[27] Karl Marx and Friedrich Engels, *The Communist Manifesto*, *www.yale.edu/lawweb/avalon/treatise/communist_manifesto/mancont.htm*.

[28] Anderson, *Imagined Communities*; C. E. Black, *The Dynamics of Modernization: A Study in Comparative History* (New York: Harper & Row, 1966), partially reprinted in Jason Finkle and Richard Gable, eds., *Political Development and Social Change*, 2nd edition (New York: Wiley, 1971); Gellner, *Nations and Nationalism*; Ernst Haas, "What Is Nationalism and Why Should We Study It?" *International Organization*, v.40, no.3, 1986.

[29] Rogers Brubaker, *Nationalism Reframed* (New York: Cambridge University Press, 1996).

[30] Eugen Weber, *Peasants into Frenchmen: The Modernization of Rural France, 1870–1914* (Stanford, CA: Stanford University Press, 1976).

[31] Weber, *Peasants into Frenchmen*; Ernst Haas, *The Uniting of Europe: Political, Social and Economic Forces 1950–1957* (Stanford, CA: Stanford University Press, 1958).

[32] For example, Eric Hobsbawm, *Nations and Nationalism Since the 1780s: Programme, Myth, Reality* (Cambridge: Cambridge University Press, 1990).

[33] Rawi Abdelal, *National Purpose in the World Economy: Post-Soviet States in Comparative Perspective* (Ithaca, NY: Cornell University Press, 2001); Alexander Wendt, "Collective Identity Formation and the International State," *American Political Science Review*, v.88, no.2, June 1994, pp. 384–96.

became aware of their national identities but how boundaries between groups are maintained.[34]

These "pure constructivist" theories, however, typically do not amount to a fundamental explanation of ethnicity because they beg some of the most significant questions: Why is it that people have the capacity to develop group consciousness in this way? What drives people to "buy into" the national project, to be susceptible to such socialization? As Posner puts the question, are they simple "sponges," naturally absorbing any social categories put forth by authority figures?[35] What are the psychological underpinnings for this sort of behavior? And what are the limits of construction? Can a powerful state with the proper social institutions ultimately generate any form of consciousness that it wants in individuals? This school generally does not base itself on psychological research, largely taking for granted that consciousness can form in the described way.

Virtually the only scholars working in the ultrasoft tradition who have deeply engaged psychological research in order to provide microlevel theoretical underpinnings are Rogers Brubaker and his various coauthors. They draw heavily on cognitive psychology to argue that ethnic and national identities, and the action that flows from them, might best be conceptualized as "schemas" or other mental mechanisms that place oneself in the world, represent views on the world, and define a course of action. The degree to which a purported group actually behaves like a group (displays "groupness") depends on the historical processes, institutional environments, and elite strategies that help shape ethnic schemas and cue their activation, among other things.[36]

The Brubaker team's important analysis of psychological research makes tremendous headway, but begs two major questions. For one thing, as the notion of ethnicity is stripped to a cognitive core, it appears to lose almost all of the value component that ethnicity-as-conflictual theories hold tends to drive ethnic politics. If ethnicity is merely a type of cognition, such as a schema, then why are particular values or behaviors attached to it? Why are schemas ethnic at all? In fact, Brubaker's cognitive approach suggests that there might actually be no values inherent to ethnic cognition. This then leads us outside the realm of ethnicity-as-conflictual theory and requires different approaches, some of which will be considered later. A bigger question concerns what will replace ethnicity-as-conflictual theory. Brubaker suggests ethnicity may merely be a way of seeing the world and provides an important vocabulary for describing the cognitive mechanisms that produce this way of seeing the world, thereby helping pioneer

[34] John A. Armstrong, *Nations Before Nationalism* (Chapel Hill: University of North Carolina, 1982); George M. Scott, Jr., "A Resynthesis of the Primordial and Circumstantial Approaches to Ethnic Group Solidarity: Towards an Explanatory Model," *Ethnic and Racial Studies*, v.13, no.2, April 1990, pp. 147–71; Edward H. Spicer, "Persistent Cultural Systems," *Science*, v.174, no.4011, November 19, 1971, pp. 795–800.

[35] Daniel N. Posner, *Institutions and Ethnic Politics in Africa* (New York: Cambridge University Press, 2005), p. 24.

[36] Rogers Brubaker, "Ethnicity Without Groups," *Archives Europeennes de Sociologie*, v.43, no.2, 2002, pp. 163–89; Brubaker, Loveman, and Stamatov, "Ethnicity as Cognition."

the understanding of ethnicity as being primarily "relational."[37] But we are left to wonder why this particular way of seeing the world is so widely associated with such a great range of important political and quotidian phenomena. We need, in short, to build on this very important description to develop a true theory of ethnicity, a core systematic logic that can explain why ethnicity in particular becomes associated with cognitive mechanisms like schemas, why ethnic cognition is so prevalent, and how it impacts politics. Rather than discard the concept of identity, as Brubaker and Cooper recommend in response to the challenge of such questions, we need to develop a better theory of identity.[38]

ETHNICITY-AS-EPIPHENOMENAL THEORIES

The works discussed prior to Brubaker see ethnicity as the expression of values that inherently facilitate intergroup discord; however, a very large literature rejects completely the notion that ethnicity contains its own intrinsic value. Instead, both ethnicity and ethnic politics are seen as a function of other pursuits, as means by which people struggle for more mundane goods like power, material resources, security, or status.[39] Many of these theorists stress the role of Machiavellian elites, said to manipulate otherwise peaceful, cooperative populations into "ethnic frenzies" or less intense forms of ethnic conflict when they have the desire and the opportunity. Mueller, for example, rules out inherently ethnic passions as causes of the Rwandan genocide and the Yugoslav civil war, blaming "thugs" who ran rampant, fomenting conflict in order to enrich or empower themselves. He writes, "In all this, nationalism was not so much the impelling force as simply the characteristic around which the marauders happened to have arrayed themselves."[40] Brass advances a similar ethnicity-as-epiphenomenal view in his account of ethnic riots, suggesting that ethnicity serves not even as a coordinating device but almost entirely as a discourse that guilty elites invoke to obscure the real, venal causes of violence that they incite.[41]

Such "elite manipulation" theories beg some very important questions, the chief of which is: If ethnicity has no inherent meaning for individuals, why do followers follow the elites' calls to ethnic battle? The most sophisticated works advance some answers. Snyder ventures that elites control mass media, thereby

---

[37] Brubaker, *Nationalism Reframed*; Rogers Brubaker, Margit Feischmidt, Jon Fox, and Liana Grancea, *Nationalist Politics and Everyday Ethnicity in a Transylvanian Town* (Princeton, NJ: Princeton University Press, 2006). An interesting review by Zsuzsa Csergo can be found in *Nations and Nationalism*, v. 14, no. 2, April 2008.

[38] Rogers Brubaker and Frederick Cooper, "Beyond 'Identity,'" *Theory and Society*, v.29, 2000, pp. 1–47.

[39] Such an assumption constitutes the basis for a groundbreaking use of computer modeling to study separatism: Ian S. Lustick, Dan Miodownik, and Roy J. Eidelson. "Secessionism in Multicultural States: Does Sharing Power Prevent or Encourage It?" *American Political Science Review*, v.98, no.2, May 2004, pp. 209–29.

[40] John Mueller, "The Banality of Ethnic War," *International Security*, v.25, no.1, summer 2000, pp. 43–71.

[41] Paul R. Brass, *Theft of an Idol* (Princeton, NJ: Princeton University Press, 1997).

directly influencing how people think.[42] Another possible answer is that the masses expect a cut of the spoils, that they can gain opportunities to loot, to exercise greater power personally, or to reap material or political benefits through massive ethnic patronage networks led by the elites.[43] In a similar vein, Brass's account and others suggest that the masses may not share the interests of elites but may have their own private reasons for joining them.[44] For example, Kalyvas notes that individual villagers sometimes take sides in civil wars with an eye toward using the opportunity to get revenge on a neighbor who might be plausibly portrayed as part of the enemy. Likewise, whole villages often seek to plunder or settle their own scores against rival villages through the opportunities civil war brings.[45] Ethnicity, in this case, may merely be a narrative that helps all of these individual actors tie their disparate actions together in a way that proves mutually beneficial. Developing a different logic, Wilkinson shows that when India's state-level governments do not have an interest in stopping violence, elites are able to provoke intense senses of mutual threat among ordinary Hindus and Muslims. Some elites are able thereby to spark intercommunal riots so as to polarize cleavages that would give them a majority in elections that are otherwise tight.[46]

Hardin and Laitin provide another innovative answer to the question of why followers follow that also moves toward an answer to the question of exactly what ethnicity is. Hardin describes virtually all forms of ethnic politics as little more than a means by which sets of people coordinate their actions so as to collectively pursue scarce goods like jobs and material resources in competition with other sets of people. Ethnic traits, then, are primarily just "focal points" around which people can coordinate, and whether people coordinate primarily along the lines of language, religion, or something else in their pursuit of gain is essentially arbitrary. And once a critical mass of people coordinate their materialistic or security-seeking efforts along ethnic lines, a "tipping point" is reached by which other people find it profitable to coordinate their own actions with an ethnic group lest they be forced to fend for themselves as everyone else is coordinating their actions to pursue payoffs.[47] Laitin's landmark empirical work in this tradition addresses the example of language, which others frequently treat as a "given" cultural attribute and a value in and of itself. He shows that a shared language is the product of multiple, simultaneous, long-term decisions by individuals to invest in knowing (or educating their children to know) that particular language

[42] Jack Snyder, *From Voting to Violence: Democratization and Nationalist Conflict* (New York: W. W. Norton, 2000).

[43] Kanchan Chandra, "Ethnic Parties and Democratic Stability," *Perspectives on Politics*, v.3, no.2, June 2005, pp. 235–52; Paul Collier and Anke Hoeffler, "On Economic Causes of Civil War," *Oxford Economic Papers*, v.50, no.4, 1998, pp. 563–73.

[44] Brass, *Theft of an Idol*; James D. Fearon and David D. Laitin, "Violence and the Social Construction of Ethnic Identity," *International Organization*, v.54, no.4, autumn 2000, pp. 845–77.

[45] Stathis N. Kalyvas, "The Ontology of 'Political Violence': Action and Identity in Civil Wars," *Perspectives on Politics*, v.1, no.3, September 2003, pp. 475–94.

[46] Steven I. Wilkinson, *Votes and Violence: Electoral Competition and Ethnic Riots in India* (New York: Cambridge University Press, 2004).

[47] Russell Hardin, *One for All* (Princeton, NJ: Princeton University Press, 1995).

rather than (or along with) alternative tongues. Knowing a language that no one
else speaks is not useful, so people will generally invest in knowing a language
only when they are sure that enough other people are also investing in it. Thus,
ethnic Russians who found themselves "beached" outside Russia when the USSR
disintegrated decided whether to invest in learning the local languages depending
on whether they thought enough other Russians would make similar decisions,
usually with the underlying aim of best providing their families with future access
to goods like material welfare or status.[48] In his most recent book, Laitin explicitly
generalizes this logic to argue nationalist politics is primarily about coordination,
even resting his definition of "nation" on coordination processes.[49]

While we may have some answers to the question of why followers follow,
another major question remains: Since the ways people can be categorized are
nearly infinite, why is it that elites so often invoke ethnic themes as their way of
rallying or coordinating the masses? Questions can be addressed to each of the
major accounts just discussed. If media are powerful enough simply to convince
people to follow nationalist leaders, why do elites bother to invoke ethnicity (as
opposed to something else) since elites' true goals are purported to be nonethnic?
If ethnicity serves mainly to tie together the diverse elements of ethnic riots
and civil war rather than to motivate them, why does it appear to be so widely
used (and so widely successful) as a "master narrative" relative to other possible
master narratives? If ethnic riots are mainly about security concerns and electoral
competition, why does ethnicity so frequently form the basis for this form of
protection racket? And if masses back ethnic entrepreneurs so as to gain a cut of
loot or power, why is ethnicity associated with the patronage networks and other
coordination efforts that underlie this expectation?

Hardin and Laitin answer that while ethnicity is primarily about coordination
in pursuit of desired goods like resources or status, people *also* derive a benefit
Hardin labels the "comfort of home" from ethnicity. While largely an ad hoc
assertion for Hardin, Laitin explains that culture itself is a coordination equilibrium – meaning that people will adjust their behavior to it just because they
expect others to do so – but that the particular cultural aspects around which
expectations are coordinated tend to involve different values or behavioral tendencies. Plus, people derive utility from being fully privy to the nuances and
"soul" of their local culture. Minority culture thus constitutes a "consumption
item" in which individuals who can afford its costs, or have special interests in its
production, will invest. This theoretical move essentially resolves the difficulties
of ethnicity-as-epiphenomenal theory by bringing back ethnicity-as-conflictual
assumptions, raising some of the same questions discussed previously regarding
that approach. Indeed, Laitin explicitly regards ethnic divides as the source of
major disputes over public goods at the same time he denies such disputes any
special potential to escalate into violence.[50]

---

[48] David D. Laitin, *Identity in Formation* (Ithaca, NY: Cornell University Press, 1998).
[49] David D. Laitin, *Nations, States, and Violence* (New York: Oxford University Press, 2007), pp. 40–1.
[50] Hardin, *One for All*; Laitin, *Nations, States, and Violence*.

Among theories remaining true to ethnicity-as-epiphenomenal tenets, many explain ethnicity's involvement in political entrepreneurship or coordinated resource pursuits by appealing to the notion of constructed consciousness, delving into specific historical experiences and patterns of institutional influences said to inculcate in people "commonsense" notions as to which social cleavages are proper or useful for pursuing various goods.[51] Posner, for example, details how historically contingent institutions from the colonial period embedded specific "identity repertoires" in Zambian citizens, repertoires primarily including tribe and language group as opposed to other possibilities like religion or class. With history and institutions predetermining the range of social categories that can be the basis for coordinated political action, Posner shows that both elites and masses repeatedly "switched identities" (within their repertoires) rationally so as to maximize their access to patronage resources given Zambia's changing election system.[52] This approach is highly reasonable as a pragmatic way to produce particular explanations, but as a fundamental theory it provides little insight into the general question of why historical processes appear so frequently to have produced identity repertoires with strong ethnic components (or why people think they have).

Others posit that ethnicity possesses special properties making it particularly useful in the pursuit of power, security, welfare, or other goods. One hypothesis is that shared ethnicity lowers the transactions costs associated with differences in language or cultural understandings. Thus, Deutsch argues this explains the association between modernization and ethnic politics: Industrialization and the rise of the modern state place premiums on efficiency at the same time that they bring formerly isolated peoples into closer contact for purposes of state building and economic development. States promote cultural homogeneity because they reap efficiency gains, and minorities resist when the costs of learning the dominant language and culture are too great for them relative to potential benefits.[53] More recently, economists have found the proposition that cultural commonality lowers transactions costs a fruitful basis for explaining why ethnicity persists and why it frequently forms the basis for important networks in the economy.[54] A

---

[51] Dmitry P. Gorenburg, *Minority Ethnic Mobilization in the Russian Federation* (New York: Cambridge University Press, 2003); Anya Peterson Royce, *Ethnic Identity: Strategies of Diversity* (Bloomington: Indiana University Press, 1982).

[52] Posner, *Institutions and Ethnic Politics*.

[53] Karl W. Deutsch, *Nationalism and Social Communication: An Inquiry into the Foundations of Nationality*, 2nd edition (Cambridge, MA: The MIT Press, 1966). Gellner (*Nations and Nationalism*) makes a similar argument, but he does not hold that nationalism is essentially epiphenomenal as does Deutsch.

[54] For example, Samuel Bowles and Herbert Gintis, "Persistent Parochialism: Trust and Exclusion in Ethnic Networks," *Journal of Economic Behavior and Organization*, v.55, no.1, September 2004, pp. 1–23; Janet T. Landa, "The Law and Bioeconomics of Ethnic Cooperation and Conflict in Plural Societies of Southeast Asia: A Theory of Chinese Merchant Success," *Journal of Bioeconomics*, v.1, 1999, pp. 269–84; Ronald Wintrobe, "Some Economics of Ethnic Capital Formation and Conflict," in Albert Breton, Gianluigi Galotti, Pierre Salmon, and Ronald Wintrobe, eds., *Nationalism and Rationality* (New York: Cambridge University Press, 1995), pp. 43–70.

related view is that ethnic traits are distinguished by being visible and/or relatively unchangeable, making them very useful for people who want to selectively distribute benefits along lines that are known to all and cannot easily be crossed by outsiders who are meant to be excluded.[55] In this view, American slavery was facilitated by the existence of a starkly obvious and hard-to-change difference in skin color between the slaves of African descent and the ruling whites of European descent: Escaped slaves could not easily "pass" as a member of a free group, facilitating white enforcement of the cruelly exploitative institution. Bates further posits that ethnicity tends to correspond to territory and hence to variation in modernization, which also tends to be geographically concentrated. Ethnicity, therefore, essentially becomes a useful proxy for territoriality (at least in the Africa he describes).[56] In sum, ethnic groups are merely a particularly convenient way of organizing the pursuit of interests that in and of themselves have nothing to do with ethnicity or any supposedly inherent "ethnic values," not to mention conflict-facilitating values. Ethnicity is epiphenomenal.

Even these highly sophisticated ethnicity-as-epiphenomenal theories leave key questions unanswered, however, even when taken together. For one thing, they are only weakly grounded in psychological research, which very few ethnicity-as-epiphenomenal theorists cite in anything more than a token manner. Perhaps the most prominent exception is Fearon, who relies heavily on Erikson and argues that identity has intrinsic value only in the realm of "personal identity," not "social identity," which includes ethnicity.[57] A good deal of psychological research, however, poses serious challenges to ethnicity-as-epiphenomenal theory. For one thing, what explains the group-oriented behavior observed in the aforementioned psychological experiments where participants knew that one's actions would not have any implications for one's own reward and when no opportunity or need for coordination was involved? There must be something to the phenomenon of group behavior that goes beyond coordination or the mere pursuit of material, political, status, or security interests, and ethnicity-as-epiphenomenal theorists have not yet shown that this something is irrelevant to ethnic politics.

In taking the ethnicity-as-epiphenomenal argument to a logical conclusion, Chandra is even led to wonder whether ethnicity might not matter at all. That is, if all that matters about ethnicity are particular properties of ethnicity (she singles out visibility and constraints to change) that might also be shared by other social

[55] Kanchan Chandra, *Why Ethnic Parties Succeed* (New York: Cambridge University Press, 2004); James D. Fearon, "Why Ethnic Politics and 'Pork' Tend to Go Together," mimeo, May 21–23, 1999.

[56] Robert H. Bates, "Ethnic Competition and Modernization in Contemporary Africa," *Comparative Political Studies*, v.6, no.4, January 1974, pp. 457–84.

[57] James D. Fearon, "What Is Identity (As We Now Use the Word)?" mimeo, November 3, 1999, *http://www.google.com/search?hl=en&ie=ISO-8859-1&q=James+Fearon+what+is+Identity*; and some of his writing (for example, Fearon and Laitin, "Violence and the Social Construction") with Laitin, whose view appears to have later evolved into a soft ethnicity-as-conflictual approach, as noted previously.

categories (such as gender and age), then perhaps ethnicity should be discarded entirely as an explanatory factor in favor of variables like "identities based on sticky or visible attributes."[58] But this would seem to be "throwing out the baby with the bathwater" in much the same way that Brubaker recommends discarding the concept of "identity" after running into the difficulties that psychological research poses for ultrasoft ethnicity-as-conflictual theory. Indeed, it is striking that cutting-edge work in both the ethnicity-as-conflictual and the ethnicity-as-epiphenomenal schools seems to be leading scholars to destroy the very concept (ethnic identity) that is so widely thought to be important and that originally inspired their own extraordinarily insightful research. It is the contention of this volume that the best way forward is not to reject "ethnic identity" as a factor but to rethink the foundational question of just why ethnicity might be important and to build new theory from the bottom up.

CONCLUSION: MOVING BEYOND UTILITY MAXIMIZATION AS A MICROLEVEL THEORY OF ETHNICITY

We are now in position to draw four important conclusions about the state of "ethnic studies." First, there is fundamental disagreement among scholars as to the most basic questions of ethnic politics, including the very nature of ethnicity itself, not to mention the dynamics of ethnic politics. Though there are many variations on these themes, many scholars see ethnic identification as being inherently conflictual while others see it as being almost entirely epiphenomenal.

Second, this disagreement has major implications for how we understand ethnic politics and how we recommend solutions. Debates over the most pressing issues of the day tend to center around this very divide between ethnicity-as-conflictual and ethnicity-as-epiphenomenal theories. What is the root cause of ethnic violence: elites' pursuit of power and wealth[59] or emotional struggles over group identity, relative status, and symbols?[60] Why is democratic politics sometimes organized along ethnic lines: because of institutional arrangements that shape ways of obtaining patronage or other resources[61] or because ethnic diversity is inherently divisive and inevitably makes democracy difficult?[62] What are the driving forces of multiethnic state collapse: historically and institutionally

[58] Kanchan Chandra, "What Is Ethnicity and Does It Matter?" *Annual Review of Political Science*, v.9, 2006, pp. 377–424.
[59] Brass, *Theft of an Idol*; James D. Fearon and David D. Laitin, "Ethnicity, Insurgency, and Civil War," *American Political Science Review*, v.97, no.1, February 2003, pp. 75–90; Snyder, *From Voting to Violence*.
[60] Horowitz, *Ethnic Groups in Conflict*; Kaufman, *Modern Hatreds*; Petersen, *Understanding Ethnic Violence*; Varshney, "Nationalism, Ethnic Conflict, and Rationality."
[61] Chandra, *Why Ethnic Parties Succeed*; Posner, *Institutions and Ethnic Politics*.
[62] Horowitz, *Ethnic Groups in Conflict*; Arend Lijphart, *Democracy in Plural Societies: A Comparative Exploration* (New Haven, CT: Yale University Press, 1977); Rabushka and Shepsle, *Politics in Plural Societies*.

constructed nationalism[63] or bargaining failures and patterns of resource distribution?[64] And what determines state attitudes toward international integration projects: senses of national purpose and identity[65] or the material and political interests of states and their leaders?[66] Similar divides structure the debate on secessionism, as will be discussed in the following chapter.

These differences as to cause have important implications for solutions. In the most general terms, if one believes ethnicity involves inherently conflictual human drives, then the solutions to ethnic conflict are likely to be aimed primarily at "containing" nationalism.[67] If one understands ethnic conflict to be not really ethnic and to be motivated mainly by the pursuit of material resources, then solutions might go beyond containment to addressing the resource distribution issues that fuel it.[68]

Third, despite the fact that disagreement is so deep, there appears to be no obvious cause for declaring one approach better grounded than the other. As was documented earlier, there are reasons to question the capacity of both theoretical traditions to provide a fundamental theory of ethnicity. Even though many of these theories supply brilliant explanations of particular events or kinds of events, they often run into problems when implications for other types of events are considered.[69] They also frequently encounter difficulties when basic assumptions are weighed against research into human psychology.

Fourth, despite the great divide in the literature, both ethnicity-as-conflictual and ethnicity-as-epiphenomenal theories are based on a particular kind of logic, a commonality suggesting that an alternative might be possible. The logic in which these approaches are grounded is the notion that some form of utility maximization, broadly conceived, lies at the heart of ethnicity as a phenomenon. This claim is obvious for the many theories on both sides of the divide that explicitly adopt rational choice approaches to explaining ethnic identification.[70] But it is also true of almost all the other theories in a crucial sense. To take ethnicity-as-conflictual theories first, all posit that people identify with ethnic groups so as to directly satisfy an important human need or to pursue culturally

---

[63] Beissinger, *Nationalist Mobilization*; Brubaker, *Nationalism Reframed*; Valerie Bunce, *Subversive Institutions* (New York: Cambridge University Press, 1999); Ronald Grigor Suny, *The Revenge of the Past* (Stanford, CA: Stanford University Press, 1993).

[64] Daniel Treisman, *After the Deluge* (Ann Arbor: University of Michigan Press, 1999); Susan Woodward, *Balkan Tragedy* (Washington, DC: Brookings, 1995).

[65] Abdelal, *National Purpose*; Wendt, "Collective Identity Formation."

[66] Haas, *The Uniting of Europe*; Andrew Moravcsik, *The Choice for Europe: Social Purpose and State Power from Messina to Maastricht* (Ithaca, NY: Cornell University Press, 1998).

[67] For example, Hechter, *Containing Nationalism*, and Horowitz, *Ethnic Groups in Conflict*.

[68] For example, Treisman, *After the Deluge*.

[69] Some of the most sophisticated studies explicitly recognize this difficulty and set the divergence up as a subject for future research. From different starting perspectives, see Posner, *Institutions and Ethnic Politics*, and Varshney, "Nationalism, Ethnic Conflict."

[70] For example, Hechter, *Containing Nationalism*, in the ethnicity-as-conflictual school and Fearon, "What Is Identity," in the ethnicity-as-epiphenomenal tradition. Antirationalist works also exist in both camps, including Kaufman, *Modern Hatreds*, and Brass, *Theft of an Idol*.

distinctive and/or socially constructed values. The concept of "utility," however, is not limited to narrowly defined material self-interest, instead connoting the personal value one attaches to all the different things one might desire for any reason. Thus, to say that people identify with ethnic groups so as to attain self-esteem, dignity, and/or a sense of belonging is to say that people are choosing to identify with ethnic groups as a way of pursuing utility, which for them comes from these particular things. Similarly, people are also pursuing utility if they are identifying with ethnic groups so as to satisfy desires for culturally specific goods, assumed to be a source of utility for these particular people.

Importantly, all this is *not* to say these works claim people are necessarily *rational* in their attempts to maximize utility. This is because rationality means that people not only maximize utility but remain consistent in their definition of exactly what generates utility. It is precisely this proposition, the tenet that preferences must remain stable and be transitive, that rational choice theory's harshest critics among ethnicity theorists reject. For example, both Kaufman and Petersen contend that emotions and symbols function by altering preferences on short notice, leading one preference to suddenly and overwhelmingly override other preferences that might previously have prevailed.[71] But they are both still arguing that people act to maximize utility, just rejecting the notion that people are rational in doing so and avoiding the terminology used here. In general, virtually all of the preceding theories do at a minimum assume people identify with ethnic groups as a way of maximizing utility, be this utility derived from group-based self-esteem at the expense of other groups, a sense of belonging, the achievement of "finding oneself," the enjoyment of the comforts of home, the acquisition of power, or the realization of naked material interest.

We note here one possible exception to the prevalent assumption of utility maximization. This would include any theory positing that ethnicity is pure consciousness, that people simply absorb ethnic identity like sponges absorb water, without any purpose and without any other explanation. Some ultrasoft ethnicity-as-conflictual theories and a few ethnicity-as-epiphenomenal theories may in fact fall into this category. But so long as one is not satisfied with a sponge theory of human nature, the larger point of this section is the following: Perhaps one could build a better, more powerful explanation of ethnicity and ethnic behavior by founding it on an assumption other than utility maximization. But if utility maximization is defined as broadly as it is here, as the almost tautological notion that people do whatever they think best subject to constraints, what else could possibly be the driving force behind ethnic identification? The next chapter attempts an answer.

---

[71] Kaufman, *Modern Hatreds*, pp. 27–9; Petersen, *Understanding Ethnic Violence*, pp. 32–3. Their other main objection is that rational choice theory does not appear to be borne out empirically.

3

A Relational Theory

Ethnicity Is about Uncertainty, Whereas Ethnic Politics
Is about Interests

The second core argument of this book is that ethnicity is primarily about uncertainty while ethnic politics is mainly about interests. That is, we must begin by distinguishing what drives ethnicity itself as a phenomenon from what drives actual ethnic behavior. This helps us see that the human drive explaining ethnicity itself is uncertainty reduction, which is shown to be distinct from utility maximization – it is not simply a value inserted into the utility equation that people then pursue or maximize. In fact, uncertainty reduction must occur *before* utility-maximizing behavior is possible. Uncertainty reduction thus ushers us into the realm of actual political behavior, the domain of ethnic politics, which *is* utility-maximizing behavior. This leads us to several conclusions. For one thing, because reducing uncertainty says nothing about how any resulting certainty will be used, we find new ground for the argument that there are no values inherent in ethnicity at all. But we also find that ethnicity is not epiphenomenal, not a secondary phenomenon. Instead, ethnicity is *primary* in that it precedes the politics of interest, helping make the pursuit of interest possible. All this is dubbed a "relational theory" of ethnicity for reasons that will become clear later.

This chapter proceeds by recognizing the crucial separation between the motives explaining ethnic identification and the motives explaining the group and individual behavior based on this identification. It begins by examining the former and then turns to the latter before discussing important implications. This logic, it is argued, provides better ground for future theory development, leveling more closely with psychological research as well as other key findings made previously by theorists of ethnic politics from both the ethnicity-as-conflictual and ethnicity-as-epiphenomenal schools.

UNCERTAINTY REDUCTION AS THE HUMAN DRIVE EXPLAINING ETHNICITY

What does it mean to posit that the drive behind ethnic identification is uncertainty reduction? Here it is helpful to begin with a basic theory of identity, which will help us understand how ethnicity is special.[1]

Identity as Points of Personal Reference

The theory begins with the proposition that *identity* is the *set of points of personal reference on which people rely to navigate the social world they inhabit*, to make sense of the myriad constellations of social relationships that they encounter, to discern one's place in these constellations, and to understand the opportunities for action in this context. It is, in a certain sense, a kind of social radar, a perceptual device through which people come to see where they stand in relation to the human environment. In the most basic sense, then, *groups* are defined by common relationships to points of reference.

This core claim harkens back to some of the founders of modern social psychology. Mead was perhaps the first to argue that perceptions of self are inherently about the relationship between the self and the social community, of which the self is a part and in which the self is uniquely positioned. Self-consciousness, he argues, is the process of being able to conceive of oneself from the perspective of others.[2] While Freud wrote little about "identity" and placed great emphasis on behavioral drives coming from the id (which is internal), the id never had free rein in his conception as it was always constrained by, and struggling against, the ego and superego, both of which are structures that mediate relations with the outside world.[3] Developing the psychoanalytic tradition to address the concept of identity, Erikson took Freudian notions to a more social conclusion, arguing identity cannot be understood apart from the social world: "In fact, the whole interplay between the psychological and the social, the developmental and the historical, for which identity formation is of prototypical significance, could be conceptualized only as a kind of *psychosocial relativity*."[4]

Identity and the Fundamental Human Drive for Uncertainty Reduction

Uncertainty is inherently linked to identity for three interconnected reasons. First, for all but the most isolated tribes, the social world is immensely complex, involving virtually infinite potential relationships and dimensions of behavior. Second, much of the social world is simply unknowable, such as the inner

---

[1] Parts of this chapter draw on Hale, "Explaining Ethnicity."

[2] George H. Mead, *Mind, Self, and Society*, ed. Charles W. Morris (Chicago: University of Chicago Press, 1934), pp. 200–2. See also Morris, "Introduction," in Mead, 1934, pp. x, xxiii.

[3] Sigmund Freud, *The Ego and the Id* (New York: W. W. Norton, 1960 [1923]); Erik H. Erikson, *Identity: Youth and Crisis* (New York: W. W. Norton, 1967), pp. 20–2.

[4] Erik Erikson, *Identity and the Life Cycle* (New York: W. W. Norton, 1980 [1959]), pp. 18–20; Erikson, *Identity: Youth*, p. 23.

thoughts and future actions of other people one encounters. Third, and most crucially, the human brain is a less-than-perfect information-processing organ with limited cognitive capacity; it is incapable of perfectly, speedily, or costlessly processing all information about all individuals who are directly and indirectly encountered.[5]

When we combine this limited human cognitive capacity with an impossibly complex and largely unknowable social world, it is obvious that uncertainty is going to play a very large role in how people attempt to establish personal points of reference so as to navigate this social world. Stated otherwise, any attempt to perfectly assess one's own relationship to every single individual is a futile task in all but the smallest of societies, and even then one is unlikely to fully know the inner thoughts of others one encounters. As Brown notes, "the world is simply too complex a place for us to survive without some means of simplifying and ordering it first."[6] From this logic, then, we begin to see that identity at its core is a means of reducing uncertainty, of making sense of the social world so as to survive and thrive.

Not surprisingly, then, many social psychologists have found a great deal of experimental confirmation for the proposition that *uncertainty reduction is a fundamental human motivation driving the near-universal tendency for humans to divide themselves into groups*.[7] People tend to categorize themselves and others in ways that help them make sense of the social world they inhabit. This facilitates recognition and response to members and nonmembers of these categorizations.[8] Several types of findings bolster this conclusion. For one thing, wherever there is a social world, no matter how remote, psychologists have found group-oriented behavior.[9] The drive to categorize has been documented even in young children, and even when the objects or people being categorized are highly similar.[10]

More importantly, the groups that humans form all tend to be based on at least some sense that they share a common fate. In a rich set of experiments briefly discussed in Chapter 2, Tajfel and associates sought to pinpoint the source of human grouping tendencies by trying to find the "minimal group," the "thinnest" set of conditions that can be found to generate detectable group-oriented behavior. Tajfel discovered that the degree of common fate necessary to generate group consciousness was minimal indeed. In fact, he showed that the people he studied

---

[5] For an important debate on just how limited this capacity is, see: Herbert A. Simon, "Human Nature in Politics: The Dialogue of Psychology with Political Science," *American Political Science Review*, v.79, no.2, June 1985, pp. 293–304; Leda Cosmides and John Tooby, "Better than Rational: Evolutionary Psychology and the Invisible Hand," *The American Economic Review*, v.84, no.2, May 1994, pp. 327–32.

[6] Rupert Brown, *Group Processes*, 2nd edition (Oxford: Blackwell, 2000), p. 265.

[7] Hogg and Mullin, "Joining Groups," pp. 253–5; Rupert Brown, *Group Processes*, 1st edition (Oxford: Blackwell, 1988), p. 227; Lowell Gaertner, Constantine Sedikides, Jack L. Vevea, and Jonathan Iuzzini, "The 'I,' the 'We,' and the 'When,'" *Journal of Personality and Social Psychology*, v.83, no.3, 2002, pp. 574–91, 586.

[8] Brown, *Group Processes*, 1st edition, p. 227.

[9] Forsyth, *Group Dynamics*, p. 68.

[10] L. A. Hirschfeld, *Race in the Making* (Cambridge, MA: MIT Press, 1996), p. 195.

consistently favored their own groups even when the groups were based only on trivial commonalities such as whether they over- or underestimated the number of dots on a page. In the end, he found that simply telling people they belonged to a particular group was enough to produce group-oriented behavior.[11] While some of Tajfel's interpretations (in the form of Social Identity Theory) have been found wanting by later scholarship, as discussed in Chapter 2, the finding mentioned here has been replicated in many cultural contexts and remains what Brown has called an "empirical consensus": Even minimal categorization, which represents a minimal sense of common fate, can produce group-oriented behavior.[12] In other words, people tend to think in terms of groups that connote shared relationships to the social world.[13]

Why Some Aspects of Identity Are More Useful for Uncertainty Reduction than Others

If people think in terms of groups to simplify the world, why do some types of groups get used for this purpose more than others? Indeed, if every aspect of the social world can become the basis for at least a "minimal group" à la Tajfel, then aren't there at least as many groups as there are aspects of the social world? And if this is so, how does thinking in terms of groups *simplify* things?

The answer begins by recognizing that there is informational content in each "identity dimension" (point of personal reference), information about the relationship between the individual and the referenced object. At the most minimal level, this information is simply that the individual is in a particular category of people defined by a common point of reference. But identity dimensions can tell an individual more than "I am in this category of people," adding "therefore the following things could possibly affect me." This typically happens where one's fate is somehow perceptibly determined by one's belonging to a particular category.[14] The term "categorization" thus refers here to a person's perception of membership in a certain category, having a reference point in common with others to some aspect of the social world. In the tradition of Geertz, it is helpful to use the adjective "thick" to denote high levels of meaning.[15] Personal points of reference, groups, or categorizations, therefore, become "thicker" when they come to have greater importance in people's lives, when people's lives are seen to be affected in more significant ways by the referent.

There are at least three important reasons why some categories become thicker than others: intrinsic importance, imposed importance, and usefulness as rules of

---

[11] Tajfel, "Social Psychology," p. 23.

[12] Brown, *Group Processes*, 1st edition, p. 224.

[13] Tajfel ("Social Psychology," p. 24) also reports that when intergroup categorization and interpersonal similarity are pitted against each other, categorization prevails. This indicates that what is driving human group formation is not the quality of the potential members, as sociobiological theories sometimes posit (Van den Berghe, *The Ethnic Phenomenon*).

[14] Harvey Sacks, *Lectures on Conversation*, v.1 (Oxford: Blackwell, 1992), pp. 42, 401.

[15] Clifford Geertz, *The Interpretation of Culture* (New York: Basic Books, 1973).

thumb. The first two play significant roles in ethnic politics, but the third is the real key to understanding why ethnicity in particular appears to be so important.

1. *Intrinsic importance*. Some limitations or opportunities in life chances are intrinsic to particular kinds of distinctions. One of the most obvious involves language. Two people without a common language face potentially huge transactions costs in interaction. This will make groups of people who speak different languages and who encounter each other in almost any kind of social setting immediately aware of a relevant categorization: those who speak one's language and those who do not. Significantly higher communications costs can be associated with cultural, not just linguistic, differences because these frequently attribute different meanings to the same actions in ways that might not be clear to outsiders.[16]

2. *Imposed importance*. The bulk of categorical limitations on people's life chances are imposed by the broader social environment, not the intrinsic nature of the categories themselves. It is clear that when one set of people (or sometimes even a single person) treats another as different and has the power to affect that other's life chances according to this perceived difference, this perception of difference can be expected to become salient to the one receiving the treatment.[17] One way elites can make categorical distinctions important is to base the allocation of material resources on them.[18] Thus, for example, where white owners of a firm decide to use white skin as a way to determine whom to hire, the black–white distinction becomes significant to black applicants whether they want it to be or not because their blackness is the basis for their not attaining a job they seek and would otherwise get.

3. *Usefulness as Rules of Thumb*. When one combines the fundamental human imperative for uncertainty reduction with the limited cognitive capacity of the human brain, one is led to an even more important way in which some identity dimensions can thicken, taking on a great deal of "extra" meaning. Suppose that a relatively simple, easily perceptible social category frequently coincides with other, less perceptible and/or more complicated points of reference that are important for independent reasons. In such situations, the simpler, more obvious ones can serve as *rules of thumb* (or shorthand, clues) for determining whether someone else belongs to a group defined by the less detectable or more complicated traits.

For example, a stranger's accent would typically tell nineteenth-century English people far more than the bare fact that the stranger pronounced certain words differently. It might also tell them with reasonable accuracy what city the person hailed from and what class he or she belonged to, from which

---

[16] As with Geertz's famous winks and eye-twitches in *The Interpretation of Culture*.

[17] Forsyth, *Group Dynamics*, pp. 378–83.

[18] Forsyth, *Group Dynamics*, pp. 378–83; Michael Banton, *Ethnic and Racial Consciousness*, 2nd edition (New York: Longman, 1997).

people might additionally infer all kinds of other information (correct or otherwise) regarding the person's tastes, experiences, or even beliefs, political loyalties, morals, and abilities. The actual accent the person had would probably not be important at all so long as they could still understand each other, but the other information that the accent connoted could have enormous consequences as to whether the stranger might be hired, trusted, respected, or welcomed into one's home.

Points of personal reference, then, even group labels themselves, can become thick with meaning not only when the original referents become important in their own right, but also when they come to connote relationships to *other* referents seen to be correlated with the originals. At their most robust, these rules of thumb can involve whole patterns of recognition and can imply appropriate relational action to such an extent that they can be fruitfully analyzed as cognitive schemas.[19] Psychologists Hogg and Mullin find that by identifying themselves strongly as group members, individuals are effectively replacing aspects of their own individuality (including their unshared attitudes and behaviors) with stereotypical beliefs, attitudes, and/or behaviors.[20] Likewise, categorizing others in this way leads people to assume individuals in these other groups are much more alike than they actually are. Perhaps the most obvious example to an American is the extremely meaningful category of race.[21] By serving as rules of thumb for interpreting the social world, then, these simple and more perceptible traits can powerfully guide people in interpreting a social situation and choosing how to respond to it.

The Situational Essence of Identity as an Uncertainty-Reduction Device

If some identity categories become rules of thumb for social navigation while others do not, and if no single hyper-thick categorization comes to define and prescribe all elements of human interaction, what determines which rules of thumb will be activated? Research suggests that people tend to categorize others depending upon both the *accessibility* of the category and the *fit* between the category and observed social reality.[22]

---

[19] Brubaker, Loveman, and Stamatov, "Ethnicity as Cognition"; George P. Knight, Martha E. Bernal, Camille A. Garza, and Marya K. Cota, "A Social Cognitive Model of the Development of Ethnic Identity and Ethnically Based Behaviors," in Bernal and Knight, eds., *Ethnic Identity: Formation and Transmission Among Hispanics and Other Minorities* (New York: SUNY Press, 1993), pp. 213–34.

[20] Hogg and Mullin, "Joining Groups."

[21] Banton, *Ethnic and Racial Consciousness*, pp. 165–6; Anthony W. Marx, *Making Race and Nation: A Comparative Study of South Africa, the United States, and Brazil* (New York: Cambridge University Press, 1998).

[22] Penelope J. Oakes, S. Alexander Haslam, and Katherine J. Reynolds, "Social Categorization and Social Context: Is Stereotype Change a Matter of Information or of Meaning?" in Dominic Abrams and Michael A. Hogg, eds., *Social Identity and Social Cognition* (Malden, MA: Blackwell Publishers, 1999), pp. 55–79, 59; Abrams, "Social Identity." On categorization, see also Andreas Wimmer, "Does Ethnicity Matter? Everyday Group Formation in Three Swiss Immigrant Neighbourhoods," *Ethnic and Racial Studies*, v. 27, no. 1, January 2004, pp. 1–36; and Wimmer, "The Making and Unmaking of Ethnic Boundaries: A Multilevel Process Theory," *American Journal of Sociology*, v. 113, no. 4, January 2008, pp. 970–1022.

1. *Accessibility*. Psychologists have distinguished between two types of accessibility. A social category is said to be *chronically accessible* if it is available to people through memory. Someone told throughout her life that blacks are different from whites, for example, is more likely to interpret a given situation in terms of race. Sometimes people can have a particular motivation to think in terms of a category, as when it might excuse them from some blame – this also makes a category chronically accessible.[23] A social category is *situationally accessible* if it is somehow immediately available in the situation itself through direct contact, active suggestion, or cues in the environment.[24] For example, when an investigator asks an American to describe a compatriot who happens to be of African American descent, just mentioning or subliminally suggesting the category "black" right beforehand – a sort of process called "priming" – is found to make the describer more likely to use this category and related stereotypes.[25] A category can also be situationally accessible if it repeatedly comes up in conversations or mass media.[26] This creates great opportunity for "identity entrepreneurs" to identify categories, portray them as having importance for people's life chances (creating identity discourses), and actively promote their accessibility so as to shape how people actually understand their relationship to the social world in given situations.[27]

2. *Fit*. Nevertheless, important research makes clear that mere accessibility does not guarantee a category's use, but that people also tend to invoke categories based on how well they *fit* a situation. That is, accessible categories are more likely to be used to interpret a situation if they help make sense of it, accounting at least somewhat accurately for similarities and differences among people.[28] The notion of fit is not absolute, of course. People frequently use categories that are far from 100 percent accurate.

The chief question is whether there is available *another* category that *fits better* and is sufficiently easily applicable given the complexity and stakes of the situation at hand. Kurzban, Tooby, and Cosmides show that by altering a situation in the right way, even Americans, whose culture is steeped in racial consciousness, can be made to stop thinking even unconsciously in terms of race (at least in that situation).[29] Their experiment was quite clever. People were first shown a series of pictures of a dispute involving individuals of different racial appearances. Subjects

---

[23] Abrams, "Social Identity"; Hogg and Mullin, "Joining Groups," p. 252.

[24] Brubaker, Loveman, and Stamatov, "Ethnicity as Cognition," p. 25; Hogg and Mullin, "Joining Groups," p. 252.

[25] Brown, *Group Processes*, 2nd edition, pp. 273–4.

[26] Emanuel A. Schegloff, "Reflections on Talk and Social Structure," in Deirdre Boden and Don H. Zimmerman, eds., *Talk and Social Structure* (Cambridge: Polity, 1991), pp. 44–70.

[27] An outstanding work on identity discourses is Ted Hopf, *Social Construction of International Politics: Identities and Foreign Policies, Moscow, 1955 and 1999* (Ithaca, NY: Cornell University Press, 2002).

[28] Oakes, Haslam, and Reynolds, "Social Categorization," p. 59; Hogg and Mullin, "Joining Groups," p. 252; Abrams, "Social Identity."

[29] Robert Kurzban, John Tooby, and Leda Cosmides, "Can Race Be Erased? Coalitional Computation and Social Categorization," *Proceedings of the National Academy of Sciences, USA (PNAS)*, v.98, no.26, December 18, 2001, pp. 15387–92.

of the experiment were then asked to recall who said what. Strikingly, the mistakes that people made in their recollections revealed that they had unconsciously used racial categories to help keep track of who was on what side. For example, if they mistakenly identified a black person as the speaker, odds were that the person who had actually made the statement was also black *even though the dispute was not "blacks" versus "whites."* This was the result, at least, when the psychologists included no other visible clues that were likely to help people keep track of who was on which side of the dispute. That is, people knew there was no perfect correlation between the race of the individual and the side they took in the dispute, but they subconsciously reverted to racially encoded thinking anyway because they had no better way of keeping track of a situation that was too complex for them to perfectly understand.[30] The researchers' key finding, however, came when they introduced a fully arbitrary but visible distinction among people (different colored shirts) that *did* correspond well to sides in the dispute. The subjects almost entirely dropped race as a categorization, even on an unconscious level, instead structuring assessments of the situation in terms of shirt color. "Any readily observable feature – however arbitrary – can acquire social significance and cognitive efficacy when it validly cues patterns of alliance," the researchers conclude.[31]

Such findings strongly suggest that what we observe in social categorization and groupness is not usually the operation of "constructed consciousness" or "cognitive representations" that are "ways of thinking" that invariably impose themselves on all social interaction, as some self-avowed constructivist scholars appear to have it. Instead, we see a process by which people develop thick points of personal reference enabling them to navigate the social world as efficiently and successfully as possible, yet can nimbly disregard even seemingly all-encompassing identity categories when they lose their relative uncertainty-reducing value. Of course, thick categorizations are often quite stable due to their pervasive availability, their relative usefulness in multiple types of important situations, and the fact that some of these situations themselves are quite stable. When slavery was enshrined in the American constitution, for example, even the legal system openly enforced race as a category that was pervasively relevant in a most tragic way. But research is also clear that how people categorize others and the subjective content ascribed to these categories can alter radically as context (points of common reference) shifts.[32] People are even found to ascribe different values or traits to *themselves* as context varies [33]

Explaining Ethnicity as an Especially Useful Uncertainty-Reducing Device

It is usually good practice for social scientists to begin by defining a term like ethnicity before seeking to explain it and examine its effects. Yet due to the

---

[30] Noting this resistance to disconfirmation, Sacks (*Lectures on Conversation*, p. 336) calls categories "knowledge protected against induction."
[31] Kurzban, Tooby, and Cosmides, "Can Race," p. 15388.
[32] Oakes, Haslam, and Reynolds, "Social Categorization," pp. 59–60.
[33] Abrams, "Social Identity," p. 200.

fundamental and widespread disagreement as to just what ethnicity actually is, the standard practice has led to some deeply diverging conclusions, as described extensively in Chapter 2. Some definitional efforts, attempting to be as precise as possible in specifying ethnicity's essential components, have led to the conclusion that ethnicity as such may not cause anything at all.[34]

The present volume has taken a somewhat unorthodox approach. The idea has not been to begin with a definition of ethnicity, but to start with a basic theory of identity that will hopefully allow us to understand why we even have a concept like "ethnicity" in the first place, however defined. That is, perhaps there is a reason why all the different elements that get differential emphasis in the literature are widely associated with a common term even if this term has defied precise specification by the brightest of scholars.

We are now ready to tie together much of the preceding discussion to show that there is an important logic underlying the concept of ethnicity and most of the diverse attributes scholars have attached to it, a logic that has uncertainty reduction in a highly complex world at its core. Crucially, we have argued that certain points of personal reference have properties that facilitate their use in uncertainty reduction, properties that might be broken down into four categories. First, group-oriented behavior derives primarily from categories associated with a sense of commonality of fate, senses that can arise naturally or be deliberately manipulated by people in power. Second, categories that have intrinsic importance (especially those involving barriers to communication) can be expected to stand out for people as they navigate the social world; they can thus be important in and of themselves and also serve as rules of thumb due to their ability to stand out. Third, categories that are otherwise highly perceptible have the potential to serve as rules of thumb for interpreting and guiding social interaction. Fourth, categories that correlate with other highly important categories also have the potential to serve as rules of thumb in uncertainty reduction.

These four properties are associated with virtually all the core features frequently referred to through the term "ethnicity." Indeed, in perhaps the most widely cited definition, Weber famously referred to shared perceptions of common descent and culture as lying at the heart of ethnicity. "Common descent" and "culture" usually imply some mix of shared language, physical resemblance, and common ritual regulation of life, especially religion.[35] It is not necessary to rehash the seemingly interminable definitional debate on ethnicity, since we are only interested here in establishing the range of concepts commonly (though not necessarily always) considered under the rubric of ethnic. In fact, scholars sometimes vigorously debate what should be left on or off Weber's list (e.g., Is religion part of ethnicity?), but they have generally not added too many new elements. Here it is worth mentioning a couple that are sometimes appended by leading theorists. Horowitz introduces a requirement of scale: The group defined by the

---

[34] Chandra, "What Is Ethnicity."

[35] Max Weber, "Ethnic Groups," from G. Roth and C. Wittich, eds., *Economy and Society*, v.1 (Berkeley: University of California Press, 1978), pp. 389–95, as reprinted in John Hutchinson and Anthony Smith, eds., *Ethnicity* (New York: Oxford University Press, 1996), pp. 35–8.

ethnic categorization must transcend face-to-face relationships.[36] Brass argues that ethnicity implies a group contains, in principle or practice, the elements for a complete division of labor and reproduction.[37] The following paragraphs demonstrate that these various components are united (at least in part) by a strong potential to be useful for individuals in reducing the uncertainty they face in the social world through both their *accessibility* and their *fit* with important situations people face.

1. *Connotation of common fate.* As discussed earlier, social categories are more likely to be used as rules of thumb to the extent that they are both accessible (situationally and chronically) and capable of making "sense" of particular social situations with some reliability and efficiency. Ethnic symbols can be seen as serving to evoke (cue, make situationally accessible) ethnic categorizations (even ethnic schemas) *as well as* to further thicken these categorizations by evoking them in a wider range of situations than would otherwise be the case. This increases the chances that thick ethnic categorizations will actually be activated for social interpretation and behavior. In particular, symbols linked to myths of common origin, often said to be the distinguishing feature of ethnic groups, have properties as rules of thumb that help account for the special force often attributed to ethnicity.[38] Ethnic symbols gain much of their power by quickly communicating a sense of the shared history, blood relationships, or past commonalities of fate experienced by ethnic group members. This, in turn, lends credibility to suggestions of *future* commonalities of fate for those who have a certain relationship to these symbols. Just as mentioning the word "black" can induce a European American to describe an African American in racial terms, so can propagating ethnic symbols promote "ethnic ways of thinking."[39] And not just any old ways of ethnic thinking: These ethnic symbols, from flags to stereotypical media images to ethnic group names themselves, can evoke particularly strong senses of common fate since they imply a whole history that seems to confirm it.[40] Moreover, these symbols can be made broadly "situationally available" through such easy actions as flag placement, inserting myth-bearing rhetoric in widely heard speeches, and other almost costless moves. Intuitively understanding this power and mobilizational potential, charismatic politicians often cultivate symbols that have the gravitas of age and history behind them in their efforts to mobilize

---

[36] Horowitz, *Ethnic Groups in Conflict.*

[37] Paul R. Brass, *Ethnicity and Nationalism* (London: Sage, 1991), p. 19.

[38] Armstrong, *Nations Before Nationalism*; Kaufman, *Modern Hatreds*; Smith, *Myths.*

[39] By making them situationally accessible.

[40] We must, however, keep in mind Abner Cohen's (*Two-Dimensional Man*, Berkeley: University of California Press, 1974) insight that symbols are by their very essence ambiguous, frequently and characteristically imbued with new meaning. The continuity of ethnic symbols in no way necessitates the continuity of their meaning.

a following.[41] Symbols that actually *are* old (as documented in historical texts and oral traditions, for example) can be among the most plausible.[42] The rhetoric of ethnic blood relationships is especially powerful because it implies the very close commonality of fate typical of families, kin.[43]

2. *Barriers to communication.* Many of the "ethnic" traits identified by Weber and others inherently tend to involve barriers to communication. This is most obvious in the case of linguistic differences, but it is also true of cultural differences.[44] Since communication is intrinsically important to social life, the presence of a communication barrier renders such differences immediately relevant (situationally accessible) in social encounters, making it more likely that they will be used as rules of thumb. Moreover, barriers to communication also inhibit disconfirmation of the simplifications that social rules of thumb imply.

3. *Visible physical differences that are hard to change or disguise.* People are very good at identifying physical differences among themselves and can do so quickly. For example, two Americans meeting on a street at noon might have a hard time guessing whether the other person is a Republican or a Democrat, but they can typically tell immediately what color skin the other has. Furthermore, it can be very costly if not impossible for one to change the color of one's skin in a way that would not be noticed. Visible physical differences, then, can be very attractive as social rules of thumb due to their ease of use, their high situational accessibility. Indeed, their ease of use helps explain why they are employed even when they are highly imperfect; more accurate indicators might be much more difficult to invoke. It must be remembered, of course, that there is nothing inevitable about any physical difference being used in this way.[45] As noted earlier, Kurzban and his colleagues have shown that even in America race can be "erased" as a rule of thumb given the right circumstances.[46]

4. *Correlation with other important factors.* Ethnic traits can be not only unusually visible and self-evident but also unusually correlated with less visible

---

[41] Connor, "Beyond Reason"; Jack Snyder and Karen Ballantine, "Nationalism and the Marketplace of Ideas," *International Security*, v.21, no.2, autumn 1996, pp. 5–40.

[42] There is thus an element of path dependence to ethnic symbolic forms that helps us account for the continuity we see in the national symbolism of groups like Greeks and Jews described by authors like Armstrong (*Nations Before Nationalism*), Smith (*Myths*), and Aviel Roshwald, *The Endurance of Nationalism* (New York: Cambridge University Press, 2006). On path dependence, see Douglass C. North, *Institutions, Institutional Change and Economic Performance*, New York: Cambridge University Press, 1990. Plausibility also hinges on media and access to falsifying data (Snyder and Ballantine, "Nationalism and the Marketplace").

[43] Horowitz, *Ethnic Groups in Conflict.*

[44] Pierre Bourdieu, *The Logic of Practice* (Stanford, CA: Stanford University Press, 1990); Geertz, *The Interpretation of Culture.*

[45] Hirschfeld, *Race.*

[46] Kurzban, Tooby, and Cosmides, "Can Race." See also Banton, *Ethnic and Racial.*

and less self-evident traits that are nevertheless extremely powerful determinants of a person's life chances. That is, they often have a significant
degree of "situational fit" with other important aspects of the social world.
This can make ethnic thinking very attractive as a rule of thumb for efficiently drawing inferences about these other important traits. Such a correlation can come about in several ways, three of which will be stressed
here: by development, by design, and by coordination.

"By development" refers first to the fact that modes of communication and
physical differences, both of which are frequently implicated in ethnic difference,
have historically tended to be territorially concentrated.[47] This is understandable since both communication (which passes on culture and beliefs) and reproduction possibilities (which pass on inherited physical traits) depend on social
contact. And opportunities for social contact tended to be quite limited territorially for most people up until the industrial age. Critically, *other* things important
to people's life chances have *also* historically tended to be territorially concentrated. Among other things, this includes economic development and sometimes
even class or peculiar economic specializations.[48] Ethnic distinctions, then, are
frequently correlated with levels of economic development and class, and sometimes with particular economic niches. When this correlation is relatively strong,
people can be tempted (even if unconsciously) to use ethnicity as a rule of thumb
for inferring a lot of information about another person, including his or her likely
socioeconomic background, likely economic power, likely beliefs, and likely status trajectory. Indeed, the latter traits are often less immediately perceptible than
are ethnic characteristics but are extremely important to people's life chances. A
classic work by Bates provides an excellent example. Studying Africa, he demonstrates that economic development took place unevenly in terms of geography
and that pockets of development and underdevelopment often tended to coincide
with territorially concentrated cultural differences, producing long-lasting dis-
parities in power and wealth. Competition over resources, he found, thus tended
strongly to be structured along ethnic group lines.[49]

In referring to correlation "by design," we have in mind how powerful people
can consciously use ethnic categories in exercising their power. In a state that
privileges whites over blacks, for example, knowing the color of a person's skin
can tell one a lot about how a person is likely to be treated. Dawson illustrates
how a social structure long imposed by white leaders in the United States renders the life chances of African Americans so heavily dependent on a particular
conception of race, even in the spheres of economics and social interaction,
that many African Americans have tended to find it more cost-effective to
calculate the benefits of governmental policies for the race as a whole than for
themselves as individuals. Dawson dubs this race-based calculation the "Black

---

[47] Hechter, *Containing Nationalism*, p. 24.
[48] Bates, "Ethnic Competition"; Michael Hechter, *Internal Colonialism* (Berkeley: University of California Press, 1975).
[49] Bates, "Ethnic Competition."

Utility Heuristic."[50] This helps explain a finding of Lublin's statistical analysis of U.S. voting patterns between 1972 and 1994: By far, the strongest predictor of African American voting was race, not socioeconomic position.[51] The role of race in politics differs in Brazil, however, and one of the most important sources of such variation is how whites in power have intentionally used racial categories to achieve their own goals.[52]

An additional way in which ethnic traits can become correlated with other things that are important to people is through the logic of coordination developed by Hardin and Laitin, whose work was discussed in Chapter 2.[53] Their core insight is that ethnic divides, either because of inherent importance in social interaction (as with language distinctions) or pure perceptibility (as with skin color differences), can become focal points around which people coordinate their actions in pursuit of a wide variety of goods. This might help explain, for example, why particular economic niches are often occupied disproportionately by members of particular ethnic groups.[54] In such a case, the fact that people coordinate along ethnic lines in their economic behavior can make ethnicity a useful rule of thumb for quickly determining who is likely to be in what line of work and then inferring other information associated with that determination.

Of course, ethnic traits are not the only ones possessing any of the four key properties just discussed. Age and gender differences, for example, are visible in ways that are hard to conceal or change and frequently do roughly correspond to some other important dimensions of the social world, such as senses of certain social obligations and status. Social class can involve visible distinctions among people, as in modes of dress or the degree to which one's hands show calluses or other signs of hard manual labor. Citizens of countries that are not based on ethnic principles, such as the United States, can share symbols connoting a strong sense of common fate.

Even though each of these alternative dimensions of social cleavage is important in its own right, none possesses ethnicity's range or depth in the tendency to be used as a rule of thumb in the modern social world. For example, age and gender do not usually divide whole peoples by socioeconomic class or territorial settlement patterns, as ethnic distinctions are wont to do since ethnic groups generally contain the elements for a complete division of labor and reproduction, which age and gender categories as a rule do not.[55] Class distinctions can indeed be perceptible and hard, but they are arguably usually less perceptible and hard than "ethnic" traits and do not so clearly and so often correspond to all of the other important aspects of life that ethnic divides frequently coincide with, such

---

[50] Michael Dawson, *Behind the Mule* (Princeton, NJ: Princeton University Press, 1994).

[51] David Lublin, "The Election of African-Americans and Latinos to the U.S. House of Representatives 1972–94," *American Politics Quarterly*, v.25, no.3, July 1997, pp. 269–86.

[52] Marx, *Making Race and Nation*.

[53] Hardin, *One for All*; Laitin, *Nations, States, and Violence*.

[54] Horowitz, *Ethnic Groups in Conflict*; Landa, "The Law"; Brian Shoup, *Conflict and Cooperation in Multi-Ethnic States* (Oxford: Routledge, 2007).

[55] Brass, *Ethnicity and Nationalism*, p. 19.

as macroterritorial differences in levels of development. Cleavages that are purely ones of class also do not link as strongly to symbols and myths of common origin and history, which help make ethnicity credible as an inescapable indicator of long-term common fate, as with extended family. Similarly, state membership is not readily visible or difficult to disguise in and of itself.

In fact, it is more likely that ethnic divisions will come to serve as rules of thumb for interpreting these other cleavages than the other way around (with the exception of gender and age, of course). Moreover, when these other cleavages correspond with ethnic divides, they arguably become much more powerful determinants of social interaction. Recognizing a woman or elder as part of an ethnic group is more likely to lead one to impute particular values or practices to that person than if one merely sees a woman or an elder but has no other grounds for guessing at his or her likely behavior. Hechter's seminal work on Great Britain makes a similar case for class: Ethnic differences can become fused with class differences in a "cultural division of labor." This can facilitate the rise of "internal colonialism" by which cultural markers (in Hechter's book, Irish ones) come to be widely associated with class differences, thereby binding whole ethnic groups to a limited range of economic and social opportunities.[56] Ethnicity, then, reinforces the class divide, creating a powerful potential for political mobilization. Similarly, ethnic nationalism can produce extraordinarily strong senses of state solidarity, an insight that several classic works have used to help explain the widespread phenomenon of the nationalizing state in the modern age.[57]

This conduciveness for use as a reality-simplifying rule of thumb also helps explain other assumptions about ethnicity that frequently appear in seminal works. For one thing, we better understand why elites frequently turn to ethnicity in their efforts to manipulate perceptions of their actions, as Brass documents,[58] and why populations frequently buy into the ethnic discourse. We also learn how ethnic divides can be broadly correlated with differences in values,[59] including different preferences regarding public goods, without necessarily being the actual source or product of these value differences. Different local modes of life and different local histories tend to give rise to distinct local values, and ethnic divides are frequently correlated with these modes of life and histories for reasons just described. To the extent that these distinct local values and behavioral expectations reflect coordination equilibria,[60] ethnic markers can also be useful to both insiders and outsiders in recognizing these equilibria so as to react to them.

---

[56] Hechter, *Internal Colonialism*.

[57] For example, Anderson, *Imagined Communities*; Brubaker, *Nationalism Reframed*; and Gellner, *Nations and Nationalism*.

[58] Brass, *Theft of an Idol*.

[59] As Hechter (*Containing Nationalism*) and many economists (e.g., Alesina, Baquir, and Easterly, "Public Goods") posit.

[60] Laitin, *Nations, States, and Violence*. Some ethnic traits, like language, are of course themselves coordination equilibria. But even though coordination is important in much of ethnic identity, it is only one aspect of a broader phenomenon that is more fundamentally rooted in uncertainty reduction.

Overall, it is the combination of all these properties that makes "ethnicity" useful as a concept and that, indeed, underlies its widespread use and the importance that scholars and ordinary people so often attach to it. For the rest of this book, therefore, an "ethnic group" is defined broadly, as a set of people who (a) have a common point of reference to at least one ethnic dimension of the social world; (b) share the view that they indeed have this in common; and (c) capture this similarity in a label, the ethnic group's name. By "ethnic," we follow Weber in referring to perceptions of common descent and culture along with at least some traits usually associated with these things, including shared language, physical resemblance, and common ritual regulation of life, including religion.[61] "Ethnic identity," then, is simply the corresponding subset of the ethnic points of personal reference that define any given individual. The term "ethnicity" is taken to be simply another word for ethnic identity.

Ethnicity as Conceptually Prior to Utility Seeking and Emotional Behavior

To say that ethnicity is a product of the drive to reduce uncertainty is to say that ethnicity is conceptually *prior* to the realm of interest-driven or emotional behavior. Here it is important to distinguish between the concepts of uncertainty and risk.[62] Both concepts refer to situations where a precise outcome is unknown, but the unknown can take two different forms. We are in the realm of *risk* when we do not know which among many possible outcomes will obtain, but when we can at least attach probabilities to the different possible outcomes. For example, flipping a coin is usually considered a matter of risk because one can say with confidence that there is a 50 percent chance of a heads outcome and a 50 percent chance of tails. We are in the realm of *uncertainty* when we cannot attach any probabilities to the various outcomes, as when we might not even be able to ascertain what the possible outcomes are or when we have no basis upon which to judge likelihood. When one can assess risk, utility-maximizing behavior is possible because one can choose a strategy that one believes will result in the most desirable outcome, somehow weighting each outcome by its likelihood of actually occurring. One is in no such position under uncertainty: Action might as well be random because the person has no idea how to consider what the consequences will be. When one is faced with a situation of uncertainty, therefore, one must find a way of reducing this uncertainty before any kind of purposive action is possible.[63]

As noted earlier, there is little that is certain about the social world, making a theory of how people cope with this fact quite pertinent. This lack of certainty is due both to the social world's enormous complexity (at least, in all but

---

[61] Weber, "Ethnic Groups."

[62] I am grateful to Michael Hechter for calling my attention to this distinction.

[63] Debra Friedman, Michael Hechter, and Satoshi Kanazawa, "A Theory of the Value of Children," *Demography*, v.31, no.3, August 1994, pp. 375–401.

small isolated communities) and to natural variation in human personality and the resulting impossibility of fully knowing the mind of another person. A theory of behavior in the social world, therefore, must consider the mechanisms by which people cope with this uncertainty. This is not to say that humans are perfect and accurate calculators of probabilities, nor that they make decisions to act based on unbiased estimates. It is not even to say that people cope with uncertainty by assigning probabilities, by consciously turning uncertainty into risk. It turns out that much of this coping is through ingrained mental mechanisms that merely approximate the turning of uncertainty into risk, with certain kinds of situations automatically activating schemas, cuing perceptual categories, or triggering emotions that are associated with particular responses – as if uncertainty is turned directly into certainty, skipping the stage of actually assessing probabilities to various potential outcomes. Either way, theory building is likely to be most promising if it fits closely with the various mechanisms by which people effectively reduce uncertainty in their lives.

The phenomenon of ethnicity reflects just such a mechanism, a mechanism doing its work before people act on the basis of desires or emotions. It manifests a human drive to reduce social uncertainty by organizing the world into thick social categories that imply probabilities as to how the actions of others are likely to affect one and that sometimes prescribe immediate reactive action, thereby effectively turning uncertainty directly into "certainty," as least as far as choosing one's actions is concerned. That is, ethnicity interprets the world, making action on the basis of interests or emotion (a mechanism for changing the saliency of desires[64]) possible.

Crucially, uncertainty reduction (at least, as discussed here) is not just another form of utility maximization. That is, it is not just another value that one can "plug in" to a person's utility function and that the person can then be expected to pursue along with other sources of utility. For one thing, uncertainty reduction through ethnicity is primarily an unconscious behavior. Psychological evidence suggests that adopting a category-based rule of thumb (like a "thick" ethnic categorization) is not a controlled cognitive process. Instead it is unconscious, rapid, effortless, and involuntary.[65] Hence, for example, many well-intentioned people who genuinely detest racism on principle sometimes find themselves lapsing into thoughts or behaviors based on racial stereotypes. Such processes, however abhorrent particular examples may be, are explained in psychological terms as a way people's brains attempt to draw quick, easy conclusions about how the world is likely to affect them and how they should react.[66] This example also illustrates that the uncertainty-reducing mechanism of ethnicity can sometimes enter the realm of consciousness, especially as people learn about psychology or come to disapprove of the injustice of rules of thumb based on a given thick categorization.

[64] Petersen, *Understanding Ethnic Violence*, pp. 17–18.
[65] Forsyth, *Group Dynamics*, p. 77.
[66] Gordon W. Allport, *The Nature of Prejudice* (Reading, MA: Addison-Wesley, 1954), p. 19; Brown, *Group Processes*, 1st edition, pp. 227–8; Erikson, *Identity and the Life Cycle*, p. 30; Forsyth, *Group Dynamics*, p. 78; Hirschfeld, *Race*; Hogg and Mullin, "Joining Groups."

More generally, however, these processes occur outside of awareness.[67] Indeed, the fact that ethnicity as an uncertainty-reducing mechanism operates primarily in the realm of the unconscious makes ethnic identification feel more natural, real, and intense than the conscious choices people make based on motives that they both perceive and/or decide whether to pursue, such as deciding to become a lawyer or to join the local choir.

Of course, there are certain benefits that a person may obtain directly from the very process of uncertainty reduction. One is a "feeling of certainty," which is sometimes valued in its own right. As Hogg and Mullin put it, "people have a fundamental need to feel certain about their world and their place within it – subjective certainty renders existence meaningful and thus gives one confidence about how to behave, and what to expect from the physical and social environment within which one finds oneself."[68] A feeling of certainty can also be valued because its opposite, a feeling of uncertainty, is aversive. It is aversive because it correlates with a lack of control over one's life and can give rise to feelings like unease and fear.[69] Thus, in some realms of human behavior, people are found to maximize a feeling of certainty, defined as a form of utility. For example, Friedman, Hechter, and Kanazawa find that the desire for uncertainty reduction better explains fertility patterns than do people's normative beliefs or their pursuit of instrumental values like material well-being.[70]

There is also evidence that people can derive self-esteem from successfully reducing the level of uncertainty in an uncertain situation, and fascinatingly this may provide a better explanation for some of the psychological findings on which the "hard ethnicity-as-conflictual" theories described in Chapter 2 are based. That is, the self-esteem generated in Tajfel's original "minimal group" experiments may not have derived from the denigration that ingroups inflicted on outgroups, but instead from uncertainty reduction that also took place during the course of the experiments. Hogg and Mullin thus provide a head-to-head test of the uncertainty reduction and self-esteem hypotheses by replicating Tajfel's minimal group experiments in conditions of greater and lesser uncertainty. Remarkably, they find that the self-esteem produced in such experiments tends to *depend on levels of uncertainty*. That is, the results were stronger under conditions of uncertainty (in this case, the first time a subject had participated in such an exercise) than in conditions of greater environmental certainty (when participants had previous experience in such experiments, getting used to the format and expectations).[71] People, this and other research suggests, derive self-esteem from their ability successfully to impose some modicum of cognitive order

---

[67] Brown, *Group Processes*, 2nd edition, p. 264.

[68] Hogg and Mullin, "Joining Groups," pp. 253–5.

[69] Hogg and Mullin, "Joining Groups," pp. 253–5; Johan M. G. van der Dennen, "Ethnocentrism and In-group/Out-group Differentiation: A Review and Interpretation of the Literature," in Vernon Reynolds, Vincent Falger, and Ian Vine, eds., *The Sociobiology of Ethnocentrism* (Athens: University of Georgia Press, 1987), pp. 1–47, 39–46.

[70] Friedman, Hechter, and Kanazawa, "A Theory."

[71] Hogg and Mullin, "Joining Groups."

(meaningful social categories) on an uncertain social world, not from the fact of disadvantaging groups of which they are not a part.

Even though uncertainty reduction may be associated with tangible benefits like self-esteem and a positive feeling of certainty, these largely remain *by-products* of the underlying uncertainty-reduction drive rather than the *reasons why* uncertainty reduction takes place. That is, people do not think in terms of ethnicity and invoke ethnic categories primarily because they just happen to find it a useful way of achieving a good feeling. Instead, the most important drive is to actually reduce uncertainty, and the positive feeling and self-esteem that may result are best interpreted as feelings that would naturally accompany a process that by its nature allows people to more effectively engage the world that surrounds them to obtain things they desire. That is, the general, fundamental need to reduce uncertainty in order to navigate the social world is the primary motive driving ethnicity, while any self-esteem or other associated forms of utility are secondary.

Moreover, the drive to reduce uncertainty through identity is not a drive to *maximize* a feeling of certainty. Indeed, psychologists have found that people do not seek to reduce uncertainty in all situations and in all areas of life, as they would do if they were primarily subjective certainty maximizers. Instead, because uncertainty reduction is primarily a mechanism for making social action possible for the purpose of obtaining other ends, people tend to invoke these uncertainty-reducing mechanisms mainly in situations that are subjectively important, where something else of value to them is at stake.[72] One set of research findings helps illustrate this point. If people were certainty maximizers, we would expect them to consistently invoke the thickest possible categorizations in their attempts to understand their world, thereby eliminating all sense of uncertainty. Yet research has found that the degree to which people resort to such categorizations to explain their world can change dramatically as the situation changes, rendering their need to reduce uncertainty more or less immediate. Thus, massive uncertainties like economic collapse and social upheaval – as in Weimar Germany – are widely associated with the newly broad appeal of very thick (encompassing, compelling) social categories involving ethnic stereotypes and group conspiracy theories.[73] Similarly, the appearance of a category-based threat also tends both to enhance the thickness of the category and to expand the range of activities it guides.[74]

Ethnicity, then, is a prior first step to utility-maximizing behavior, making the social world intelligible so that one better understands how to pursue what one desires. It is instrumentally useful, not a good that is pursued due to immanent value.[75] Ethnicity is the realm not of the irrational, but of the *pre*-rational.

---

[72] Hogg and Mullin, "Joining Groups," pp. 253–5.

[73] Hogg and Mullin, "Joining Groups," pp. 266–7; Stephen E. Hanson, *Ideology, Uncertainty, and Democracy: Party Formation in Third Republic France, Weimar Germany and Post-Soviet Russia* (New York: Cambridge University Press, forthcoming).

[74] Tajfel, "Social Psychology," p. 15; Forsyth, *Group Dynamics*, p. 388; Van der Dennen, "Ethnocentrism," pp. 35–6.

[75] On immanent and instrumental values, see Michael Hechter, "Should Values Be Written Out of the Social Scientist's Lexicon?" *Sociological Theory*, v.10, no.2, autumn 1992, pp. 214–30.

Functionalism and Consistency with a Theory of Human Evolution

This theory of ethnicity could well be interpreted as a functionalist argument. In part, this is true because the theory starts with the premise that identity is something that serves a particular function. This need not be a problem, though. For one thing, there is a place for functionalist arguments in the sciences. Biology, for example, considers it progress to identify an important function of, say, a particular gene or an organ – this provides a premise upon which theories of the organism can be further developed. To the extent that the capacity for perceiving the social world is located in the brain, the present analysis is quite analogous to the mode of theory development in biology just described.

Arguments that start by positing a function of something can also constitute part of a valid explanation for that something if a plausible and testable causal mechanism that can account for why something's function should bring it into existence is also hypothesized. The present chapter does this in two ways. First, it explains *why* ethnicity serves this function more universally than other traits or potential cleavages extant in human society like class or gender: Ethnic traits have special (though not entirely unique) properties that, taken together, make them particularly useful as rules of thumb for interpreting and navigating the social world.

Even more fundamentally, the notions of evolution and natural selection potentially provide the required plausible and testable mechanism by which the general human capacity for categorical thinking came into existence by virtue of its function. This is not a "social Darwinian" hypothesis: The thing that is posited to have evolved is not a social structure of any kind, but the human brain itself. Because it is widely accepted that humans are an evolved species and that the brain is an organ subject to processes of mutation, it is certainly plausible to suspect that certain kinds of cognitive mechanisms (capacities in the brain) might have evolved over evolutionary history. To make this argument, as evolutionary psychologists have averred, one must ground the case for adaptive favorability in periods long before human civilization appeared.[76]

The notion of identity presented here is fully consistent with what evolutionary psychologists say is a convergence of research on the general finding that the human brain consists of multiple, coordinated domain-specific problem-solving mechanisms (such as a mechanism for language acquisition) rather than a single domain-general mechanism (such as "social learning" or "trial-and-error induction") that approaches perfect rationality. These domain-specific mechanisms can be loosely characterized as "instincts."[77] The tendency for social categorization is

---

[76] Jerome H. Barkow, Leda Cosmides, and John Tooby, *The Adapted Mind: Evolutionary Psychology and the Generation of Culture* (New York: Oxford University Press, 1992); Leda Cosmides and John Tooby, "Evolutionary Psychology: A Primer," January 13, 1997, *http://www.psych.ucsb.edu/research/cep/primer.html*.

[77] John Tooby and Leda Cosmides, "The Psychological Foundations of Culture," in Jerome H. Barkow, Cosmides, and Tooby, eds., *The Adapted Mind: Evolutionary Psychology and the Generation of Culture* (New York: Oxford University Press, 1992), pp. 19–136; Cosmides and Tooby, "Evolutionary Psychology."

likely to be just such a mechanism or instinct, adaptively favorable in evolutionary historical terms because of its ability to quickly and efficiently detect and predict behavior (such as coalitional activity) that can have a direct effect on a person's or people's reproductive chances, for example, by altering one's access to scarce resources necessary for survival.[78]

Of course, the central argument made here about ethnicity and identity does not hinge on the claims of evolutionary psychology; it stands on its own for all of the reasons presented in this volume. Nevertheless, the fact that it is consistent not only with such an array of empirical evidence but also with a more fundamental theory of human biology only reinforces our confidence in the conclusions and suggests additional avenues for research.[79]

BEYOND UNCERTAINTY REDUCTION: ETHNIC POLITICS AS THE REALM OF "ORDINARY" INTERESTS

If ethnicity is essentially a social uncertainty-reducing device that is useful for pursuing whatever individuals desire, then the realm of ethnic *politics* is driven by these desires. To say that ethnicity is about uncertainty reduction, as the previous section of this chapter does, is to say nothing about what people might want to do in their newly-less-uncertain worlds nor about why they might want to do things that require social navigation in the first place. *Uncertainty reduction, then, is a domain-specific motive*, one that applies only in situations of subjective importance where attempts to uniquely evaluate all involved individuals and their relationships to every other relevant individual are either beyond human capacity or too costly in the time and effort they would require. *Other motives, therefore, must determine what situations are subjectively important and drive the particular use to which categorical thinking (including ethnic thinking) is put.* This leads us to a very important conclusion: *There is no such thing as an inherently ethnic interest or ethnic preference.* Instead, we should assume ethnic group behavior is motivated by the same kinds of motives that drive human behavior more generally in all kinds of situations.

One such motive includes the desire for material goods and economic welfare. Material resources are very widely desired because they can be vital to survival in conditions of shortage and, more generally, have a large impact on one's life chances. Hence, as has been well documented, material motives have been associated not only with the need for uncertainty reduction[80] but also with a great deal of intergroup hostility and discriminatory behavior.[81] In fact, it has been shown that group categories (including ethnic ones) can become important to people as rules of thumb at least in part because they help people make sense of social situations that have great implications for their material well-being.[82]

[78] Kurzban, Tooby, and Cosmides, "Can Race."
[79] Also see Van der Dennen, "Ethnocentrism," p. 47.
[80] Forsyth, *Group Dynamics*, pp. 375–83.
[81] Van der Dennen, "Ethnocentrism."
[82] Forsyth, *Group Dynamics*, pp. 375–83.

Experiments have also found that introducing material objects of competition increases intergroup hostility.[83] This is intuitively obvious – just reflecting on the local nightly news will likely turn up quite a bit of evidence that people can get very emotionally involved in an issue when they have something material at stake and when they feel that they may be denied by the actions of a coalition of others.

Surprisingly, a number of leading specialists on ethnicity sweepingly dismiss theories giving material motives central roles, calling materialism completely unable to account for the passion and emotion involved in intergroup conflict. They claim that we need to look instead to what they portray as the intrinsically nonrational psychology of the ethnic bond or emotion for the explanation. But as noted previously, such critics rarely themselves cite actual psychological research to justify these claims.[84] Horowitz is a very prominent exception; he does make such claims but also grounds them in an extensive discussion of psychological research as well as a sophisticated analysis of multiple cases of ethnic relationships.[85] In part, Horowitz's conclusions can be explained by his heavy reliance on parts of the Social Identity Theory tradition of the 1970s and 1980s that were critiqued in Chapter 2.[86] But because Horowitz's position is based on more than this and has come to inform other important works, his argument against materialism deserves to be taken very seriously by anyone making a different case.

Horowitz presents a great deal of case study evidence that ethnic group leaders and even masses are often quite willing to undergo enormous economic hardship for the sake of nonmaterial gains, such as recognition or symbolic status.[87] But to conclude from this that material concerns have no role requires a major oversimplification of what is at stake. If all that is at stake in such situations is a single, one-time tradeoff between economic welfare and, say, symbolic gain, then Horowitz might be right. But in a later passage, without exploring the implications for his previous argument, Horowitz writes that ethnic groups are involved not just in a "single game" but in lifelong games where people believe that one loss now can lead to a permanent disability.[88] In this light, we can clearly see why the emotion involved in ethnic conflicts sometimes seems out of proportion to the material stakes of the moment – what is really at stake is not just the momentary object, but a whole future stream of gains that may depend on the precedent set at that particular moment. If group members fear that their existence or future well-being might be at stake if they do not secede, for example, it may well be more than worth intense short-run costs to procure national independence and thereby secure what they see as a greater long-run

---

[83] Ibid., p. 378.
[84] For example, Scott, "A Resynthesis"; Smith, *Myths*.
[85] Horowitz, *Ethnic Groups in Conflict*.
[86] Ibid., pp. 104, 131–4, 144–6. Similar are Kaufman, *Modern Hatreds*, and Petersen, *Understanding Ethnic Violence*.
[87] Horowitz, *Ethnic Groups in Conflict*, pp. 131–4.
[88] Ibid., p. 147.

stream of material benefits.[89] Since material resources are undoubtedly a very important determinant of one's life chances, it is eminently understandable that these conflicts could become quite emotional. It is premature, therefore, for Horowitz to claim that it is "obvious" that economic theories cannot explain the extent of emotion involved in ethnic conflict. That economic motives may not be conscious does not mean that they are not there, hardwired into the human brain and operating through the reality-simplifying social radar of ethnic identity.

Horowitz also criticizes materialist theories for being unable to explain the struggle over symbols that have no intrinsic material value. The struggle over symbols is better interpreted through at least two insights, however. In part, the group that is able to establish its symbols most firmly in state institutions is also thereby sending a signal to others about who has the greatest likelihood of success in obtaining material (and other) resources in the future and who needs to be reckoned with by those seeking exchange. Moreover, in light of the preceding discussion of what makes ethnicity special, it is clear that ethnic group symbols can have real implications by evoking "ethnic behavior" (making ethnicity situationally available as a guide to interpretation and behavior) and perhaps cuing particular responses through the activation of "ethnic schema" that may exist. It is no leap to imagine that expectations of long-run access to material resources might be at stake in these "symbolic" struggles. In light of this reasoning and the evidence presented earlier, then, it is no surprise that elites promoting group identification would be willing to sacrifice short-run material well-being for the purpose of establishing their group's symbolic framework in state institutions, thereby promoting a much greater long-run stream of material resources. Materialism, then, can fully be expected to serve as a key motive involved in ethnic group behavior.

The desire for material gain is certainly not the only motive driving the behavior of ethnic groups. Another is *security*, what one might call a "survival instinct" associated with feelings like fear or anxiety. Such a motive is likely to be quite important in those cases where physical well-being is potentially at stake along group lines due to either the natural or social environment. Additionally, the seeking of fungible resources like *power* can also constitute an important motivation because those with, for example, political influence can often translate this into many other goods they might seek, be they material resources, security, or something else.[90] Laitin also finds evidence that people pursue *status* in their choice of language repertoires and that these status considerations are reflected in the attitudes they take toward those who speak different languages.[91] Indeed, *self-esteem* can also be a motive behind the behavior of ethnic groups once they are formed – even as we deny self-esteem pride of place as the primary motivation

---

[89] For example, Abdelal (*National Purpose*, p. 113) shows that Ukrainian separatists saw the short-term costs of breaking with Russia as necessary to bear for the sake of longer term gain.

[90] Atul Kohli, "Can Democracies Accommodate Ethnic Nationalism? Rise and Decline of Self-Determination Movements in India," *Journal of Asian Studies*, v.56, no.2, May 1997, pp. 325–44.

[91] Laitin, *Identity in Formation*.

behind the actual formation of groups and group-oriented thinking.[92] Indeed, Petersen is convincing that self-esteem considerations are at least partly behind the resentment that has fueled much of the ethnic violence in twentieth-century Eastern Europe.[93]

Overall, ethnicity is not a motive for behavior but a form of social radar that guides *how* people interpret the social world and pursue their interests. These interests might include material, political, and other forms of gain as well as goods that are valued in their own right like security or self-esteem. Ethnicity, then, is the realm of uncertainty reduction, whereas ethnic politics is the domain of interests.

CONCLUSION

The motive behind ethnic identification is uncertainty reduction, whereas the motives behind the behavior of the resulting ethnic groups derive from the various interests people have. Ethnicity is thus most usefully described as neither primordial nor constructed, neither inherently conflictual nor epiphenomenal, but as *relational* at its core. Ethnicity defines the individual in relation to the social world, a process that occurs prior to purposive action. People have many points of personal reference that help them navigate the social world, and ethnicity possesses several properties that, in combination, greatly facilitate its usage as a rule of thumb for inferring much information about the social world and for acting within it. These properties (which may not all be involved in any given ethnic category) include perceptibility, high costs of change, inherent importance in social interaction, association with perceived important commonalities of fate, and correlation with other cleavages that are important to people. Although utility-maximizing behavior is certainly important, it is possible only after uncertainty reduction, a function that ethnicity serves. Ethnicity, then, is neither a motive in its own right nor epiphenomenal. Instead, it is a primary device for uncertainty reduction that precedes interest-oriented behavior.

The insight that ethnicity is about making sense of the world is not new, of course. Many other works have acknowledged that ethnicity serves this purpose in at least some realms of human experience.[94] Hardly any of these accounts, however, explore the full ramifications of this idea, assuming instead that ethnic identification derives primarily from some form of utility maximization, be this utility defined in terms of a sense of relative group worth[95] or "rewards to which it provides access."[96] In other words, the relational aspect of ethnicity gets remarkably short shrift in the literature on ethnic politics, overpowered

[92] Hogg and Mullin, "Joining Groups."

[93] Petersen, *Understanding Ethnic Violence.*

[94] For example, Fearon, "What Is Identity"; Horowitz, *Ethnic Groups in Conflict,* p. 82; Posner, *Institutions and Ethnic Politics,* p. 11.

[95] Horowitz, *Ethnic Groups in Conflict.*

[96] Posner, *Institutions and Ethnic Politics,* p. 12.

by assumptions that the previous chapter showed are not as well supported by research into human behavior.

The exceptions in the literature can be regarded as the pioneers of what this volume calls a relational approach to understanding ethnicity, perhaps beginning with the aforementioned seminal work of Mead and other psychologists who built upon his insights. In other social sciences, the relational aspect of identity has been given a central role in important work by such theorists as Young (who termed identity "relational" as early as 1976), Hopf (who considers identity in international relations to be explicitly "relational"), and the Brubaker team (which, as described in Chapter 2, has made some of the pathbreaking connections between the concept of ethnicity and cutting-edge psychological research on how people see the world).[97] The approach also resonates with interpretivist research on the variable meaning actors invest in identity categories in defining their relationships to the social world.[98]

The present volume builds on this foundation, seeking to establish a tighter and more powerful version of relational theory, to go well beyond describing and documenting identity's relational nature (the chief contribution of past relational works) to systematizing and explaining it through a specific logic. This logic should be capable of generating distinct, testable hypotheses and significantly improving our understanding of the most important ethnic phenomena. The success of such a broad theoretical initiative would be impossible to fully demonstrate in one volume, so this book seeks to persuade readers of its viability though "case comparisons within a case study." That is, the following chapter considers the case of separatism, one variety of ethnic politics, in order to show how the general relational theory can undergird new, more specific theories of ethnic politics. The advantages of this version of relational theory compared to its rivals are then illustrated through systematic case comparisons involving ethnic groups in the former Soviet region.

---

[97] Crawford Young, *The Politics of Cultural Pluralism* (Madison: University of Wisconsin, 1976), p. 41; Hopf, *Social Construction*; Rogers Brubaker, *Ethnicity Without Groups* (Cambridge, MA: Harvard University Press, 2004).

[98] For example, Lloyd I. Rudolph and Susanne Hoeber Rudolph, "Engaging Subjective Knowledge: How Amar Singh's Diary Narratives of and by the Self Explain Identity Formation," *Perspectives on Politics*, v.1, no.4, December 2003, pp. 681–94; Lisa Wedeen, "Conceptualizing Culture: Possibilities for Political Science," *American Political Science Review*, v.96, no.4, December 2002, pp. 713–28.

4

A Theory of National Separatism in Domestic and Interstate Politics

To demonstrate the potential of the broad relational theory of ethnicity just outlined, this chapter uses it to develop a more concrete theory of national separatism. Separatism thus serves as a case of the more general phenomenon of ethnic politics that the relational theory is intended to illuminate. It is a useful case for several reasons. For one thing, it is reflective of what this volume has called the great puzzle of ethnic politics. Next to nearly every region with a strong separatist movement (Slovenia in Yugoslavia, Ukraine in the USSR, the Igbo territory in Nigeria's First Republic, and Quebec in Canada, among others), one also finds regions where the main ethnic minority representatives favor continued political integration (Montenegro in Yugoslavia, Uzbekistan in the USSR, the Yoruba-land in Nigeria, and Nunavut in Canada). The puzzle even reaches international relations, as Turkey has been challenging the European Union (EU) to admit it, while Norway remains a stalwart of separation. These differences are extremely important, with separatism linked to the breakup of states like the USSR and the outbreak of civil war in countries like Nigeria. Of course, separatism is not necessarily bad: Many members of oppressed minority groups see it as their best hope of escaping repression in states dominated by representatives of other groups.

The present chapter begins by showing that despite some seminal insights, the dominant theories of secession (generally rooted either in ethnicity-as-conflictual or ethnicity-as-epiphenomenal theory) do not satisfactorily account for observed patterns. It then builds the relational theory of separatism, locating its source in a collective action problem that is exacerbated by ethnicity's uncertainty-reducing mechanism. Variation in separatism depends on factors influencing how this collective action problem is interpreted by the minority group, especially the nature of ethnic divides, the behavior of any preexisting central government, leaders' framing strategies, institutionally mediated interests, and whether the potentially separatist region is already an independent state.

Before moving forward, please note that since separatism inherently concerns territory, the ethnic groups in question are almost always territorially concentrated ones. And since a territorially concentrated ethnic group is a nation by the definition given in this book, both terms are used interchangeably in what follows.

Most studies of separatism – in both domestic politics and international relations – are generally rooted in the assumptions of ethnicity-as-conflictual theory or ethnicity-as-epiphenomenal theory.[1]

Ethnicity-as-Conflictual Theories of Separatism

Many theories locate the driving force for separatism in conflictual tendencies inherent in ethnicity: When ethnic difference coincides at least roughly with territorial concentrations, self-conscious groups defined by these differences tend either to try to dominate the state or separate their territory from it. This basic proposition has generated three kinds of explanations for patterns of national separatism:[2]

1. *National Consciousness arguments* consider separatism primarily an expression of national consciousness.[3] Explaining separatism, then, largely boils down to explaining the rise of national consciousness, often attributed to identity itself,[4] contingent historical processes of identity construction and contestation,[5] broad historical processes like industrialization or globalization,[6] or institutions like ethnofederalism.[7]

2. *Capabilities arguments* suppose that the potential for separatism exists within every nation but that the ability actually to pursue it does not.[8] Variation in separatism, then, depends on factors that influence what a given group

[1] Since many do not explicitly or completely identify their underlying assumptions about the nature of ethnicity, we are forced to extrapolate in some of what follows.

[2] The three kinds of explanations are each compatible with hard, soft, or ultrasoft ethnicity-as-conflictual assumptions as to the actual source of ethnicity's conflictual tendencies. See Chapter 2.

[3] "National consciousness" refers to an active belief that one belongs to a particular nation. This notion will also be called "national identification" or a personal "sense of national distinctiveness."

[4] Taylor, "The Politics of Recognition"; Geertz, "The Integrative Revolution."

[5] Ralph R. Premdas, "Secessionist Movements in Comparative Perspective," in Premdas, S. W. R. de A. Samarasinghe, and Alan B. Anderson, eds., *Secessionist Movements in Comparative Perspective* (London: Pinter Publishers, 1990), pp. 12–29; Anthony Smith, ed., *Nationalist Movements* (London: The MacMillan Press Ltd., 1976); Franke Wilmer, *The Social Construction of Man, the State, and War: Identity, Conflict, and Violence in Former Yugoslavia* (New York: Routledge, 2002).

[6] Anderson, *Imagined Communities*; Black, *The Dynamics of Modernization*; Deutsch, *Nationalism and Social Communication*; Gellner, *Nations and Nationalism*; Huntington, *The Clash*.

[7] Gail W. Lapidus, "From Democratization to Disintegration," in Lapidus and Victor Zaslavsky, with Philip Goldman, eds., *From Union to Commonwealth* (New York: Cambridge University Press, 1992); Carol Skalnik Leff, "Democratization and Disintegration in Multinational States," *World Politics*, v.51, January 1999, pp. 205–35; Hudson Meadwell, "Nationalism in Quebec," *World Politics*, v.45, 1993, pp. 203–41; Suny, *The Revenge*.

[8] This approach draws on sociological theories of "political opportunity structure" (Sidney Tarrow, *Power in Movement: Social Movements, Collective Action and Politics*, New York: Cambridge University Press, 1994) and "resource mobilization" (John D. McCarthy and Mayer N. Zald, "Resource

is capable of, including: the repressive capacity of an existing union state;[9] activity-sustaining resources such as those ethnofederalism might provide,[10] and less tangible resources like the ability to conceive of independence as being possible or templates for action provided by the prior actions of others.[11]

3. *Countervailing Incentives arguments* also assume a universal tendency toward separation among self-conscious nations, but hold that material or political incentives can override the separatist ethnic impulses. These countervailing incentives might include (expected) political upward mobility in the central government,[12] ideological differences with union authorities,[13] and considerations of relative economic well-being – specifically, the poorest regions and groups are usually expected to be the most eager seceders within a given state because they have incentive to escape the position of poverty and denigration in which they find themselves.[14] Some work on international integration posits that nations generally prefer independent states but might willingly surrender some sovereignty to a larger entity for economic gain or security against third parties.[15]

Mobilization and Social Movements: A Partial Theory," *American Journal of Sociology*, v.86, no.6, 1977, pp. 1212–41).

[9] Jane Dawson, *Eco-Nationalism: Anti-Nuclear Activism and National Identity in Russia, Lithuania, and Ukraine* (Durham, NC: Duke University Press, 1996); Sumit Ganguly, *The Crisis in Kashmir: Portents of War, Hopes of Peace* (Cambridge: Cambridge University Press, 1997); Paul Mojzes, *Yugoslavian Inferno: Ethnoreligious Warfare in the Balkans* (New York: Continuum, 1994); Alexander Motyl, *Sovietology, Rationality, Nationality: Coming to Grips with Nationalism in the USSR* (New York: Columbia University Press, 1990); Donna Lee Van Cott, "Explaining Ethnic Autonomy Regimes in Latin America," *Studies in Comparative International Development*, v.35, no.4, winter 2001, pp. 30–58.

[10] Beverly Crawford, "Explaining Cultural Conflict in Ex-Yugoslavia," in Crawford and Ronnie D. Lipschutz, eds., *The Myth of Ethnic Conflict* (Berkeley: International and Area Studies Research Series, University of California, Berkeley, 1998, no.98); Gorenburg, *Minority Ethnic Mobilization*; Philip G. Roeder, "Peoples and States After 1989," *Slavic Review*, v.58, no.4, winter 1999, pp. 854–82.

[11] Beissinger, *Nationalist Mobilization*; Ted Robert Gurr, *Minorities at Risk* (Washington, DC: United States Institute of Peace Press, 1993); Edward W. Walker, *Dissolution: Sovereignty and the Breakup of the Soviet Union* (New York: Rowman and Littlefield, 2003).

[12] Horowitz, *Ethnic Groups in Conflict*, pp. 229–88; Subrata K. Mitra, "The Rational Politics of Cultural Nationalism: Subnational Movements of South Asia in Comparative Perspective," *British Journal of Political Science*, v.25, January 1995, pp. 57–78; Ronald Rogowski, "Causes and Varieties of Nationalism: A Rationalist Account," in Edward Tiryakian and Rogowski, eds., *New Nationalisms of the Developed West: Toward Explanation* (Boston: Allen & Unwin, 1985), pp. 87–108.

[13] Stephen E. Hanson, "Ideology, Interests, and Identity: Comparing the Soviet and Russian Secession Crises," in Mikhail A. Alexseev, ed., *Center-Periphery Conflict in Post-Soviet Russia: A Federation Imperiled* (New York: St. Martin's Press, 1999), pp.15–46.

[14] Horowitz, *Ethnic Groups in Conflict*; Mitra, "The Rational Politics"; Joseph R. Rudolph and Robert J. Thompson, "Ethnoterritorial Movements and the Policy Process: Accommodating Nationalist Demands in the Developed World," *Comparative Politics*, v.17, no.3, April 1985, pp. 291–312; John R. Wood, "Secession: A Comparative Analytical Framework," *Canadian Journal of Political Science*, v.14, no.1, March 1981, pp. 107–34. Hechter makes a similar argument in *Internal Colonialism* and "The Dynamics of Secession" (*Acta Sociologica*, v.35, 1992, pp. 267–83), but argues in his later *Containing Nationalism* that secessionism can be associated with regional wealth as well as poverty.

[15] Haas, *The Uniting of Europe*.

Just as Chapters 2 and 3 have found problems in the core propositions of ethnicity-as-conflictual theory, so do we find difficulties facing the specific theories of separatism that it spawns. National Consciousness arguments often flirt with tautology, interpreting history in a way that is strongly colored by already knowing the outcome. Capabilities arguments face a similar peril: The capacity to engage in separatist mobilization is most easily identified when separatist mobilization is actually observed, but it is less easily distinguished before the fact. For example, arguments stressing the separatism-inducing effects of ethnofederal institutions do not explain well why some nations seem to respond to these forces, while others do not.[16]

Countervailing Incentives arguments avoid some of these problems by suggesting a range of variables that explain why some groups do not seem to be following the expected urge for independence even when they have the chance. But they leave us uncertain as to how much material or political benefit it takes to override the inherently conflictual tendencies supposedly involved in ethnic difference. Indeed, if any behavior that would seem to compromise the goal of sovereignty can be explained away with reference to other factors, the theory becomes unfalsifiable and unhelpful as an explanation. Moreover, the proposition that material or political considerations routinely override purely "ethnic" considerations sits quite uneasily with the psychological foundations of hard ethnicity-as-conflictual theory, which stresses the primacy of self-esteem and personal dignity as motives and often explicitly denies that materialism can trump the "passion" associated with ethnic desires.

Ethnicity-as-Epiphenomenal Theories of Separatism

Other theories of separatism draw on ethnicity-as-epiphenomenal assumptions, denying that ethnicity provides any motive for separatism. Instead, separatism is said usually to come from economic or political interests. Because these interests can be calculated in myriad ways, so do we find myriad permutations of ethnicity-as-epiphenomenal theories of separatism. Turning to economic considerations, some argue that richer regions are more likely to display separatism than poorer ones because they want to avoid having their resources redistributed,[17] while others explicitly reject this "wealth hypothesis" and point instead to perceptions of group-based economic injustice or ethnic labor competition.[18] Political considerations are also widely thought to matter, especially expectations of upward mobility in a (potential) union state and intergenerational competition for jobs within groups.[19] Holding such material and political interests constant, other

---

[16] Some cite other factors ad hoc (e.g., Bunce, *Subversive Institutions*) or attribute unexplained variation to contingency.

[17] Bates, "Ethnic Competition"; Milica Zarkovic Bookman, *The Economics of Secession* (New York: St. Martin's Press, 1993).

[18] Elise Giuliano, "Secessionism from the Bottom Up: Democratization, Nationalism, and Local Accountability in the Russian Transition," *World Politics*, v.58, no.2, January 2006, pp. 276–310.

[19] Laitin, *Identity in Formation*; Laitin, "The National Uprisings in the Soviet Union," *World Politics*, v.44, no.1, October 1991, pp. 139–77.

ethnicity-as-epiphenomenal theories stress variation in the ability of political entrepreneurs to mobilize these interests to their advantage. Such variation comes from such factors as differential bargaining power (which depends on power over resources)[20] or the existence of important allies (such as neighboring "kin states").[21] There is strong disagreement, though, over the effects of some resources that may fall into the hands of ethnic group leaders. Some theorists warn that granting political autonomy to minority regions will only give elites there more resources to use for advancing separatist agendas,[22] though others argue autonomy can successfully appease such elites.[23] International relations (IR) theories nearly all fall into the ethnicity-as-epiphenomenal category since most hold that ethnic distinctiveness is not a factor influencing whether states choose to integrate politically with other states.[24] What matter are state interests pure and simple.[25]

In general, these theories are very promising in pointing to some of what this study will argue are the right variables. But as more general theories they leave room for improvement. Their biggest weakness lies in explaining why ethnicity is ever implicated in the separatist calculus in the first place. Fearon provides one intriguing answer: Ethnicity's relative visibility and hard-to-change nature make ethnic divides useful for leaders who want hard lines for deciding whom to include and exclude in resource allocation.[26] This is far from a satisfying answer, however. For one thing, there are many other "hard" lines that could form the basis for distribution decisions and coordination, including preexisting territorial-administrative divisions and, as Chandra points out, age and gender.[27] Why would ethnic content become associated with separatism when simple territoriality could suffice quite nicely for this purpose, especially when the latter is already institutionalized as a mechanism of selective resource distribution, as it often is? The problem of ethnicity's role is even more severe for bargaining theory, which cannot by itself explain why ethnic rhetoric has any bargaining value and which, crucially, has a hard time explaining why a region would *actually*

---

[20] Daniel S. Treisman, "Russia's 'Ethnic Revival': The Separatist Activism of Regional Leaders in a Postcommunist Order," *World Politics*, v.49, no.2, January 1997, pp. 212–49.

[21] James D. Fearon, "Commitment Problems and the Spread of Ethnic Conflict," in David A. Lake and Donald Rothchild, eds., *Ethnic Conflict* (Princeton, NJ: Princeton University Press, 1998), pp. 107–26; David D. Laitin, "Secessionist Rebellion in the Former Soviet Union," *Comparative Political Studies*, v.34, no.8, October 2001, pp. 839–61; Pieter Van Houten, "The Role of a Minority's Reference State in Ethnic Relations," *Archives Europeennes de Sociologie*, v.1, 1998, pp. 110–46.

[22] Paul R. Brass, *Ethnicity and Nationalism: Theory and Comparison* (London: Sage Publications, 1991); Svante E. Cornell, "Autonomy as a Source of Conflict: Caucasian Conflicts in Theoretical Perspective," *World Politics*, v.54, no.2, January 2002, pp. 245–76.

[23] Lustick, Miodownik, and Eidelson, "Secessionism in Multicultural States."

[24] See Abdelal, *National Purpose*.

[25] Robert O. Keohane and Joseph S. Nye, "International Interdependence and Integration," Fred Greenstein and Nelson Polsby, eds., *Handbook of Political Science*, v.8, 1975, pp. 363–414; Andrew Moravcsik, *The Choice for Europe: Social Purpose and State Power from Messina to Maastricht* (Ithaca, NY: Cornell University Press, 1998).

[26] Fearon, "Why Ethnic Politics."

[27] Chandra, "What Is Ethnicity."

secede and then sustain that independence if the whole purpose of bargaining is to maximize transfers from a central government.

Thus, we sense that scholars have already identified many of the key factors involved in separatism, but we also see that these factors have not yet been systematized and grounded in theory capable of making generalizations that are satisfying beyond answering a particular, isolated empirical puzzle. The rest of this chapter seeks to show how a more satisfying theory might be developed on the basis of a relational approach to ethnicity.

TOWARD A THEORY OF SEPARATISM BASED ON A RELATIONAL APPROACH
TO ETHNICITY

The relational approach to ethnicity outlined in Chapter 2 proves to be strong ground upon which to construct a powerful theory of separatism. The starting point is different from those of other theories. Ethnicity is not a product of utility maximization or the outcome of a spongelike absorption of consciousness. It is neither inherently conflictual nor epiphenomenal. Ethnicity, then, cannot supply the motive for separatism, but it also cannot be ignored. Instead, ethnicity is a mechanism for uncertainty reduction. And the way in which ethnicity reduces the uncertainty inherent to political integration tends to lower the expected value of cooperative strategies, making separatist ones more attractive.

A Behavioral Assumption: The Maximization of Life Chances

It is important to base theory on a clear statement of one's assumptions as to what drives behavior in the theory. This book's relational theory of ethnicity posits that uncertainty reduction drives ethnic identification, but that what people do with their identities depends on other motivations. It does not specify what these motivations are, though it does argue that there are no inherently "ethnic" motivations. Theory building requires further specification of these motivations. Thus, consistent with the relational approach, we assume that people primarily seek to increase their *life chances*, the opportunity individuals have to pursue whatever it is that they desire. This behavioral assumption has several major merits. For one thing, it subsumes other desires that are frequently attributed to individuals, such as wants for wealth, personal security, and power. This is because the latter are desired primarily because they afford opportunity to pursue whatever individuals actually value, be it wealth and power for their own sake or something for which wealth or power are useful, such as the ability to help the poor or achieve progressive change in a political system.[28] Both leaders and masses can be usefully characterized as seeking to maximize life chances: Leaders' life chances are usually maximized by staying in power, while masses pursue

---

[28] Even though people are concerned with relative status considerations, status is interpreted here not as an immanent good but as something that is desirable because it connotes the ability to get what one wants in a world filled with others who may also want the same scarce goods.

life chances in a variety of other forms, with personal material welfare being one of the most obvious.[29] While the concept of life chances is very broad, a general sense of "opportunity" is arguably not significantly more difficult to measure than the concepts it subsumes, such as power. That is, it does not require knowing the mind of the individual, as the even broader concept of utility would. Finally, the notion that people seek to maximize life chances is consistent with biological and evolutionary research. Indeed, life chances are tightly linked to survival and reproductive opportunities. This behavioral assumption proves fruitful for theory building, though future studies may benefit from assuming more specific motivations.

Collective Action Problems, Separatist Politics, and Ethnofederalism

One of the central arguments of this chapter is that separatism can largely be explained as the result of a collective action problem faced by individuals seeking to maximize their life chances. A collective action problem is a situation in which everyone as a group could be better off by cooperating but in which cooperation can fail because the individuals involved face incentives that put their individual interests at odds with group interests.[30] There are several hurdles to collective action that must be overcome for separatism to emerge in a polity.[31] Two are "microlevel" collective action problems, focusing on the individuals involved. One of these is a problem of coordination: How do people agree on the specific lines along which "center" and "periphery" are divided when alternative definitions are possible and people might disagree on the particulars despite agreeing on the big picture? That is, what are the "group" and "region" that would secede? Another microlevel collective action problem is a problem of social choice: After people have agreed on boundaries, how does one aggregate the variety of values and preferences that individuals have so as to determine a "regional preference" or a "group strategy for action?" It is often the case that majority votes could be won for multiple different strategies since an incremental change could win a few new "votes" at the same time that it loses a few old votes. Also, after a group is defined and decides on a collective interest to pursue, it encounters a macrolevel collective action problem in its interaction with the central government (this will be described in detail later). States that are already independent but that are considering integration can expect to encounter this macrolevel collective action problem should a union state be created.

It is helpful to study this macrolevel collective action problem by focusing on the case of union states with ethnofederal institutions, institutions that effectively resolve the microlevel collective action problems and thus isolate the macrolevel

---

[29] The observed willingness of some to die for a cause can be explained not only by belief in an afterlife but also by the element of risk. Most people who die for a cause do not actually *prefer* to die. Instead, they make a decision to *risk* their lives for a cause, hoping to survive but calculating that the potential rewards in expanded life chances if they succeed are worth it.

[30] Mancur Olson, *The Logic of Collective Action* (Cambridge, MA: Harvard, 1965).

[31] Hechter, "The Dynamics of Secession."

problem. Ethnofederalism is a federal system of government in which federal regions are invested with ethnic content.[32] Yugoslavia was an obvious example, with Slovenia being designated as a homeland for ethnic Slovenes, Croatia for Croatians, and so on. In such systems, the regional administrative boundaries are typically established as key lines along which coordination occurs for issues of center-periphery relations. They also supply a particular institutional framework that provides a solution to the social choice problem: Ethnofederal regions have governments that typically claim to represent the "titular" ethnic group. Alternative claims may be voiced and may be considered more legitimate, but the claim voiced by the regional government has the institutions of the local state apparatus backing it up. Largely for this reason, actual secession in ethnofederal systems has tended to occur only when a regional government has opted for secession (including instances where grassroots movements have taken over the regional government). Additionally, because already-independent states also typically have in place the same sorts of mechanisms to resolve the microlevel collective action problems, focusing on ethnofederations allows us to generate a theory that also applies to international relations. This study, therefore, focuses on the behavior of the leadership of ethnofederal regions, treating ethnofederalism as effectively having provided a solution to the social choice problem as well as the coordination problem. Later in this chapter, we return to how separatism in international relations can be expected to differ from patterns within ethnofederations.

Focusing on ethnofederal states and the macrolevel collective action problems they entail has a great deal of promise. For one thing, the macrolevel collective action problem (the relationship between regions and central governments) is the core problem of separatism. Indeed, we are most interested in understanding the conditions under which two or more territorially concentrated ethnic groups can successfully live in a single polity. Moreover, many of the world's most important states are at least nascent ethnofederations, including India, Russia, Nigeria, Canada, and even China.[33] Thus, a theory taking ethnofederalism as a starting point is directly relevant to a large number of important countries. By isolating the implications of the macrolevel collective action problem, we also provide a good basis for future theory, which can concern itself with addressing the additional complexities involved in other ways of solving the microlevel collective action problems. To add these at this early stage of theory development would only complicate the task at hand, which is to illustrate the capacity of a relational theory of ethnicity to generate new and useful insights. It is nevertheless suggested that the macrolevel dynamics of secessionism will remain highly similar even where ethnofederalism is not around to solve the microlevel collective action problem. This study, therefore, seeks to explain separatism by focusing on

---

[32] Bunce, *Subversive Institutions*; Henry E. Hale, "Divided We Stand: Institutional Sources of Ethnofederal State Survival and Collapse," *World Politics*, v.56, no.2, January 2004, pp. 165–93; Leff, "Democratization and Disintegration"; Philip G. Roeder, "Soviet Federalism and Ethnic Mobilization," *World Politics*, v.43, no.2, January 1991, pp. 196–232.

[33] Hale, "Divided We Stand."

the macrolevel collective action problem between regional and (potential) central governments.

To elucidate the particulars of the macrolevel collective action problem facing ethnic minority regions and central governments, it is helpful to begin by using some of the language of game theory. Readers are asked to indulge a bit of mathematical terminology because this adds efficiency to the discussion as well as precision, making it absolutely clear which assumptions are being made and which outcomes are associated with which kinds of situations. That is, the theory's underlying logic is initially characterized as a series of "extended-form games" that are "played" by one minority *Region* and the federal *Center* in an ethnofederal state. In this bare-bones world, let us assume that the Center effectively represents a dominant ethnic group that is distinct from a minority ethnic group concentrated in the Region. Let us also treat the Region as if it were an individual, having its own interests defined in terms of life chances. For this initial stage of theory building, then, we can think of regional interests as reflecting an aggregation of all regional citizens' interests, an aggregation carried out by ethnofederal institutions. This is obviously an oversimplification. But it efficiently captures and will help clarify a core dynamic that is essential to further understanding the fundamental issues involved in separatism. In fact, by identifying this core logic, we gain a conceptual foundation upon which the true complexity of secessionist decision making can be examined later in this chapter. The hyper-simple core logic helps us better understand what is at stake when we delve into the complex process by which regional leaders, regional citizens, and central leaders interact to produce regional strategies on the question of separation and integration.

The Basic Secession Game

The basic framework for all of the following secession games, as diagrammed in Figure 4.1, is simple but reasonable. The Region must choose whether to *secede* or to stay in the *union* and then the Center decides how to react, with each combination of possible moves resulting in particular outcomes that have differing values (payoffs) to the Center and Region. To begin, if the Region opts to secede, the Center resolves either to go to *war* as a way to preserve its territorial integrity or to *acquiesce*, letting the separatist Region peacefully become an independent state through some sort of negotiated process. If the Center takes the path of war, we assume with historical justification that it wins after a bloody, destructive battle and that it then imposes an exploitative arrangement on the disloyal region.[34] By "exploitative," we refer to incorporation of the Region into the union on terms such that the Region is worse off (has lower life chances) than

---

[34] Most agree with Horowitz (*Ethnic Groups in Conflict*) that separatists rarely win such wars. Cases where they could win (as with Croatia's secession from Yugoslavia in 1991) are considered later.

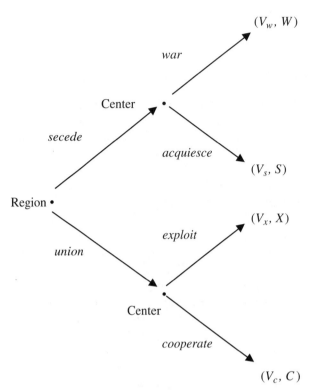

FIGURE 4.1. Extended Form Secession Game: General Framework.

would most likely be the case if the Region were instead an independent state encountering no resistance on the part of union authorities. If the Region opts for secession but the Center opts for war, then, the Region receives its worst possible payoff value, designated in the diagram as V_W, while the Center gets the payoff designated by W. This W payoff represents an outcome whereby the Center exploits the defeated Region but must subtract the major costs incurred in war from the value of this exploitation. If the Region attempts to secede but the Center gives in, letting the region go free, the Center receives the payoff associated with enduring a secession (S) while the Region gets the value associated with peacefully seceding V_S. Because, as Young has noted, there has never been a case of successful reunification after secession, we assume here that secession is irrevocable once it has occurred.[35] If the Region chooses union instead of separation, the Center has two basic choices. On one hand, the Central government can *exploit* the region, giving the Region a payoff designated as V_X and the Center a payoff designated as X. On the other hand, the federal authorities can *cooperate* with the Region.

[35] Robert A. Young, "How Do Peaceful Secessions Happen?" *Canadian Journal of Political Science*, v.27, no.4, December 1994, pp. 773–92, 789. A possible exception is Yemen, although the Yemeni breakup is not generally held to have involved ethnic distinctions.

By "cooperation," we mean here incorporating that Region on favorable terms, ensuring that gains from union are distributed such that the Region is better off than it would most likely have been as an independent country. In this case, the Region receives the payoff V_C and the Center gets C

This game plays out in different ways depending on how both the Central government and the Region in question value the different outcomes. More specifically, if we posit different preference orderings for the two players, we can expect the Region to decide differently between secessionism and unionism. One can run through the different possible preference orderings to identify the most likely patterns.

The Center's Preferences and Types of Central Governments

Let us start with the Center. Given world experience, it is reasonable to posit that Central state leaders prefer to avoid any secession attempt on the part of minority regions. Thus, we can confidently assume that the Center considers either of the payoffs involving a secession attempt (W or S) to be of lesser value than either of the payoffs that do not involve such an attempt (C or X). That is, (C or X) > (W or S).

Beyond this uncontroversial claim, however, we have no historical or theoretical grounds for assuming that all central governments value different outcomes in the same way. Let us first take the issue of whether the Center might prefer an outcome where it exploits a Region (an outcome with value X) to one where it implements a cooperative arrangement (a value of C). It is certainly the case that some governments have seen fit to exploit minority regions, revealing a preference ordering of $X > C$ Examples might include Nigeria vis-à-vis Igboland in the 1960s or Great Britain vis-à-vis Ireland prior to the twentieth century. Some hard ethnicity-as-conflictual theories imply that exploitation is actually the top preference of central governments: If group esteem ("positive social identity") is primarily gained by establishing superiority over other groups, and if this can be achieved by maximizing an economic advantage over other groups, then exploitation should be the norm. Such claims are rejected here for reasons elaborated in Chapters 2 and 3. Nevertheless, there are still reasons why a central government might opt to exploit an ethnic minority Region rather than cooperate with it in the union. The obvious one is that the Center can simply take the resources of the Region, thereby making itself better off at the latter's expense.

There are at least two reasons why we cannot expect central governments always to be exploitative, however. First, exploitation is costly. Since the Region will not voluntarily go along with exploitation, resources must be expended in order to coerce it. Of course, cooperation also usually involves some transactions costs, but there is a crucial difference: The expenditure involved in coercion is typically destructive. Some form of destruction is usually necessary to establish a credible threat so as to induce the Region to give in to the exploitation. For this reason, a Central government exploiting a Region involves at least some net transactions costs for the Center, not pure gain.[36] It is at least possible, then, that the expected costs of coercion could outweigh the expected benefits that the Center could gain from exploitation in at least some cases. Second, exploitation is not likely to benefit the Central government in the long run. While "resource theft" might bring new resources to the Center at the actual moment of theft, continued exploitation is likely to lead to the underutilization of the Region's resources as it is deprived of investment and as opportunities to take full advantage of economies of scale are lost. Regional citizens may also become less willing to work hard, deprived of opportunities to benefit from simple work or from innovation. Their administrative and other talents will also be lost to the union as a whole if their upward mobility is restricted geographically. The point is not that this is always the case, but that some Central governments may well see things this way.

In fact, there is a great deal of evidence that at least some central governments have been motivated by a longer term vision of balanced growth to subsidize the development of impoverished regions or even to pay off certain regions so as to keep them content to stay in the union. The emerging EU provides one example, adopting policies explicitly aimed at boosting the economies of its least developed members. Even the USSR, despite the generally odious nature of its political system, effectively transferred resources (largely but not solely in the form of oil and natural gas) to nearly all of its ethnic minority republics at the expense of the dominant nation's Russian Republic and explicitly sought to develop the economies of its most lagging provinces. After the USSR collapsed, the emergent Russian Federation also become known for transferring significant resources domestically both to underdeveloped regions and to potentially secessionist ones with the aim of keeping them from attempting actual secession.[37]

We thus have no theoretical or empirical grounds for simply assuming that Central governments always prefer an exploitative outcome to a cooperative one, whether $X > C$. This is likely to depend on the Center's time horizons and its assessments of the transactions costs involved in exercising the coercion necessary to sustain exploitation.

Similarly, we have no theoretical or empirical grounds for definitively answering the question of whether $W > S$. That is, once a region has declared secession, federal governments have not been found to consistently opt either for or against violent suppression of the separatist drive. The contrast between Yugoslavia and the USSR is telling. The former sought to prevent Croatia's and Slovenia's secession using military might, whereas the latter did not attempt to use force in response to the republics' 1991 declarations of independence. Whereas secession deprives a Central government of the gains of integration, antisecessionist war can be very costly, possibly outweighing the benefits of recovering the territory

---

[36] Thus, exploitation is never the socially optimal outcome. The best collective good is achieved through cooperation.

[37] Vladimir Popov, "Fiscal Federalism in Russia: Rules Versus Electoral Politics," *Comparative Economic Studies*, v.46, 2004, pp. 515–41; Treisman, "Russia's 'Ethnic Revival.'"

should the violence succeed. Different central governments might weigh these eventualities in different ways. In some countries, a peaceful response may be dictated by a general pacifism, a high value attached to peace and all the activity war would disrupt. Even at the height of Quebec's secessionist movement in 1995, for example, hardly anyone seriously thought that the Canadian central government would send in the troops to stop it. In other cases, the same response might be motivated by the central government's recognition of its own weakness, as arguably was the case with the USSR after the August 1991 coup attempt, which will be discussed later in this book. Other governments might opt for war out of fear that a precedent could be set by secession, one leading to the separation of multiple other regions.[38]

Overall, in terms of our model's assumptions as to the Center's preferences, we cannot make blanket assertions as to whether $X > C$ or $W > S$. In essence, this discussion establishes that Central governments can be seen as coming in "types" that are defined on two dimensions. On one dimension, when a union exists, the union government can be *exploitative* (when $X > C$) or *nonexploitative* (when $C > X$). On the other dimension, once a Region has declared secession, the Central regime can be *peaceful* (when $S > W$) or *war-ready* (when $W > S$).

The Region's Preferences

Turning to the ethnic minority Region in our game-theoretic world, global experience and commonsense allow us safely to assert that cooperation is preferred to being exploited within a union ($V_C > V_X$)and that peace is preferred to war after secession is declared ($V_S > V_W$)Moreover, we can confidently assume that simple exploitation is preferred to the combination of war and subsequent exploitation ($V_X > V_W$).

Whether a Region can be expected to prefer national independence to cooperation in a union (whether $V_S > V_C$), however, is a hotly contested question, as is clear from the preceding discussion of existing theory. Indeed, ethnicity-as-conflictual theories frequently posit that national independence is a good in its own right due to the status it brings a group relative to other groups. For such theories, ethnic Regions are essentially value-rational, regarding independence as the chief value in its own right, a value not subject to compromise ($V_S > V_C$)[39] If ethnic Regions are value-rational in this way, they will always strive for independence, failing to do so only when the state is so powerful that to try would mean certain national annihilation. But the prediction that ethnic minority regions secede whenever they can is clearly false. In virtually every ethnofederal country with more than one ethnic group, some regions have demonstrated a markedly greater propensity to secede than others. Even in the USSR, where the state essentially disintegrated and presented countries with a golden opportunity to

---

[38] Monica Duffy Toft, *The Geography of Ethnic Violence: Identity, Interests, and the Indivisibility of Territory* (Princeton, NJ: Princeton University Press, 2003).

[39] On value-rationality, see Varshney, "Nationalism, Ethnic Conflict."

achieve secession peacefully, many ethnic regions such as Uzbekistan still sought to preserve the union.

The relational theory of ethnicity facilitates another view of Regional preferences: *The true top preference of any given Region is in fact to be part of a cooperative union*, a union in which that Region is incorporated on favorable terms. Joining a Region to an existing union is at least *potentially* beneficial to both the Region and the rest of the union since this union eliminates transaction costs involved in international borders and reduces the per capita cost of public goods,[40] thereby resulting in a *net* increase in wealth and opportunity (life chances).[41] The resultant benefits could theoretically (ideally) be distributed in such a way that all expect to gain from unification. Very importantly, it is also theoretically possible that political decentralization could be effected in those policy areas where differences in preference or culture between a given Region and the Center exist. Language laws, for example, can be adopted so as to ensure that losses in this sphere do not outweigh the overall gains of unity. Other possible arrangements, such as consociational systems, are infinite.[42]

Critics of such arrangements will be quick to reply that these are very often unrealistic, but this is precisely the point being made here. The difficulty is not that different nations would not want such an ideal union were it possible but that they very frequently cannot count on this "good scenario" ever happening because it depends on the goodwill and competence of the Central government, traits that are all too often very difficult to imagine. Central governments, typically controlling the military and other instruments of power, generally have the capacity not only to ensure that a Region benefits but also to exploit any individual Region, making it less well off than it would be as an independent country. *What is expressed as value-rational nationalism, then, may simply reflect a belief that a Central government will not allow or follow through on a truly cooperative arrangement, an eventuality having major long-run implications for life chances.* Nationalism becomes vocalized as a supreme value in its own right not so much because it actually is a supreme value in its own right but because nationalists firmly believe that the ideal is not possible in a state controlled by another ethnic group and that giving in now might set a precedent for long-term constriction of life chances.

The example of the EU perhaps makes this as clear as any other example. Groups like the Baltic nations, which absolutely and emphatically ruled out ceding even a single drop of sovereignty to the newly democratic and highly decentralized union that Gorbachev promised, have proven quite willing to dissolve a great deal of their own decision-making authority and sovereignty in the EU. The EU, arguably, is widely seen in many post-Soviet and even older European states as something rather close to an ideal union. This is a very important point because it helps us distinguish the actual underlying preferences of ethnic Regions from beliefs about the structure of the game they face, that is, their beliefs regarding the

---

[40] Specifically, nonrival public goods.

[41] Alberto Alesina and Enrico Spolaore, "On the Number and Size of Nations," *Quarterly Journal of Economics*, v.11, no.4, November 1997, pp. 1027–56.

[42] For example, Ugo M. Amoretti and Nancy Bermeo, eds., *Federalism and Territorial Cleavages* (Baltimore: Johns Hopkins University Press, 2004); Lijphart, *Democracy in Plural Societies*.

preference ordering of the Center (crucially, whether the Center is exploitative or cooperative).

A note is in order here regarding the distinction between a Region (whose interests are considered here) and that Region's individual citizens (whose aggregated interests constitute the Regional interest). There may well be some value-rational *individuals* in a given ethnic group, understood as people who have developed tremendously thick and chronically accessible ethnic schema.[43] There may indeed be many such people in a few groups. But there are just as undoubtedly at least some in every ethnic group who are more skeptical of, indifferent to, or even opposed to the separatist or more broadly nationalist enterprise. Where there are "patriots," there can almost always be found at least some "traitors." When we look at aggregate units like ethnic groups, nations, or, as in the present case, ethnic Regions, we have no historical justification for an assumption of homogeneity, much less 100 percent community-wide value-rationality. Indeed, it has been authoritatively established that ethnic populations do not uniformly support nationalism even in the most extreme cases. Instead, there is a great deal of variety in the degree and intensity of support for ethnic separatism across individuals within every society. This has been convincingly argued through a variety of means, including the seminal historical sociological analysis conducted by Hroch in Europe; survey data employed by scholars like Gorenburg in Russia and Nadeau, Martin, and Blais in Quebec; and ethnographic anthropological research like that of Royce.[44] Moreover, these same studies find that this variation is not entirely random but is highly correlated with a person's particular location in social structure. Research also shows that the thickening of identity categories and the invocation of ethnic schema are in principle reversible and that whether or not certain schemas are activated typically depends at least in part on environmental cues and the schema's degree of fit with the situation.[45]

By implication, we arrive at a complete preference ordering for ethnic minority Regions. The adoption of what appears to be value-rationality, even at the individual level, likely involves individuals' reactions to situations that lead to extremely negative evaluations of national prospects within a union state dominated by another group. Thus, while some or even many individuals may in fact behave value-rationally in the way they treat national independence at any given moment, from a theoretical perspective it is more appropriate to treat prosecession value-rationality as reflecting a situation whereby an ideal union might *in theory* be possible but where the union state is very strongly perceived to be exploitative, rendering continued integration unpalatable.[46] We thus have strong

[43] See Chapter 3.
[44] Dmitry Gorenburg, "Not With One Voice: An Explanation of Intra-Group Variation in Nationalist Sentiment," *World Politics*, v.53, no.1, 2000, pp. 115–42; Miroslav Hroch, *Social Preconditions of National Revival in Europe: A Comparative Analysis of the Social Composition of Patriotic Groups among the Smaller European Nations* (New York: Cambridge University Press, 1985); Richard Nadeau, Pierre Martin, and Andre Blais, "Attitude Towards Risk-Taking and Individual Choice in the Quebec Referendum on Sovereignty," *British Journal of Political Science*, v.29, 1999, pp. 523–39; Royce, *Ethnic Identity*.
[45] Brubaker, *Ethnicity Without Groups*; Kurzban, Tooby, and Cosmides, "Can Race."
[46] That is, a situation where the Region is certain that for the Center, $X > C$

theoretical and empirical grounding to adopt the theoretical assumption that $V_C > V_S$. This then gives us the following preference ordering for ethnic minority Regions: $V_C > V_S > V_X > V_W$. This assumption runs counter to a fundamental principle of ethnicity-as-conflictual theory.

Implications: The Sources of Separatism and Variation in It

Having gone as far as we can in specifying Regional and Central preferences, we are now in position to flesh out the secession game sketched in Figure 4.1, showing what happens when we fill in the Region's preferences and create different versions of the game based on whether the Center is peaceful or war-ready, cooperative or exploitative. This gives us four different versions of the game, illustrated in extended form by Figures 4.2 through 4.5. The numbers in the parentheses to the right of each outcome reflect how both the Region and Center rank these outcomes: The left-hand number refers to the Region and the right-hand number refers to the Center. For example, in Figure 4.2, the "war" outcome (top right) is the fourth-best (i.e., worst) outcome for the Region but the third-best outcome for the Center. An asterisk (∗) denotes the equilibrium outcome of each game. This is the outcome that would be reached if both Center and Region acted rationally, accurately assessing both their own and the other's preferences and then choosing the option that, given these constraints, gives them the best available payoff.

This analysis leads us to three closely related conclusions that form the basis for the rest of this book. First, in this simple game, *the key factor determining whether a given Region will secede is whether or not the Central government of a union state is exploitative and peaceful*. If the Center is willing and able to accommodate the interests of the ethnic Region in the union or clearly willing or able to employ military might to preserve its territorial integrity, then the Region will find it in its interests to remain in the union. In the former scenario, the optimal cooperative union will result, whereas in the latter the Region will suffer exploitation but at least avoid the costs of war. Where the Center is seen as exploitative and unable to employ force to save the union, secession is the result.

Second, since at least some uncertainty is intrinsic to any real-world assessment of central government intentions and capacities, we reach an even bigger conclusion: *The politics of separatism is fundamentally about shaping regional beliefs regarding the nature of the (potential) Central government*. This can be restated in a more technically precise way that will later help show the connection to other important findings. Regions face inherent uncertainty as to whether a future Central government will prove to be exploitative and peaceful. Their task, though, is not usually to turn uncertainty into certainty, since true certainty is a rarity in the world of human beings. Instead, the primary task is to *convert uncertainty into risk*. The difference between uncertainty and risk, it will be recalled, is that probabilities can be attached to potential outcomes under risk whereas people are unable to assess probabilities in a situation of uncertainty. Thus, separatist

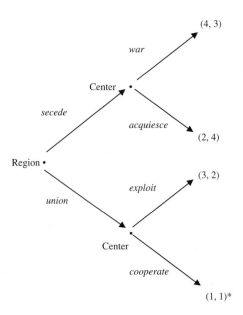

* = equilibrium outcome with perfect information.

FIGURE 4.2. Secession Game. *Union*: War-Ready, Nonexploitative.

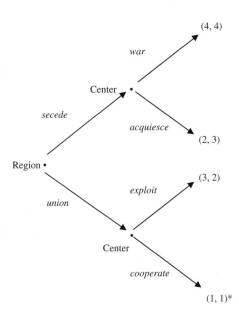

* = equilibrium outcome

FIGURE 4.3. Secession Game. *Union*: Peaceful, Nonexploitative.

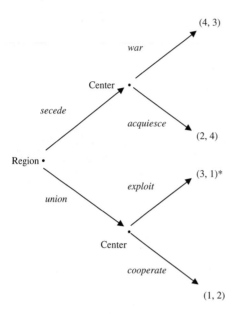

* = equilibrium outcome

FIGURE 4.4. Secession Game. *Union*: War-Ready, Exploitative.

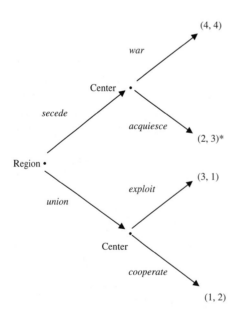

* = equilibrium outcome

FIGURE 4.5. Secession Game. *Union*: Peaceful, Exploitative.

politics is largely the process by which Regions' perceptions are influenced as to the risk involved in union and separation.

This leads us to a third conclusion. Converting uncertainty into risk is desirable because it enables a Region to assess the value of different possible strategies, which are actions that are chosen based on calculations of what another actor may do. And *secession represents a strategy, not an outcome or a preference.*[47] Under uncertainty, a Region has no idea whether a secessionist strategy would result in peaceful independence or war followed by exploitation at the hands of the union's dominant group, not to mention all the possibilities in between. Under risk, that same Region can identify a whole array of eventualities associated with each strategy and weight them according to their probabilities of actually occurring. The Region is thus able to choose the option that produces the most attractive *portfolio of possibilities*. In terms frequently used by economists, this is a calculation of *expected gains*. This means that the choice between a secessionist strategy and a unionist one is not a simple matter of deciding for sure whether a union will be exploitative and peaceful. Instead, it is a matter of weighing the potential gains against potential losses and weighting each potentiality according to the chances of each being realized.[48]

This has the following critical implication: An ethnic Region may elect to stay in a union that it deems highly likely to be exploitative if it would reap a very large gain in life chances should exploitation not happen to occur in the future. In such a case, the possible gains might be "worth the risk." The idea of something being "worth the risk" is lost in standard credible commitment models,[49] but it can be incorporated into the secession model as illustrated in Figure 4.6. The terms P_C and P_W are probabilities, with P_C denoting the likelihood perceived by a Region that the Center will behave cooperatively should the region stay in the union and P_W referring to the chance perceived by a Region that the Center would resort to war should the Region attempt to secede. An elementary calculation shows that Regions valuing the cooperative outcome (V_C) highly enough will be willing to stay even in a union where exploitation is the most likely outcome (that is, where $P_C < 0.5$).[50] Crucially, this is true even when the likelihood of war is zero should the Region attempt to secede. Conversely, the driving force behind

---

[47] I am grateful to Celeste Wallander for calling to my attention the importance of distinguishing clearly between preferences and strategies.

[48] Such calculations are of course rarely made explicitly, quantitatively, or perfectly by individuals. This does not mean that some form of risk assessment is not made, for example, through "instincts" or other cognitive mechanisms that do tend to resemble explicit calculations in the judgments they produce, taken together over time.

[49] On the more general need to incorporate indeterminacy into social science models, see Russell Hardin, *Indeterminacy and Society* (Princeton, NJ: Princeton University Press, 2003).

[50] In precise formal terms, a region will opt to stay in the union whenever:
$$(P_C - 1)V_X + P_C V_C > P_W V_W + (1 - P_W)V_S$$
or, by implication, when
$$V_C > (P_W/P_C)(V_W - V_S) + (V_S/P_C) + V_X(1/P_C - 1).$$
Since this equation has solutions for $P_C < 0.5$, we can see that if the potential value of the union (V_C) is great enough, it is logical to expect a Region to be willing to take a chance on exploitation.

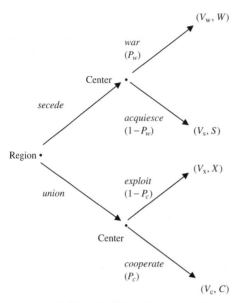

FIGURE 4.6. Extended Form Secession Game Introducing Uncertainty.

Regions' secessionism can be better understood as a fear, not certain knowledge, of exploitation in a union – a fear incorporated into a calculation made by Regional leaders that the likelihood and potential cost of exploitation are too high to accept for the sake of whatever gains may be possible in the union state.

The key to understanding variation in separatism across time and space, therefore, is to understand both the *assessment of the risk* and the *assessment of the benefits and losses* that each ethnic Region attaches to the various possible outcomes on which it gambles by opting for either a unionist or a separatist strategy. It turns out that ethnicity is strongly implicated in the assessment of risk and generally unrelated to the assessment of benefits/losses.

ETHNICITY AND VARIATION IN SEPARATISM OVER TIME AND SPACE

If separatism is at root a region's strategic response to a collective action problem with the central government, how can we explain why some regions are more separatist than others and why levels of separatism might change over time? And since such collective action problems do not inherently derive from ethnicity, is this approach really distinct from ethnicity-as-epiphenomenal theories? The key lies in the concluding paragraph of the previous section: Variation in separatism will depend upon regions' assessments of the *risks* and the *potential benefits and losses* that could result from political integration. Ethnic divides can powerfully shape these risk assessments, making "separatism" seem like a reasonable risk management strategy where it would otherwise not even be considered. Ethnicity, then, is far from epiphenomenal yet also cannot be said to supply the motivation for separation. At the same time, ethnicity is not the only factor affecting perceptions of risk and potential losses and benefits in the union. The paragraphs that follow unpack these notions, exploring five factors that are found to be crucial in influencing assessments of risks and benefits/losses.

1. *Ethnicity.* Thick ethnic divides heighten the degree of risk that a region's leaders and masses attach to being in a union state, strengthening the perception that a significant collective action problem exists.

2. *Central state policies.* The actions undertaken by central governments can powerfully alter regional leaders' and masses' perceptions as to whether they are likely to experience exploitation or cooperation in a future union state.

3. *Framing.* Regional leaders, through their agenda-setting power and influence over media, can influence mass perceptions of central actions and the underlying nature of the collective action problem, manipulating the way risk is factored into important decisions on separatism (i.e., in a referendum).

4. *Institutionally mediated interests.* The interests of the masses (especially material interests) influence the potential mobilizing power of all the various "frames" that regional leaders might employ to manipulate interpretation of the collective action problem. Regional leaders, competing to gain or stay in power according to the institutional rules that link them to mass opinion, adopt frames that will at a minimum keep them in power given the mass interests (involving potential gains and losses) they perceive in their regions.

5. *International relations versus domestic politics.* Independent countries face lower potential losses and probabilities of losses (or higher expected gains) from opting for independence than do ethnofederal regions in a preexisting union state. Thus, a region that may have been unionist while in a disintegrating union will become more separatist after that union breaks up.

These five factors are briefly elaborated next.

Ethnicity

One of the overarching arguments of this book has been that ethnicity is about uncertainty-reduction, whereas ethnic politics is about run-of-the-mill interests, which we have specified in this chapter to mean a desire to maximize life chances. Ethnicity is important in politics because it has properties facilitating its use as a rule of thumb for interpreting highly complex or inscrutable situations in the world of relations among human beings. The possibility of a region joining a larger union state is one such situation, laden with uncertainty due in part to the collective action problem involved. That is, there is always a chance that a central government could forego the socially optimal outcome (cooperation in a union) for the sake of short-term gains it might reap from an attempt to exploit the region.

Ethnicity frequently comes into play for several reasons, none of them having to do with any ethnic desire for independence but all of them having to do with ethnicity's attractiveness as an uncertainty-reducing mechanism. First, ethnic categories as defined in Chapter 3 are among the few that can coincide with the territorial distribution of communities, at least roughly.[51] This means that ethnicity becomes a viable candidate for the role of rule of thumb in interpreting issues of political integration because these issues inherently involve uncertainties based on territorial relationships and the distribution of goods that are important for people's life chances. Second, all the other properties of ethnicity discussed in Chapter 3 (frequently including perceptibility, resistance to change, and the "thick" connotation of common fate) make ethnicity quite an attractive rule of thumb. It is easy to invoke and capable of doing a great deal of uncertainty reduction by allowing people to make a wide range of inferences as to the likely behavior of other groups, including groups associated with the central government. That is, they prove very helpful by providing an easy conversion of uncertainty into risk, giving people in the region a better sense of the likelihood that the central government will treat them in a given way.

Since ethnicity is only a rule of thumb and not a *perfect* means by which people calculate probabilities associated with outcomes, its use turns out to have a significant impact on people's assessments of risk involved in a given union. Ethnicity does not create the commitment problem involved in political integration, but it has a strong tendency to exacerbate it, to heighten the degree of risk that minority-region people associate with a union state. In large part, this is because ethnic symbols invest extra meaning in territorial-administrative divisions that may not be very thick with meaning in their own right. This extra meaning includes symbolized representation of mutual histories or historical myths that may not before have revolved around a particular territorial division but that have had major implications for people's life chances.[52] When a thick ethnic distinction fraught with symbolism of past conflict is overlaid upon an administrative territorial unit that had previously not had great implications for people's lives, we would expect minority-group residents of that region to attribute more danger of exploitation than would be the case without this overlaying. In the most extreme cases of hyper-thick ethnic identification, such as those that might develop in the heat of intense conflict or grievous crimes like genocide, ethnicity can come to involve cognitive phenomena like schemas, which essentially suggest an action script for individuals to follow when relating to members of another ethnic group. In such a case, ethnicity can serve not so much to convert uncertainty into risk, but essentially to turn uncertainty directly into a form of "certainty" whereby

---

[51] Many other highly visible and hard-to-change social categories like age and gender obviously do not because they cut across all human social units, even the nuclear family.

[52] In an extreme case, for example, a genocide attempted by members of one group against members of another.

one acts as if exploitation were certain in any kind of union. It is arguably this sort of phenomenon that is witnessed by those who study what appears to be value-rational behavior in deeply divided societies. Even in such a case, however, the ethnic divide is not the cause of the collective action problem, though it certainly accentuates it quite heavily. The core question is ultimately whether a cooperative outcome is possible, not whether it is desirable, even though many people who are actually wrapped up in such thick ethnic schemas might not be conscious of this distinction.

But ethnic differences do not necessarily have to be bound up with a history of group conflict to exacerbate the collective action problem central to separatism. Group identity in general, as was shown in Chapter 3, is important to people because it connotes a commonality of fate. Ethnic group identity – due to the special properties of ethnic markers discussed earlier – stands out for its ability to quickly thicken, to rapidly produce a strong sense of commonality of fate, a feeling of "groupness." Even when two ethnic groups do not define themselves as being in conflict with the other, the sense of common fate and distinctiveness within each group can be strong. One way of putting this is to note that people can be "nationally conscious," perceiving a common history and fate with other members of their nation, without being in conflict. Thus, when this kind of divide in national consciousness is overlaid onto a territorial divide where the question of integration or separation is at hand, the result will be a stronger sense of distinction between the groups defined by the territorial divide despite the fact that there is no actual history of conflict. By extension, individuals within such a group are more likely to feel disconnected from control over their own fates when members of another group are predominantly in charge of a union state. Ethnic divides, then, can be seen as introducing a sense of separation from control among nondominant groups. And psychological research has found that people tend to underestimate dangers that they can take steps to manage and to overestimate dangers that they cannot control.[53] For example, people tend to fear flying in an airplane more than driving a car even though statistics show that the latter is more dangerous: One surrenders control when boarding the airplane, whereas one can hope to swerve or slam on the brakes if danger arises while one is driving.

One implication of all this is the following: When members of a minority nation possess a strong sense of national distinctiveness (thick identification with their nation) relative to the dominant group in the union, it is likely to lead members of this nation to attach a higher probability to the potential for exploitation than they would have had there been no such ethnic division and hence no such sense that a union involved control "by another group." Ethnicity, then, is not just any means by which people turn uncertainty into risk, but one that leads people to exaggerate the dangers of exploitation in a union seen to be dominated by members of other ethnic communities.

---

[53] Some seminal research on risk perceptions is usefully summarized by Paul Slovic, "Perception of Risk," *Science*, v.236, 1987, pp. 280–5. See also Friedman, Hechter, and Kanazawa, "A Theory."

We thus arrive at a different and more accurate understanding of the relationship between ethnicity and separatism. For one thing, we see how ethnic divides can frequently accompany separatism but not motivate it. There are no ethnic motives and no values inherent to national consciousness that drive separatism. Instead, the driving force behind separatism is the fear of exploitation resulting from the collective action problem facing regions and central governments. Ethnicity is a mechanism for assessing the risks involved. But no claim is made that it is a perfect or unbiased mechanism: Instead, when people are conscious of ethnic differences between the minority and dominant groups, ethnicity makes separatism more likely by leading people to see the danger of exploitation as being greater than it would otherwise seem. Ethnicity affects outcomes not by influencing preferences, but by *informing strategy*. Ethnicity, at root, is thus neither simply a coordination mechanism nor merely a tool that is "used strategically" by elites or other actors, as ethnicity-as-epiphenomenal theories typically conjecture. Instead, ethnicity helps provide the risk assessments that influence what strategy people believe will lead to the greatest expected gains. Introducing ethnic difference, then, can make the difference between separatism and unionism under certain conditions; it is not simply a way to realize one of these strategies after they have already been chosen. Ethnicity is neither inherently conflictual nor epiphenomenal. It does not make a region prefer separation to other outcomes, yet it can lead people to emphasize the danger of exploitation that is inherent in any political union, thereby putting separatism on the table among the set of potentially viable solutions.

Central State Policies

If regional perceptions of central government intentions are crucial in generating or preventing separatism, then it would seem obvious that central state policies are also an important influence on secessionism. Four particularly important types of policies are discussed here as strongly influencing whether masses and leaders in a minority region are likely to view the central government as being exploitative or war-ready, impacting people's perceptions of what game they are in.

Past Union–State Treatment of Minority Groups. It stands to reason that minority-region representatives will find past central government policies useful in judging whether that government is likely to be exploitative and war-ready in the future. Just what conclusions regions will draw from a past use of force is not straightforward, however. If coercion is exercised in the context of the clear rule of law to preserve the union, as has usually been the case in India, it can establish a credible deterrent to would-be separatists, reducing separatism.[54] If it is used arbitrarily, it can be seen as an instrument of exploitation and can lower a region's expected value of staying in a union. Treatment fresh in memory and directly tied

---

[54] Paul R. Brass, *The Politics of India Since Independence*, 2nd edition (New York: Cambridge University Press, 1994).

to particular incumbent authorities is likely to be the most chronically and situationally accessible, hence the most influential, in impacting regions' assessments of potential risks and gains from union.

Institutional Design. Perhaps the most common way in which union states attempt to convince subject nations that they are cooperative (even as they claim war-readiness) is to create political institutions that add credibility to these claims. Although some scholarly controversies remain, research has suggested that central governments are more credible in claiming they will behave cooperatively when they create potential "checks" on their power through "constitutional" documents[55] and permutations of democracy that protect against the tyranny of the majority, including various forms of consociationalism and federalism.[56]

Institutional Change. We must distinguish between new institutions that provide assurances for minority groups and the actual transition from old institutions to new ones. This is because the transition itself creates uncertainties, sometimes leading people to invoke ethnicity as a way of assessing the risks involved. This, arguably, is one reason why ethnic mobilization is frequently associated with democratization, even where the intended democratic endpoint is meant to ensure minority protection.[57]

The Process of Institution Building. The process by which new institutions are developed can help mitigate the uncertainties involved in institutional change and can reinforce the trust-building intent of new institutions by getting them off to a good start. Researchers have found that institution-building processes are likely to promote perceptions of cooperative intent when they are transparent,[58] when negotiating parties are in regular communication with each other,[59] when these parties interact face-to-face,[60] and when there is some sanction in place to punish those who attempt to use the transition period as an opportunity to

---

55 Douglass C. North and Barry R. Weingast, "Constitutions and Commitment," *Journal of Economic History*, v.49, no.4, December 1989, pp. 803–32; John M. Veitch, "Repudiations and Confiscations by the Medieval State," *Journal of Economic History*, v.46, no.1, March 1986, pp. 31–6; Barry R. Weingast, "The Political Foundations of Democracy and the Rule of Law," *American Political Science Review*, v.91, no.2, June 1997, pp. 245–63.

56 Amoretti and Bermeo, *Federalism and Territorial Cleavages*; Hechter, *Containing Nationalism*; Donald L. Horowitz, "Comparing Democratic Systems," *Journal of Democracy*, v.1, no.4, fall 1990, pp. 73–9; Lijphart, *Democracy in Plural Societies*.

57 See Barry Posen, "The Security Dilemma and Ethnic Conflict," in Michael E. Brown, ed., *Ethnic Conflict and International Security* (Princeton, NJ: Princeton University Press, 1993), pp. 103–24; Snyder, *From Voting to Violence*.

58 Hechter, *Containing Nationalism*, p. 153.

59 Elinor Ostrom, James Walker, and Roy Gardner, "Covenants With and Without a Sword: Self-Governance Is Possible," *American Political Science Review*, v.86, no.2, June 1992, pp. 404–17, 413.

60 Elinor Ostrom, "A Behavioral Approach to the Rational Choice Theory of Collective Action," *American Political Science Review*, v.92, no.1, March 1998, pp. 1–22, 7.

exploit the others.[61] Interestingly, the findings on face-to-face negotiations hold even for people who represent large organizations in such talks.[62] These findings are firmly in line with other research demonstrating the importance of leadership "crafting" of pacts and sequences of reforms precisely so as to build credibility and confidence in new institutional arrangements.[63]

Framing

While central governments influence regional perceptions of risk through what their representatives do and say, regional leaders have a great deal of influence in shaping how these words and actions translate into policy outcomes due to the great deal of complexity involved. So far we have assumed that regional leaders act upon an aggregation of regional mass perceptions as to the risks involved in a potential union, aggregation that takes place through ethnofederal institutions. It would of course be folly to believe there is in fact only one possible aggregation, even in a pure democracy. This is true for several reasons. First, the true choice is not simply between "union" and "secession" but myriad varieties of each. Unions can be more or less democratic, more or less decentralized, more or less accommodating to minority rights, and generally handcrafted to placate particular group concerns. That is, separation is not the only strategy by which a region can conceivably address the collective action problem described earlier. Second, there is uncertainty as to whether a strategy of pursuing any of these arrangements will in fact lead to the desired cooperation or the feared exploitation both in the short run and the long run. Complexity in the secession calculation thus exists along two conceptual dimensions, *possibility* (the different forms of union and secession that are possible) and *risk* (the chances of each happening if a given strategy is chosen). Third, we cannot assume that all people in a region will identically sort out this multidimensional complexity. Instead of thinking in terms of united regional opinion or even in terms of opposed but well-defined camps, therefore, it is helpful to understand public opinion on secession as reflecting a multidimensional *pattern of distribution* of individuals' views. Individual views will tend to cluster in different places in different societies, generating the cross-regional or cross-national differences that are found in public opinion polling and everyday encounters that one might have.

Even in full democracies, such complexity in both possibility and risk allows regional leaders to generate majority support for a wide variety of strategies, sometimes enabling them effectively to choose between independence and

---

[61] See Jon Elster, "Ulysses and the Sirens," in Elster, ed., *Ulysses and the Sirens* (New York: Cambridge University Press, 1979); Russell Hardin, *Collective Action* (Baltimore: The Johns Hopkins University Press, 1982), pp. 211–13.

[62] Olson, *The Logic*, pp. 33–6; Elinor Ostrom, *Governing the Commons* (New York: Cambridge University Press, 1990), pp. 189–90.

[63] Guillermo O'Donnell and Philippe C. Schmitter, *Transitions from Authoritarian Rule* (Baltimore: Johns Hopkins University Press, 1986); Weingast, "The Political Foundations," p. 98.

union.[64] One leadership tactic is simply to opt for one of the many majority-supported strategies and to ask people to select either it or the status quo. For example, if leaders of a unitary state with a history of group exploitation decide to liberalize, people in a minority region may well prefer either independence or federalization to the existing situation (a unitary state). If the minority region's leadership has independent reasons for wanting to stay in the union, then, it can win majority endorsement for this strategy by asking people in a yes/no referendum whether they support federalization, with "no" implying continuation of the status quo. But this same leadership could have also gained majority support for independence in the same way.

Furthermore, leaders can pose *hypothetical* possibilities to voters. For example, suppose a majority in an ethnic region would support a union over independence, but only if this union democratized and decentralized. Suppose also that this same majority also shares the view that this outcome is highly unlikely and, on this basis, calculates that its expected gains are greater with independence. In such a situation, a clever regional leader who has a personal preference for retaining the union can ask people in a referendum whether they would support the creation of a "democratic, decentralized" union. Such a question, by stripping the risk out of the equation, could generate a majority vote in favor of a union if people vote sincerely. Yet a question that just asked voters to choose between independence and union would have generated a vote for independence. "Framing" is the general term given to such processes by which elites influence mass expressions of support for given options by shaping how the options are interpreted and how the set of alternatives is conceived.[65]

One of the most significant tools of framers is the referendum. A referendum result is easily portrayed as a popular mandate, convincing many that "the people have spoken" on a given issue. Referenda sometimes actually have the force of law. Referenda, then, are critical *frame freezers*. Thus, the wording of a referendum on separatism can sometimes become an issue of union-breaking import.

---

[64] Such situations have been extensively studied both through game theory (see in particular the literatures on agenda setting and legislative majorities) and psychological behavioral analysis (in which people can be found to answer very differently when the very same structural situation is presented with different situational cues). Sources for game-theory perspectives include: Josephine T. Andrews, *When Majorities Fail: The Russian Parliament, 1990–93* (New York: Cambridge University Press, 2002); Kenneth Arrow, *Social Choice and Individual Values*, 2nd edition (New Haven, CT: Yale University Press, 1963); Jeffrey S. Banks, *Signaling Games in Political Science* (New York: Harwood, 1991); Anthony Downs, *An Economic Theory of Democracy* (New York: Harper & Row, 1957). On psychological research, see Amos Tversky and Daniel Kahneman, "The Framing of Decisions and the Psychology of Choice," in Jon Elster, ed., *Rational Choice* (New York: NYU Press), pp. 123–41.

[65] An important body of sociological work on the subject is discussed in Douglass McAdam, Sidney Tarrow, and Charles Tilly, "Toward an Integrated Perspective on Social Movements and Revolution," in Mark Irving Lichbach and Alan S. Zuckerman, eds., *Comparative Politics: Rationality, Culture, and Structure* (New York: Cambridge University Press, 1997).

Institutionally Mediated Interests

One of the central tenets of this book has been that ethnic politics revolves around the pursuit of banal interests people have in pursuing wealth, power, security, and other things associated with expanded life chances. We thus expect leaders and masses to evaluate the various possible separatist and unionist strategies according to the expected value they have for their own life chances. For ethnofederal regional leaders, maximizing life chances generally depends on staying in power since this affords great opportunity to pursue whatever else they may want. Such leaders have reason to be sensitive to even *potential* public opinion on any issue that may be potent enough (tied overtly and closely enough to mass life chances) to be used by an opponent to unseat them, ceteris paribus.[66] The previous subsection has already demonstrated, of course, that leaders may have a great deal of latitude in their ability to orchestrate majority support for policies they desire through framing. We thus must assume that the personalities or idiosyncratic preferences of leaders will play at least some role in real-world separatism.

Yet certain kinds of institutions can restrict this latitude for leaders. Democratic institutions, for example, constrain leadership behavior through electoral competition.[67] Leaders in such systems do not promote frames in isolation, but in the face of rivals' attempts to find and invoke more powerful frames as a way of unseating them. When there exists real political competition, regional leaders have incentive to seek out and utilize the most powerful frames on important issues, those generating the most popular support. Autocrats can also be subject to political competition, even if this is manifested only in riots, demonstrations, or the more general potential for extra-system opposition activity. In general, though, the more political competition exists in society, the more tightly leaders will be pressed to seek out and mobilize the frame with the greatest potential to gain popular support. Separatism thus can be seen as involving two essentially sequential games played by regional leaders: They play the first game with their populations and rival politicians to determine a master strategy regarding relations with the union (a set of strategies to be played in different contingencies) and the second with the central government as modeled in Figure 4.6.

The economic issues involved in separatism are likely to be among those to which leaders are responsive. It is uncontroversial that people's senses of their own life chances are bound extremely tightly to their understandings of their economic prospects. Furthermore, as noted in Chapter 3, people frequently perceive a correlation between the economic prospects of individuals and those of the ethnic groups to which these individuals belong. Additionally, real economic issues

---

[66] In terms of a regional-level theory like the present one, it makes little difference whether regional leadership and public opinion are brought into alignment through the self-adjustment or replacement of the leadership.

[67] Democracy is a political system in which a country's most important decision makers are elected in free, fair, and competitive elections on a regular basis. This follows Samuel P. Huntington, *The Third Wave* (Norman: University of Oklahoma Press, 1991).

(especially taxation, transfers, trade, and investment in public goods) are involved in center-periphery interaction in a union. And finally, perceived economic needs and prospects are frequently correlated with territories that can consider independence or integration, territories that may also coincide with ethnic differences to a significant degree. Thus, even though some scholars have dismissed economic theories of separatism for leaving out the passion frequently associated with it, the present study suggests to the contrary that people can become passionate about national independence in part *because* it is associated strongly with long-term economic expectations that they see as having very direct and important effects on their life chances. As the psychological research described earlier suggests, the economic motivation may not be consciously or fully thought through by individuals involved. When leaders seek popular support in their bids to stay in power, therefore, they are strongly likely to pay attention to widespread regional economic concerns.

There is reason to expect different regions' populations (taken as wholes) to have different economic interests in a given union, helping us explain why some regional governments appear more willing than others to take on risks that would seem to be equal for all regions. In particular, populations in relatively underdeveloped regions are likely to perceive they have more to gain in a given union than do masses in more-developed regions of the same union.[68] Most basically, this is because economically developed regions already have access to important "goods of modernity" and cannot get much more from regions that are at lower levels of development, whereas the less-developed regions can in fact hope to get such access (as well as the goods themselves) from the more-developed regions.[69] For example, a relatively developed region cannot hope to obtain much new technology from a less-developed region that will help it move "up" the cycle of production – for this, it generally must look to the world market. The more-developed region, of course, still potentially accrues economic benefits (a share of the gains from trade) from its association with a less-developed region, including remittances from businesses that operate outside of the more-developed region. But these benefits do not involve the direct prospect of rapid economic *development* and are thus less compelling to the region's population as a whole, making the more-developed region less willing to take on a significant risk of

---

[68] Economic development is more important than ordinary wealth because it is a form of wealth that is to a significant degree self-sustaining and self-augmenting, providing not only for immediate consumption but also for the prospect of long-term access to streams of wealth and greater future life chances. Very importantly, it involves and generally requires investments in infrastructure and human capital (highways, railroads, telecommunications, sanitation, education, etc.). By Bates's ("Ethnic Competition") operational definition, a region is more developed to the extent that it attains higher levels of education, per capita income, urbanization, industrial employment, and media of mass communication.

[69] Even though a group's members may consider their group wealthy if their region possesses vast and valuable natural resources, the wealth of development is what people primarily desire; natural resources are desired only as a means to that end, and a means requiring several uncertain steps before average people can expect actually enjoy the benefits of development that they really desire.

exploitation for the sake of them. And major differences in levels of development tend to be readily, even inherently, noticeable by people.[70] The less-developed region's population, therefore, has more incentive to risk exploitation by staying in the union because its potential payoffs are higher.[71] As the risk of exploitation rises, then, the most developed regions are likely to be the first to abandon the integration project.

There is an additional reason why regional leaders are likely to act in ways that coincide with their constituents' economic concerns vis-à-vis a union: Leadership and mass interests are likely to be congruent on this issue, at least in the broadest sense. Simply put, a regional leader is likely to prefer commanding a more powerful economy to a lesser one, while the population as a whole is likely to prefer living in a richer economy to a poorer one. This simple claim, of course, does not touch on likely immense differences in views on how the gains should be distributed and will of course also depend on leaders' calculations as to whether they can stay in power during any transition to or from political independence. But to the extent that union or independence will produce greater expected gains for a region as a whole, there is at least some tendency for mass and leader interests to be aligned.

A number of additional considerations deserve mention here. For one thing, popular perceptions of interests in a given union will depend partly on the alternatives. Thus, a poor region may display greater separatism than a rich region regarding the prospect of joining a Russian-led union if the poor region (but not the rich region) also has the option of joining the more economically developed European Union and if the two unions are mutually exclusive. Similarly, ethnic regions located next to major world markets or with ready access to oceans or other maritime trade routes may have less need to rely on their union state as a source of economic development than do ethnic regions that would be landlocked or otherwise isolated as independent states.[72]

Past state policies may factor in as well. Some countries, as was noted previously, have explicit policies designed to raise poorer regions' levels of development. Other countries may have long traditions of exploitation, letting the rich get rich while the poor get poorer. In countries with the latter sort of tradition, as

[70] There is no assumption that people know or calculate economic statistics here. Instead, these conclusions are often based on what might be called lived experience, including personal travel, oral accounts from friends or trusted colleagues who have traveled or have other sources of knowledge, and images from movies and television or other media. Of course, when development differences are rather small and not obvious to ordinary travelers, there is great scope for elites to manipulate perceptions of relative economic standings (Yoshiko Herrera, *Imagined Economies: The Sources of Russian Regionalism*, New York: Cambridge University Press, 2005). But the greater are the differences in development, the less successful elites are likely to be in manipulation. People's assessments of relative wealth tend to be accurate; however, they may not be updated mechanically. Thus, when development differentials persist for decades or even centuries, perceptions of relative wealth can work their way into national consciousness and become part of a status hierarchy of nations that takes time to erode as contradictory evidence mounts.

[71] In essence, this latter logic is outlined by Bates, "Ethnic Competition."

[72] Jeffrey Sachs, "Geography and Economic Transition," mimeo, paper presented at Hebrew University, Jerusalem, Israel, in memory of Dr. Michael Bruno, December 1997.

is arguably the case for many countries formerly subject to colonial rule, we might expect poor-region masses to assess the likelihood of exploitation as being very high, whereas rich-region masses might see it as being very low, possibly reversing the "normal" pattern whereby, ceteris paribus, the most developed regions tend to be the leading seceders.

International Relations Versus Domestic Politics

Finally, the strategic choices made by independent states considering integration will be somewhat different from those made by ethnofederal regions considering whether to remain in a preexisting union state, although the fundamental logic remains the same in each case. The primary differences arise from the different starting points of each type of unit: Ethnic regions contemplating secession are already in some form of union, whereas independent states contemplating integration are not.[73] The key argument of this subsection is that, for several reasons, the very same administrative unit is less likely to support joining a given union (in which it would be a minority) from a position as an already-independent state than from a position as a member of that same union. Initially, the expected cost of rejecting a union is lower for an already-independent state than for an ethnic region because the latter is much more likely to be subjected to unionist coercion. This is because union troops are most likely already in the ethnic region's but not the independent state's territory, and because the international community is more likely to tolerate unionist coercion if it is an "internal affair" rather than conquest. Moreover, because any major institutional change involves transition costs and risk, the status quo will be preferred, ceteris paribus. In the cases of separation and integration, examples of such costs include merging or separating currencies and changing economic policies, all also involving significant risk. Thus, when an ethnic region is already a member of a union state, the transition costs militate in favor of preserving that union, whereas transition costs work in the opposite direction when the region is already an independent state.

For these reasons, and without any change in national consciousness being involved, even regions that had been highly pro-union when they were in a union can be expected to be less supportive of reconstituting that union after it may happen to dissolve. A region would thus require a greater degree of expected gain (either greater potential gain or a more credible union commitment not to exploit) to support the very same union after the union's breakup than before. It is thus quite possible that pro-union regions can become anti-union simply by virtue of becoming independent, even if they become independent against their own will. This is the case if the expected costs of transition involved in reintegration, combined with the expected value of independence, outweigh the expected returns to reconstituting the union.[74]

---

73 Kenneth Waltz, *Theory of International Politics* (Reading, MA: Addison-Wesley, 1979).
74 On such costs of transition and other economic factors involved in integration decisions, see Chad Rector, *Federations* (Ithaca, NY: Cornell University Press, forthcoming 2009).

At the same time, the *relative* degrees of unionism or separatism *across units* are likely to remain relatively stable when they transition from being ethnic regions to being independent states. This is because the difference between belonging to and being outside of a union can be seen as affecting all of the units equally. All regions will be less likely to support integration after they become independent states; however, those that were the most separatist before independence are likely to remain so after independence.

CONCLUSION

The overarching purpose of this chapter has been to demonstrate that the relational approach to ethnicity outlined in Chapter 3 can facilitate the development of a powerful theory of separatism, one that differs from existing alternatives in important ways. The chapter began by showing that existing theories of separatism tend to be based on the two competing views of ethnicity that drive much of the broader ethnic politics literature today: ethnicity-as-conflictual theory and ethnicity-as-epiphenomenal theory. Not only do these views inadequately relate to research into human psychology, as was shown in Chapters 2 and 3, but they also beg major questions on the issue of national separatism. Ethnicity-as-conflictual theories tend to overpredict separatism, to court tautology, or to resort frequently to other variables in an ad hoc manner. Ethnicity-as-epiphenomenal theories often do a good job of systematizing these other variables but tend not to explain adequately why ethnicity ever gets bound up with separatism in the first place – particularly where separatism revolves around administrative divides that eliminate the need for ethnic divides as lines along which resources can be allocated or action coordinated. The relational theory enables a coherent alternative that corresponds well with microlevel psychological evidence and accounts for the importance of key variables identified by many ethnicity-as-epiphenomenal theories (including economic factors), while also explaining why ethnicity is so often implicated in separatist politics and why it so often involves high degrees of emotion and short-term sacrifice. Indeed, ethnicity is not merely a tool that is used instrumentally to pursue strategies that are already chosen, but instead is a conceptual mechanism that provides the *basis* upon which strategies are chosen.

Specifically, the relational approach to ethnicity uniquely underpins a theory that the driving force behind separatism is an ethnically charged collective action problem. In principle, both minority regions and majority-group-dominated central governments could benefit from integration, but regional uncertainty as to (for example) whether central government time horizons are short or long can lead a regional government to fear that the center will pursue the short-term gain of exploitation in the union. Separation is one strategy for dealing with this sort of commitment problem. Whether a given region's leadership opts for this particular strategy or some other one (including options like consociationalism or federalism) will depend in part on how it assesses central government intentions. Ethnicity has important qualities as a rule of thumb for evaluating the degree of risk involved in such situations, for assessing the center's intentions. Specifically, thick ethnic divides tend to raise regional assessments of danger in the union by increasing the sense that the region lacks control over its own fate. Ethnic divides also potentially introduce symbolically communicated fears of historically patterned exploitation at the hands of the dominant group. Other factors influencing regional choices of separation as a strategy are found to include actual central state policies, regional leaders' ability to frame policy choices for their constituents, the institutionally mediated interests of the masses (with the least economically developed regions most often having the greatest interest in a given union), and whether the region is an independent state considering integration or an ethnofederal province considering separation from a preexisting union.

As a shorthand, subsequent pages refer to all this as "the relational theory of separatism," but this semantic decision does not imply a claim that this particular theory of separatism is the only theory of separatism consistent with a relational approach to ethnicity. Along with relational assumptions, this theory of separatism also builds on other assumptions that have nothing intrinsically to do with ethnicity, such as the proposition that we are dealing with federal state institutions that tie provincial leaders to public opinion in certain ways. It thus may be that other theorists will find better ways to build a theory of separatism consistent with relational assumptions. Nor is any claim made that this theory is fully *derived from* the relational approach. Instead, the claim is only that the relational approach makes this particular theory of separatism possible. That is, the theory of separatism presented here gains core insights from the relational approach to ethnicity at the same time that its central propositions contradict the fundamental claims of the ethnicity-as-conflictual and ethnicity-as-epiphenomenal approaches. With this understanding, Part II demonstrates the advantages of relational theory over its rivals in explaining important patterns of national separatism.

CASE COMPARISONS

Separatism in Eurasia

S pecialists tend to be divided on the role of ethnicity in separatism, as described in Chapter 4. Ethnicity-as-conflictual theorists hold that ethnic divides are inherently fraught with conflict potential and that, in the absence of constraining or countervailing factors, a group that is conscious of its own national distinctiveness will naturally gravitate toward demands for a state of its own. These scholars may vigorously disagree on whether national consciousness is an age-old primordial bond or a contingent and constructed product of history and institutions, but they concur that it is the most fundamental motivating force behind separatism. The other side in the debate takes a starkly different view, denying that ethnicity has any intrinsic meaning for separatism. Instead, ethnicity-as-epiphenomenal theorists see nationality as simply a set of useful lines along which greedy or ambitious elites can divide spoils, foment conflict instrumentally, or coordinate their self-interested activities. The purpose of Part II is to illustrate empirically how an alternative approach, a relational theory of ethnicity, can provide a better cornerstone for building theories of separatism.

The rival theories, as established in Chapter 4, produce four broad explanations for separatism that will be weighed against the relational theory. Ethnicity-as-epiphenomenal theory posits that ethnic factors do not drive separatism and that any apparent relationship reflects the usefulness of ethnicity's hard and visible boundaries for elites and masses wishing to act collectively in pursuing goods like money or power. The ethnicity-as-conflictual approach produces the remaining three alternatives to the relational theory of separatism. National Consciousness theory is the simplest, positing that groups with the strongest senses of national consciousness will tend to be the most separatist. Capabilities theory agrees that national consciousness is the impetus behind separatism but concedes that this expression can be constrained: Ethnic groups will tend to express separatist demands only to the extent they have the opportunity to do so. Countervailing Incentives theory also agrees that national consciousness impels separatism but acknowledges that groups have other, nonethnic interests that can override the ethnic ones if strong enough.

The relational theory of separatism, as developed in Chapter 4, generates five sets of expectations that can be set against these alternatives. They are stated only in general terms here, with specific predictions elaborated in the chapters that follow. Assuming a ceteris paribus clause applies to each, these expectations are

1. *Ethnicity.* Regions whose titular group members are less conscious of a significant ethnic divide between themselves and the dominant group will display less separatism than other regions. Ethnicity will matter specifically by accentuating the collective action problem of union not as a source of motive and not soley as an instrument or coordinating device.

2. *Central state policies.* Separatism will vary in response to actions of the central state (including institutional initiatives) that impact the credibility of union commitments not to exploit a given member region, with credibility being assessable according to established research on collective action.

3. *Framing.* Under certain circumstances, leaders can manufacture mass majority votes in favor of either separation or union by differently framing the collective action problem involved in the union or the various possible solutions to it.

4. *Interests.* Mass and leadership interests, as mediated through institutions, will generally determine how leaders choose to frame a given union and alternative strategies for dealing with it.

5. *International relations versus domestic politics.* A transition from the realm of domestic politics to international relations (as when a union dissolves) will tend to raise the absolute level of separatism of all regions, though the factors influencing variation in separatism across regions will generally remain the same.

The introductory chapter already described the ample opportunities for comparative analysis afforded by the many states and ethnic regions of the former USSR, including variation not only in these regions' levels of separatism but also in the factors treated as causal by the rival theories. To take advantage of the depth of material available, Chapters 5–9 engage in cross-sectional, cross-temporal, and cross-individual comparative analysis concentrating mainly (although not exclusively) on Ukraine and Uzbekistan, chosen because they provide highly illustrative variation that facilitates this analysis.[1] Part II thus begins with five chapters (5–9) that correspond to the five sets of expectations arising from the relational theory, with each expectation evaluated carefully against relevant rival expectations using the best method available. Other republics/countries are brought in when necessary to make certain points or to show how Ukraine and Uzbekistan fit into a bigger picture. Chapter 10 then adds both breadth and quantitative rigor to the argument, presenting statistical analyses of policy patterns in nearly all the USSR's fifty-three ethnic regions and of public opinion patterns in as many as twelve of them.

---

[1] Ukraine and Uzbekistan are not simply "two cases" here; many of the subsequent chapters define cases not as regions/countries but as country–periods or individual human beings. On this approach to defining cases, see: Alexander L. George and Andrew Bennett, *Case Studies and Theory Development in the Social Sciences* (Cambridge, MA: MIT Press, 2005); Gary King, Robert Keohane, and Sidney Verba, *Designing Social Inquiry* (Princeton, NJ: Princeton University Press, 1994).

5

Ethnicity

Identity and Separatism in the USSR 1917–1991

One of the starkest clashes in the scholarship of ethnicity pits experts who explain separatism as the natural expression of national consciousness (be it primordial or constructed) against theorists who deny that ethnicity plays any significant causal role. This chapter begins our empirical discussion of separatism by arguing against both of these approaches (termed here ethnicity-as-epiphenomenal theory and the National Consciousness version of ethnicity-as-conflictual theory) and starting to build the empirical argument for the relational theory.

We begin by considering the puzzling contrast between Ukraine and Uzbekistan, back when they were component parts of the USSR. If National Consciousness theories of separatism are to escape the tautology of considering separatism a defining feature of national consciousness, the crucial causal element of national consciousness is a sense of national distinctiveness vis-à-vis the dominant ethnic group in the union. Prior to the Gorbachev era, leading experts frequently argued that Uzbeks and other Central Asians were highly conscious of national distinctions separating them from the dominant Russians and that the degree of national consciousness of Ukraine's population was lower than that of the Uzbeks due to the large part of its culture and history that it shared with Russia. They thus frequently expected Uzbekistan, not Ukraine, to pose the greatest challenge to Soviet unity.[2] Yet it was Ukraine, not Uzbekistan, that willfully sought secession and dealt the death blow to the USSR. Thus, more recent National Consciousness accounts posit that national identification was actually weak in unionist Central

[2] Alexandre Bennigsen and Marie Broxup, *The Islamic Threat to the Soviet State* (New York: St. Martin's Press, 1983); Helene Carrere d'Encausse, *Decline of an Empire: The Soviet Socialist Republics in Revolt* (New York: Harper & Row, 1981); Bohdan Nahaylo, *The Ukrainian Resurgence* (Toronto: University of Toronto Press, 1999), pp. xii, 1; Orest Subtelny, *Ukraine – A History*, 2nd edition (Toronto: University of Toronto Press, 1988/1994), p. 532. Other leading accounts of the time that imply similar views but do not address the question directly include Michael Rywkin, *Moscow's Muslim Challenge: Soviet Central Asia*, revised edition (Armonk, NY: M. E. Sharpe, 1990); Roman Szporluk, "Nationalities of the USSR in 1970," *Survey*, v.17, no.4, 1971, pp. 67–100, reprinted in Szporluk, *Russia, Ukraine, and the Breakup of the Soviet Union* (Stanford, CA: Hoover Institution Press, 2000), pp. 29–70.

Asia and strong in secessionist Ukraine, raising serious questions of circular reasoning.[3]

One might reasonably suppose that the earlier accounts were in fact wrong, but close analysis demonstrates something different from either National Consciousness interpretation. *Both* Ukrainians and Uzbeks had developed strong senses of a national self distinct from the dominant group in the USSR by the dawn of the Gorbachev-era national uprisings, and that of the Uzbeks was at least as powerful as that displayed by the Ukrainians. Also in both cases, this national consciousness was laced with strong senses of grievance against the Russian-dominated union. This indicates national consciousness is insufficient to explain separatism.

At the same time, this chapter finds ethnicity to be far from epiphenomenal. Instead, a sense of ethnic distinctiveness does appear to be something like a necessary (although insufficient) condition for separatism to take root: Those republics with little "ethnic material" distinguishing the local population from the dominant Russians (the Russian Republic itself and the unusually Russified Belorussian Republic) tended to be highly unionist. This is puzzling for ethnicity-as-epiphenomenal theorists: If the motives for secession are not "ethnic," why would the least ethnically distinct not have behaved like the others? Ethnicity's role cannot be attributed to the hard and bright lines ethnicity can provide to facilitate elite coordination, predation, or exclusion because the federal and lower-level territorial boundaries of the USSR provided ample and preinstitutionalized lines along which elites could coordinate, predate, or exclude – ethnicity was neither necessary nor cost-effective for this purpose.

The relational theory of separatism is better suited to explain observed patterns: Ethnic distinctions exacerbated a collective action problem involved in ethnofederal center–periphery relations. That is, national consciousness is neither a motive nor a tool; instead, it raises regional senses of danger that put separatism on the table as a viable response. The more moderate ethnicity-as-conflictual theories (the Capabilities and Countervailing Incentives versions) are, like relational theory, broadly consistent with the evidence in this chapter. These theories are explored further in subsequent chapters.

LIFE CHANCES AND NATIONAL IDENTIFICATION IN THE USSR

Goble once ventured that about 70 percent of the 400 ethnic groups identified in the 1989 Soviet census have names that simply translate as "human being" in their native languages. In 1921–2, when Stalin forced individuals across the country to name their ethnic identity for state records, many apparently gave

[3] For example, Gregory Gleason, *The Central Asian States: Discovering Independence* (Boulder, CO: Westview Press, 1997). Some posit Ukrainian national consciousness developed rapidly as the USSR's demise approached: Philip Goldman, Gail Lapidus, and Victor Zaslavsky, "Introduction: Soviet Federalism – Its Origins, Evolution, and Demise," in Lapidus and Zaslavsky, with Goldman, eds., *From Union to Commonwealth: Nationalism and Separatism in the Soviet Republics* (New York: Cambridge University Press, 1992), pp. 1–21.

state ethnologists puzzled looks and simply replied "We are human beings."[4] Indeed, despite the popular image of the USSR as a "prison of nations," the young Bolshevik regime not only tolerated non-Russian cultures, but actually promoted identification with ethnic groups by explicitly tying individuals' life chances to these distinctions and seeking to make people conscious of them. Stalin later led significant reversals, but early Soviet policy laid much groundwork for the nationalist movements that accompanied the USSR's dissolution.

Some groups, to be sure, entered the union with highly developed senses of national distinctiveness. Darden and Grzymala-Busse trace such strong senses in the Baltic republics and Moldova to the pre-Soviet introduction of mass schooling, which taught ethnic distinctions as robust ways of interpreting the broader world. In the Baltics, this was backed up with the full panoply of nation-state institutions during the interwar period, making ethnicity highly relevant to understanding interactions with outside powers including Russia. Similarly, the future Moldovans of the USSR were educated as Romanians, a distinct status vis-à-vis Russians that was also reinforced by interwar Romanian state institutions.[5] Despite having far less pre-Soviet national schooling, Armenians were also highly ethnically conscious upon joining the USSR, having experienced the nation-galvanizing tragedy of the 1915 genocide.[6]

Even these nations' strong pre-Soviet senses of ethnic distinctiveness should not be confused with the very different idea of enduring anti-Russian sentiment, however. As the relational theory would expect, historic patterns of ethnic sympathy among these groups have been highly variable depending on the situation. Lithuanians for a time tended to see Poland, which contained their "historic" and future capital Vilnius during the interwar period, as the main threat and often treated Russians as national allies even after the start of World War II.[7] The rural Latvians generally backed the Bolsheviks over their own nationalist parties in 1917 due to promises of economic redistribution.[8] And Armenians, upon joining the USSR, widely saw Russians as allies against various Muslim groups.[9]

Most ethnic groups in the USSR, however, first experienced mass schooling and widespread minority national consciousness under Bolshevik rule. While most know Lenin as a champion of strict state centralization, he was also the strongest Bolshevik advocate of organizing the state along national lines.[10] Like

---

4 Paul A. Goble, "CIS, Boom, Bah: The Commonwealth of Independent States and the Post-Soviet Successor States," in Allen C. Lynch and Kenneth Thompson, eds., *Soviet and Post-Soviet Russia in a World of Change* (New York: University Press of America, 1994), pp. 181–205, 184.

5 Keith Darden and Anna Grzymala-Busse, "The Great Divide: Literacy, Nationalism, and the Communist Collapse," *World Politics*, v.59, no.1, October 2006, pp. 83–115.

6 Ronald Grigor Suny, *Armenia in the Twentieth Century* (Chico, CA: Scholars Press, 1983).

7 Timothy Snyder, *The Reconstruction of Nations: Poland, Ukraine, Lithuania, Belarus* (New Haven, CT: Yale University Press, 2003), pp. 81–2.

8 Aviel Roshwald, *Ethnic Nationalism and the Fall of Empires: Central Europe, Russia and the Middle East, 1914–1923* (New York: Routledge, 2001), p. 101.

9 Suny, *Armenia*.

10 Richard Pipes, *The Formation of the Soviet Union: Communism and Nationalism 1917–1923*, revised edition (Cambridge, MA: Harvard University Press, 1964); Gerhard Simon, *Nationalism and Policy*

most communists at the time, he believed nationalism was a by-product of capitalism that would become irrelevant as socialism developed. Lenin and other early Soviet leaders also believed, however, that most regions of the Russian Empire had not yet even reached the stage of capitalism and that the state would therefore have to artificially accelerate the historical process. This line of reasoning led the Bolsheviks to think that national consciousness needed to be promoted as part of this historical process, that nations had to be "liberated" in the short run so that they could *later* merge into a single harmonious human community.[11] Thus, as Soviet nationalities policy emerged in the cauldron of the Russian Civil War, Bolshevik leaders opted to push the development of nations and to institutionalize them in a "federal" state structure. This was also an attractive strategy for winning the civil war, since it enabled them to align with minority nationalists against the Russian White Army.[12]

Combining brute force with nationalist alliances, the Bolsheviks slowly reunited most of the former Russian Empire. After taking power in 1917, they created the Russian Soviet Federated Socialist Republic (RSFSR, or simply "Russian Republic"). In 1918, they formed the Turkistan Autonomous Soviet Socialist Republic (ASSR), which was made a constituent part of the RSFSR.[13] The Belorussian Soviet Socialist Republic (SSR) appeared in 1919, after the Bolsheviks seized much of what is today Belarus.[14] In 1920, the Bolsheviks retook much of modern Ukraine, establishing the Ukrainian SSR.[15] Also in 1920, Lenin ordered the invasion of three Transcaucasian republics that had enjoyed brief periods of independence during World War I: Georgia, Armenia, and Azerbaijan. These were soon united into a single Transcaucasian republic.[16] By 1922, four "union republics" (the RSFSR, Ukraine, Belorussia, and Transcaucasia) were ready to sign a Union Treaty founding the Union of Soviet Socialist Republics (USSR), which they did on December 30.[17]

The number of union republics subsequently multiplied. In 1924, the regime created the Uzbek and Turkmen SSRs, and in 1929, the Tajik SSR was separated from the Uzbek one. In 1936, Stalin's new constitution formed the Kazakh SSR one and the Kyrgyz SSR as full-fledged union republics[18] and split the Transcaucasian Republic into its constituent parts: Georgia, Armenia, and Azerbaijan.[19] And finally, during World War II, the Soviet Union annexed the Baltic states (Estonia, Latvia, and Lithuania) and Moldova as part of the infamous "secret

Toward the Nationalities in the Soviet Union: From Totalitarian Dictatorship to Post-Stalinist Society (Boulder, CO: Westview Press, 1991).

[11] Francine Hirsch, *Empire of Nations: Ethnographic Knowledge and the Making of the Soviet Union* (Ithaca, NY: Cornell University Press, 2005).
[12] Simon, *Nationalism*, pp. 21–3.
[13] William Fierman, "The Soviet 'Transformation' of Central Asia," in Fierman, ed., *Soviet Central Asia: The Failed Transformation* (Boulder, CO: Westview Press, 1991), pp. 11–35, 16.
[14] Hirsch, *Empire of Nations*, pp. 149–50.
[15] Nahaylo, *The Ukrainian Resurgence*, p. 9.
[16] Pipes, *The Formation*, p. 224.
[17] Pipes, *The Formation*, p. 275.
[18] Fierman, "The Soviet," p. 16.
[19] Simon, *Nationalism*, p. 147.

protocol" of the Nazi–Soviet Pact. These new acquisitions each became union republics. The USSR also expanded Belorussia and Ukraine westward through wartime territorial conquests.

All this by 1990 gave the USSR fifteen *union republics* (SSRs), the highest rank awarded to national-territorial units, with each possessing a foreign border and the formal (although not actual) right to secede. Some union republics contained *autonomous republics* (ASSRs) or lower-level *autonomous regions* (*oblasts*) or *districts* (*okrugs*), with the two latter categories frequently called simply AOs. ASSRs and AOs were almost always official ethnic minority homelands, although they were also component parts of union republics just like run-of-the-mill regions (*oblasts* and *krais*, which were not ethnically defined). Unlike union republics, ASSRs and AOs lacked the formal right to secede, almost never shared a border with a foreign state, and tended to be designated for relatively small ethnic groups. AOs typically represented the smallest such groups.[20] All in all, by Gorbachev's accession to power, the USSR contained fifty-three ethnic units (union republics, autonomous republics, and AOs).

The Soviets went to surprising lengths to imbue these formations with real ethnic meaning for people's life chances. For one thing, they drew ethnic boundaries in ways intended to reinforce shared preexisting determinants of life chances, including local economies, language families, and ways of life, which were all considered important parts of national identity by the Bolsheviks.[21] In their zeal to accelerate history and win local allies, the Soviet leadership worked actively to deepen both the reality and the perception of these commonalities.[22] This process, called *nativization* (*korenizatsiia*), lasted until the early 1930s and involved efforts both to promote local cultures and to replace ethnic Russians with "natives" (those of the *titular* nationality of the given ethnic region) in both political and economic jobs in the non-Russian republics. The Bolsheviks deliberately fostered "national proletariats," giving minority nationalities preference in hiring for industrial employment, promotion into the elite Communist Party, and "election" to legislatures (*soviets*) of all levels.[23] At the same time, the famous slogan "nationalist in form, socialist in content" communicated that these national formations did not have the freedom to oppose Communist Party policy.[24] Thus, even though the state structure was formally federal, the Communist Party of the Soviet Union (CPSU) remained strictly centralized.[25]

---

[20] Aleksei M. Salmin, "From the Union to the Commonwealth: The Problem of the New Federalism," in Stephen White, Rita Di Leo, and Ottorino Cappelli, eds., *The Soviet Transition: From Gorbachev to Yeltsin* (Portland, OR: Frank Cass, 1993), pp. 33–53, 37–8; Pipes, *The Formation*, p. 250.

[21] Strategic considerations were also involved, as in breaking up the large Muslim Turkistan ASSR: Nazif Shahrani, "Central Asia and the Challenge of the Soviet Legacy," *Central Asian Survey*, v.12, no.2, 1993, pp. 123–35.

[22] Terry Martin, *The Affirmative Action Empire: Nations and Nationalism in the Soviet Union, 1923–1939* (Ithaca, NY: Cornell University Press, 2001).

[23] Simon, *Nationalism*, pp. 23–36.

[24] Pipes, *The Formation*, pp. 242–3.

[25] Ibid., p. 242.

   The Bolsheviks, in accordance with Stalinist theory, placed special emphasis on language as the expression and indicator of national culture and identity and hence extensively promoted the use of national languages. Stalin wrote:

What distinguishes a national community from a state community? The fact, among others, that a national community is inconceivable without a common language, while a state need not have a common language. The Czech nation in Austria and the Polish in Russia would be impossible if each did not have a common language, whereas the integrity of Russia and Austria is not affected by the fact that there are a number of different languages within their borders. We are referring, of course, to the spoken languages of the people and not to the official governmental languages. Thus, *a common language* is one of the characteristic features of a nation. This, of course, does not mean that different nations always and everywhere speak different languages, or that all who speak one language necessarily constitute one nation. A *common* language for every nation, but not necessarily different languages for different nations![26]

Here we see not only how Stalin gave great pride of place to language in defining a nation, but also how early Soviet leaders considered diverse national cultures not to pose an immediate threat to the USSR's unity. Language development and education thus became key goals in the nativization campaign, with Moscow codifying languages, promoting their use in administration, and using them for instruction in local schools, which in turn were to teach local national history.[27] Language nativization sometimes even went against the local will: In Belorussia, local elites tended to be either Polonized or Russified, and it took Moscow to convince them to use their "own" language.[28] Darden and Grzymala-Busse argue that nativization went farthest in Armenia and Georgia, where pre-Soviet nation-building initiatives, including national curricula, were sustained and even deepened under the banner of the Transcaucasian republic.[29]

   Starting in the mid-1930s, the regime reversed many of the most radical nativization policies and promoted Russian language and culture much more heavily than before, although the core linkage of ethnic divides to life chances was largely kept in place within the many republics and AOs that survived.[30] In fact, the process of national identification in the union republics in some ways came to fruition under Soviet leader Leonid Brezhnev. Brezhnev's "stability of cadres" policy, a reaction to the rapid reshufflings of the Nikita Khrushchev years and the purges under Stalin, meant that republic leaders had ample leeway to build their own political machines and promote their own groups' cultures.[31] The emergence of local national intelligentsias gave added impetus to

---

[26] Joseph Stalin, *Marxism and the National Question* (1913), *http://www.marxists.org/reference/archive/stalin/works/1913/03.htm.*
[27] Simon, *Nationalism*, pp. 42, 48.
[28] Ibid., p. 43.
[29] Darden and Grzymala-Busse, "The Great Divide," pp. 97–8.
[30] Yuri Slezkine, "How a Socialist State Promoted Ethnic Particularism," *Slavic Review*, v.53, no.2, summer 1994, pp. 414–52.
[31] John P. Willerton, "Reform, the Elite and Soviet Center-Periphery Relations," *Soviet Union/Union Sovietique*, v.17, nos.1–2, 1990, pp. 55–94, 59.

this trend.[32] Thus, while Russians prevailed in central party and government institutions by the late 1980s, the minority nationalities tended to dominate republic-level and local party and government posts.[33] People's life chances came to depend "thickly" on the national identities ascribed to them by the state, identities that before the Soviet era frequently had little to no meaning for "group" members.

REJECTING THE PURE NATIONAL CONSCIOUSNESS EXPLANATION:
UKRAINE AND UZBEKISTAN

Several important works have traced the Soviet Union's destruction to the processes just described. The USSR's own institutions and policies created strong consciousness of national distinctiveness where none had existed before.[34] Some of these works appear to stop here. They seem to assume that an explanation of national consciousness is the most important part of the story of the USSR's collapse, accounting for the secessionism that produced it. There are some major difficulties with this sort of claim. For one thing, most of the Soviet republics sought to *preserve* some form of union rather than to gain independent statehood, and public opinion to be discussed later suggests this was also true at the mass level.

Theorists of National Consciousness might issue the following rejoinder: The truly secessionist Soviet republics had more fully developed national consciousness than the more unionist ones. By these lights, Central Asia's unionism is explained by the fact that its republics were artificial creations of the USSR, with their people seeing themselves in subethnic terms – as members of clans or citizens of cities or of regions – for many of the most important aspects of their daily lives. Uzbekistan's people, the story goes, simply had not yet developed a sense that ethnic identity was important to them, unlike most Ukrainians. Yet this runs squarely into the point made earlier: Leading works on Soviet nationalities written prior to the Soviet breakup often argued that virtually the opposite was the case, raising concerns of circular reasoning.

The rest of this section engages in a focused comparison of Ukraine and Uzbekistan to show that "levels of national consciousness" cannot alone explain patterns of separatism witnessed in the former USSR. It is shown that Soviet and pre-Soviet history had produced strong senses of national distinctiveness in both Ukraine and Uzbekistan, that major grievances were linked to this national consciousness in both republics, and that leaders in both of these entities acted on the basis of this consciousness and these grievances – with actual secessionism resulting only in Ukraine.

---

[32] Suny, *Armenia*.
[33] Mark Beissinger and Lubomyr Hajda, "Nationalism and Reform in Soviet Politics," in Hajda and Beissinger, eds., *The Nationalities Factor in Soviet Politics and Society* (Boulder, CO: Westview Press, 1990), pp. 305–22, 306, 309–10.
[34] For example, Brubaker, *Nationalism Reframed*; Lapidus, "From Democratization"; Leff, "Democratization and Disintegration"; Suny, *The Revenge*.

Ukraine in the USSR

Before Gorbachev came to power, only the staunchest of Ukrainian nationalists seriously believed Ukraine would break with the Russian-dominated USSR in the foreseeable future, even if given the chance.[35] Ukrainians are quite near to Russians culturally as well as geographically, with the two groups speaking closely related Slavic tongues and claiming the same historical roots in Kievan Rus'. There are no reliable physical markers dividing the two groups, and Ukrainians tended to enjoy great upward mobility in the Soviet and even Russian Imperial systems.[36] In addition, Ukrainians had never before produced a generally recognized state of their own, and large numbers of them claimed Russian as their first language. Thus, a highly esteemed Western historian of Ukraine, Orest Subtelny, was able to write in 1988: "By and large, it seems that most Soviet Ukrainians accept the Soviet regime as their legitimate government and identify with it."[37] Despite such early assessments, this chapter agrees with more recent accounts that Ukraine had in fact developed a robust sense of national consciousness by the time Gorbachev came to power.

Ukrainian historians, like their Russian counterparts, trace their nation back to the storied grand princes of Kievan Rus', which existed between the tenth and fourteenth centuries.[38] The name "Ukraine," in several Slavic languages, literally means "on the periphery," and indeed, the region and people now associated with Ukraine were situated on a frontier zone, at the intersection of the continually shifting borders of the Grand Duchy of Lithuania, the Ottoman Empire, the Polish-Lithuanian Commonwealth, the Crimean Tatar Khanate, and the infant Russia (Muscovy). While nothing resembling a Ukrainian state emerged at that time, a ragtag army of escaped peasants and other drifters, now known as Cossacks, did appear in the late seventeenth century under Bohdan Khmelnytsky and establish a political entity known as the Hetmanate. But it and two associated entities were missing key attributes of statehood and quickly lost their independence to Poland and Russia.[39]

By the late eighteenth century, the territory that is today Ukraine was largely divided between the Russian and Habsburg Empires. While Russia had long controlled the bulk of Ukraine, the Habsburgs ruled the western provinces of Galicia (including the famous capital Lviv), Bukovina, and Transcarpathia. This division was significant because Austrian policies, as part of a "divide-and-rule" effort to distinguish Ukrainians from and pit them against both Russians and Poles, created a Ukrainian intelligentsia in Galicia and allowed the publication of Ukrainian periodicals, the formation of Ukrainian political parties, and the

---

[35] See Nahaylo, *The Ukrainian Resurgence*, pp. xii, 1.

[36] Laitin, *Identity in Formation*.

[37] Subtelny, *Ukraine*, p. 532.

[38] Andrew Wilson, *The Ukrainians: Unexpected Nation*, 2nd edition (New Haven, CT: Yale University Press, 2002).

[39] Alexander J. Motyl, *Dilemmas of Independence: Ukraine after Totalitarianism* (New York: Council on Foreign Relations Press, 1993), pp. 26–8; Wilson, *The Ukrainians*, pp. 58–65.

opening of Ukrainian educational institutions intentionally promoting a sense of Ukrainian distinctiveness.[40] This western part of Ukraine remained outside both Russia and the USSR until World War II. Between the wars, however, it fell under the control of Poland (Galicia), Romania (Bukovina), and Czechoslovakia (Transcarpathia). The former two interwar states oppressed and attempted to forcibly assimilate their Ukrainians, although the latter country was more tolerant, permitting a mild level of cultural autonomy.[41] The repression arguably served to strengthen Ukrainians' sense of distinctiveness still further. Overall, historians generally agree that most western Ukrainians had developed a fairly strong sense of national identification before their incorporation into the USSR.

The situation was quite different in the rest of Ukraine, for which the USSR provided the primary nationalizing impulse. Before the Russian Revolution, most Ukrainians in the empire remained rural agriculturalists, with Poles, Jews, and Russians dominating the industrializing cities.[42] Moreover, eastern Ukrainians published their first daily Ukrainian-language newspaper only in 1905, and just one survived until 1914.[43] Some Ukrainians led by Mykhailo Hrushevsky utilized the chaos of World War I to declare a Ukrainian People's Republic, but it was highly unstable, and the Bolsheviks easily stepped into the power vacuum in 1920.[44] Nevertheless, the interlude between the start of World War I and the Bolshevik takeover did give the eastern Ukrainians unprecedented opportunity to mobilize. Many peasants were primarily interested in legitimating land seizures, although other Ukrainians took the chance to publish in Ukrainian and establish a rudimentary political organization based on Ukrainian identity. The result was additional meaning invested in the category "Ukrainian" for the people who fell under this label.[45]

The Bolsheviks then institutionalized Ukrainian national identity, thickening it with meaning for life chances, much as they did for all the major nationalities they recognized. Krawchenko reports that this effort was remarkably successful in Ukraine:

> Overall, the proportion of state business conducted in the Ukrainian language grew from 20 percent in early 1925 to 70 percent by the spring of 1927. The rural apparatus was virtually completely Ukrainised, and in major urban centers it made impressive inroads. In the city of Dnipropetrovsk, for example, three-quarters of all paper work was Ukrainised.... Where Ukrainians predominated, regimental schools and business were completely Ukrainised.[46]

---

[40] Keith Darden, "Families, Schools, and the Durability of National Loyalties," draft manuscript, May 3, 2006, *http://www.umich.edu/~iinet/iisite/dgi/PDF/paper%20Darden.pdf*; John-Paul Himka, "Western Ukraine in the Interwar Period," *Nationalities Papers*, v.22, no.2, 1994, pp. 349–50.

[41] Himka, "Western Ukraine," pp. 351–5; Simon, *Nationalism*, pp. 191–2.

[42] Bohdan Krawchenko, *Social Change and National Consciousness in the Twentieth-Century Ukraine* (New York: St. Martin's Press, 1985).

[43] Ibid., p. 27.

[44] Motyl, *Dilemmas*, pp. 30–1; Nahaylo, *The Ukrainian Resurgence*, p. 9.

[45] Krawchenko, *Social Change*, pp. 56–8.

[46] Ibid., pp. 110–1.

Moreover, many officials from the 1917 Ukrainian government found new life in Soviet institutions, where they were able to promote some nationalist ideas.[47]

If things were looking up for Ukrainian nationalists in the 1920s, they took a terrible turn downward in the 1930s. For one thing, Stalin sharply scaled back Ukrainianization policies. More gravely, some 80 percent of Ukraine's writers and creative intelligentsia disappeared in his infamous purges.[48] The Great Famine was the most egregious atrocity to befall Ukrainians, as Stalin gave orders for state organs to confiscate virtually all agricultural production in the most important grain-growing areas, killing millions.[49] The first two decades of Soviet rule thus created massive grievances, or a sense of negative common fate with regard to Russian domination, at the same time that it generally raised Ukrainians' awareness of the importance of nationality distinctions in determining their life chances.

After the war, the regime further broadened the "situational availability" of "Ukrainian" as an interpretive category and laid the institutional foundations for future mobilization along the lines of nationality. The USSR granted Ukraine its "own" ministry of foreign affairs and eventually won a symbolically important seat for "Ukraine" in the United Nations. It attached the adjective "Ukrainian" to the names of armies and fronts.[50] And most important of all, after the war, Stalin united all territories predominantly populated by Ukrainians into a single, explicitly "Ukrainian" political entity for the first time in history. There thus emerged a single institutional representation of "Ukraine" that then began to take on additional ethnic meaning.

After Stalin died, Ukrainian politics revolved around a covert competition between two factions in the republic's branch of the Communist Party, one advocating greater Ukrainian autonomy and the other preferring tighter ties with Russia.[51] The "national communists," personified by Petro Shelest, gained local power under Brezhnev, taking advantage of Brezhnev's stability in cadres policy to nurture nationalistic ideas subtly before finally going too far and being removed.[52] The republic helm was then bestowed on Volodymyr Shcherbitsky, who was reputed to be devoid of the Ukrainian national idea and kept a tight lid on nationalism in Ukraine, stifling Ukrainian language schools and producing virtually all records in Russian.[53]

---

[47] Karen Dawisha and Bruce Parrott, *Russia and the New States of Eurasia: The Politics of Upheaval* (New York: Cambridge University Press, 1994), pp. 35–6.

[48] Krawchenko, *Social Change*, p. 134.

[49] International Commission of Inquiry into the 1932–99 Famine in Ukraine (Jacob W. F. Sundberg, President), *The Final Report* (Toronto: the International Commission, 1990); Simon, *Nationalism*, p. 99.

[50] Krawchenko, *Social Change*, pp. 169–70.

[51] Wilson, *The Ukrainians*.

[52] Krawchenko, *Social Change*, p. 242; Subtelny, *Ukraine*, p. 513.

[53] Author's interview with Konstantin Sytnik, chair of the Ukrainian Supreme Soviet 1980–85, June 29, 1993; Bohdan Krawchenko, "Ukraine: The Politics of Independence," in Ian Bremmer and Ray Taras, eds., *Nations and Politics in the Soviet Successor States* (New York: Cambridge University Press, 1993), p. 89.

Shcherbitsky was also at the helm in 1986 when the huge Chernobyl nuclear reactor exploded, killing about 30, contaminating large swaths of Ukrainian land, and imposing untold psychological trauma on masses of Ukrainians fearful of developing cancer or other radiation-related illnesses.[54] Moscow at first tried to cover the accident up, and Shcherbitsky took no immediate measures to warn or evacuate the endangered population.

Until Gorbachev forced Shcherbitsky to resign in September 1989, any open advocacy of anything close to Ukrainian independence was brutally quashed.[55] Yet the Ukrainian republic itself remained, and the new repression imposed on Ukrainian culture under Shcherbitsky in some ways heightened Ukrainians' sense that their fate depended on their Ukrainianness.

Overall, despite Ukraine's cultural similarity and commonalities with Russia, and despite the long division of Ukrainian land among different empires, the material was clearly in place for a separatist movement by 1989. Not only were Ukrainians highly aware of a national identity distinguishing them from Russians, but they also had many negative experiences associated with this history that could form the basis for a negative evaluation of the prospects for a cooperative union with Russia.

Uzbekistan in the USSR

Historical accounts of the origins of Ukrainian national consciousness are frequently deemed sufficient to explain Ukrainian separatism in the 1990s; however, one could make an analogous case for the emergence of national consciousness in Uzbekistan during the Soviet period. Looking at history objectively might even lead us to expect Uzbekistan to have been *more* prone to secede than Ukraine. Crucially, the goal here is not to judge Uzbekistan according to some absolute standard of national consciousness but to show that the bulk of its people possessed the cultural resources for a secession drive to at least roughly the same degree as did the bulk of the Ukrainian people.

Most obvious were linguistic and physical distinctions, taught in the USSR as important group identity markers. Most Uzbeks spoke a tongue belonging to the Turkic family, completely different from the Slavic linguistic family to which Russian and Ukrainian belong. The stereotypical Uzbek was also characterized by a darker complexion and more Asiatic features than the stereotypical Russian.

It is true that no nation-state had ever existed in Central Asia before the Soviet conquest.[56] The region had been the seat of several great rulers, including the Samarkand-based Amir Timur (Tamerlane) in the fourteenth and fifteenth

---

54 David Marples, *Ukraine under Perestroika: Ecology, Economics and the Workers' Revolt* (New York: St. Martin's Press, 1991), p. 8; Subtelny, *Ukraine*, p. 535.

55 See the personal account of the nationalist dissident Levko Luk'ianenko, *Spovid' u Kameri Smertnykiv* (Kyiv: Vitchyzna, 1991).

56 Donald Carlisle, "Islam Karimov and Uzbekistan: Back to the Future?" in Timothy J. Colton and Robert C. Tucker, eds., *Patterns in Post-Soviet Leadership* (Boulder, CO: Westview Press, 1995), pp. 191–216, 191.

centuries, but his was not a true "state" and no one would have called it "Uzbek" at that time. Much like Ukraine claims the Hetmanate and its two associated realms as predecessors, modern Uzbekistan can assert ties with three putative city-states that controlled most of the area that is now Uzbekistan (and more) in the nineteenth century: the Emirate of Bukhara and the Khanates of Khiva and Kokand. But as with the Hetmanate, these did not survive for long as independent entities, with Russia expanding vigorously into the region in the 1800s.[57]

But the Soviet state did much to tie the life chances of Uzbeks systematically to the social category "Uzbek" and to invest it with meaning. In fact, the idea of an Uzbek nation first appeared as the Soviets launched their early ethnicity policies in 1920.[58] Stalin's henchmen drew up Uzbekistan's borders in 1924, and in December, its first governing body appeared. The early Soviet regime carefully balanced different regionally based elite networks in the new leadership, thereby helping unify the republic while retaining the ability to play one group against the other as a divide-and-rule strategy.[59] Critchlow summarizes how other Soviet policies had tied the category "Uzbek" tightly to people's life chances by 1991:

Under Stalin and his successors, Uzbek nationality, however artificial its original premises, has been shaped and consolidated by the federal institutions of the Soviet system. For nearly seven decades, citizens of Uzbekistan have been carrying passports in which their identity is stamped as "Uzbek." They have been going to school in the "Uzbek" language. They have been consumers of "Uzbek" newspapers and "Uzbek" radio and television programs. The offices with which they have dealt, in a system where the citizen turns instinctively to officialdom to provide for his or her needs, have said "Uzbek" on the door, even when the top people inside were Russians. When they have traveled outside of Uzbekistan, or when their sons have served in the Soviet Army, they have been treated as "Uzbeks." In this way, the idea of being "Uzbek" has become internalized in the minds of those who comprise the nationality.[60]

The Brezhnev period proved particularly significant in thickening Uzbek national identification. On one hand, the Uzbeks were denied visible aspects of upward mobility that were allowed other groups, including Ukrainians. Most dramatically, Uzbekistan's longtime party leader, Sharaf Rashidov, was never given full Politburo status whereas Ukraine's party leaders were consistently full Politburo members. On the other hand, Brezhnev's stability of cadres policy gave Rashidov (who ruled the republic 1959–83) the opportunity to build his own local political machine and co-opt Slavic officials whom Moscow assigned to key republic posts as its "watchdogs."[61] All Rashidov had to do was put on the formal appearance that he was delivering ever more cotton from his republic

[57] James Critchlow, *Nationalism in Uzbekistan: A Soviet Republic's Road to Sovereignty* (Boulder, CO: Westview Press, 1991), p. 8; Fierman, "The Soviet," p. 12.
[58] Carlisle, "Islom Karimov," p. 191.
[59] Ibid., p. 194.
[60] Critchlow, *Nationalism in Uzbekistan*, p. 15.
[61] Carlisle, "Islom Karimov," p. 194; Critchlow, *Nationalism in Uzbekistan*, p. 20; James Critchlow, "Prelude to 'Independence': How the Uzbek Party Apparatus Broke Moscow's Grip on Elite Recruitment," in William Fierman, ed., *Soviet Central Asia: The Failed Transformation* (Boulder, CO: Westview Press, 1991), pp. 131–58, 20; Fierman, "The Soviet," p. 25.

to the Soviet regime. As one strategy to entrench himself in power, Rashidov used his autonomy and authority to strengthen elements of Uzbek culture and identification. Islam was quietly accepted as "a matter of individual consciousness."[62] Uzbek intellectuals could publish works glorifying the Uzbek nation and calling for the "de-Russification" of its language, officialdom, and history. Russians' share of positions in local institutions was reduced. Uzbek-language schools were created, and publications expanded as a new native elite and intelligentsia emerged.[63] Such developments are one important reason why many of the West's top experts on Soviet nationalities believed that serious nationalist challenges to the regime could come from Central Asia, including Uzbekistan.[64]

This increasingly robust "Uzbek" category also took on symbolism of negative commonalities of fate linked to the Russian-dominated union. Nationalists rallied public opinion most passionately against the "cotton monoculture" that Soviet authorities had imposed on the republic, leaving its economy warped, relatively unindustrialized, and poor. They decried how the water-intensive cotton economy devastated much of Uzbekistan's natural environment, resulting in the virtual disappearance of the Aral Sea due to overirrigation from the region's two major rivers. The Aral's demise was portrayed as both a tragedy for national heritage in its own right and a cause of other major long-term disasters, such as the destruction of a once-vital fishing industry.[65] Moreover, the newly exposed sea bed sent salts through the wind to ruin surrounding arable lands. And without the sea's moderating effects, according to nationalist accounts, summers became hotter and frost seasons longer, causing blizzards in the spring and drought in the summer.[66] Increased infant mortality was also directly traced to the pollution resulting from cotton production, irrigation, and the Aral's decline.[67]

Uzbek nationalists additionally found grounds to charge late Soviet leaders with seeking to destroy the newly consolidated Uzbek national elite. Brezhnev's successors after 1982 launched a full-scale "anti-corruption" purge of Central Asian officials that became known in Moscow as the "Uzbek affair."[68] This purge was correctly understood in Uzbekistan to be less about actual corruption than about reclaiming the authority that Brezhnev had effectively ceded to local party leaders during the stability in cadres era. This implied halting de-Russification and reducing the republic's de facto autonomy.[69] Uzbeks as an ethnic group consequently lost their majority in the ruling republic party bureau.[70] As Carlisle writes: "Because it was personalized and generalized to an entire ethnic group, the scandal came to have national overtones. This was deeply resented in the

[62] Critchlow, *Nationalism in Uzbekistan*, p. 18.
[63] Ibid.
[64] Bennigsen and Broxup, *The Islamic Threat*; Critchlow, *Nationalism in Uzbekistan*; d'Encausse, *Decline*.
[65] Critchlow, *Nationalism in Uzbekistan*, pp. 63–81.
[66] Ibid., p. 82; *Pravda Vostoka*, June 27, 1989, p. 1.
[67] Critchlow, *Nationalism in Uzbekistan*, pp. 81–2, 4.
[68] Gorbachev later added Turkmenistan and a "number of oblasts" in Kazakhstan. Ibid., p. 42.
[69] Critchlow, *Nationalism in Uzbekistan*, pp. 40–2.
[70] Ibid., p. 44.

republic as a slur on the whole titular nationality."[71] The Uzbek press was full of articles in 1990 on the wrongs committed by Moscow's investigative team.

Additional grounds for concluding that Uzbeks' sense of national distinctiveness relative to Russians was at least as strong as that of Ukrainians can be found in nationalist policies other than secessionism that Uzbek leaders pursued once Gorbachev's reforms afforded them the opportunity. These included strong "culturalist" initiatives that are hard to explain if one believes national sentiment was understood to have no potential mobilizing power. The Uzbek tongue was enshrined as the sole "state language." Streets and territories were renamed with vigor, gaining a distinctively national character.[72] Key state posts were reconcentrated in the hands of ethnic Uzbeks.

Overall, the grounds are strong for the claim that Uzbekistan had sufficient national consciousness and grievance to have supported a powerful secession drive.[73] Had Uzbekistan actually seceded, it would have been easy to construct an account linking national consciousness to this outcome much as has actually been done for Ukraine.

The Insufficiency of National Consciousness

The comparison between Uzbekistan and Ukraine illustrates that one cannot explain Ukraine's separatism and Uzbekistan's unionism by arguing only that Ukraine possessed a sense of national consciousness that Uzbekistan lacked. Not only did historical accounts produced prior to the USSR's breakup often suggest the opposite, but careful analysis finds that Uzbeks had developed at least as much of a sense of cultural distinctiveness and grievance vis-à-vis Russians as did Ukrainians in the crucial 1990–1 period. Separatist politicians had as much "ethnic material" to work with in Uzbekistan as in Ukraine, and perhaps even more since Uzbeks faced more overt discrimination in the union (including in the highly visible Politburo) and had a culture and language that were more starkly different from Russian culture and language. Western Ukrainians had a longer history of distinctly national consciousness than did Uzbeks, but western Ukrainians were still a minority in their republic. For the majority of Ukrainians, the foundations for a strong sense of national identification created by Soviet institutions were

---

[71] Carlisle, "Islom Karimov," p. 195.

[72] *Komsomolets Uzbekistana*, December 26, 1990, p. 2.

[73] Since different dimensions of one's identity can be differentially useful for uncertainty reduction in different situations, the present argument must not be misunderstood as denying the prominence of nonethnic identity dimensions in Uzbekistan (e.g., clan or region) when different issues are at stake. See Kathleen Collins, "The Logic of Clan Politics: Evidence from the Central Asian Trajectories," *World Politics*, v.56, no.2, January 2004, pp. 224–61; William Fierman, "Introduction," in Fierman, ed., *Soviet Central Asia: The Failed Transformation* (Boulder, CO: Westview Press, 1991), pp. 1–7; Pauline Jones Luong, *Institutional Change and Political Continuity in Post-Soviet Central Asia* (New York: Cambridge University Press, 2002); John Schoeberlein-Engel, "Identity in Central Asia: Construction and Contention in the Conceptions of 'Ozbek,' 'Tajik,' 'Muslim,' 'Samarqandi' and Other Groups," Ph.D. dissertation in Anthropology, Harvard University, Cambridge, MA, 1994.

roughly the same as in Uzbekistan, if not stronger in the latter given Rashidov's greater promotion of the national idea than Shcherbitsky's. Thus, Uzbeks did not behave like a group that lacked the ethnic basis for a secession movement: Their official leadership pursued ethnic favoritism in language status and state employment, moves hard to explain if one denies that Uzbek ethnicity had any mobilizational potential or local meaning.

Uzbekistan's combination of national consciousness and unionism is not unique. In other work, the author has made an analogous argument that unionist Kazakhs also possessed at least as much national consciousness and grievance as Ukrainians. Indeed, those citing the famine as key to Ukraine's secession must explain why the Kazakhs did not mount a similar drive despite the fact that the Kazakh nation lost almost *half* of its members to the Soviet "sedentarization" campaign of the 1930s, yet its leaders still broadly supported the union with Russia during the late Soviet period.[74] While it remains for the next chapter to test some more nuanced versions of ethnicity-as-conflictual theory, the preceding analysis has allowed us to rule out that National Consciousness alone is the explanation, as some versions of ethnicity-as-conflictual theory would hold. There can be strong national consciousness without separatism.

REJECTING ETHNICITY-AS-EPIPHENOMENAL THEORIES OF SEPARATISM: RUSSIA AND BELARUS

Having ruled out the simplest of the ethnicity-as-conflictual theories of separatism, we now turn to the opposite end of the theoretical spectrum, to ethnicity-as-epiphenomenal theories. Such works posit that ethnicity is involved in separatism only as a useful line along which people can coordinate their actions, exclude other people from spoils, or foment conflict. If these are the only roles that ethnicity itself plays, then one would expect actual ethnicity to have nothing to do with separatism in countries with a federal system like the USSR's. This is because late Soviet federalism provided premade territorial-administrative lines along which people could coordinate their pursuits, go to war, or exclude others from spoils within a union state. There were also ample subfederal territorial-administrative lines (*oblasts, krais, raions,* etc.) available for selective distribution within a given federal unit. Moreover, all these lines were already highly institutionalized channels of resource allocation in the Soviet system.[75] Thus, the

---

74 One could argue that the Kazakh potential for separatism was offset by the large numbers of Russians in Kazakhstan, but the fact that Kazakhs did not strongly mobilize this grievance for secession reinforces the argument that national consciousness alone (even when linked to major grievances) does not necessarily lead to separatism. A strong argument can also be made, though, that the presence of the Russians was not really the cause of Kazakhstan's unionism. See Henry E. Hale, "Cause Without a Rebel: Kazakhstan's Unionist Nationalism Meets Theories of Secession and Post-Secession Foreign Policy," paper presented at the Annual Meeting of the Association for the Study of Nationalities, New York, April 14, 2005.

75 Jerry F. Hough, *The Soviet Prefects* (Cambridge, MA: Harvard University Press, 1969).

costs of using such channels for purposes of coordination and selective resource allocation should have been far lower than the costs involved in creating, retasking, or augmenting exclusively ethnic networks for this purpose.[76] Ethnicity-as-epiphenomenal theory thus supplies no reason why ethnically distinct regional governments should have behaved any differently from those that were not ethnically distinct from the group dominating the central government in the USSR. Yet this is not what we find.

The following pages show that ethnicity matters even in federal systems like that of the late Soviet Union. They illustrate how the only two union republics that were significantly lacking in a sense of national distinctiveness relative to Russians (Belorussia and Russia) were key unionists. That is, despite operating in the same institutional framework and facing the same collective action problems as the separatist republics, their leaders lobbied for saving a union (albeit a restructured one).

The Russian Republic (RSFSR)

The RSFSR's dominant group, ethnic Russians, was also dominant in the USSR both in terms of population and occupation of the most important political and economic posts. Because the dominant group in the union and the republic were one and the same, there was no sense of ethnic distinctiveness between them.

Of course, the situation was not without nuance. The Russian Republic was not formally *ethnically* defined, and, accordingly, the official word used for "Russian" in the republic name was not *russkaia*, the narrowly ethnic designation, but *rossiiskaia*, a broader term including all peoples of the territory ruled by Russia. Partly as a result, notions of ethnic identity as Russians were surprisingly thin for citizens of the Russian Republic even as late as 1990. What held greater meaning for their lives in most situations was their connection to the institutions of the USSR as a whole.[77] Partly for this reason, the state-propagated concept of a Soviet identity ("Soviet person," *sovetskii chelovek*) did take on significant meaning in the RSFSR. This Soviet identification, however, was not mutually exclusive with a more narrow notion of also being ethnically Russian. Indeed, an identity as Soviet was bound to be important because the Soviet Union as a whole was important, but it was hardly ever argued (even in official state rhetoric) that Soviet identity had completely supplanted Russian or any other ethnic identity. Ethnic Russians may have identified strongly with the Soviet Union, but that did not mean that the category of Russian lacked any meaning for them. The essential point is that ethnic Russians could be both Russian and Soviet, whereas Uzbeks and Ukrainians could be Soviet but not Russian. Thus, no matter whether they saw the union as being dominated by "Russians," "Russified peoples," or "Russian Soviets," ethnic Russians experienced no sense of national distinctiveness

---

[76] This is demonstrated explicitly in Jones Luong, *Institutional Change*.
[77] Szporluk, *Russia, Ukraine*; Astrid Tuminez, *Russian Nationalism since 1856* (New York: Rowman and Littlefield, 2000).

separating them from the Soviet leadership, whereas Ukrainians and Uzbeks quite often did. Indeed, surely no one thought the USSR was run by "Uzbek Soviets" or "Ukrainian Soviets" under Gorbachev.

Despite the absence of a clear ethnic divide cleaving between the Russian nation and the Soviet leadership, the Russian Republic under Yeltsin was certainly implicated in the collapse of the USSR, although this was not for any desire to secede from the greater union.[78] This is not an uncontroversial claim; many have asserted that Russia's leadership did in fact aim to destroy the USSR. Some argue Yeltsin was hell-bent on subverting the union from the beginning because it was the fiefdom of his personal nemesis, the imperious Gorbachev, or because it embodied the Communist regime he hated, or because its destruction was his fastest path to "ultimate power."[79] No one doubts the intensity of Yeltsin's ambition and rage against Gorbachev, but close examination of his actions and statements makes it hard to escape the conclusion that he was in fact committed to saving a *union*, although not Gorbachev's, up until the very end. His aim, supported by most of the Russian elite, including many Communists, was to restructure the union to Russia's advantage, relying on its overwhelming size and economic might to prevent other republics from being a burden on the Russian economy.

It is helpful to begin by noting the widespread perception among both Yeltsin's team and the Russian population that Russia was actually being denied its proper position in the union. First, despite its obvious demographic and cultural dominance, the Russian Republic had faced some important handicaps in its treatment by the Soviet center, mostly deriving from Lenin's original determination to stamp out "bourgeois" Russian chauvinism. For example, Russia was not given its own party organization separate from the union organization. Thus, there was no Central Committee of any RSFSR Communist Party, even though there were central committees for the Ukrainian and Uzbek Communist Party organizations. The Russian Republic also lacked a republic-level academy of sciences, which in other republics was important in promoting a sense of national distinctiveness through historical and cultural scholarship. In terms of the economy, the economist who was Yeltsin's right-hand man in the Russian parliament, Ruslan Khasbulatov, explained that the Soviet leadership had ruled Russia more or less directly in the past, giving Russia's parliament and other organs almost no autonomy and exporting its wealth in an unequal exchange with other republics (read: selling oil at below-market prices).[80]

[78] See John B. Dunlop, *The Rise of Russia and the Fall of the Soviet Empire* (Princeton, NJ: Princeton University Press, 1994); Henry E. Hale, "The Makeup and Breakup of Ethnofederal States: Why Russia Survives Where the USSR Fell," *Perspectives on Politics*, v.3, no.1, March 2005, pp. 55–70; Stephen Kotkin, *Armageddon Averted* (New York: Oxford University Press, 2001).

[79] Archie Brown, *The Gorbachev Factor* (New York: Oxford, 1997), pp. 24, 39; Jerry F. Hough, *Democratization and Revolution in the USSR* (Washington, DC: Brookings, 1997), p. 340; Michael McFaul, *Russia's Unfinished Revolution* (Ithaca, NY: Cornell University Press, 2001), pp. 111, 136–8; Wisla Suraska, *How the Soviet Union Disappeared* (Durham, NC: Duke University Press, 1998), pp. 5–6.

[80] *Argumenty i Fakty*, no.28, July 14–20, 1990, p. 2.

Little survey work was done on such questions during this period; however, existing relevant evidence indicates the public was generally in agreement that Russia deserved better. The 1991 New Soviet Citizen survey, designed by a University of Iowa team, found that a strong plurality (47 percent) of RSFSR residents west of the Urals believed Russians had "too little" influence "on life and politics" in the USSR, with 36 percent stating that Russians had the right amount of sway and 17 percent "too much."[81] Only 13 percent named Russians as a disadvantaged group in the union, however – what was in question was what Russians deserved.[82]

Moreover, Russian elites and masses shared a growing perception that the central government was not adequately coping with the challenges of the day as the economy continued to slow. For example, over 90 percent of those RSFSR residents queried in both the 1990 and 1991 New Soviet Citizen surveys asserted that the economy had worsened during both 1989–90 and 1990–1.[83] The 1991 survey also asked people to name the most important problem facing the union and to evaluate the union government's performance on that issue: A whopping 76 percent of the interviewed Russian Republic citizens rated this performance as either "poor" or "very poor."[84]

What we saw unfold in Russia during 1990–1, then, was not a secessionist strategy but a very strong, even reckless, renegotiation effort designed to address these deficiencies by demanding a combination of decentralization and a greater role for Russia in controlling what union functions remained. Some have treated Russia's June 1990 "sovereignty declaration" as a Yeltsin move aimed at destroying the union, but it was not purely Yeltsin's doing and was instead a compromise document that did not portend secession and did not even involve very radical claims compared to declarations being made by other republics around that time.[85] For example, the Russian compromise declaration laid claim to all resources located on Russian territory but strikingly did not seek to appropriate the "economic and scientific potential" (e.g., state enterprises) in the republic, a standard clause in the sovereignty declarations of all other republics except Tajikistan, Uzbekistan, and Belorussia. Although it reserved Russia's right to secede, formally bestowed by the Soviet Constitution ever since Stalin, it explicitly stated that the purpose

---

[81] Arthur H. Miller, William Reisinger, and Vicki T. Hesli, "New Soviet Citizen Survey, 1991, Monitoring Institutional Change" [Computer file]. ICPSR06521-vI. Iowa City, IA: Iowa Social Science Institute [producer], 1991. Ann Arbor: Inter-university Consortium for Political and Social Research [distributor], 1995; Miller, Reisinger, and Hesli, *Public Opinion and Regime Change: The New Politics of Post-Soviet Societies* (Boulder, CO: Westview, 1993). The figures are the frequencies reported by Miller et al. in the codebook. About 1,400 RSFSR respondents were surveyed in a four-stage stratified representative sample. Hereafter these data are called "New Soviet Citizen Survey, 1991."

[82] Ibid., author's calculation using supplied sample weights.

[83] Ibid. and Arthur H. Miller, "New Soviet Citizen Survey, 1990: Problems of Peace and Security" [Computer file]. ICPSR version. Des Moines, IA: Arthur H. Miller [producer], 1992. Ann Arbor: Inter-university Consortium for Political and Social Research [distributor], 1994, hereafter cited as "New Soviet Citizen Survey, 1990." Frequencies are those reported by Miller et al. in each case.

[84] New Soviet Citizen Survey, 1991, question 18. Frequencies from Miller et al.

[85] *Izvestiia*, May 23, 1990, p. 4; May 24, 1990, p. 2; June 12, 1990, p. 1; Hough, *Democratization and Revolution*.

of the declaration was to be the basis of a "New Union Treaty" to preserve the USSR.[86]

The subsequent infamous "war of laws" between Yeltsin and Gorbachev also reveals not an attempt to destroy the union but moves designed to renegotiate it and force change. Many of the key battles were Russian leadership efforts to gain more control over federal and economic reforms, which Gorbachev had previously been attempting to impose on republics after only cursory consultations.[87] The Russian leadership essentially sought to present Gorbachev with a *fait accompli*, creating a situation in which the Soviet center had no choice but to let the republics administer economic reform themselves. In July 1990, Russia's parliament practically liquidated the USSR banking system, the linchpin of the center's capacity to appropriate republic resources and distribute them as it deemed fit.[88] It also claimed veto power over foreign deals involving resources on Russian territory and created institutions (including a State Bank) to control such activity.[89] Nevertheless, this whole time Yeltsin's leadership was assuming the USSR would be preserved and even continue to administer some property in Russia. Thus, almost immediately after dealing the body blow that was the banking legislation, the Supreme Soviet that Yeltsin chaired ordered its Council of Ministers to draw up a list of Russian assets to be given over to USSR management.[90] Moreover, the famous "500-Day Plan" of economic reform that Yeltsin was vigorously pushing during 1990 was premised on retaining a union (e.g., for monetary policy), although it did call for significant decentralization.[91]

---

[86] For the sovereignty declarations, see Eduard Bagramov, ed., *K Soiuzu Suverennykh Narodov: Sbornik Dokumentov KPSS, Zakonadatel'nykh Aktov, Deklaratsii, Obrashchenii i Prezidentskikh Ukazov, Posviashchennykh Probleme Natsional'no-Gosudarstvennogo Suvereniteta* (Moscow: Institut Teorii i Istorii Sotsializma TsK KPSS, 1991).

[87] For example, Postanovlenie S'ezda Narodnykh Deputatov Rossiiskoi Sovetskoi Federativnoi Sotsialisticheskoi Respubliki, "O razgranichenii funktsii upravleniia organizatsiiami na territorii RSFSR (osnovy novogo Soiuznogo dogovora)," *Vedomosti S'ezda Narodnykh Deputatov RSFSR i Verkhovnogo Soveta RSFSR*, no.4, st.63, 1990, pp. 81–3; *Izvestiia*, August 2, 1990, p. 2. See also Hough, *Democratization and Revolution*, pp. 364–5.

[88] Postanovlenie Verkhovnogo Soveta RSFSR, "O Gosudarstvennom banke RSFSR i bankakh na territorii respubliki," *Vedomosti S'ezda Narodnykh Deputatov RSFSR i Verkhovnogo Soveta RSFSR*, no.6, st.98, 1990, p. 142. See also Juliet Johnson, *A Fistful of Rubles* (Ithaca, NY: Cornell University Press, 2000), pp. 26–63.

[89] Postanovlenie Prezidiuma Verkhovnogo Soveta RSFSR, "O zashchite ekonomicheskoi osnovy suvereniteta RSFSR," *Vedomosti S'ezda Narodnykh Deputatov RSFSR i Verkhovnogo Soveta RSFSR*, no.10, st.133, 1990, pp. 173–4; *Izvestiia*, August 21, 1990, p. 2; Postanovlenie Prezidiuma Verkhovnogo Soveta RSFSR, "O merakh po vypolneniiu postanovleniia Verkhovnogo Soveta RSFSR ot 13 iiulia 1990 goda 'O gosudarstvennom banke RSFSR i bankakh na territorii respubliki,'" *Vedomosti S'ezda Narodnykh Deputatov RSFSR i Verkhovnogo Soveta RSFSR*, no.11, st.146, 1990, pp. 188–9.

[90] Zakon Rossiiskoi Sovetskoi Federativnoi Sotsialisticheskoi Respubliki, "O sobstvennosti na territorii RSFSR," *Vedomosti S'ezda Narodnykh Deputatov RSFSR i Verkhovnogo Soveta RSFSR*, no.7, st.101, 1990, p. 147; Postanovlenie Verkhovnogo Soveta RSFSR, "O podgotovke perechnia imushchestva RSFSR, funktsii upravleniia kotorym peredaiutsia soiuznym organam," *Vedomosti S'ezda Narodnykh Deputatov RSFSR i Verkhovnogo Soveta RSFSR*, no.7, st.105, 1990, p. 149.

[91] Russia's Prime Minister Ivan Silaev, for example, declared that this reform required the conclusion of a New Union Treaty. *Izvestiia*, June 18, 1990, p. 1.

Accordingly, while campaigning for the Russian Republic's new directly elected presidency in spring 1991, Yeltsin did not oppose a union but instead trumpeted his ability to work with Gorbachev to produce an agreement on a "New Union Treaty," convincing Gorbachev to provide a more decentralized union. In fact, he cited his success in promoting such a "Union of Sovereign States" as one of his top four achievements during his first year at Russia's helm.[92] While Yeltsin did make some blustery moves, such as calling on Gorbachev to resign and suggesting the republics themselves should govern without Gorbachev's government during late 1990 and early 1991, these are best understood as part of a bargaining strategy to eventually get a better deal in the union.[93] He effectively said as much in an April 1991 warning: If Gorbachev did not live up to his promises on the New Union Treaty, the republics might just launch their own agreement without including central authorities at all.[94] This interpretation makes much better sense of the fact that, prior to the August 1991 coup, Yeltsin was among the union republic leaders who had promised to sign the New Union Treaty that Gorbachev had long sought in order to save his teetering state. Indeed, while Yeltsin applied more rhetorical pressure on his nemesis after his June 1991 victory in the RSFSR presidential elections, he reaffirmed his pledge to sign the new treaty after Gorbachev acceded to a final set of demands on republic tax authority in late July.

In pursuing a radically restructured yet preserved union, Yeltsin was in line with Russian public sentiment. In a March 1991 referendum that Gorbachev orchestrated, over 70 percent of those RSFSR citizens who voted opted to preserve the USSR.[95] The New Soviet Citizen surveys, while covering only that part of Russia west of the Urals, also detected strong support for a decentralized union there: When asked in April 1991 what measures the USSR government should take to preserve the union, only 9 percent replied it should not be preserved, and when asked whether they supported a "full transfer of power to the republic level," 61 percent wanted the center to retain some authority.[96]

The essential unionism of Russian leadership actions remained in place even after the August 1991 coup sent Soviet institutions reeling. It is important first to consider what the Russian leadership did *not* do yet could easily have done had it in fact wanted to ensure the actual dissolution of the union. Russia is the only former Soviet republic *never* to have issued a formal declaration of independence from the USSR, which could have ended all talk of reviving the union before it had even started.[97] Yet Yeltsin met with Gorbachev and eight other republic leaders just two days after he himself had played the leading role in defeating the

---

92 Radio Russia, June 1, 1991, 1110 GMT, FBIS-SOV-91-106, p. 71. See similar Yeltsin statements in *Izvestiia*, March 30, 1991, p. 3.
93 For example, his February 1991 televised speech, described in *Izvestiia*, February 22, 1991, p. 2.
94 *Izvestiia*, 26 April 26, 1991, p. 1.
95 Of course, the referendum wording was carefully manipulated as will be discussed in Chapter 7.
96 New Soviet Citizen, 1991, survey questionnaire, frequencies from questions 107, 108.
97 Roman Solchanyk, "Russia, Ukraine and the Imperial Legacy," *Post-Soviet Affairs*, v.9, no.4, October–December 1993, pp. 337–65, 348.

coup. At that meeting, he declared that a New Union Treaty was still necessary, an opinion supported by Khasbulatov, Russia's new congressional speaker, in his speech to the first post-coup meeting of the USSR parliament on August 26.[98] Thus, Yeltsin's own decree ordering the expropriation of all Communist Party property contained the following sentence in Article 1: "The funds of the CPSU located abroad are distributed by agreement between the republics *after the signing by them of a Union treaty*" [emphasis added], a clause that surely would have been left out had Yeltsin not actually wanted to save some form of union.[99] Yeltsin saw no problem with formally recognizing the Baltic states' independence shortly after the August coup, but evidence suggests his leadership saw them as special cases that did not keep him from strongly supporting continued union with the other republics, especially important ones like Ukraine. Indeed, Russian leaders even resorted to threatening other republics, including Ukraine, not to leave the union, as will be discussed in Chapter 6.

In the end, it was Ukraine's move to secede that essentially forced Yeltsin to follow. In a December 1, 1991, referendum, Ukraine voted overwhelmingly to become an independent state over the objections of both Yeltsin and Gorbachev. Faced with this fact, Yeltsin calculated that the only way to keep Ukraine in *some* kind of a union was to liquidate the old one and to create whatever Ukraine would agree to – in this case the CIS.[100] Explaining his actions to the Russian parliament after it ratified the CIS Treaty, Yeltsin called "criminal" the idea that Russia should simply have ignored Ukraine's referendum vote and fortified a union without Ukraine.[101] Then-Foreign Minister Andrei Kozyrev confirms this interpretation, stressing that Russia's leaders saw the CIS as a way to prevent the outbreak of violence while still achieving some kind of union ties with Ukraine.[102] Public opinion clearly buttressed Yeltsin's incentives to keep Ukraine in a union. The respected VTsIOM polling agency asked 994 people in December 1991 how they were responding to Ukraine's referendum vote in favor of independence. A full 40 percent reacted with "alarm" and another 10 percent cited "outrage," while just 23 percent approved of the results and a mere 12 percent confessed indifference. And even at this late date, in the same survey, two-thirds of RSFSR respondents affirmed that their republic should sign a union treaty.[103]

The Russian case is useful because it helps rule out ethnicity-as-epiphenomenal theories of separatism. If ethnicity in and of itself does not matter and if what matters are elite drives for power and resources, then we cannot explain why the

[98] Mikhail Gorbachev, *Zhizn' i Reformy*, v.2 (Moscow: Novosti, 1995), pp. 583–4; Gorbachev, *The August Coup: The Truth and the Lessons* (New York: Harper Collins Publishers, 1991), p. 50; *Biulleten' No.1 Sovmestnogo Zasedaniia Soveta Soiuza i Soveta Natsional'nostei*, Verkhovnyi Sovet SSSR, Vneocherednaia Sessiia, August 26, 1991, pp. 39–40.

[99] Ukaz Prezidenta Rossiiskoi Sovetskoi Federativnoi Sotsialisticheskoi Respubliki, "Ob imushch-estve KPSS i Kommunisticheskoi partii RSFSR," *Vedomosti S'ezda Narodnykh Deputatov RSFSR i Verkhovnogo Soveta RSFSR*, no.35, st.1164, 1991, pp. 1434–5.

[100] Boris Yeltsin, interview in *Argumenty i Fakty*, December 12, 1991, p. 1.

[101] *Rossiiskaia Gazeta*, December 13, 1991, p. 1.

[102] *Nezavisimaia Gazeta*, December 8, 1992, p. 5.

[103] Survey results obtained directly from the polling agency VTsIOM.

authorities in a republic like Ukraine would want to secede while those in Russia would not. Indeed, Russian leaders stood to gain more in terms of both immediate power and resources because Russia was a bigger state that had long been subsidizing almost all of the other republics, including Ukraine, through greatly underpriced oil and gas, among other things.[104] Yet Russia's leader forewent opportunities to secede that opened up after August 1991, while Ukraine's leaders seized them, and Yeltsin agreed to dissolve the union only after it became clear that Ukrainian secession could not be stopped. The relational theory provides a better explanation: Secessionism is a response to an ethnically charged collective action problem in a union, one that Russians did not feel both because they did not see an ethnic divide separating them from control of union policies and because their republic's size meant they had resources that could be used to prevent the union from exploiting Russia in the future. Of course, some ethnicity-as-epiphenomenal theories might respond that the latter reasoning is compatible with their logic, that Russia was unionist only because its size assured its people that they could be no worse off in a union than outside it. This response, however, runs into trouble with the case of Belarus.

Belarus

Belarus, as the Belorussian SSR came to be called after gaining political independence and as it will sometimes be called here, also constitutes a case where there was relatively little cultural or other material to become the basis for a strong sense of distinctiveness vis-à-vis Russia. There are three main grounds for this claim. First, most objectively, Soviet censuses regularly showed that Belorussians in the Belorussian Republic were by far the most Russified among all the populations of the different union republics. In fact, only 74 percent of Belorussians claimed their "own" titular language as their native language in 1989. This is striking because *all* of the other union republics registered figures in the 90 percent range, and most republics claimed 97–99 percent. The significance of this is magnified given the emphasis that Soviet thinking and education put on language as a defining feature of national identity, as described earlier. Second, most media and historical accounts have noted that Belorussians did widely lack a sense they were distinct from Russians in a meaningful way throughout the Soviet period. Crucially, accounts written both before and after the USSR broke apart are consistent.[105] Third, the claim of weak Belorussian national consciousness finds strong support in an analysis of formative events in Belorussian history, a brief treatment of which now follows.

In some ways, Belorussian national development parallels that of Ukraine. Both groups could claim independent "states" in the midst of both World Wars

---

[104] William W. Hogan, "Oil and Gas in the Former Soviet Union: Market Impacts and Reform Challenges," working paper in the series of the Center for Business and Government, John F. Kennedy School of Government, Harvard University, Cambridge, MA, March 1993, p. 19.

[105] A telling title is: David Marples, *Belarus: A Denationalized Nation* (Amsterdam: Harwood, 1999).

I and II. Like much of western Ukraine, western Belarus was also part of Poland between the wars and only joined the USSR after World War II.[106] Many western Belorussians, like western Ukrainians, also adhere to a Catholic tradition in contrast to the Orthodoxy that characterizes the history of their eastern coethnics as well as of most Russians.[107]

There are some important reasons why Belorussians, unlike Ukrainians, did not develop a strong sense of national distinctiveness relative to Russians, however. One is that western Ukrainians, and not western Belorussians, were part of the Austro-Hungarian Empire in the nineteenth century and were explicitly given autonomy to develop their own intelligentsia, literature, political parties, and native-language schools.[108] With this critical state-supplied opportunity, Ukrainian elites were able to thicken ethnic Ukrainian points of personal reference by developing them and promoting them as explaining the world and demonstrating shared fate. Belarus, on the other hand, did not experience this historical opportunity to develop a national intelligentsia and thereby tie the masses' sense of life chances to a national idea.[109] Belorussians in fact became part of the Polish and then Russian intellectual-cultural traditions. Accordingly, the USSR met little resistance in implementing an aggressive Russification program in Belarus after World War II, whereas it shied away from such policies in western Ukraine for fear of sparking resistance that could prove a threat to the regime.[110]

Additionally, virtually every other Soviet nation had developed *some* plausible national grievance directed against Russian authority, but historians widely agree that the temporal span of Russian–Belorussian relations actually provided few symbols with which political entrepreneurs might mobilize a strong separatist movement. There were no major wars that could easily and plausibly be portrayed as having occurred between these peoples, and the Great Famine that devastated Ukraine did not greatly affect neighboring Belarus. The most likely candidate for anti-Russian symbolism would seem to have been the Chernobyl nuclear disaster. But there was little sense that this tragedy reflected Russian anti-Belorussian attitudes or behavior given the fact that Chernobyl itself was in Ukraine. There were some attempts to link the Belorussian nation to the 1569–1795 Grand Duchy of Lithuania, which was effectively finished off by the Russian Empire.[111] But given how far from living memory these events were, and given that the republic of "Lithuania" had a more direct claim on this legacy based on its name and possession of the historic capital city of Vilnius, such interpretations were not likely to have been seen as plausible or important by a broader society that already possessed a dense array of myths linking Belorussians closely to Russians. At least, this was not likely without an extended period of education and

---

[106] Simon, *Nationalism*, pp. 174, 382.
[107] Abdelal, *National Purpose*, p. 124.
[108] Himka, "Western Ukraine."
[109] Simon, *Nationalism*, pp. 173–227.
[110] Abdelal, *National Purpose*, pp. 124–5; Szporluk, *Russia, Ukraine*, pp. 109–38.
[111] Snyder, *The Reconstruction*.

propagation, something that was not needed by separatists in Ukraine or Uzbekistan. And unlike Uzbeks, Belorussians did not generally possess clear physical markers distinguishing them from Russians. The Russian and Belorussian languages were also quite similar. Large numbers of Belorussians, then, simply did not see themselves as distinct from Russians to a significant degree in a way that might have provided a strong potential basis for a separatist movement by the early 1990s.

Accordingly, Belarus was consistently among the most unionist of republics. Belarus issued a declaration of sovereignty, but it did so after the RSFSR had blazed this path. And naturally, the Belorussian document advocated the preservation of the Soviet Union.[112] Thus, when Gorbachev's representatives invited the republic leadership to submit its own New Union Treaty proposal for consideration, Belorussian experts included a long list of issues to be in the Union's purview.[113] Belarus was also never in doubt as a signatory to the New Union Treaty, which was finalized and ready to sign in August 1991. After the putsch of that month, Belarusian leader Stanislau Shushkevich joined Yeltsin in dissolving the USSR and creating the CIS as a last-ditch effort to preserve some form of union after Ukraine ratified its own secession in a referendum.[114]

In short, if ethnicity-as-epiphenomenal theories are correct that ethnicity is nothing more than a set of lines for coordination, resource distribution, or conflict fomentation, we are unable to explain why the Belorussian leadership forewent secession at the same time that Ukrainian authorities embraced it. Belarus was just as close to the prosperous European Community as was Ukraine, and its relative wealth should have made it particularly attractive for resource-grabbing or power-seeking politicians. If the authorities needed a way to divide spoils locally, they could easily have done so along *oblast* (regional) or *raion* (district) lines, long institutionalized as channels of resource distribution and administration. The relational theory of ethnicity provides a better explanation: Belorussians, on the whole, simply lacked a sense that a meaningful ethnic divide separated them from control over the union state and thus did not attach much significance to the collective action problem involved in that union.

CONCLUSION

The focused comparison of Ukraine, Uzbekistan, Russia, and Belarus lends confirmation to one of the central claims of the relational theory of separatism outlined in Chapter 4: A strong sense of minority ethnic distinctiveness (particularly when fraught with the symbolism of past exploitation) leads group members in ethnofederal regions to attach greater risks of exploitation to continued

---

[112] Document in Bagramov, *K Soiuzu.*
[113] Document, copy in possession of author.
[114] See preceding discussion of the RSFSR and Shushkevich, interview in *Argumenty i Fakty,* January 8, 1992, p. 3.

integration but does not privilege any particular strategy for dealing with this risk. This means, for one thing, that ethnic regions with low senses of national distinctiveness are likely to avoid true secessionism even when they do favor greater autonomy to correct perceived overcentralization. This accounts for the consistent unionism of Russia and Belarus. On the other end of the spectrum, the republics whose populations' national awareness was steeped in pre-Soviet schooling (especially Estonians, Latvians, Lithuanians, and Moldovans[115]) or forged in genocide (Armenia[116]) are generally characterized by experts as featuring unusually thick national identification. These republics were among the first to claim autonomy and the most reluctant to accept central promises of cooperation. This indicates that ethnic consciousness does matter, that ethnic divides are not simply lines along which people coordinate action, divide spoils, or provoke conflict, as ethnicity-as-epiphenomenal theories tend to posit.

At the same time, ethnically conscious groups that fear exploitation in ethnofederal states have several strategies available, not just secessionism. These other strategies might include pushing for greater decentralization or power-sharing arrangements in the central government, perhaps along with privileges for the local group in regional political appointments. Thus, national consciousness is not a sufficient explanation for separatism, as some ethnicity-as-conflictual theories appear to imply. This was confirmed by contrasting the Uzbek case with that of Ukraine: Uzbeks possessed at least as great a sense of national distinctiveness relative to Russians as did Ukrainians, and both distinctions involved significant national grievances. Yet only Ukraine opted for secession in the end. Indeed, one can make a strong argument that every republic except Russia and Belarus possessed national consciousness that was at least as thick as most Ukrainians possessed, yet there was much variation in actual separatism among these republics.[117]

To sum up the performance of the rival theories of ethnicity so far, ethnicity-as-epiphenomenal theory and the National Consciousness version of ethnicity-as-conflictual theory are inadequate fits with observed events. The three other theories weighed here, though, are consistent with these events and cannot yet be distinguished from each other in terms of accuracy. Thus, even though relational theory is strongly in line with what we have examined so far, we cannot

---

[115] As coded by Darden and Grzymala-Busse, "The Great Divide." Accounts on each country include: Rasma Karklins, *Ethnic Politics and Transition to Democracy: USSR/Latvia* (Baltimore: Johns Hopkins University Press, 1994); Charles King, *The Moldovans: Romania, Russia, and the Politics of Culture* (Stanford, CA: Hoover Institution Press, 2000); Toivo Raun, *Estonia and the Estonians* (Stanford, CA: Hoover Institution Press, 2001); Ronald Grigor Suny, *The Making of the Georgian Nation* (Bloomington: Indiana University Press, 1994); Vytas Stanley Vardas, Judith Sedaitis, and Stanley V. Vardas, *Lithuania: The Rebel Nation* (Boulder, CO: Westview, 1996).

[116] Suny, *Armenia*.

[117] See fn. 117–18 for works on the Baltic republics, Moldova, Armenia, and Georgia. On Kazakhstan, see Hale, "Cause Without a Rebel." On Azerbaijan, Kazakhstan, Kyrgyzstan, Tajikistan, and Turkmenistan, see Bremmer and Taras, *Nations and Politics*.

yet rule out the Capabilities and Countervailing Incentives versions of ethnicity-as-conflictual theory: Perhaps national consciousness does naturally lead ethnic groups to desire political independence, but other factors can differentially constrain or override this desired. The next chapter takes up this possibility by examining changes in republic attitudes toward secession over time.

6

Central State Policies and Separatism

The previous chapter has shown that patterns of Soviet-era separatism cannot be explained as a simple resource grab or as the pure expression of national consciousness, so what can it be? At least three possibilities remain. Ethnicity-as-conflictual theory may still hold that separatism is an expression of national consciousness while pragmatically making one of two arguments. Capabilities arguments posit that groups or regions can lack the capability to engage in this expression. Countervailing Incentives arguments anticipate that the ethnic separatist impulse can be overridden by important nonethnic interests that a group might have in a union. The third argument is that the relational theory of separatism is correct, that the impulse behind separatism is an ethnically charged collective action problem. This chapter weighs these three theories against each other through a comparative, process-tracing study of variation in Ukrainian and Uzbek separatism over time.

This strategy is effective because the explanatory factors central to each theory do not vary together over time during the Gorbachev era. The relational theory holds that where levels of national consciousness are equal, variation in secessionism will depend first and foremost on the degree to which central state policies demonstrate credible commitments not to exploit minority regions and a willingness to use force to preserve the union, as described in Chapter 4. During 1985–91, the Soviet government changed its policies three times in ways that prominent research on credible commitments suggests should be important. These changes thus define four periods, with relational theory generating distinct expectations for each. The policy changes are such that the relational theory expects increasing separatism in both Ukraine and Uzbekistan during the first two periods, declining separatism in the third, and then rising separatism in the fourth.

This expectation diverges from what we would expect were Capabilities and Countervailing Incentives theories correct. The Capabilities version of ethnicity-as-conflictual theory holds that a region should change its level of separatism over time as its capacity to engage in separatist activity changes. Because most accounts of the Gorbachev years paint a picture of steadily declining central institutional capacity and a steadily rising sense that republic independence was a real possibility, this theory would expect a steady rise in secessionism throughout all four periods. The Countervailing Incentives version of ethnicity-as-conflictual theory holds that a region will alter its degree of separatism as incentives to pursue nonethnic goods in the union change. Almost all accounts of late Soviet history concur that not only was Soviet institutional capacity consistently weakening, but prospects for the economy were also worsening as reform was delayed, growth ground virtually to a halt, inflationary pressures rose, and economic institutions descended into chaos. Objective republic interests in the union were thus deteriorating consistently during this period, so we would expect steadily rising republic secessionism as countervailing interests in the union were declining throughout all four periods.

The rest of this chapter demonstrates that the detailed flow of events in Ukraine and Uzbekistan fit better with the relational theory than with the Capabilities or Countervailing Incentives versions of ethnicity-as-conflictual theory.[1] The chapter also has implications for the theories that were discredited in the previous chapter. The part of relational theory evaluated here does not violate any ethnicity-as-epiphenomenal assumptions; in fact, the findings from this particular chapter generally support ethnicity-as-epiphenomenal theory as well as relational theory. The results provide further reason to question the National Consciousness version of ethnicity-as-conflictual theory, though. If national consciousness alone influences separatism, we would have expected either constant levels of separatism among Uzbekistan and Ukraine (since both had developed significant national consciousness by the dawn of the Gorbachev era) or steadily growing separatism (if one assumes that national consciousness was growing during this period), yet we find neither.

THE UNILATERAL PERIOD: MARCH 1985–MAY 1990

This first period is labeled "unilateral" because Gorbachev's regime sought to preserve the union during this time primarily by imposing what its representatives saw as a solution to the collective action problem on the republics. All the theories considered in this chapter would expect rising separatism in this period, although the relational theory also generates specific expectations that can be confirmed or disconfirmed by tracing the process through which the general pattern emerged.

The key to the relational theory's expectations is the degree to which union policies communicate credible central government commitments to forcefully

---

[1] Much of the material on Ukraine comes from Henry E. Hale, "The Double-Edged Sword of Ethnofederalism: Ukraine and the USSR in Comparative Perspective," *Comparative Politics*, v.40, no.3, April 2008, pp. 293–312.

resist secession and not to exploit constituent minority regions. Rather than simply assert that a given policy has the requisite credibility, it is useful to begin by consulting relevant research on credible commitments more generally. A starting proposition for such researchers is that cooperation is much more likely to succeed when negotiating parties are constrained in their ability or desire to renege on their agreements ("defect") to the detriment of other negotiating parties.[2] Experimental research by Ostrom and her colleagues finds that mutually profitable cooperation is far more likely to emerge in situations where not only is there a sanction involved to punish defectors, but the prospective cooperators are also in regular communication with each other on these issues.[3] The first phase of Gorbachev's union-saving activity can be seen as a classic failure to satisfy either condition.

In the 1960s and 1970s, nationalist incidents in the Soviet Union were few and far between.[4] Thus, when Mikhail Gorbachev became general secretary of the Communist Party of the Soviet Union in March 1985, he did not anticipate that they would become a major issue under his rule.[5] Thinking the days of serious ethnic problems were over, Gorbachev's initial policies were actually aimed at recentralizing the USSR, withdrawing much of the de facto autonomy that republic leaders had come to enjoy under Brezhnev's stability of cadres policy. Gorbachev stressed "internationalism" (as opposed to "localism"), with the Russian language as the lingua franca.[6] Gorbachev's first Central Committee and Politburo were the most Russian in Soviet history, with Central Asians bearing the brunt of the shift.[7]

But during his first four years, Gorbachev was surprised to witness a striking eruption of ethnic conflicts and nationalist demands. In some cases, the conflicts appear generated by Gorbachev's own anti-ethnic-autonomy policies. Most notably, riots flared up in the Kazakh SSR after Gorbachev replaced the ethnically Kazakh head of the republic's Communist Party organization with an ethnic Russian in December 1986. In others, liberalization appeared to give voice to longstanding conflicts of interest between different minority republics, as with the dispute between Armenia and Azerbaijan over who should control the Nagorno-Karabakh AO that turned gruesomely violent in 1987–8. In still other cases, *glasnost'* allowed old minority grievances against the Soviet regime

[2] Elster, "Ulysses"; Hardin, *Collective Action*, pp. 211–13; Thomas C. Schelling, *The Strategy of Conflict* (Cambridge, MA: Harvard University Press, 1980).

[3] Ostrom, Walker, and Gardner, "Covenants," p. 413.

[4] Those few that did arise were punished severely. See Luk'ianenko, *Spovid'*.

[5] *M.S. Gorbachev v Sverdlovskoi Oblasti 25–27 Aprelia 1990 goda* (Moscow: Politizdat, 1990), pp. 37–8, published in A.B. Veber, V.T. Loginov, G.S. Ostroumov, and A.S. Cherniaev, eds., *Soiuz Mozhno Bylo Sokhranit': Belaia Kniga: Dokumenty i Fakty o Politike M.S. Gorbacheva po Reformirovaniiu i Sokhraneniiu Mnogonatsional'nogo Gosudarstva* (Moscow: Gorbachev-Fond, Aprel'-85, 1995), p. 104.

[6] Ronald J. Hill, "Managing Ethnic Conflict," in Stephen White, Rita Di Leo, and Ottorino Cappelli, eds., *The Soviet Transition: From Gorbachev to Yeltsin* (Portland, OR: Frank Cass, 1993), pp. 57–74, 61–2.

[7] Beissinger and Hajda, "Nationalism and Reform," p. 312.

to be aired. The Baltic republics, which had been full-fledged independent states before the USSR conquered them during World War II, experienced the highest levels of nationalist ferment.[8] Moreover, these initial expressions of ethnic tensions had important demonstration effects on other republics.[9] Not only did acts such as Estonia's 1988 declaration of sovereignty show other republics that such actions were possible without provoking a crackdown, but Baltic nationalists in particular recognized that their own goals would be served if they could directly promote nationalist movements in other republics. Thus, they not only encouraged but actively sent emissaries to help organize nationalist movements in other republics, including Ukraine's *Rukh*.[10]

The events in Kazakhstan, Transcaucasia, and the Baltics compelled Gorbachev's regime to admit there was a "nationalities problem" and to address it.[11] The Soviet leader's first instinct was to demonstrate his goodwill by unilaterally enacting what he saw as concessions to growing republic demands for autonomy while using his bully pulpit to persuade minority peoples to accept the new structures.[12] Soviet leaders thus worked furiously to put in place a legal framework that would channel these demands. Key acts included allowing all republics to freely elect their own parliaments in early 1990, restructuring the Communist Party Politburo along national lines, naming a Ukrainian the official "second secretary" of the party, granting the Uzbek party leader full Politburo membership for the first time in nearly three decades, and legislating substantial autonomy for republics. Gorbachev also directly promoted liberalization in republics that had been lagging, replacing both the Uzbek and Ukrainian party bosses in 1989.[13]

It is important to recognize another central part of Gorbachev's strategy that endured straight up until the August 1991 coup attempt: the threat of state violence against activists or republic officials who egregiously flouted his attempts to control the reform process. Thus, in April 1989, Soviet troops brutally quashed a demonstration of about 10,000 people who had begun to call for Georgian independence in Tbilisi. The Georgian party leadership was then removed.[14] Although Gorbachev denied approving this highly unpopular military action, his disavowals were widely disbelieved.[15] He did take responsibility, however, for an even more forceful act that occurred in January 1990 in Baku, where Soviet troops killed over a hundred people while reasserting central control after a series

---

[8] Juris Dreifelds, "Latvia: Chronicle of an Independence Movement," in Miron Rezun, ed., *Nationalism and the Breakup of an Empire: Russia and Its Periphery* (Westport, CT: Praeger Publishers, 1992), pp. 43–56, 47; Nils Muiznieks, "Latvia: origins, evolution, and triumph," in Ian Bremmer and Ray Taras, eds., *Nations and Politics in the Soviet Successor States* (New York: Cambridge University Press, 1993), pp. 182–205, 190.

[9] Beissinger, *Nationalist Mobilization*.

[10] Goble, "CIS, Boom, Bah," pp. 88–9.

[11] Lapidus, "From Democratization," p. 46.

[12] Mikhail Gorbachev, *Zhizn' i Reformy*, v.1 (Moscow: Novosti, 1995), p. 512.

[13] Carlisle, "Islom Karimov."

[14] Nikolai Ryzhkov, *Perestroika: Istoriia Predatel'stv* (Moscow: Novosti, 1992).

[15] For example, Leonid Ivashov, *Marshall Yazov: Rokovoi Avgust 91-ogo: Pravda o "Putsche"* (Moscow: Bibliotechka Zhurnala "Muzhestvo," 1992), p. 60.

of deadly anti-Armenian pogroms there. Later that year, Gorbachev shepherded through a series of laws aimed at legitimizing the center's use of coercion: laws on secession and on delimiting powers between the union and the republics. The Soviet leader repeatedly declared after the spring of 1990 that republics were welcome to discuss secession but only in the context of the new legislation; otherwise, the state had the right to enforce its law by force if necessary. Ukraine and Uzbekistan were both spared violent central intervention during this period, however.

This early Gorbachevian combination – liberalization, the imposition of legislation on center-republic relations from above, the unleashing of demonstration effects, and the partially botched use of force – opened up space for Uzbek and Ukrainian leaders to air old grievances and call for autonomy while sometimes providing new cause for these autonomy demands. Thus, in response to the aired national grievances that were discussed extensively in Chapter 5, as well as to a general bureaucratic desire for less oversight that had reportedly been shared even by Shcherbitsky,[16] Volodymyr Ivashko began to request more autonomy for Ukraine almost immediately upon being confirmed as Shcherbitsky's successor. Even before the first competitive republic elections scheduled for March 1990, Ivashko's Ukrainian leadership began work on a declaration of sovereignty and adopted a law on language that declared Ukrainian to be a state language of the republic.[17] In his opening remarks to the February 1990 Plenum of the republic's party branch, Ivashko praised its election platform for grounding itself in a call for "the economic independence of Ukraine in the framework of a Soviet federation on the basis of a new union treaty."[18] Economic independence, backed by a declaration of sovereignty, would give Ukraine control over enterprises on its own territory (and associated revenues) and enable the republic to retaliate against other republics that did not fulfill contractual obligations for the delivery of vital goods.[19] In the bigger picture the Ukrainian communists painted at this time, however, sovereignty was clearly not the top priority, playing only a minor role in the party's lengthy election platform for the 1990 parliamentary elections, adopted in late 1989.[20]

As the spring of 1990 progressed, the USSR announced certain policies that drove Ivashko's communist organization to back even greater autonomy from Moscow. Most prominently, in early May 1990, Soviet Prime Minister Nikolai Ryzhkov unveiled a major economic reform that included such unpopular measures as a 300 percent hike in the officially set price of bread, which sparked mass hoarding before the prices were to go into effect.[21] Ivashko took a strong stand:

---

[16] Vitaly Vrublevsky, *Vladimir Shcherbitsky: Pravda i Vymysly: Zapiski Pomoshchnika: Vospominaniia, Dokumenty, Slukhi, Legendy, Fakty* (Kyiv: Dovira, 1993), pp. 239–40.

[17] Leonid Kuchma, *Ukraiina – Ne Rosiia* (Moscow: Vremia, 2004), p. 406; TASS (English), 2028 GMT, February 22, 1990, FBIS-SOV-90-037, February 23, 1990, p. 64.

[18] *Pravda Ukrainy*, February 24, 1990, p. 2.

[19] Ibid.

[20] *Pravda Ukrainy*, December 3, 1989, pp. 1–2.

[21] *Izvestiia*, May 24, 1990, p. 1; *Izvestiia*, May 26, 1990, p. 1.

No price hikes could be permitted, he declared, without a reliable compensation mechanism and a referendum.[22] Around this time, Ivashko cited other economic grievances against the USSR, for example decrying the heavy-industry bias in the Ukrainian economy and averring that sovereignty was a way to rectify it.[23] Ivashko's vision was thus of a sovereign Ukraine in "mutually profitable relations with other republics," which could only come about if the Soviet Union were turned into a real federation replete with a great deal of republic autonomy.[24]

Changes in the Uzbek Republic's official attitude toward sovereignty closely resembled developments in Ukraine during this period. The Uzbeks' new party leader Islom Karimov, like the new Ukrainian party boss Ivashko, had come to call openly for more autonomy in the union by the spring of 1990. During this period, Uzbekistan became the first republic to create the post of republic president and the first holder of this title, Karimov, justified it as necessary to strengthen "economic and political independence . . . within the framework of a single Union federation."[25] The statements of Shukurulla Mirsaidov, chairman of the Uzbek Council of Ministers, also made clear that the Uzbek leadership favored remaining in a union, but wanted significantly more autonomy.[26] Accordingly, Uzbekistan imposed restrictions on some goods it exported to the other republics in the spring of 1990, arguing this was necessary to keep goods available locally and to keep shelves from emptying during the transition to the market.[27]

Overall, Gorbachev did almost the opposite of what credible commitment theorists would have recommended for avoiding secessionism and reaped the predictable results. He promised an ideal world of interethnic harmony and progress but provided republics with no way to be sure that this was not simply a trap to lure them back into a repressive union. He did not even consult regularly with the top republic leaders who, in 1990, became responsible to their own people rather than Gorbachev through newly competitive regional elections. This strategy was accompanied by Soviet policies that were easily portrayed in both Ukraine and Uzbekistan as not representing republic interests. As a result, communist leaders as well as nationalists in these republics moved to support greater and greater levels of autonomy from Moscow. At the same time, through the famous policies of *glasnost'* and *perestroika*, the union government was providing more and more opportunity for separatists to mobilize and voice their demands, culminating in the early 1990 parliamentary elections. And this liberalism not only gave Ukrainians and Uzbeks themselves more time to mobilize but also provided opportunities for them to learn from other republics, particularly Baltic nationalists who were

---

[22] *Izvestiia*, May 30, 1990, p. 1; *Pravda*, May 29, 1990, p. 2.

[23] *Pravda*, May 3, 1990, p. 2.

[24] *Pravda Ukrainy*, May 3, 1990, p. 2; *Pravda Ukrainy*, May 10, 1990, p. 3.

[25] *Vremia*, 1430 GMT, March 26, 1990, FBIS-SOV-90-060, pp. 117–18.

[26] *Izvestiia*, April 1, 1990, p. 2, FBIS-SOV-90-065, p. 88; *Moscow Domestic Service*, 1500 GMT March 27, 1990, FBIS-SOV-90-060, p. 118.

[27] *Pravda Vostoka*, April 28, 1990, p. 1, FBIS-CHI-90-105, p. 103; *Izvestiia*, June 1, 1990, p. 6, FBIS-SOV-90-108, p. 103.

actively promoting separatist movements throughout the USSR. Events during this period, then, are broadly consistent with all of the theories studied in this volume. As all of them would predict, both the Ukrainian and Uzbek republic leaderships increasingly called for autonomy at the same time that they continued to back the union between 1986 and early 1990.

THE BILATERAL PERIOD: JUNE 1990–MARCH 1991

This second period is dubbed "bilateral" because Gorbachev endeavored then to win confidence in a proposed federal solution through bilateral negotiations with republic representatives, continuing to use violence rather arbitrarily. The evident failure of its attempts both to present republics with institutional accommodation and to "reason" with the nationalists forced a rethink in the Soviet leadership. In some ways, the new central policies were an advance in the effort to counteract the collective action problem at the heart of the union. The centerpiece was to be a New Union Treaty, a successor to the old Union Treaty of 1922 that marked the official founding of the USSR. This alone had some potential to reassure republic representatives that they would not be exploited: Research has found that "constitutional" documents generally help make rulers' promises not to exploit constituents credible because these documents can provide clear guidelines to these constituents on when they need to coordinate their efforts to "punish" a central government for violating the trust.[28] Moreover, the specifics of the treaty promised republics greater resources that they could then have used to resist future central exploitation attempts: greater autonomy and control over important resources.[29]

Nevertheless, this early New Union Treaty effort did not alter the fundamental structure of the situation from the perspective of Chapter 4, a situation in which the central government was holding all the cards and essentially seeking to impose a deal on the republics, albeit a more reasonable deal from the republics' point of view. Research on institution building and collective action often stresses that the *process* by which an institutional framework is developed can go a long way in building the initial trust (credibility) needed to make the transition from one institutional equilibrium to another. Ostrom, in addition, presents extensive behavioral research concluding that people are far less likely to succeed in cooperating when they do not interact face-to-face (even when they may otherwise be communicating).[30] Moreover, she elsewhere shows that this logic applies even to the interaction of relatively small numbers of people representing large organizations.[31] Research on negotiations specifies that without

---

[28] North and Weingast, "Constitutions and Commitment"; Veitch, "Repudiations and Confiscations"; Weingast, "The Political Foundations."
[29] Schelling, *The Strategy of Conflict*, p. 43; Hardin, *Collective Action*, p. 212.
[30] Ostrom, "A Behavioral Approach," p. 7.
[31] Olson, *The Logic*, p. 33–6; Ostrom, *Governing the Commons*, pp. 189–90.

transparency and visibility of outcomes in the negotiating process, even a struc-
turally sound institutional arrangement might be subverted because the relevant
actors may never have enough faith to make the leap from old institutions.[32]

This illuminates the inadequacy of Gorbachev's bilateral stage of unionist
activity. The Soviet leader went about this effort by forming a working group
consisting of lower-level representatives of the republics to hammer out a first
draft of the New Union Treaty.[33] The republics' representatives on the working
group, however, did not have any significant power to make binding commitments or compromises on behalf of their republics and grew to act more as
technical advisers than representatives.[34] Gorbachev's representatives thus dominated the concrete work of the committee. Moreover, the group tended to meet
bilaterally with mid- or low-level delegations from the republics in order to ascertain republics' positions, taking the sum of these separately expressed views into
account while composing the first draft of the treaty. The fact that republic leaders were largely left out of the process undermined their faith in what objectively
represented some significant concessions.[35]

The union republic leaders' doubts as to the cooperative nature of the union
continued to grow when Gorbachev at times revealed the coercive side of his
union-saving strategy in arbitrary ways rather than in a clearly rule-based manner
that would have been more compatible with democratic law enforcement and
nonexploitative intent. Most notable was the Kremlin's crackdown on the highly
separatist Baltic republics. The Soviet government first openly threatened and
then sent troops into the capitals of Lithuania and Latvia in January 1991, killing
at least a dozen people.[36] Such acts communicated that at least some Soviet leaders
were quite willing to use force to repress national movements. But these same
acts also failed to eliminate the movements completely and were easily portrayed
as ham-handed attempts to repress the will of the Baltic peoples, adding fuel to
nationalist fires.

Additionally, Gorbachev's economic policies continued to flounder, lending
credence to nationalist claims that the central government, through either incom-
petence or indifference, could not be counted upon to adopt policies suitable to
republics like Ukraine and Uzbekistan. Most prominently, Gorbachev wavered
throughout much of 1990 on whether to back his own prime minister's reform
plan (involving the price hikes noted previously) or the alternative 500-Day
Plan promoted by Yeltsin's Russian Republic. This waffling degenerated into a
protracted effort to merge the two largely incompatible plans, resulting in
the near paralysis of reform efforts as the economy descended into chaos.[37]

---

[32] Hechter, *Containing Nationalism*, p. 153.

[33] *Izvestiia*, June 13, 1990, p. 1.

[34] Author's interview with Mykola Shulha, a Ukrainian representative in these negotiations, July 5,
1993.

[35] *Izvestiia*, December 8, 1990, p. 2; *Vedomosti Verkhovnogo Soveta Ukrainskoi SSR*, 1991, p. 171.

[36] *Izvestiia*, January 10, 1991, p. 1; *Izvestiia*, January 14, 1991, p. 1; David Remnick, *Lenin's Tomb*
(New York: Vintage Books, 1994), p. 387.

[37] Gorbachev, *Zhizn' i Reformy*, v.1, pp. 590–1.

Making matters worse, the most prominent actual reform was new Prime Minister Valentin Pavlov's surprise January 1991 declaration that 50- and 100-ruble notes were no longer legal tender and that people would have only a small window of time to exchange them. Pavlov said the aim was to hit criminals who supposedly accumulated vast quantities of these large bills, but it also harshly punished ordinary citizens who did not trust banks and frequently kept savings in such notes at home. Ukrainian leader Leonid Kravchuk, who took over from Ivashko as parliamentary chairman in the summer of 1990, later wrote that the banknote reform "undermined the remaining faith in the bankrupt system."[38]

The impact of all of this on republics' choices of strategy can be seen in both Ukraine's and Uzbekistan's accelerating calls for more autonomy between June 1990 and March 1991, as all theories considered here would expect. First, both republics reacted sharply against Soviet government efforts to raise prices and confiscate large ruble notes in the absence of any progress on deeper economic reform as the situation deteriorated. Ukraine announced in late 1990 its own republic-level marketization plan that would insulate itself against central policies through complete customs and taxation autonomy.[39] Envisioning an eventual national currency, in November 1990 Ukraine introduced a system of "coupons" required along with rubles to purchase certain staple goods.[40] Uzbekistan reacted less radically but still strongly, de facto seizing autonomy by openly defying central policies it did not like and calling on the regime to better take republic interests into account. For example, it rescinded a 5 percent tax that Pavlov had placed on essential foodstuffs and industrial goods.[41] Nevertheless, statements by various top officials left absolutely clear that the Uzbek leadership favored remaining in a union – just one that would give the republic significantly more autonomy.[42]

The accelerating separatism of both republics was also evident in the New Union Treaty process. Ukrainian representatives were skeptical of union intent from the beginning, avoiding giving concrete recommendations to Gorbachev's initial New Union Treaty working group while hinting that the future union should be a very loose one, perhaps little more than a common "market space" with national defense responsibilities. Uzbek negotiators were more cooperative, supporting more autonomy than the status quo afforded but generally being in accord with what Gorbachev's group was proposing.[43] In fact, Uzbekistan submitted its own draft treaty to the working group in summer 1990, and it was

---

[38] Leonid Kravchuk, *Maemo Te, Shcho Maemo: Spohady i Rozdumy* (Kyiv: Stolittia, 2002), p. 77.

[39] Documents in various issues of *Vedomosti Verkhovnogo Soveta Ukrainskoi SSR* and *Vidomosti Verkhovnoi Rady Ukraiins'koi RSR* from 1990.

[40] *Izvestiia*, October 29, 1990, p. 2; *Izvestiia*, November 1, 1990, p. 2; *Izvestiia*, December 26, 1990, p. 7; *Izvestiia*, December 26, 1990, p. 7.

[41] All-Union Radio *Maiak* 1030 GMT, March 29, 1991 FBIS-SOV-91-063, p. 83.

[42] *Izvestiia*, March 31, 1990, p. 2; Moscow Domestic Service 1500 GMT, March 27, 1990, FBIS-SOV-90-060, p. 118.

[43] Unpublished participant report on republic positions expressed during the summer 1990 New Union Treaty working group consultations. Copy in possession of author.

quite similar to the first draft that Gorbachev was to publish a few months later.[44] But when this first Gorbachev draft finally appeared in the press in November 1990, Uzbekistan's leadership expressed no more willingness than Ukraine's to sign it.

Kravchuk and Karimov primarily lambasted the way the treaty had been developed. Kravchuk argued that the future union should not be handed down from above, but should be negotiated by the republics alone.[45] He thus embarked on a series of demonstrative "negotiations" to conclude "treaties" or agreements with each of the other union republics, mostly pledging economic cooperation, pointedly leaving Gorbachev out, and generally not mentioning the New Union Treaty.[46] During the same period, Kravchuk declared that Ukraine would not fix any position on the New Union Treaty until after Ukraine adopted its own constitution, which would determine the legal foundation for such a signature.[47] Accordingly, Ukraine did not actively participate in the production of the second draft New Union Treaty, published in March 1991.[48] Uzbekistan's leader similarly complained about the treaty process: "We are only formally heard out and then given the fifth or tenth, but nevertheless their own, version of a treaty in which nothing of what we are proposing is taken into account."[49] Uzbek leaders and media thus pilloried the draft, finding at least technical fault with almost every article, despite the fact that side-by-side comparison reveals it was very close to what Uzbek representatives had themselves proposed just months before.[50] Criticism of details of the treaty continued through the publication of the second draft in March 1991.[51] Overall, even though the New Union Treaty may have been a positive step for Gorbachev, his bilateral approach to going about it did not augur success, pushing Ukraine perilously close to outright secessionism with Uzbekistan not too far behind.

A rise in Ukrainian and Uzbek separatism was also evident in several other ways during this period. For one thing, both republics adopted their landmark declarations of sovereignty then. These documents asserted the superiority of republic over union law but also claimed to be starting points for negotiating a New Union Treaty. Ukraine's was more radical than Uzbekistan's, however, claiming the right to Ukrainian armed forces.[52] Calls for greater republic

---

[44] Unpublished draft treaty proposed by Uzbek experts in the summer of 1990. Copy in possession of author.

[45] *Izvestiia*, December 8, 1990, p. 2.

[46] *Izvestiia*, November 19, 1990, p. 1; *Izvestiia*, January 12, 1991, p. 1; *Izvestiia*, February 1, 1991, p. 2.

[47] *Izvestiia*, December 8, 1990, p. 2.

[48] Author's interview with Mykola Shulha, head of the Rada Commission on State Sovereignty, Interrepublic and Internationality Relations, July 5, 1993.

[49] *Izvestiia*, January 28, 1991, p. 3.

[50] For example, *Krasnaia Zvezda*, January 30, 1991, p. 1; *Pravda*, December 18, 1990, p. 4; *Izvestiia*, January 28, 1991, p. 3.

[51] For example, *Sovet O'zbekistoni*, April 5, 1991, p. 3.

[52] Documents reprinted in Bagramov, *K Soiuzu*.

control over the instruments of coercion, including in Uzbekistan, also followed the Soviet crackdown in the Baltics.[53] The link between the Baltic bloodshed and Ukrainian policies was openly stated. On one hand, Kravchuk interpreted the Baltic events to mean that the union was willing to use violence and would be likely to use it even more decisively on Ukraine given its greater strategic importance for the USSR.[54] On the other hand, it also gave Ukrainian leaders the incentive to build up their ability to resist a potential crackdown as best they could, taking advantage of the continued opening that Gorbachev was providing. Thus, Ukraine's parliament reinforced earlier measures to restrict republic citizens' participation in the Soviet military and even to take over Soviet police troops on Ukrainian territory.[55]

Overall, the June 1990–March 1991 period featured a decline in Soviet state capacity, a continued buildup of economic problems, some boneheaded central policies, expanded liberalization, and attempts to shore up the union that were mishandled and sometimes violent. The result, as all the theories considered here would expect, was continued divergence between the positions of Gorbachev's government on the one hand and Ukraine's and Uzbekistan's on the other.

THE MULTILATERAL PERIOD: APRIL–AUGUST 1991

Among the four periods considered here, this third stage has the greatest potential for distinguishing the relational theory of separatism from all versions of ethnicity-as-conflictual theory because this is where their expectations most clearly diverge. Indeed, hardly any expert on Soviet politics would deny that the opportunity for separatist mobilization continued to expand and that economic problems and state capacity continued to deteriorate during this period.[56] And if national consciousness in the minority republics was changing at all, it was surely strengthening.[57] In the spirit of ethnicity-as-conflictual theory, then, we would expect to have seen continued divergence between the position of the central government and the positions of both Ukraine and Uzbekistan on the issue of remaining in the union. And this is what many accounts seem to have presumed happened without examining events during this period in detail.

The relational theory generates another expectation because, after the second round of New Union Treaty negotiations failed in early 1991, Gorbachev made a move that appears almost as if it came right from a specialists' handbook on institution crafting, trust building, and credible commitment. The big

53 *Krasnaia Zvezda*, January 30, 1991, p. 1.

54 Kravchuk, *Maemo Te*, p. 72.

55 Postanovlenie Prezidiuma Verkhovnogo Soveta Ukrainskoi SSR, "O nekotorykh merakh po zashchite gosudarstvennogo suvereniteta Ukrainskoi SSR," *Vedomosti Verkhovnogo Soveta Ukrainskoi SSR*, no.9, st.96, 1991, p. 232.

56 Beissinger, *Nationalist Mobilization*; Dunlop, *The Rise*; Jack F. Matlock, *Autopsy on an Empire* (New York: Random House, 1996).

57 Beissinger, *Nationalist Mobilization*.

break with past strategy came at the villa of Novo-Ogarevo in April 1991, where nine top republic officials and Gorbachev announced a pledge to complete work speedily on the New Union Treaty, conceiving of the future entity as a "Union of Sovereign States."[58] Henceforth, negotiations were to be face-to-face, with Gorbachev engaging republic leaders directly, collectively, and frequently. This facilitated communication and transparency, which many studies have argued are crucial for building trust and allaying security concerns.[59] The multilateral nature of the negotiations, as well as Gorbachev's willingness to concede more autonomy, also afforded republic leaders a greater sense of collective power.[60] To the extent that Soviet separatism was driven by worries about the center's credibility in promising nonexploitation, therefore, we would expect the new strategy to have had a serious chance to stem or reverse the centrifugal dynamic. Thus, unlike ethnicity-as-conflictual theories, the relational theory would predict these republics to have moved closer to a compromise with the central government on preserving a union.[61] The bulk of evidence bears out this expectation.

The crucial case is Ukraine, whose leadership as of March 1991 seemed to be on the verge of supporting outright secession, held back mainly by Soviet coercive might. Ukrainian leader Kravchuk, who had sent his prime minister to the April 1991 meeting, later wrote that Gorbachev during this multilateral period demonstrated a remarkable ability to avoid the temptation to try dictating terms or "sermonize" the republics, creating a "democratic" working atmosphere in which the republics really could come to agreement.[62] In addition, just after the initial Novo-Ogarevo accord took place, Kravchuk publicly recognized that it marked a major turning point. He noted that at long last, Gorbachev had effectively accepted the formulation "Union of Sovereign States," which Kravchuk had previously advocated in contradistinction to Gorbachev's earlier concept of a "renewed federation."[63] After the initial Novo-Ogarevo meeting, Kravchuk personally joined the union negotiations for the first time. The Uzbek authorities had not ventured as close to actual secessionism as had the Ukrainian leadership,

---

[58] The agreement also included economic anticrisis measures that were hailed as progress, although they were primarily stopgaps to deal with immediate pressures, such as ongoing strikes, and did not in and of themselves constitute anything like a comprehensive economic reform plan. The New Union Treaty was seen as the key first step to stabilizing the union and providing the mechanism for true future economic reform.

[59] Ostrom, "A Behavioral Approach," p. 7; Ostrom, *Governing the Commons*, pp. 33–6; Hechter, *Containing Nationalism*, p. 153; Weingast, "The Political Foundations."

[60] Steven Solnick, "Is the Center Too Weak or Too Strong in the Russian Federation?" in Valerie Sperling, ed., *Building the Russian State* (Boulder, CO: Westview, 2000), pp. 137–56.

[61] As noted previously, ethnicity-as-epiphenomenal theory is compatible with the aspect of the relational theory's logic examined here.

[62] Kravchuk, *Maemo Te*, pp. 81–3.

[63] Solchanyk, "Russia, Ukraine," pp. 349–50. After the USSR in fact collapsed, in his 2002 memoirs, Kravchuk (*Maemo Te*, pp. 81–2) moderates his interpretation and writes that the Novo-Ogarevo accord only temporarily strengthened Gorbachev's hand, just staving off conservative forces. He reports that at this time he (Kravchuk) was pushing for something close to the European Union but was willing to compromise.

but a turnaround centering on Novo-Ogarevo was noticeable there as well. This is nicely illustrated in two roundtable discussions of legal scholars on the New Union Treaty: In one held prior to Novo-Ogarevo, a top legal scholar (Bahtiar Karimov) absolutely lambasted the document, but by early May he was talking of a major improvement.[64]

Momentum for negotiated decentralization gathered over the summer 1991, and in June the Novo-Ogarevo negotiators completed the third major draft New Union Treaty, explicitly recognizing the republics' own sovereignty declarations in the first line of the preamble and neglecting to allot any state property to the reconstituted union. In a final series of negotiations, Gorbachev, Yeltsin, and other republic leaders ultimately hammered out an agreement that seven republic leaderships (Belarus, Russia, and the five Central Asian republics) publicly declared they would sign come August 20. Gorbachev and his supporters have since asserted that Ukraine's and Azerbaijan's leaders stated privately that they, too, might add their signatures as early as October.[65]

Close examination of Ukrainian events strongly suggests that its leaders genuinely intended to sign eventually. First, shortly before Novo-Ogarevo, in March 1991, 70 and 80 percent of Ukraine's citizens had voted to preserve a union in referendum questions posed not only by Gorbachev but also by the Ukrainian leadership (respectively). The mere fact that Ukrainian authorities carried out the referendum was also significant because the leadership of the hard-core separatist republics like the Baltics had refused to do so. Second, as noted previously, Kravchuk had publicly stated that the Novo-Ogarevo initiative represented a fundamental change that addressed Ukrainians' primary concerns. While Ukraine's leadership had not yet agreed with the union treaty in August 1991,[66] the grounds for reaching agreement had been established.

There is also a third reason to suppose Ukraine's leaders were actually intending to sign a version of the New Union Treaty: They had consistently said over the course of much of the previous year that Ukraine would first adopt its own constitution before acceding to a union treaty.[67] Some regard these statements as a tactic to delay the treaty indefinitely; however, work on the Ukrainian constitution had in fact proceeded apace since November 1990, and the original intent was to conclude this by April 1991. Although the process dragged on for longer than originally planned, it directly involved an effort to hammer out Ukraine's attitude to the union. In June 1991, the Rada adopted a blueprint for the constitution, a "constitutional conception." This document explicitly allowed Ukraine to join the newly constituted union. It did not require Ukraine to join, but laid out criteria by which Ukraine's leaders were to make this decision. These criteria were the republic's declaration of sovereignty (which the June 1991 version of

[64] *Molodezh' Uzbekistana*, May 4, 1991, p. 2; *Sovet O'zbekistoni*, April 5, 1991, p. 3.
[65] Gorbachev, *Zhizn' i Reformy*, v. 2, p. 552; Author's interview with Grigory Revenko, Gorbachev aide on the New Union Treaty process, October 20, 1993.
[66] Nahaylo, *The Ukrainian Resurgence*, pp. 370–1.
[67] *Vidomosti Verkhovnoi Rady Ukraiins'koi RSR*, no.50, 1990, p. 935.

the New Union Treaty had already explicitly recognized in the very first line), along with the following principles:

Voluntariness of entry and exit; sovereign equality and mutual profitability; the rejection of the use of force or the threat of the use of force or any other means of pressure; territorial integrity, the nonviolability of existing borders; the peaceful regulation of disputes and conflictual situations; noninterference in internal affairs; respect for the rights of the individual, national minorities and peoples; equal rights and the right of the peoples to decide their own fate; cooperation and mutual respect; good neighborly fulfillment of agreed obligations; the realization of joint activity according to mutual agreement and in a volume acceptable to each state and the non-imposition of harm to the interests of each other and the union as a whole.[68]

There is nothing in these conditions that Gorbachev was not already essentially offering. Approving this document in June 1991, the Rada ordered that a full draft constitution be presented when it reconvened in early September 1991 after the usual summer break.[69]

Indeed, despite claiming to have dreamt of Ukrainian independence since March 1990, Kravchuk reports in his memoirs that he also believed until the failed August 1991 putsch that this was unrealistic in the near future and that it was thus necessary to create some form of confederation with the other Soviet republics. Only with the collapsed coup did he realize actual independence was an immediate possibility.[70] Future president Kuchma, who in 1990 was a Rada member and head of the military-industrial giant Yuzhmash, likewise recalls in his memoirs that the New Union Treaty looked like a "done deal" during that crucial summer, a necessary "lesser evil" with full Ukrainian independence possible only in the distant future.[71]

One finds some additional evidence in the research of Beissinger, who has created a database of all reported protests at which secessionist demands were raised in the USSR. Figure 4.4 in his landmark book reveals that the number of Ukrainians participating in secessionist demonstrations dropped during the "multilateral period" discussed in this section, reaching a point near zero for the month of July, when the treaty agreement was in its final stages. It spiked up again only in August, as Soviet hardliners torpedoed the process by attempting a coup.[72]

In short, the Ukrainian leadership seemed to be getting what it wanted given the perceived constraints of the time. It had established a framework for signing the New Union Treaty and had signaled its intent to sign in the autumn of 1991. Soviet coercion also remained a factor keeping Ukraine in the union despite the fact that violence used in the Baltics and Transcaucasia during 1989–91 had been only half-hearted: Ukraine perceived itself as being far more strategically valuable

[68] *Vedomosti Verkhovnogo Soveta Ukrainskoi SSR*, 1991, p. 991.
[69] *Vedomosti Verkhovnogo Soveta Ukrainskoi SSR*, 1991, p. 987.
[70] Kravchuk, *Maemo Te*, p. 102.
[71] Kuchma, *Ukraiina – Ne Rosiia*, pp. 410–11.
[72] Beissinger, *Nationalist Mobilization*, p. 183. These are not simply seasonal effects; his data reveal much higher levels of demonstration participation in previous months of July.

and hence more likely to bring about the resolute use of force if it attempted actual secession.[73] Gorbachev thus felt confident enough to leave for vacation at a Black Sea resort on August 4, 1991.

Some analysts have characterized this multilateral stage of Gorbachev's activity as a last ditch effort that had no better chance of succeeding than past efforts in the face of deeper centrifugal forces, in keeping with the expectations of ethnicity-as-conflictual theory. But most of these accounts either do not note what was fundamentally distinct about the multilateral period and/or simply wrote off the moderation of separatist demands during this time as a temporary aberration.[74] The findings and perspective presented here are quite different and do not require resort to ad hoc factors to explain this variation: Gorbachev's new strategy represented a fundamental change, rendering the union's promises to respect republic interests in the union much more credible, just as the theory and research on collective action and institutional origins cited before would have predicted. Ethnicity was not driving a desire for independence; instead, it was accentuating a commitment problem that Gorbachev had finally begun to find a way to solve.

THE PERIOD OF CENTRAL STRATEGY COLLAPSE: AUGUST–DECEMBER 1991

On August 18, the USSR's vice president, prime minister, KGB chief, interior minister, and defense minister all announced that Gorbachev, actually healthy and vacationing, was gravely ill, and that they were therefore taking over his duties and introducing a national state of emergency. They did not, however, arrest their most prominent opponents. Russian Republic President Yeltsin led a bold resistance, publicly appealing for people to take to the streets in defiance of the coup plotters. As Konovalev has crucially noted, the military leadership grossly miscalculated that their subordinates would follow them should developments point to bloodshed.[75] Key commanders disobeyed their coup plotting superiors, generally citing an unwillingness to tolerate civilian carnage in any effort to seize Russian Republic headquarters, known informally as the "White House." While the crowd there was smaller than many in Yeltsin's camp had hoped, it was large enough to ensure that any effort to capture the White House would be bloody. Thus, key military figures like Grachev, Lebed, Shaposhnikov, and Gromov chose to disobey their orders, opening up a major split in military leadership and forcing Defense Minister Yazov to call off the assault on Yeltsin's White House.[76]

---

[73] Kravchuk, *Maemo Te*, p. 72.

[74] For example, Beissinger, *Nationalist Mobilization*, pp. 390, 422–5; Donna Bahry, "The Union Republics and Contradictions in Gorbachev's Economic Reform," *Soviet Economy*, v.7, no.3, 1991, pp. 215–55.

[75] Valery Konovalev, "Marshal Yazov: Triumf i Tragediia Odnogo Predatel'stva (22.08.91)," in *Radio Svoboda: Avgust 19–21* (Moscow: Radio Free Europe/Radio Liberty, 1992), p. 195. Some coup plotters later claimed they themselves were reluctant, knew from the start they might not succeed, and did not want to shed blood, but considered their act a last-ditch effort to save the union: Ivashov, *Marshal Yazov*.

[76] V. G. Stepankov and Ye. K. Lisov, *Kremlevskii Zagovor* (Moscow: Ogonek, 1992), p. 180.

In one fell swoop, then, the putschists undermined Gorbachev's laborious efforts to build the trust of the republics *and* shattered the military "stick" that he had brandished to keep his restive regions at the negotiating table and that he had held in reserve as a plan of last resort. Although Gorbachev furtively approached the military leadership in late 1991 and demurely "raised the possibility" of military intervention at that late date,[77] by then new brass was in place that realized the coup had at least temporarily destroyed the unity of the army and thenceforth its ability to intervene effectively in such affairs. This military split was also evident at the republic level, including Ukraine, although Kravchuk and the Rada quickly won the support of top military officials on Ukrainian soil for Ukrainian independence.[78]

The events surrounding the coup thus had two important implications for Ukraine and Uzbekistan in terms of the relational theory of separatism. First, the coup attempt itself confirmed that minority republics faced real long-term dangers in even a reformed union, reducing the credibility of Gorbachev's promises that the union would be cooperative. It revealed that Gorbachev had not, in fact, reined in the hardline opponents of republic autonomy as he had earlier claimed. While defeat had temporarily incapacitated the hawks, it remained possible that they would regain strength in the future. Mass media afterwards widely portrayed the coup plotters as bumbling incompetents and/or drunks,[79] which implied that a better organized effort could succeed in the future. Kravchuk thus describes his thinking at the time: "The only relief from future putsches is to build an independent Ukrainian state." Kuchma and many of his fellow Rada members concurred.[80] Shaposhnikov, who after disobeying the coup plotters became defense minister of the dying union, reports his frustration while trying to convince Ukrainian leaders that the new military commanders posed no threat and that Ukraine thus had no need for its own army: "I got the impression," Shaposhnikov writes somewhat resentfully in his memoirs, "that the deputies did not quite trust me, as if I was somehow trying to trick them."[81]

Ironically, the way in which the RSFSR resisted the coup and then attacked Gorbachev's authority actually heightened Ukrainian fear of a future union. In defeating the putsch, Yeltsin's Russia quickly filled the power vacuum, taking advantage of its victor's aura and possession of the USSR's capital city to assume operation of key union institutions and dominate the new temporary organs set up to govern the USSR. This led Kravchuk on August 30 to blast the provisional union government for being Russian-dominated, questioning "whether this committee, which is composed of representatives of one republic, can defend the interests of other republics."[82] Yeltsin's press secretary and vice president

---

[77] Hough, *Democratization and Revolution*, p. 486.

[78] Konstiantyn P. Morozov, *Above and Beyond: From Soviet General to Ukrainian State Builder* (Cambridge, MA: Harvard University Press, 2000).

[79] Remnick, *Lenin's Tomb*, p. 452.

[80] Kravchuk, *Maemo Te*, p. 103; Kuchma, *Ukraiina ne Rosiia*, pp. 415–16.

[81] Yevgeny Shaposhnikov, *Vybor: Zapiski Glavnokomanduiushchego* (Moscow: PIK, 1993), p. 104.

[82] Solchanyk, "Russia, Ukraine," pp. 350–1.

both exacerbated the situation by declaring that if Ukraine followed through with secession, Russia might lay claim to some Ukrainian territory dominated by Russian-speakers. Despite some Russian attempts at damage control after Ukrainian officials objected, these claims helped convince the latter that they needed their own full-fledged military.[83]

The putsch's second major implication for Ukraine lay in the "window of opportunity" its failure opened for actual secession. Even though the divided and decapitated Soviet military might one day regroup, the chances of central violent retaliation for secession were as low as they were ever likely to be. This perception was reinforced not only by the Baltic republics' immediate declarations of complete independence but also by Yeltsin's quick decision to recognize them as full-fledged foreign states. Acknowledging the fait accompli, Gorbachev himself recognized their independence in early September.

The importance of this window of opportunity can be seen in how Ukraine's leadership behaved during the coup and how it dramatically changed course after it became obvious the putsch had failed. Upon learning of the coup, Ukraine's first official reaction was for the Rada Presidium (the elite organ of the parliament) to pass a resolution on August 20, 1991, calling on the people of Ukraine *not* to engage in strikes and demonstrations and ordering a study that would eventually determine whether the putschists' acts would go into effect.[84] Some follow Kravchuk's personal recollections in interpreting this response and other Ukrainian nonactions as a subtle form of resistance.[85] Others have seen it as equivocation or bet hedging,[86] and Valentin Varennikov, the coup plotters' representative who flew to Kyiv during the putsch, later claimed that Kravchuk had appeared quite cooperative.[87] Either way, the clear implication is that Ukrainian leaders' initial inaction bespoke an understanding that the coercive threat to Ukraine was real.

Thus, only on August 22, after the coup had clearly failed and the Soviet military was obviously incapacitated, did the Rada Presidium order the full parliament to convene, which it did two days later. The Rada then took some very radical steps, most dramatically adopting a declaration of independence that would need to be confirmed in a referendum slated for December 1. The resolution explicitly declared that this move was a response, in part, to "the deathly insecurity that was hanging over Ukraine in connection with the state coup in the USSR on August 19, 1991."[88] Moreover, on the very same day, the Rada claimed ownership of all Soviet military formations in Ukraine in order to create its own armed

[83] Vitaly Masol, *Upushchennyi Shans* (Kyiv: Molod', 1993), p. 73.

[84] Postanovlenie Prezidiuma Verkhovnogo Soveta Ukrainskoi SSR, "O Zaiavlenii Prezidiuma Verkhovnogo Soveta Ukrainskoi SSR," *Vedomosti Verkhovnogo Soveta Ukrainskoi SSR*, no.40, st.529, 1991, p. 1122.

[85] Kravchuk, *Maemo Te*; Kuchma, *Ukraiina – Ne Rosiia*; Georgy Shakhnazarov, *S Vozhdiami i bez Nikh* (Moscow: Vagrius, 2001), p. 378.

[86] Wilson, *The Ukrainians*, pp. 165–7; Nahaylo, *The Ukrainian Resurgence*, pp. 373–84.

[87] Valentin Varennikov, *Sud'ba i Sovest'* (Moscow: Paleia, 1993), p. 32.

[88] Postanova Verkhovnoi Rady Ukraiins'koi RSR, "Pro proholoshennia nezalezhnosti Ukraiiny," *Vidomosti Verkhovnoi Rady Ukraiins'koi RSR*, st.502, 1991, pp. 1062–3.

forces.[89] It also announced a number of economic measures designed to insulate Ukraine from the union economy.[90] The fact that Ukraine's leadership waited until the outcome was clear and then took such *radical* steps to create its own security infrastructure, combined with its public statements, strongly suggests that Moscow's threat to use force had originally been highly credible in the eyes of Ukrainian elites and that the breakdown of this threat produced a critical change in their government's chosen strategy vis-à-vis the union.

While campaigning for a pro-independence vote in the referendum, Ukraine's leadership did not completely reject talks with Gorbachev representatives but obviously placed far more emphasis on state-building activities such as creating a separate military and seizing what Soviet assets it could.[91] Ukraine flirted with an "economic community" that Gorbachev proposed during fall 1991, but this was largely an attempt to keep Russia from unilaterally liberalizing prices, which it had just said it would do and which Ukrainian leaders feared would harm their economy.[92] Thus, this agreement disappeared from memory almost entirely after Ukraine's referendum confirmed its independence in a 90 percent vote and after Russia refused to veer from its reformist course. And just a week later, the USSR effectively disappeared from the geopolitical map.

Uzbekistan behaved very similarly to Ukraine in adopting a more nationalist strategy after the coup, yet its leadership did not follow Ukraine in calling for outright secession. Uzbek President Karimov initially hedged his bets much as Kravchuk had done in Ukraine.[93] By August 21, after it was clear the coup had failed, Karimov acted rapidly to consolidate his own administration's power in Uzbekistan. He nullified the coup plotters' acts, seized control of the local interior ministry and KGB, broke with the CPSU, and appropriated its property in Uzbekistan.[94]

The most significant Uzbek act, however, requires careful interpretation. On August 31, 1991, Uzbekistan's parliament convened and declared that Uzbekistan was an independent state. Uzbekistan's declaration, however, represented not an effort to seize actual state independence as with Ukraine but instead a move to

---

[89] Postanova Verkhovnoi Rady Ukraiiny, "Pro viis'kovi formuvannia na Ukraiini," *Vidomosti Verkhovnoi Rady Ukraiins'koi RSR*, st.506, 1991, p. 1068; Morozov, *Above and Beyond*.

[90] See various issues of *Vidomosti Verkhovnoi Rady Ukraiins'koi RSR*, 1991.

[91] Gorbachev, *The August Coup*, pp. 60–1; Morozov, *Above and Beyond*; Postanovlenie Prezidiuma Verkhovnogo Soveta Ukrainy, "O proekte Dogovora o Soiuze Suverennykh Gosudarstv," *Vedomosti Verkhovnogo Soveta Ukrainskoi SSR*, no.44, st.585, 1991, p. 1263; *Vedomosti Verkhovnogo Soveta Ukrainskoi SSR*, no.37, 1991, pp. 1058–9; *Vidomosti Verkhovnoi Rady Ukraiins'koi RSR*, no.45, 1991, p. 1315; *Vedomosti Verkhovnogo Soveta Ukrainskoi SSR*, 1991, p. 1491.

[92] *Vedomosti Verkhovnogo Soveta Ukrainskoi SSR*, 1991, p. 1491; Krawchenko, "Ukraine," p. 92.

[93] Carlisle, "Islom Karimov," p. 198; Interfax 0944 GMT, August 20, 1991, FBIS-SOV-91-161, p. 76.

[94] *Izvestiia*, August 30, 1991, p. 2; Ukaz Prezidenta Uzbekskoi Sovetskoi Sotsialisticheskoi Respubliki, "Ob imushchestve KPSS na territorii Uzbekskoi SSR," *Vedomosti Verkhovnogo Soveta Uzbekskoi SSR*, no.10, st.220, 1991, p. 23; Ukaz Prezidenta Uzbekskoi Sovetskoi Sotsialisticheskoi Respubliki, "ot 21 avgusta 1991 goda," *Vedomosti Verkhovnogo Soveta Uzbekskoi SSR*, no.10, st.217, 1991, p. 21; Ukaz Prezidenta Uzbekskoi Sovetskoi Sotsialisticheskoi Respubliki, "ot 25 avgusta 1991 goda," *Vedomosti Verkhovnogo Soveta Uzbekskoi SSR*, no.10, st.218, 1991, pp. 21–2.

gain bargaining position for anticipated negotiations on restructuring the union. This is clear in the declaration of "independence" itself, which actually presumed Uzbekistan's continued membership in a union. It stated that Uzbekistan was to participate in the creation of collective security forces and the maintenance of the strategic troops of the USSR. Moreover, it called for a unified economic space "in the union."[95] Uzbekistan followed up on these policies during the fall of 1991, creating its own intelligence service and defense ministry, though clearly intending these to play a role in a unionwide defense framework.[96] The picture is thus one of Uzbekistan claiming a much greater right to defend itself in the security realm in the wake of the coup plotters' defeat, but also seeking to maintain a strong association with the other republics in a decentralized but still substantial union.

Overall, the plotters of the August coup tried to prevent decentralization but in their clumsiness succeeded only in heightening republics' senses of danger in the union while simultaneously undermining the coercive threat that Gorbachev had successfully wielded to devalue secessionist strategies. That is, the putsch attempt raised the perceived probability of an exploitative long-run outcome in the union at the same time that it raised the perceived probability of a peaceful response were secession to be attempted in the short run. This change was enough to put Ukraine firmly in the separatist camp. It also convinced Uzbekistan's authorities that they needed to demand more autonomy in a future union and thus caused their strategy to diverge from that of the union, although this strategy remained essentially unionist. Thus, while the strategies of the Ukrainian, Uzbek, and central governments had been converging in the preceding period, they came to diverge again after the putsch. This broad pattern over time is just what one guided by the relational theory of separatism would expect, yet it does not fit comfortably with any version of ethnicity-as-conflictual theory.

TAKING STOCK: RULING OUT ALTERNATIVE THEORIES AND
POSING A REMAINING PUZZLE

Chapters 5 and 6, taken together, enable us to draw three important conclusions. First, existing theory does not provide an adequate account of patterns of separatism in the former USSR. Ethnicity-as-epiphenomenal theory cannot explain (without ad hoc suppositions) why ethnicity is implicated in separatism and thus cannot account for why Belarus and Russia, the two union republics with the lowest senses of national distinctivness in the USSR, did not ultimately seek secession like Ukraine. Ethnicity-as-conflictual theories also do not satisfy. Those focusing

---

[95] Postanovlenie Verkhovnogo Soveta Respubliki Uzbekistan, "O provozglashenii gosudarstvennoi nezavisimosti Respubliki Uzbekistana," *Vedomosti Verkhovnogo Soveta Uzbekskoi SSR*, no.11, st.245, 1991, pp. 68–9.

[96] *Krasnaia Zvezda*, September 26, 1991, p. 2; Ukaz Prezidenta Respubliki Uzbekistan, "Ot 26 sentiabria 1991 goda," *Vedomosti Verkhovnogo Soveta Uzbekskoi SSR*, no.11, st.244, 1991, p. 67; Ukaz Prezidenta Respubliki Uzbekistan, "Ob obrazovanii Ministerstva po delam oborony Respubliki Uzbekistana," *Vedomosti Verkhovnogo Soveta Uzbekskoi SSR*, no.11, st.230, 1991, p. 61.

mainly on National Consciousness as the driving force of separatism are stymied
by the case of the Uzbeks, a group that was consistently unionist yet had at least
as strong a sense of national distinctiveness vis-à-vis Russians as did Ukrainians.
More complex ethnicity-as-conflictual theories might still posit that the impulse
behind separatism is a historically developed sense of national distinctiveness,
but suppose that this was simply constrained by a lack of Capabilities or overridden by Countervailing Incentives. Yet separatism in the USSR did not always
vary along with changes over time in capabilities and interests in the union. The
opportunities for separatist mobilization were increasing at the same time that
the immediate value of the union was decreasing between April and August 1991,
yet this accompanied a distinct convergence between the official strategies of the
union and the republics of Ukraine and Uzbekistan.

Supporters of the Countervailing Incentives approach might argue that the
New Union Treaty itself opened the way for republic leaders to perceive greater
countervailing incentives in terms of long-run union benefits, and that this
explains the convergence of April–August 1991. But the spirit of the underlying ethnicity-as-conflictual theory rests quite uncomfortably with such an interpretation. Indeed, to detend the Countervailing Incentives approach in this way
implies that precious little incentive is necessary to countervail the supposed ethnic urge to independence given that (a) virtually all experts treat the entire period
of 1990–1 as a process of mounting economic problems and growing institutional dysfunction; (b) the New Union Treaty agreement provided very little new
information as to whether or how the economic and state-building crises could
be reversed or overcome; and (c) accordingly, the treaty did little more than add
credibility to Gorbachev's promises that a future union would be a cooperative
one. Indeed, such facts are frequently cited as reasons to doubt that Gorbachev
could in fact have saved the union even had the treaty been signed.[97] To salvage
the Countervailing Incentives argument in the face of such a situation, then, one
must conclude that the supposed ethnic motivation for seeking independence is
extremely weak and easily overpowered. Yet this is not satisfactory because the
major theories positing an ethnic motive for behavior generally treat it as one of
the most important forces in world politics.

The relational theory better accounts for observed patterns of secessionism
and does not have to resort to uncomfortable or arbitrary claims in so doing. The
impulse driving separatism is a collective action problem in which ethnic distinctions influence how probabilities of exploitative and cooperative outcomes are
assessed in a given union. Where people are not conscious of an ethnic divide
distinguishing them from the central government or when such perceived divides
do not involve significant indicators of danger, a region's representatives are less
likely to perceive much risk of exploitation associated with the collective action
problem. Thus, locally based authorities as well as the masses in Belarus and
Russia generally supported a union. Where people are conscious of an ethnic
divide with the central government, past and future central state actions will

97 For example, Beissinger, *Nationalist Mobilization*.

be crucial in shaping whether a given region sees the union as too likely to be exploitive. The process-tracing case studies of Ukraine and Uzbekistan thus show how changes in Gorbachev's strategies and actions over the course of 1985–91 had crucial consequences for the separatism of these republics. In particular, Gorbachev adopted a series of multilateral, face-to-face negotiations during April–August 1991 that promised a great degree of decentralization through a New Union Treaty, all elements that independent research on collective action would recognize as significant departures from previous central policies. Thus, the policies of both Ukraine and Uzbekistan started to converge with those of the central government on the union after earlier periods of divergence.

The relational theory would also expect groups with the thickest senses of national distinctiveness to collectively perceive the greatest degree of separation from control over their fate in the union and thus to perceive the greatest risks of exploitation. This should lead them to be least likely to accept any given central promise of nonexploitation as credible. In the USSR, this created a kind of vicious separatist cycle: The Soviet government saw the deep suspicion in such republics (especially the Baltics, Moldova, and Georgia[98]) as intransigence and was more willing there to employ economic coercion or deadly force, but this only exacerbated these republics' mistrust of union promises. Their representatives, more than those of other republics, tended to see the New Union Treaty initiative as a trap the center was hoping to spring and thus never engaged it seriously. In general, though, Beissinger's data on popular participation in separatist rallies do show that when all Soviet republics are taken together, there was an across-the-board drop in July 1991, as the New Union Treaty negotiations were culminating, to the lowest level of secessionist protest in two and a half years, suggesting the central policy shift was having some effect even in some of these republics.[99]

Chapters 5 and 6 still leave us with one important empirical puzzle, though: Given that Ukraine and Uzbekistan had very similar senses of national distinctiveness and experiences vis-à-vis Russians and the central government, why did Ukraine consistently display greater separatism during 1990–1? This is the subject of the next two chapters.

---

[98] Armenia was preoccupied with its conflict with Azerbaijan and tended to assess relations with the union through this lens.

[99] Beissinger, *Nationalist Mobilization*, Figure 4.2, p. 163.

7

Framing

Manipulating Mass Opinion in Ukraine and Uzbekistan

Why was Ukraine's leadership consistently more inclined to reject central union-saving initiatives than was Uzbekistan's throughout the final years of the Soviet Union? The relational theory posits that the driving force behind secessionism is an ethnically charged collective action problem, in which case variation in separatism is likely to come from factors influencing how this problem is perceived and evaluated. The previous chapter demonstrated that, in fact, both the Ukrainian and Uzbek governments regularly shifted their attitudes toward a union in response to what Soviet central authorities were proposing and how they were proposing it. Yet the actual proposals of the union center are not the only factors capable of influencing perceptions of the root collective action problem. As Chapter 4 argued, ethnofederal regional leaders are likely to have considerable power to frame center-periphery relations for their constituents, meaning that they can potentially alter mass understandings of the core collective action problem by promoting different frames. Thus, when institutions force leaders to be at least somewhat responsive to masses' perceptions of their own interests, framing strategies can enable leaders to pursue policies closer to their own personal preferences than might be otherwise possible. The relational theory, then, fits easily with the notion that leadership framing can explain why some ethnic regions display more separatism than others.

Rival theories of ethnicity generate different expectations as to the role of leadership framing in the politics of separatism. This is most obvious regarding the National Consciousness and Capabilities versions of ethnicity-as-conflictual theory: If self-conscious nations always prefer political independence, or at least do so whenever they have the capability, then we would expect framing to matter mainly with regard to what is perceived to be possible. Countervailing Incentives theories could anticipate important framing effects in influencing the tradeoffs people make between their ethnic separatist impulses and interests pulling in the opposite direction. This theory diverges from relational theory in *how* framing could produce a unionist effect, though. The relational theory would expect greater unionism to result from frames that specifically defuse the collective action problem at the heart of the union. Countervailing Incentives theory, ceteris paribus, would not expect such effects because the motivation for separatism is not a collective action problem (in which case selectively defusing it should make no difference) but an inherent ethnic desire for independence. Ethnicity-as-epiphenomenal theories, as described in Chapter 4, tend to award leading roles to elite manipulators but have a harder time explaining why ethnicity would figure in the manipulation at all if it has no intrinsic meaning for people – especially when alternative lines for mass mobilization like territorial-administrative boundaries are available. Thus, to the extent framing is found to matter, and when it matters by defusing union collective action problems linked to ethnic divides, the relational approach offers a more satisfying basis for understanding separatism.

The cases of Uzbekistan and Ukraine are very useful for evaluating the importance of framing. At key moments in both republics, their ultimate relationship to the union had to be ratified by a referendum before having the force of law. At the points when these referenda occurred, official republic policies (the specific dependent variable of this study) were identical to mass interests as aggregated in a simple majoritarian fashion through a referendum process defined by republic institutions. Moreover, multiple referenda occurred with varying connections to the policy process, and some useful public opinion data are also available on related questions. We thus gain a chance to study the relationship between expressed public opinion and actual secession in a variety of situations, including when their connection was most direct.

This chapter demonstrates that Ukrainian and Uzbek leaders did indeed adopt different framing strategies, that these strategies manipulated ethnic interpretations of the union's collective action problem, and that they quite likely made the difference between union and secession in each case. To put this more boldly, there is strong evidence that the leadership of both republics had the opportunity to generate majority popular support for both "independence" and "union" at the same time, even during the crucial fall of 1991. In fact, the pattern we saw in Ukraine could have been reversed: If its leaders had chosen a different framing strategy and pursued it with all the resources at their disposal, we might have seen a majority of Ukrainians voting for a union rather than independence. Likewise, a different framing strategy could have generated Uzbek support for independence even before Ukraine essentially destroyed the union with its secession. This claim has enormous implications. Among them are that the Soviet breakup was far from inevitable, that it was much more of a contingent outcome than is commonly recognized.

THE COMPLEXITY OF THE UNION ISSUE

The issue of secession from the USSR was extraordinarily complex, creating ample opportunity for leadership framing to impact outcomes as described in

Chapter 4. This is clear from the discussion in Chapter 6: Gorbachev alone proposed many different versions of the same union during his tenure, ranging from the 1985 model that did not concern itself much with national differences to the late 1991 variety that resembled the emergent European Union more than the USSR. And these were just Gorbachev's proposals. Soviet hardliners wanted to restore a pre-*perestroika* totalitarian regime. Moderates like Soviet parliamentary speaker Anatoly Lukianov agreed to a federal solution but insisted on retaining institutionalized socialism. Some minority republic nationalists proposed embedding resource redistribution into the union's constitution, while Russia's leadership supported a union without such redistribution. Whether one "supported the union," therefore, could depend heavily on what type of union was on offer.

The complexity did not end with the many varieties of union that were conceivable. For one thing, the different versions of union were not associated with certain outcomes. Thus, people also had to consider probabilities: To what degree could a given union arrangement be counted on to bind a central government to its promises of cooperation and nonexploitation? Republic leaders were in good position to influence not only what varieties of union people thought were possibilities, but how realistic they thought these different varieties were. Moreover, leaders often deliberately stretched terms like "union" and "independence," rendering their meanings highly unclear.

Much of the story of late Soviet-era secessionism, then, is a story of both republic and central leaders manipulating this complexity so as to frame the debate to the advantage of positions they favored. This chapter focuses primarily on 1991 because this was the decisive year and the period in which the impact of framing was most stark due to several referenda. We first briefly consider the framing strategy of the central government in early 1991 because it was Gorbachev who sharply escalated the framing battle by seeking an explicit public sanction for his union-saving efforts in the form of the March 1991 unionwide referendum. We then turn to case studies of Ukraine and Uzbekistan.

GORBACHEV AND THE MARCH 1991 REFERENDUM

As was described in detail in Chapter 6, the second half of 1990 was marked by a growing divergence between Soviet government efforts to restructure the USSR and republic leaders' strategies for determining their relationship to the union. Ukrainian and Uzbek leaders objected to central government efforts to impose a New Union Treaty from above and to Gorbachev's inability to formulate an economic reform plan that inspired confidence. Ukraine, especially, had started taking some radical steps, even introducing its own quasi-currency ("coupons") and talking about an economic reform plan separate from the union's.

In response, Gorbachev decided that his reforms' prospects would be bolstered by something he could present as a clear popular mandate. With this aim in mind, he sought a referendum that would be held in March 1991 and become a "final verdict" on whether the union should be saved.[1] Central authorities eventually decided on the following wording:

Do you consider necessary the preservation of the Union of Soviet Socialist Republics as a renewed federation of equal sovereign republics, in which the rights and freedoms of the individual of any nationality are guaranteed in full measure? Yes or no.

Observers immediately recognized the importance of how this question framed the issue, with critics calling it a blatant attempt to engineer a "yes" vote. Indeed, it characterized a future union as being a "federation," as featuring republics that are "equal" and "sovereign," and as fully guaranteeing "rights and freedoms of the individual of any nationality." The drafters of the question confirmed that this wording was quite carefully considered. One member of the Supreme Soviet expert staff who helped formulate the query admitted in 1993 that "some cunning was permitted" in this process. But even though the question may have been quite complex and contained many separate parts, he argued, the clause on human rights was necessary to show people why they needed to preserve the union.[2] Gorbachev later stated that it was necessary so that people realized they were not voting for the USSR as it had been, but as it would become.[3] In the language of Chapter 4, the question was formulated in part so as to bring out people's first preference for cooperative integration while leading them to ignore all the real-world strategic considerations that typically lead people to oppose particular integration projects, including real possibilities of exploitation grounded in historical patterns of oppression. At the same time, it is important to note that the question also stipulated that this union was to be "socialist," something that was expected by some framers to lose votes in the referendum given how discredited Marxist ideology had become in most republics. In fact, the adjective "socialist" had been retained in the union's name at the insistence of Lukianov, the moderately conservative chairman of the USSR's parliament, over the objections of some.[4]

Republic leaders clearly recognized that Gorbachev's framing strategy was likely to produce majority votes in favor of a thusly described union, especially when backed by a central media campaign. Thus, the republics whose leaderships had displayed the greatest separatist fervor (the Baltic republics, Armenia, Georgia, and Moldova) refused to carry out Gorbachev's referendum on their soil.[5] Three of these (Georgia, Latvia, and Estonia) conducted their own "polls" instead, crucially wording their questions differently and producing large

---

[1] *Izvestiia*, December 18, 1990, p. 2.
[2] Author's interview with Yevgeny Koliushin, participant in the drafting of the March 1991 referendum question, April 16, 1993.
[3] Gorbachev, *Zhizn' i Reformy*, v.1, p. 517.
[4] Author's interviews with Koliushin and one other leading Supreme Soviet official.
[5] The Soviet government did organize some polling stations in these republics, but without republic government cooperation, turnout was extremely low. The results among those who did turn out, of course, were in favor of the "union."

majorities for independence.[6] In those republics that cooperated in conducting Gorbachev's referendum, the results were predictably pro-"union," despite the fact that this union was described as socialist:

Turkmenistan	97.9%
Tajikistan	96.2%
Kyrgyzstan	94.6%
Kazakhstan	94.1%
Uzbekistan	93.7%
Azerbaijan	93.3%
Belarus	82.7%
Russia	71.3%
Ukraine	70.2%

Even in Ukraine, the most separatist of the republics to cooperate with the referendum, well over two-thirds of the voting public supported "union."[7]

Gorbachev attempted to present this as a mandate for preserving the USSR, and at first glance the results would seem to have been powerfully in his favor. What damaged his framing strategy was that some republic leaders were able to successfully counter it in ways that diluted the meaning of the mandate. Most obviously, six republics had not even conducted the referendum and three of these had generated votes for independence in their own separate polls. Additionally, several other republics had introduced their own referendum questions, with their own choices of wording on the union, that were asked side-by-side with Gorbachev's. Ukraine, for example, posed a question on its version of the union along with Gorbachev's and got a larger "yes" vote for its own question than for Gorbachev's. Uzbekistan also asked its own question along with Gorbachev's. Both the Ukrainian and Uzbek votes were for some form of "union," but these distinct queries and votes confused the mandate Gorbachev sought. Both republics and Gorbachev could plausibly claim mandates for different versions of the union. As a result, the standoff continued until Gorbachev launched the multilateral negotiations at Novo-Ogarevo in April, as described in Chapter 6. We now turn to a deeper analysis of the framing strategies of Ukraine's and Uzbekistan's leaders and their impacts.

UKRAINE: FROM "UNION" TO "INDEPENDENCE"

Ukrainians had developed a thick sense of distinctiveness vis-à-vis the dominant Russians and had certainly come to attach a high risk of future exploitation to the USSR by 1991, but the meaning of their ultimate December vote for independence is by no means straightforward. This is due largely to the complexity of the union issue, the ambiguity of key terms, and leaders' efforts to manipulate public opinion through framing. In fact, what turned Ukraine to independence

---

[6] *Izvestiia*, March 4, 1991, p. 1; *Izvestiia*, April 9, 1991, p. 1.
[7] *Izvestiia*, March 26, 1991, p. 3.

was, as much as anything else, a conscious decision by its leaders to frame the issue in a way that privileged a majority vote for "independence" rather than for "union" in December 1991.

Competing Frames and the March 1991 Referenda

It is important to start with the recognition that average Ukrainians did not have perfect information, giving Ukrainian leader Kravchuk considerable slack to work with in public opinion regarding the union. A January 1991 survey makes this clear: Only 9 percent of the respondents throughout Ukraine said they had read the draft New Union Treaty and only 24 percent said they had even skimmed it; 35 percent said they had not read it at all; and 33 percent did not even know what it was despite intense media discussion.[8] Most people were willing to venture an opinion on it, however. Asked simply whether they supported it, 11 percent recommended Ukraine sign it in its then-current state; 20 percent said it just needed to be touched up first; and 17 percent averred it should be reworked. And at this time, only 12 percent asserted definitively that it should not be signed.[9]

With public opinion potentially malleable in early 1991, Ukrainian leaders recognized that Gorbachev's framing strategy for the March referendum could generate the appearance of public support for central policies, something Kravchuk hoped to avoid. Ukrainian leaders had been backing more republic autonomy than Gorbachev throughout 1990 and did not want a referendum result that could undercut this effort. At the same time, Kravchuk rejected calls from some Ukrainians to follow the Baltic republics in boycotting Gorbachev's referendum. The Ukrainian leader had in fact called for a referendum on the New Union Treaty even before Gorbachev had officially proposed the idea.[10] Kravchuk's strategy was instead to present voters with two questions instead of one. The first would be Gorbachev's question, unedited. The second would be a "poll" sponsored by the Ukrainian government asking people a question more to its liking:

Do you agree that Ukraine should be in a Union of Soviet Sovereign States on the basis of the Declaration on State Sovereignty of Ukraine? Yes or no.[11]

Kravchuk and most observers interpreted a "Union of Soviet Sovereign States" as meaning more autonomy for the republics than a "renewed federation," which Gorbachev's question called for. Moreover, the Ukrainian question left out the reference to socialism that was in Gorbachev's question. Also crucial was the

---

[8] Ya. Shiman and L. Brust, results from survey of 1,747 residents of Ukraine taken January 3–10, 1991, commissioned by the Erasmus Foundation and the Institute of Sociology of the Ukrainian Academy of Sciences. Rounding accounts for the fact that the total adds up to 101 percent.

[9] Shiman and Brust survey, January 3–10, 1991.

[10] *Izvestiia*, December 8, 1990, p. 2.

[11] *Izvestiia*, February 14, 1991, p. 2; Postanovlenie Verkhovnogo Soveta Ukrainskoi SSR, "O provedenii referenduma v Ukrainskoi SSR 17 marta 1991 goda," *Vedomosti Verkhovnogo Soveta Ukrainskoi SSR*, no.12, st.129, 1991, pp. 312–3.

mention of Ukraine's declaration of sovereignty, which had not before been put forth for a popular vote of approval.

Gorbachev's center mounted a formidable campaign in favor of its own question in Ukraine, and the republic's locally based political forces took different positions on how to vote on the two questions. The largest nationalist movement, *Rukh*, campaigned for a "no" vote on the Gorbachev question but strongly urged voters to reply "yes" to Ukraine's own question – importantly, the latter was still a vote for some kind of Soviet Union. Only a few radical groups called for "no" votes on both questions. The Communist Party establishment, under both parliamentary chairman Kravchuk and party organization boss Stanislav Hurenko, backed a "union" vote on both questions.[12] Kravchuk reasoned that Gorbachev's question was only asking whether people thought that a union should continue, whereas the Ukrainian question was about the kind of union they wanted.

In the end, both questions won overwhelming majority votes. Over 70 percent voted for Gorbachev's "renewed federation," and even greater numbers, some 80 percent, affirmed support for a "Union of Soviet Sovereign States" based on Ukraine's sovereignty declaration.[13] Significantly, both options involved some kind of union, showing that leaders could mobilize strong support for integration at that time if given the chance to choose their words carefully.

Of course, the wording of referenda is not the only important arena for framing activity. Kravchuk during early 1991 did much to highlight the ambiguity and complexity of terms like "independence" and "union" in public minds. For example, in a live television interview in the nationalist-dominated city of Lviv, the Ukrainian leader declared:

I have recently been in various regions of the republic and did not meet one person who did not want to see [Ukraine] free. But the population wants not only sovereignty, but also that kind of union in which Ukraine, possessing corresponding rights and duties, would be a state. Only unity is the true path to independence, although the road to it is complicated and dramatic.[14]

Thus, while Kravchuk was pushing a strategy advocating greater Ukrainian autonomy within some kind of union that would be preserved, he was also shaping language itself so as to leave himself ample latitude for post hoc interpretation of what "independence" and "union" implied.

Accordingly, after the March 1991 referenda, Kravchuk frustrated Gorbachev by not recognizing any mandate for Gorbachev's version of a union and instead averring that more Ukrainian voters had voted for what the Ukrainian leadership was proposing than what the Soviet government was. He and Gorbachev thus grew further apart in the month after the referendum.[15] Yet hardly anyone at the

---

[12] Hurenko's forces basically ignored the republic question, focusing on Gorbachev's. See *Izvestiia*, February 28, 1991, p. 2; Krawchenko, "Ukraine," pp. 82–3.

[13] Bohdan Krawchenko and Alexander Motyl, "Ukraine: From Empire to Statehood," in Ian Bremmer and Ray Taras, eds., *New States, New Politics: Building the Post-Soviet Nations* (New York: Cambridge University Press, 1997), p. 254.

[14] *Izvestiia*, March 6, 1991, p. 2.

[15] *Izvestiia*, March 29, 1991, p. 2.

time denied that a majority of Ukrainians had expressed support for at least some form of union in March 1991.

Framing the Shift to Independence

The preceding discussion presents us with a puzzle when one considers that less than a year later 90 percent of Ukrainian voters cast ballots for independence. Why did the population of Ukraine, which tended to support at least some form of union according to both referenda results and mass surveys during January–March 1991, turn so dramatically and decisively in favor of Ukrainian independence by December 1991? The August coup is clearly part of the answer, since Chapter 6 showed that it starkly altered the strategies of both Ukraine's and Uzbekistan's authorities. But crucially, the failed putsch did not convert Uzbekistan's leadership to a secessionist position; Karimov's administration increased the degree of autonomy it demanded in a union but still advocated a union of some sort. The framing policy of Kravchuk and his colleagues helps explain why Ukraine's response was more radical.

Prior to the August 1991 coup attempt, Ukraine's top leaders had been calling for a restructured union, but afterward they pressed vigorously for full independence and the actual dissolution of the Soviet state, with the referendum being only the denouement. Some observers initially saw Ukraine's about-face as naked opportunism on Kravchuk's part. But after 90 percent of Ukrainian citizens voted for independence in the December 1 referendum, most analysts concluded that a massive swing in public opinion had taken place. Almost all of the 70 percent who had voted to preserve the USSR in March 1991 must have changed their minds, it was supposed, backing secession instead of union by December. This interpretation is based on a widespread misinterpretation of the nature of public opinion and what was at stake during this pivotal year.

There are three keys to understanding the Ukrainian turnaround in Ukrainian referendum results, each highlighting the importance of framing. The first is the nature of the collective action problem inherent to political integration as well as the crucial distinction between the preferences and the strategic choices involved in dealing with this problem. As Chapter 4 notes, preferences reflect the relative values (in terms of life chances) that people attach to different outcomes regardless of their probabilities of actually happening. In some sense, then, preferences are about the world of the ideal. Strategies are choices of action designed to maximize the value that is actually attained given judgments as to the likely contingent actions of others and the resulting outcomes. Unfortunately, analysts often confuse preferences with supported strategies, particularly when interpreting poll results. When a referendum or survey asks people whether they "support independence," does a "yes" mean that they are supporting it as a preference (the ideal scenario that inherently maximizes life chances relative to alternatives) or as only the best available strategy for maximizing life chances given that the behavior of others is likely to thwart the ideal? The simple "yes" does not tell us. Moreover, respondents themselves may not think through such nuances and are highly likely to be influenced in their answers to such deceptively simple questions by the probabilities they attach to different outcomes, probabilities that may not even be formulated at a conscious level. Chapter 3 presented psychological evidence that much of the work ethnicity does in reducing uncertainty in the social world occurs outside of consciousness. This means that especially when ethnicity is involved as an uncertainty-reducing shorthand for interpreting the likely actions of others, people are quite likely to be injecting probability assessments into their answers to simple questions about what options they favor. Simple surveys and referendum questions on whether people support a union or independence, then, are most likely to reflect supported strategies rather than actual preferences. It is when surveys go beyond simple questions that we start to gain analytical leverage in separating strategies from preferences. And doing so is essential to understanding separatism because preference-strategy ambiguity is a crucial framing resource that authorities use to influence political outcomes.

Much of the change in Ukrainian attitudes observed during 1991 can in fact be attributed to major developments impacting the promise of different strategies, as distinct from preferences. One perceived obstacle to the realization of an "ideal union" preference was the risk (accentuated by ethnic distinctions) that a given union would bring not cooperation but exploitation. Moreover, prior to August 1991, the union possessed a coercive capacity that Ukrainian leaders clearly saw as capable of punishing them if they tried to secede. The August coup's collapse called this coercive capacity into question at the same time that the coup attempt itself undercut the case that what Gorbachev was offering would lead to a union in which Ukraine was better off than it would have been as an independent state. The coup thus made "independence" look better than before not because people no longer preferred an ideal union but because that ideal suddenly looked much less likely to ever come about. The expected value of separatist strategies had grown while the expected value of unionist ones had declined. What changed was the relative valuation of strategies, not underlying preferences.

The second key to understanding Ukraine's referenda reversal between March and December 1991 has already been implied by bringing up the case of Uzbekistan: "Independence" was not the only plausible way to respond to the commitment problem of union, even as this problem was exacerbated by the August 1991 coup. Uzbekistan's leadership, as shown in Chapter 6, merely sought more autonomy to insulate itself against future union attempts at exploitation, not outright independence. In fact, it is quite reasonable to suspect that at least some, and perhaps even a majority, of Ukrainians could have been convinced that some kind of policies short of secession could have reduced the dangers of union enough to make it worth the risk. Another way of putting this is that Ukrainian people may well have supported *either* a significantly reformed union or independence over the status quo ante, which was a Soviet Union in which Ukraine was widely viewed as having been exploited and in which the commitment problem was perceived to be strong. Thus, although we might posit that support for "independence" as a reasonable way to deal with the collective action problem increased after the coup, it is entirely possible that majority support remained for certain unionist strategies as well.

The third key is the crucial ambiguity of the term "independence" during 1991, especially autumn. There was little "absolute" in the masses' understanding of "independence" (*nezalezhnist'* in Ukrainian, *nezavisimost'* in Russian), the term for which people were asked to vote in December 1991.[16] This terminological ambiguity was rife in the speeches of Kravchuk as well as other Ukrainian leaders. The head of the Communist-led majority Group of 239 in the Rada, Oleksandr Moroz, like Kravchuk repeatedly called the New Union Treaty a necessary element of Ukrainian "independence" (*samostiinist'*, *nezalezhnist'*).[17] There were at least two ways to interpret this ambiguity. One is that independence was not actually mutually exclusive with being part of a union: A state could have independence within a union, as Kravchuk had suggested in the run-up to the March 1991 referendum. Another interpretation is that a declaration of independence was a kind of bargaining chip, something that needed to be adopted to make sure that when a union was concluded, it would maximally guarantee Ukrainian interests. Later in the chapter, evidence is presented that Ukrainian citizens in late 1991 did not necessarily believe that a victory for "independence" in the referendum would deprive them of important associations with the other Soviet republics, including Russia.

We must interpret the difference between the March and December 1991 referenda in Ukraine in light of these three considerations. The wording of Gorbachev's March 1991 referendum had indeed made clever use of the complexity and ambiguity involved in the issue of union. It asked not whether people wanted to stay in any old union, but in a "federation" that would be "renewed," that would "guarantee" the "rights and freedoms of the individual . . . in full measure," and in which all republics would be "sovereign." This question was about the kind of ideal union that Gorbachev instinctually believed to be Ukrainians' top preference, one they would choose if all fears of exploitation could be certainly allayed. The March 1991 Ukrainian referendum question (wording given previously) was even "more ideal," as it dropped the adjective "socialist" and averred that Ukraine's declaration of sovereignty (justified precisely as a means of protecting Ukraine from exploitation) was to be the basis for the proposed union. Thus, Gorbachev's question generated a 70 percent vote for a union, and the Ukrainian question – 80 percent support.

The December 1991 question, however, asked people only: "Do you support the Act of the Declaration of the Independence of Ukraine?" This question, for one thing, presumed that the alternative was the status quo, a union whose future shape was unspecified and whose prospects involved a good degree of perceived danger. Ukraine's leaders certainly portrayed the choice in this way.

---

[16] Paul D. D'Anieri, Robert Kravchuk, and Taras Kuzio, *Politics and Society in Ukraine* (Boulder, CO: Westview, 1999), pp. 29–30.
[17] Oleksandr Moroz, *Kudy Idemo?* (Kyiv: Postup, 1993), pp. 30–1, 55, 60, 66–7.

People were pointedly not asked whether they preferred this alternative to a greatly decentralized or otherwise restructured union. Moreover, the precise definition and implications of "independence" were left unclear, and this is crucial given that top Ukrainian politicians had long been talking of independence being possible within a union. The referendum result, an overwhelming 90 percent affirmative vote, thus in no way implies that none of these 90 percent would not also have supported a genuinely democratic, nonexploitative union with Russia, nor even that they felt such a union was impossible.

Ukrainian leaders' framing decisions, not a wholesale about-face in public opinion, in the end brought political independence to Ukraine. This is further demonstrated through three additional bodies of evidence, discussed in the following section.

Supporting Evidence: Elections, Surveys, Insider Testimony

This interpretation of Ukraine's independence vote is corroborated by the results of Ukraine's presidential balloting, survey data, and Ukrainian leaders' own actions and recollections. Turning first to the presidential election, this was held on December 1 along with the independence referendum. Prior to this vote, Kravchuk was the chairman of the Rada, elected to this post only by his fellow parliamentarians. The decision to institute a full-fledged presidency had been made as early as June 1991, and in July, the Rada set the first presidential election for December 1. It was clear from the outset that much was at stake in this election, as the new president would have a great deal of power, including a limited right to issue decrees with the force of law and the ability to invalidate USSR decisions that contradicted the constitution and the laws of Ukraine.[18] The race got underway after the August putsch and pitted several candidates against each other. The main contest was between Kravchuk and Viacheslav Chornovil, the nationalist Rukh leader and chairman of the Lviv legislature. Importantly, all of the other major candidates were with Chornovil on the nationalist side of the political spectrum, and none approached the appeal of Chornovil. Yet Kravchuk ultimately won handily, garnering over 60 percent of the ballots cast, with Chornovil netting just 23 percent.[19] On one hand, Kravchuk's victory was a triumph for separatism and the declaration of independence because he had championed both in his campaign.[20] On the other hand, the vote is better interpreted as an expression of Ukrainians' moderation in their support for "independence." If the Ukrainian population had really wanted a complete break with Russia and the USSR, it could

---

[18] Zakon Ukrainskoi Sovetskoi Sotsialisticheskoi Respubliky, "O Prezidente Ukrainskoi SSR," *Vedomosti Verkhovnogo Soveta Ukrainskoi SSR*, no.33, st.446, 1991, pp. 928–9; Zakon Ukrainskoi Sovetskoi Sotsialisticheskoi Respubliky, "O vyborakh Prezidenta Ukrainskoi SSR," *Vedomosti Verkhovnogo Soveta Ukrainskoi SSR*, no.33, st.448, 1991, pp. 931–9; Krawchenko, "Ukraine," p. 92.

[19] Krawchenko and Motyl, "Ukraine," p. 269.

[20] David R. Marples, "'After the Putsch:' Prospects for Independent Ukraine," *Nationalities Papers*, v.21, no.2, fall 1993, pp. 35–46, 42.

have followed many Galician voters in opting for Chornovil, who had supported such a policy much more clearly and consistently.

Public opinion polls illustrate far more directly the argument made here, that support for independence did not necessarily mean rejecting the idea of a union. A cleverly constructed survey that pollster Ihor Burov organized during the run-up to the referendum provides some of the most remarkable evidence. His team first asked a representative sample of nearly a thousand respondents across Ukraine whether they supported "the creation of an independent state of Ukraine," to which query 71 percent answered "yes" and 15 percent said "no." Later in the very same interviews, Burov's team added the word "democratic" to the first question, asking respondents whether they supported "the creation of a democratic independent state of Ukraine." This slight change in wording, adding the positive adjective "democratic," produced an 11-percent jump in support for an independent Ukraine, with 82 percent now replying "yes." Not stopping here, after a few more questions had passed, Burov asked whether people agreed that "it is necessary for Ukraine to become a member of a new Union." Strikingly, those who agreed outnumbered those who disagreed 46 percent to 31 percent, with 22 percent replying that it was hard for them to say. If this were a referendum and only those with opinions cast ballots, the result would have been a 60 percent vote for a union. It must be stressed that this was in the very same survey of the very same individuals on the very same day. This question was also asked without any of the "idealizing" language that had beautified Gorbachev's referendum question in March 1991 and had helped it to win around 70 percent support in the republic. A few calculations add to the dramatic implications of the results: At least 20 percent of the respondents were quite capable of expressing positive support for *both* a "new Union" and a "democratic independent state of Ukraine." Put even more strongly, over 50 percent of the people surveyed saw nothing to stop them from both supporting an independent Ukraine and declining to oppose a new Union.[21]

These survey results, which through standard lenses appear to reflect mass confusion or idiocy, are fully consistent with the kind of rational preference structure described in this volume: support for a nonexploitative union under the condition of a collective action problem. Thus, people of Ukraine were found throughout 1991 to consistently back the idea of a union when the unionist option was framed as "new" or otherwise *nonexploitative*. This is true of Gorbachev's March referendum, Ukraine's March referendum, and some of Burov's questions between the August coup and the December referendum. Yet when the choice was presented as being between something vague called independence (which was not understood as necessarily entailing a complete political break with the union) and the status quo version of the union (which involved only an uncertain prospect of establishing credible guarantees against exploitation), majorities could regularly be found to support independence. The independence option was especially

---

[21] Ihor Burov, results from survey of 934 residents of Ukraine conducted between Ukraine's declaration of independence and its independence referendum, 1991.

potent after the August putsch, which highlighted the union's long-term commitment problem. We thus find strong support for Chapter 4's hypothesis that at the level of *preferences*, people are likely to favor a nonexploitative union even as they may reject a unionist *strategy* once real-world probabilities (assessed partly through the uncertainty-reducing device of ethnicity) are factored in.

There thus appears to have been no wholesale turnaround in Ukrainian public opinion. Keeping in mind the distinction between preferences and supported strategies, what had increased was backing for independence as one strategy for escaping the status quo after the coup had exacerbated the union's commitment problem.[22] But an underlying preference for an ideal union remained strong, and significant support was still available for unionist strategies even when no soothing adjectives were used to describe them. This helps explain why Gorbachev and even Yeltsin were so spectacularly wrong in predicting that Ukrainians would reject independence on December 1 despite the fact that they surely had access to reasonable polling data.[23] Ukrainians were never asked in the December referendum about a union, which they probably would have supported had the question been asked in the right way. Instead, Ukrainians were only asked about independence, which they also supported relative to the status quo.

Ukraine's leadership clearly recognized that other frames were available, that Kravchuk was imposing a particular frame on events, and that this framing was crucial in generating the referendum vote that ultimately made Ukraine an independent state. This is nicely illustrated by the fact that some members of the Ukrainian parliament actually proposed that a *second* referendum query be added to the "independence question" that was asked in December 1991. This second question would have been: Should Ukraine join a Union of Sovereign States? This move was quashed, with one presiding officer in the Rada tactically turning terminological ambiguity against this challenge: "What kind of union can one talk about if Ukraine has become an independent state?"[24] Oleksandr Moroz, a prominent Communist leader who formed the Socialist Party of Ukraine on the Communist Party's ruins after the coup's collapse, lamented his party's failure to add a second question to the December 1991 referendum. A second question, he told his "new" party colleagues in late November, could have removed the great ambiguity in the meaning of the first question by specifying what people actually meant in voting for "independence."[25]

In fact, Kravchuk and other pro-secession leaders later confirmed that they intentionally sought to engineer a pro-independence referendum result in December 1991 precisely so that they could frame it as "canceling out" the March 1991 referendum result that had been framed by Gorbachev and his allies as a

---

[22] Wilson cites survey findings that support for "independence" rose from 63 percent to 88 percent during October and November 1991, but reports no earlier figures. Andrew Wilson, *Ukrainian Nationalism in the 1990s: A Minority Faith* (New York: Cambridge University Press, 1997), p. 128.

[23] On Gorbachev's and Yeltsin's predictions, see D'Anieri, Kravchuk, and Kuzio, *Politics and Society*, pp. 26–7; Motyl, *Dilemmas*, p. 49.

[24] Masol, *Upushchennyi Shans*, p. 63.

[25] Moroz, *Kudy Idemo?*, p. 149.

"vote for the union." Supporters of the independence referendum even used the very term "cancel out" (*perecherknut'*) to describe their goals for the referendum during the fall of 1991.[26] In his memoirs, none other than Kravchuk himself confirms that the pro-independence result achieved in the December 1991 referendum result was critical to "canceling out" the March 1991 pro-union referendum result, thereby making Ukraine's secession possible.[27] The memoirs of Kuchma, then a Rada deputy and major industrialist, also confirm that the referendum was essential in legitimating Ukrainian independence.[28]

Two additional points are worth noting. First, despite the fact that the fate of the union and the prospect of an independent Ukraine were literally at stake, a large part of the Ukrainian public remained remarkably apathetic. In November 1991, according to one survey, 50 percent of all respondents nationwide said that they discussed politics rarely or never. This was actually a slight increase from January 1991, when the figure was 47 percent.[29]

Second, in keeping with the notion that ethnic difference at least partially underlay the perception of a commitment problem, evidence from various 1991 polls indicates that ethnic Russians in Ukraine tended to feel more threatened by Ukrainian independence than did Ukrainians. Accordingly, larger shares of Ukrainians tended to back independence and oppose union than did Russians during 1991, even though the plurality in each group tended to support both independence and union after the August coup (again, depending on how the survey questions were asked). Queried in January 1991 whether they supported the signing of the first draft New Union Treaty, for example, 15 percent of those identifying themselves as native Ukrainian speakers completely ruled out signing (regardless of possible amendments to the draft), whereas only 7 percent of Russians did.[30] A geographic divergence, likely linked to ethnic divides, is also observable in this survey: Complete opposition to the New Union Treaty was consistently low across most central, eastern, and southern regions of Ukraine; however, western regions (associated with the lowest degrees of Russification) tended to display quite high levels of opposition, with 47 percent in Ternopil and 50 percent in Lviv ruling out a Ukrainian signature on the document.[31]

During the second half of 1991, after Ukraine's independence declaration but before its independence referendum, there was similar evidence of an ethnic discrepancy. If the breakdown among those reporting Ukrainian nationality was 75 percent in favor of "the creation of an independent state – Ukraine" and 11 percent against, self-professed ethnic Russians were 59 percent in favor of independence and 27 percent against. Likewise, in the same survey, Ukrainians

---

[26] Masol, *Upushchennyi Shans*, p. 63.
[27] Kravchuk, *Maemo Te*, p. 124.
[28] Kuchma, *Ukraiina–Ne Rosiia*, p. 417.
[29] Ya. Shimon and L. Brust, results from survey of residents of Ukraine taken in both January 3–10 and October 16–November 4, 1991.
[30] Shimon and Brust January 1991 survey. The findings are similar if the criterion for ethnicity is the main language spoken at home.
[31] Shimon and Brust January 1991 survey.

broke down 42 percent to 37 percent in support of Ukraine's joining a new union, whereas Russian opinion was more clearly in favor: 59 percent to 18 percent.[32]

None of this means ethnicity is itself the driving force behind separatism. Instead, significant ethnic differences of the type described in Chapters 3 and 4 tend to accentuate the collective action problems at the heart of secessionism, problems to which "independence" is one solution. Accordingly, as we expect, many of Ukraine's Russians, tied geographically to the fate of Ukraine as a territorial-administrative entity, also feared they would suffer were a future union to exploit Ukraine. Hence even they voted in large numbers for independence in the December 1991 referendum. Ukrainians, however, appear to have felt the dangers more acutely and more universally.[33]

Why, then, did Ukraine secede from the USSR? The preceding discussion leads us to several conclusions. Initially, Ukraine did not "naturally" tend toward independence as if somehow culturally destined to do so. Ukraine's leaders resolutely took it there. The population as a whole was largely apathetic, and to the extent it did display preferences, Ukrainian citizens would have been quite happy to have remained in the USSR if the latter's leadership could only have been trusted not to have acted aggressively, incompetently, and exploitatively as time passed. In fact, had Ukraine's leadership chosen to do so, it likely could have generated a genuine referendum vote for a reformed union instead of the vote for independence that actually took place. Ukrainian leaders chose to ask a question that would lead to a vote for independence rather than to ask one that would have led to a vote for a union. Further evidence for the importance of framing is described in the case of Uzbekistan, which tended to frame the issue in a way advantaging unionist policies, at least until the union actually disappeared.

UZBEKISTAN: FRAMING UNIONISM

The case of Uzbekistan further demonstrates the importance of elite framing strategies. This is because Uzbek leaders sought to impose on the masses an interpretive frame quite different from the one pushed by Ukraine's leaders even though the Uzbeks could most likely have followed the Ukrainians' path in generating a majority vote for secession in late 1991. As in Ukraine, this involved the wording of referenda, although most frequently it involved the exploitation of ambiguous terms so as to manipulate public opinion and claim mandates for particular policies.

In the March 1991 referendum, the strategy of Uzbekistan's leadership was not to further cloud the mandate for a union but to strengthen it. This is evident

---

[32] Burov survey. The results are similar if one uses the language spoken at home to reflect ethnicity. Geographically, western Ukrainian regions were dramatically opposed to the new union during late 1991: Not one survey respondent supported Ukraine's joining a new union.

[33] Another poll finds that in five southern and eastern regions of Ukraine, ethnic Russians tended to fear "ukrainianization" in connection with Ukrainian independence more than did Ukrainians: V. P. Khmel'ko and V. I. Paniotto, results of survey of 1,802 residents of these five regions taken in November 1991.

when one contrasts how Ukrainian officials treated the March 1991 unionwide referendum with how Uzbekistan's authorities did. Each introduced an additional question onto the ballot, posing its own query alongside Gorbachev's. Ukraine's supplemental question was designed to secure a mandate for greater autonomy than Gorbachev's question implied, asking people to vote on a "Union of Soviet Sovereign States" based on Ukraine's sovereignty declaration. Uzbekistan's supplemental question, on the other hand, was designed to reduce the conditionality of the union mandate by de-linking it from qualities that might not characterize a future union, including democracy, human rights, and socialism. The Uzbek version thus read plainly: "Do you agree that Uzbekistan should remain within the renewed Union (federation) as a sovereign, equal republic?"[34] As can be seen, this formulation left out all of Gorbachev's language on the protection of minority rights and freedoms in the future union. Moreover, there was no reference to any republic declaration of sovereignty, a central element of Ukraine's supplemental question. Karimov, in effect, was sure that his population would produce a pro-union vote for both his and Gorbachev's question and wanted to make sure that this union mandate held clearly even were this union to be less ideal than the one Gorbachev portrayed. "If you put the question unequivocally," declared Karimov, "then the answer is unequivocal too."[35]

The results of the March 1991 union referendum in Uzbekistan gave Karimov the strong unionist mandate he sought, with the Soviet federation as Gorbachev portrayed it winning at least 87 percent in every region. The vote on Uzbekistan's own question was practically identical to that on Gorbachev's question.[36] That this reflected the desires of the republic establishment was self-evident, and the force of a leading article in one of the republic's official Uzbek-language Communist Party newspapers revealed just how strong Uzbek unionism could be. It accused referendum opponents of all kinds of evil deeds, including slander and treason, and hailed the pro-union result as "a great political event, an important stage in the democratic changes."[37] It also seems clear, however, that Karimov could have asked a question much like Ukraine's and generated similar levels of support, providing a foundation for nationalist activism not unlike that practiced by Ukrainians in the spring of 1991.

The difference between the Ukrainian and Uzbek leaders' framing strategies was also evident in the very words they chose to represent the concept of independence in their local languages (Ukrainian and Uzbek) during the critical fall of 1991. The Ukrainian officials, as described earlier in this chapter, framed the December 1991 vote on independence so as to facilitate a post hoc interpretation that a majority vote meant a mandate for a complete break with the USSR. Ukraine's media and leadership thus logically adopted the word *nezalezhnist'* to

34 *Izvestiia*, February 22, 1991, p. 1, FBIS-SOV-91-042, p. 74.
35 Moscow Central Television Vostok Program and Orbita Networks, 1615 GMT, March 9, 1991, FBIS-SOV-91-047, p. 84. Karimov's question also intentionally left out the word "socialist." See Karimov's comments in *Berliner Zeitung*, March 5, 1991, p. 3, FBIS-SOV-91-051, pp. 84–6.
36 *Narodnoe Slovo*, March 23, 1991, p. 3.
37 *Sovet O'zbekistoni*, April 2, 1991, p. 1.

denote "independence." As previously discussed, *nezalezhnist'* was ambiguous, but it still clearly implied greater autonomy than did the Ukrainian word that had been used to denote the more limited concept of sovereignty as expressed in the republic's July 1990 declaration of sovereignty (*suverenitet*). This Ukrainian terminology, chosen by Ukrainian elites, mirrored the Russian-language terms adopted by Russian media and the RSFSR government to refer to these concepts: *nezavisimost'* (independence) and *suverenitet* (sovereignty). Recall from Chapter 6 that Ukraine (like nearly all other union republics) had declared sovereignty in 1990 without understanding this as meaning complete political independence. In fact, republic sovereignty declarations came to be seen as basic principles of autonomy upon which a union would then be refounded.

Uzbekistan's leadership and state-controlled media, however, made a different choice in terminology. After the August 1991 coup, Uzbek officials quickly followed Ukrainian and some other republics' authorities in declaring a referendum on independence. But unlike Ukraine, whose leader saw the declaration and referendum on independence as a path to secession, the Uzbek leadership adopted its declaration of independence primarily to maintain equal bargaining position with other republics for negotiations on reconstituting the union. Significantly, the word in the Uzbek language that Karimov's state-controlled media and regime chose to describe a declaration of and referendum on independence (*mustaqillik*) was the very same word that had previously been used to denote the much more limited concept of sovereignty in its sovereignty declaration of 1990.[38] In part, this choice of wording reflects the advantages of the word *mustaqillik*, especially in its association with the Uzbek word *mustahkam*, which means "strong." This decision, however, was also bound to reduce the degree to which the Uzbek-speaking population would come to expect radical changes both in voting for *mustaqillik* and in interpreting the vote for it after the fact. Indeed, Uzbekistan had already officially declared *mustaqillik* (as "sovereignty") back in the summer of 1990. Very importantly, other wording was available that would have more clearly distinguished a state of sovereignty from a state of independence, notably the term *istiqlol*, which after the dissolution of the USSR did come to refer to political independence. This sheds further light on how Uzbekistan's very declaration of independence could call for the republic to join *collective* security forces, maintain *Soviet* strategic troops, and help sustain a *common* economic space "*in the union.*"[39] Thus in a very real way, a vote for the Uzbek declaration of independence was really a vote for some kind of union.

Clearly, given the ambiguity surrounding the word "independence" in Russian as well as Ukrainian and Uzbek, as other republics began declaring independence, Karimov knew his bargaining position for a future union would be stronger with a declaration of independence in hand. He thus had to find a way to get his

---

[38] The word even before this choice meant both "independence" and "sovereignty" in Uzbek.

[39] Postanovlenie Verkhovnogo Soveta Respubliki Uzbekistan, "O provozglashenii gosudarstvennoi nezavisimosti Respubliki Uzbekistan," *Vedomosti Verkhovnogo Soveta Uzbekskoi SSR*, no.11, st.245, 1991, pp. 68–9.

population to vote for independence and at the same time not undermine the mandate he had always claimed for pursuing a unionist strategy. The ambiguous term *mustaqillik* served this purpose nicely, as did the inclusion of references to future union institutions in the actual declaration of independence.

As it turned out, Uzbekistan's own independence referendum was moot. By the time it took place on December 29, 1991, Gorbachev had already resigned, and almost all union institutions had effectively disappeared or merged into the rising Russian juggernaut. In these circumstances, Karimov's regime generated a vote of over 98 percent in favor of this unionist version of independence (*mustaqillik*), but because the center had already effectively disappeared, it made no difference whether Uzbeks had ratified this state of affairs or not. As we will see in Chapter 9, however, Uzbekistan promptly went about trying to preserve key aspects of the union.

CONCLUSION: EXPLAINING FRAMES?

This chapter has shown that the different framing strategies employed by the leaders of Ukraine and Uzbekistan can account for why Ukraine ultimately seceded from the USSR while Uzbekistan stuck with the union until the bitter end. Both Ukrainians and Uzbeks generally had sufficient national consciousness and grievance vis-à-vis Russian-dominated unions to perceive grave risks of exploitation in a continued Soviet Union, and both were sensitive to Gorbachev's efforts to assuage this sense of danger. Similarly, both reacted negatively to the consequences of the August 1991 coup attempt. Where they differed sharply, however, was in the behavior of their leaders. Ukraine's Kravchuk manipulated the wording of referenda and exploited the ambiguity of words like "independence" to produce a referendum vote that he then interpreted as a mandate for complete secession. Uzbekistan's Karimov did nearly the opposite, exploiting terminological ambiguity and bending the wording of referenda and declarations so that he could later claim a unionist mandate. Even Uzbekistan's declaration of independence made references to the future union of which independent Uzbekistan would be a part. Kravchuk thus obtained his legally required popular sanction for secession, and Karimov won backing for his more unionist course. Even though relevant survey data are available only for Ukraine, evidence strongly suggests that both republic leaders could have generated reverse results had they wished, with a majority of Uzbek voters ratifying secession and a majority of Ukrainian voters opting for union. The logic of framing, then, has supplied an answer as to why Uzbekistan displayed consistently more unionism than did Ukraine in the crucial final years of the USSR.

This strong influence of framing was possible because the primary motivating impulse for separatism was not national consciousness itself, as ethnicity-as-conflictual theory tends to posit, but a collective action problem that was magnified rather than created by the ethnic lens through which people viewed the risks involved. If fully self-conscious nations naturally desire independence and if this is all that matters (i.e., if the National Consciousness version of ethnicity-as-conflictual theory is correct), then both Ukrainians and Uzbeks should have taken advantage of their opportunity to vote against *any* form of union in the various March 1991 referenda, which they did not. If these nations were just being restrained by the threat of a Soviet crackdown, as the Capabilities version would have it, then we should not have seen the ambiguity we observed in mass support for separatism after August 1991, when the threat had effectively disappeared. Finally, this account also tends to weigh against the Countervailing Incentives version of ethnicity-as-conflictual theory: The kind of framing that proved decisive involved not the manipulation of tradeoffs between a supposed ethnic desire for separation and other interests pulling toward union, but the manipulation of degrees of certainty attached to possible outcomes from the collective action problem at the heart of the union. And, most generally, all versions of ethnicity-as-conflictual theory have difficulty explaining why significant numbers of individuals would support both independence and union in the same survey, a finding that is quite in line with relational theory's expectations.

Ethnicity-as-conflictual theorists might respond that only western Ukrainians tended to display true national consciousness, and that they behaved much like ethnicity-as-conflictual theories would predict. Thus, in the fall 1991 Burov poll, as noted previously, all western Ukrainians supported either independence or had trouble answering: Not one fell into the set of those backing independence and a new union at the same time. But this objection itself weakens the connection between separatism and national consciousness since western Ukrainians are a minority in Ukraine and since many others did in fact voice support for independence, in the end producing the most important outcome of interest here: Ukraine's secession-through-referendum. Clearly, something other than the very most intense form of nationalism was driving separatist impulses in Ukraine at the same time that national consciousness does appear to be involved.

Relational theory helps us make better sense of such patterns, being quite compatible with findings that western Ukrainians had a stronger historically developed sense of national consciousness than eastern Ukrainians and that this correlates with separatism. Indeed, ethnically grounded senses of how one fits into the world can be quite stable, resembling equilibria, when they are thick with interpretive meaning and reinforced (made highly accessible, both chronically and situationally) through one's most important formal and informal social relationships, including those involving family, school, work, and community. No reference to any underlying psychological need for "belonging" or self-esteem is necessary to explain this stability, nor is there any cause to assume that separatist motives are somehow inherent to such identification. Robust national identity divides like these will then make it much more difficult for union leaders to convince a distinct minority nation that central authorities will not in the end use their dominant position in the union to exploit rather than cooperate. This is because the members of such a nation will more readily perceive a sense of separation between themselves and control of the union, heightening the degree of risk perceived to be involved. To the extent such divides are also fraught with significant and plausible historical reasons for the nation to fear exploitation by the union-dominant group, as was clearly the case with the Baltic nations, the sense of separation from control is likely to spawn assessments of even greater risks of exploitation in the union. At the same time, the actual motivation for separatism springs not from the mere fact of ethnic consciousness (however intense) but from the credible commitment problem that is exacerbated – not caused – by the pattern of national identification. Relational theory thus appears capable of accounting for important findings generated by the best ethnicity-as-conflictual theorists, but it does so in a different way that is more consistent with otherwise inconvenient details.

The relational theory also accounts better for these patterns than ethnicity-as-epiphenomenal theory. For one thing, contrary to the expectations of ethnicity-as-epiphenomenal theory, ethnic divides did correlate with separatism. Some of those ethnicity-as-epiphenomenal theories that do posit a role for ethnicity, presenting it as essentially *being* a frame (construct) that elites manipulate for self-interested ends, run into another problem that the relational theory avoids: assuming that elites are motivated by material or political self-interest yet that the masses mindlessly buy into the ethnic frame. The relational theory assumes that no one acts out of any kind of ethnic motive and that the only difference between masses and leaders is that the latter hold framing power while the former do not. What leaders do is essentially frame choices that masses must make, choices that are often likely to involve ethnicity as an uncertainty-reduction device. Masses may be aware of the manipulation, but they still must respond to the presented choice, as on a legally binding referendum question.

Ethnicity-as-epiphenomenal theorists may still posit that the observed ethnic differences in responding to frames in fact reflect different interests: Ethnic Ukrainians were more likely than ethnic Russians to support Ukrainian separatism because they believed resource distribution would likely be coordinated along ethnic lines after secession. This finding would not actually be incompatible with relational theory: If ethnicity facilitates and thereby corresponds to patronage distribution networks, that would surely be a good reason for people to invoke ethnic categories as a rule of thumb for assessing how a given policy will impact their individual fortunes. The question here, though, is whether such an explanation is sufficient as a general explanation for the connection between separatism and ethnicity, and whether it was important in the late USSR. This book will return to this question in Chapter 10, but for now we note an important observation: If coordination equilibria are stable enough to be important, and if ethnicity facilitates resource-seeking coordination precisely because of the clarity and fixity of its lines of cleavage, then we would not have expected the leaders of "winning ethnic coalitions" (Ukrainians in Ukraine, Uzbeks in Uzbekistan) to have deliberately created ambiguity. Yet the creation and manipulation of ambiguity were core parts of these leaders' framing activity. What we document in the Ukraine, for example, looks quite different from what Chandra describes in India, where identity divides really do correspond powerfully with patronage networks and where ethnic party leaders seek to communicate clarity, not ambiguity, unless their group is in a losing position.[40] It does not appear, then, that ethnic coordination for the sake of spoils was really what was motivating separatism in the post-Soviet context. A more satisfactory answer would appear to highlight the presence of an ethnically charged collective action problem and the decisions of Karimov and Kravchuk to frame it in different ways, generating different outcomes.

This leads us to one more important question: Can we go further and explain *why* these different leaders adopted these different framing strategies? One possibility is that the explanation ends here, that we should just chalk everything up to contingent leadership decisions. Kravchuk simply wanted independence while Karimov preferred union. One might be able to make a fairly strong case for doing this, but it behooves us to at least consider the possibility that these divergent leadership decisions could be explained with reference to other important factors. One such factor could be leadership personality, but there would seem to be little in the biographies of Karimov and Kravchuk that would lead one to be significantly more inclined to separatism than the other. Indeed, even as he won the vote for independence in the December 1 referendum, Kravchuk was widely seen by leading experts as being insincere in his nationalism, opportunistically riding the separatist wave to galvanize his own political power. Moreover, even the theory of contingent leadership decision making would need to explain why there appeared to be continuity in Ukraine's greater separatism relative to Uzbekistan's even before Kravchuk, when Volodymyr Ivashko was Ukrainian leader, and why all of these leaders were able to gain support for their frames and policies from so many other elites. Another leader-oriented explanation might venture that the career security of Kravchuk was threatened to a greater degree by the possibility of hardliners coming to power in the union, making him more eager to secede so as to preserve his post. Kravchuk would have been a target, however, precisely because he had proven consistently more willing to flirt with separatism than had Karimov – this argument thus becomes tautological. A more promising answer seems to be that the kind of frames that were most potent varied from republic to republic depending on certain underlying factors that elites like Kravchuk and Karimov were capable of discerning. The following chapter argues that aggregate republic interests, especially as they derived from economic development and were mediated through particular institutions, were the key differentiating factor.

[40] Chandra, *Why Ethnic Parties Succeed.*

8

Institutionally Mediated Interests

The Political Economy of Secessionism

The relational approach has explained separatism as a strategic response to an ethnically charged collective action problem in a union and has shown, through the cases of Ukraine and Uzbekistan, that individual leaders can use framing techniques to influence strongly whether their masses choose a separatist strategy. Both Ukrainian and Uzbek leaders could have framed options so as to have generated majority referendum votes for either "independence" or "union" in the crucial fall of 1991, but Ukraine's leaders chose a pro-independence frame, whereas Uzbekistan's opted for a unionist frame. These framing differences were most important at those key moments where a particular aggregation of the popular will was identical to republic policy, the independence referenda, but Ukraine tended to display more separatism than Uzbekistan at other moments, too. Two key questions thus remain. First, why did Karimov and Kravchuk adopt different framing strategies? Second, what drove the greater separatism of Ukrainian policies relative to Uzbek ones more generally, when no referenda were determining republic responses to every move Gorbachev made?

The theory of separatism presented in Chapter 4 suggests turning to the particular interests of the particular leaders and masses involved as well as to the institutions that link them. The relational theory of ethnicity holds that senses of ethnic identity are driven by a need for uncertainty reduction, whereas ethnic politics are motivated by the pursuit of interests, as described in Chapter 3 and 4. Chapters 5 and 6 indeed found that strong national consciousness was not the impulse behind separatism yet that ethnicity was not merely a coordination mechanism (nor irrelevant) in this process. The analysis of framing patterns in Chapter 7 added confirmation to these claims. Instead, separatism is better described as one of many possible strategies for escaping a perceived danger of exploitation in a union, a danger brought about by a collective action problem that ethnicity helps people interpret. Those ethnic regions that stand to gain the most from union, therefore, will tend to be willing to take the greatest perceived chance of exploitation, whereas those that stand to gain the least will be among the first to "jump ship" as the perceived danger of exploitation rises. The crucial question is what "the regional interest" means. Following the practice established in Chapter 4, it is treated here as an aggregation of all regional citizens' interests defined in terms of life chances, an aggregation carried out by ethnofederal institutions. Regional interests factor into the actual behavior of ethnic regions (understood as the behavior of these regions' official ultimate decision makers) depending on two core factors: the *interests* of leaders defined in terms of life chances and any *institutions* that force leaders to be responsive to mass interests in particular ways. One could build theory by specifying these factors in a variety of different ways, but Chapters 3 and 4 argue that material resources are likely to be a very important determinant of life chances and are hence a key part of what both leaders and masses pursue.

This general expectation is borne out in Ukraine and Uzbekistan during the USSR's final years. For one thing, economic concerns are found to be far more important than ethnic ones in both republics, even in nationalist western Ukraine. And the material interests of leaders and masses on the issue of the union are found to have been largely congruent due partly to a coincidence of narrow self-interest and partly to institutions – including elections and other forms of political contestation – that tied politicians' future prospects to mass interests. Both the masses and leaders of Ukraine stood to gain less from continued union than did those of Uzbekistan because the former republic was more economically developed than the latter and thus would benefit less in terms of development from association with other republics. Ukraine also faced better prospects for further economic development outside the union because of its proximity to the prosperous European Union. Thus, even though both of these republics' leaders could have generated majority support by either a separatist or unionist frame, as described in Chapter 7, the separatist frame had the potential to produce *greater* support in Ukraine, whereas the reverse was true in Uzbekistan as the USSR approached its end. Much of the politics of 1990 and 1991, then, is the story of how politicians in Ukraine and Uzbekistan competed with potential rivals to explore the contours of public opinion and to take the position on union that provided them with the most political support, thereby maximizing their personal life chances (including for material gain). Very importantly, these leaders were not simply pandering to public opinion but were seeking to understand its *potential* so as to shape it to their advantage *before it could be mobilized by an opponent* (or mobilize autonomously) in a way that disadvantaged them. Thus, leaders led separatism in the former USSR, but they were constrained by real and perceived mass interests and political contestation. And even though elites took the lead in highlighting the collective action problem in the union, it was the difference in mass interests that ultimately drove Ukraine's leaders to choose a separatist strategy and Uzbekistan's a unionist one in the decisive fall of 1991.

These findings continue to positively distinguish relational theory from its rivals. The evidence of this chapter is in most tension with ethnicity-as-conflictual theories, which variously presume ethnic motives are the dominant force behind separatism. Conversely, this chapter shows how the relational theory can account for the widely observed importance of material considerations while still explaining important "ethnic effects" that remain puzzling to ethnicity-as-epiphenomenal theories.

THE RELATIVE IMPORTANCE OF ECONOMIC AND ETHNIC CONCERNS

The supposition that material interests are a leading driver of separatist behavior is well founded in survey evidence, which shows that people in both Uzbekistan and Ukraine prioritized economic issues over national or cultural ones. For example, a poll of Uzbek republic residents published in 1990 found that over 70 percent indicated food supplies and inflation as being among the problems that worried them most, while 28 percent named internationality relations and only 5 percent identified inattention to national traditions and the development of national culture.[1]

Some might dismiss this as evidence that Uzbekistan did in fact lack national consciousness, but the prioritization of the economic over the ethnic was just as stark in Ukraine, even when Ukrainian separatism was at its peak in fall 1991. One survey during this period asked residents to choose the most important goals of the Ukrainian state from a list. A full 65 percent selected "welfare of the people" and 37 percent indicated "defense of economic interests," while only 13 percent affirmed "revival of the nation." Even in the most radically nationalist western regions, only 29 percent marked "revival of the nation," while 53 percent checked "welfare of the people."[2] That is, even given the option of indicating concern with multiple issues, national and cultural issues were not cited as important priorities in Uzbekistan or either eastern or western Ukraine. Similarly, the New Soviet Citizen surveys of spring 1990 and spring 1991 asked Ukraine's people to identify the most important domestic problem facing the USSR and did not provide them with a preconceived list. In both years, majorities of those answering volunteered economic concerns and less than 15 percent mentioned anything linked to ethnicity or culture. Strikingly, the same set of questions found that economic concerns strongly outweighed ethnicity-linked ones even in Lithuania, generally regarded as one of the most intensely nationalist republics in the late USSR.[3]

THE RELATIONSHIP BETWEEN ELITE AND MASS MATERIAL INTERESTS IN UKRAINE AND UZBEKISTAN

As Chapter 4 suggested would be the case, the narrowly material interests of the masses and of official ethnofederal republic leaders were largely congruent in both Ukraine and Uzbekistan *when it came to the specific issue of the union.* This is true for two reasons. First, both leaders and masses had personal interests in a

---

[1] Bureau of Sociological Research, Uzbek SSR State Committee on Statistics, *Sotsial'no-Kul'turnaia Sfera* (Tashkent: Goskomstat UzSSR, 1990), pp. 40–1.

[2] Burov survey.

[3] New Soviet Citizen Surveys, 1990 and 1991. Author's calculations.

more-developed republic economy. Predatory leaders would prefer a more-developed economy to a less-developed one because they would have more to steal from in the former, and altruistic leaders would want their people to live better for their own sake. Similarly, if masses were given the choice between being subject to a predatory leader in a more-developed economy and being subject to that same leader in a less-developed economy, they would surely choose the more-developed economy because they would either benefit directly from the development (better roads, communications infrastructure, job availability) or hope to glean at least some benefit whenever the predatory leader opted to spend some spoils locally. Thus, if the union can be expected to have any effect on the overall economic development of a given region, as this book contends is the case, then republic leaders and masses are likely to develop similar views on the economic desirability of the union even when leaders are motivated by narrow self-interest and do not care about the preferences of the masses. This kind of interest congruence is also to be expected if the leaders are not purely predatory but sit atop locally based patronage machines that gain resources from the central government, as was closer to the situation in Ukraine and, especially, Uzbekistan during the period in question. In this case, both masses and leaders are likely to prefer richer regional political machines than poorer ones and are thus likely to perceive coinciding interests in "union issues" that stand to make a region richer or poorer. Chapter 4 also explained that the least-developed regions in a given union tend to have the greatest interest in that union because they stand to gain more from it in terms of economic development. This supposition correctly leads us to expect consistently lower separatism in the less economically developed Uzbekistan than in more economically developed Ukraine.

Some might object to the idea that the material interests of predatory or patronal leaders regarding the Soviet Union could have coincided with mass material interests. Perhaps republic leaders required central Soviet sanction to enable their stealing or patronage activity. By implication, such republic leaders might have backed USSR membership even when the economy would have been richer without it and thus the masses would have opposed it. This supposition, though, does not explain why Ukrainian leaders would have opted for secession. Moreover, the central government had in the 1980s cracked down on the most extreme varieties of corruption and patronage politics and that crackdown primarily targeted Central Asia, especially Uzbekistan, as Chapter 5 noted. Thus, this "centrally sanctioned stealing" hypothesis would lead one to expect Uzbekistan's leadership to have been more inclined to secede than Ukraine's, yet the reverse was the case. And indeed, the politics of these countries since independence surely demonstrates that no Soviet sanction was actually necessary for either corrupt gain or patronage politics.

Another objection might hold that central authority was necessary not so much for sanctioning stealing or patronage politics as for suppressing internal political contestation that could complicate such activities. Yet here too, we would have expected republics with the greatest internal divisions and most political competition to have been the strongest unionists because their leaders would have hoped that the union could help them dampen this competition, yet the opposite seems sooner the case. Hotly contested Ukraine and the ethnically fractious republics of Georgia, Azerbaijan, and Moldova were among the leading separatists. And developments in Central Asia quickly proved that republic leaders were perfectly capable of repressing dissent on their own. Indeed, as has been noted earlier, the union under Gorbachev played a key role in pushing conservative Communist Party organizations to liberalize in both Ukraine and Uzbekistan.

One might also posit that republic leaders' material interests in union would have diverged from mass interests if they believed their greatest prospects for self-enrichment lay in the opportunity to advance in the central Soviet hierarchy. Yet it was the Ukrainians, not the Uzbeks, who consistently had greater upward mobility ("most favored lord status") in the union.[4] This was nicely symbolized in Gorbachev's 1990 decision to make not an Uzbek, but a Ukrainian (Ivashko) the second secretary of the unionwide Communist Party organization. But it was the Ukrainian, not the Uzbek, leadership that pursued secession in the fall of 1991.

Mass and leadership material interests on the union did not merely coincide, however. They were tied together by institutions that gave leaders specific incentives not to venture too far from public opinion on issues that had significant import for people's material well-being. This was most clearly true in Ukraine, which experienced a major political opening after Gorbachev removed the hardline Shcherbitsky in late 1989. Especially after the union repealed the Communist Party's official monopoly on party politics in early 1990, Ukraine featured a vibrant nationalist movement with considerable mobilizational potential across Ukraine, the Popular Movement for Restructuring Ukraine, more widely known as *Rukh* ("The Movement"). In March 1990, voters for the first time chose a republic parliament in elections that were, for the most part, free and competitive.

The 1990 elections were certainly not truly fair. Rukh had virtually no access to electronic media and even had trouble finding a publishing house to print its newspaper. Also, foreign observers were denied entry visas into the country.[5] But residents of Ukraine did enjoy a real choice in most voting districts, with an average of over six contenders for each seat and candidates running unopposed in only four constituencies.[6] Shortly after these elections, the Ukrainian leader at the time, Ivashko, sanctioned a split in the Communist Party, averring that it was better for more liberally inclined communists to leave the party than to undermine its message.[7]

The freshly elected Rada thus contained many different political viewpoints, and Rukh supporters were capable of using their seats to help mobilize supporters and of influencing outcomes due to institutional rules that will be described later.

---

[4] Laitin, "The National Uprisings."

[5] Marko Bojcun, "The Ukrainian Parliamentary Elections in March–April 1994," *Europe-Asia Studies*, v.47, no.2, 1995, p. 229.

[6] *Sel'skaia Zhizn'*, March 13, 1990, p. 3; *Izvestiia*, February 17, 1990, p. 1.

[7] *Pravda Ukrainy*, April 3, 1990, pp. 1–2, FBIS-SOV-90-087, May 4, 1990, p. 95.

Additionally, in June 1990, Ivashko to some degree separated state and Communist Party power. Shortly after being elected chairman of the Rada, he resigned from his position as party leader in June 1990 and ceded that post to a more conservative figure, Hurenko.[8] Even though Communists still remained the major force in the parliament, the Rada chairman (Ivashko and, as of July 1990, his successor Kravchuk) became both the true and official leader of Ukraine. Yet because the Rada chairman's power depended on his ability to secure majority votes in the parliament, which was popularly elected and contained many different organized viewpoints, he had significant reason to be responsive to public opinion as mediated through the 1990 elections that produced the extant Rada. Moreover, during summer 1991, the Rada created a new post of president that was to be filled in December 1991 elections, giving Kravchuk even more reason to be attentive to perceived mass material interests so that he could maximize his chances of winning election to that post. Since Kravchuk faced significant political competition throughout his tenure, he had incentive to frame issues in ways that would generate the greatest degree of support.

Uzbekistan's ruling elites had even more power to frame situations for the masses because the republic was more autocratic and thus faced little potential competition from those advocating alternative frames. To describe Uzbekistan's leadership as completely insulated from mass influence in 1990–1 would be a mistake, however. Ukrainian leaders responded to mass sentiment primarily because open political competition forced them to seek out and exploit the most potent contours of public opinion before their rivals did; however, Uzbekistan's top authorities responded (at least somewhat) for two different reasons highlighted here.

First, President Karimov was initially quite beholden to a coalition of regionally based political machines *cum* patronage networks on which power in Uzbekistan had been largely based even in the Soviet period. The Communist Party of the Soviet Union had enjoyed a firm grip on power in Uzbekistan, but during the Brezhnev era it came largely to exercise authority through these political machines. The machines delivered economic goods (especially cotton) to the Uzbek and Soviet central governments and in return gained patronage resources and a good deal of autonomy in distributing them and running local affairs. As the central CPSU structures that subordinated them weakened or were captured by local interests, Uzbek regional governments became primary sources of authority in the transitional period due to their critical positions in the patronage network.[9] Because patronage networks involve at least some distribution of resources to lower levels of the network, the interests of regional bosses and their regions'

---

[8] *Izvestiia*, June 22, 1990, p. 1; *Izvestiia*, June 23, 1990, p. 2.
[9] Carlisle, "Islom Karimov"; Alisher Ilkhamov, "The Limits of Centralization: Regional Challenges in Uzbekistan," in Pauline Jones Luong, ed., *The Transformation of Central Asia* (Ithaca, NY: Cornell, 2004), pp. 159–82; Jones Luong, *Institutional Change*; Idil Tuncer, "Understanding Violent Conflict: A Comparative Study of Tajikistan and Uzbekistan," Ph.D. dissertation in Central Eurasian Studies, Indiana University, Bloomington, IN, 2007; and Erika Weinthal, *State Making and Environmental Cooperation* (Cambridge, MA: The MIT Press, 2002).

masses also tended to coincide when it came to whether more or fewer resources would be transferred to the region from the republic or union budgets. There was thus at least some sense in which pressures from these regional machines reflected mass wishes. Karimov also relied on these regional machines to deliver votes in the early 1990 parliamentary elections, the late 1991 presidential contest, and the 1991 referenda. And Karimov was in a particularly vulnerable position vis-à-vis these machines in 1990–1: He had originally come to power as an outsider, primarily from economic rather than regional machine structures and as part of a compromise between Moscow and rival Uzbek provincial bosses. Lacking his own machine, he had to be careful not to give any of the major regional bosses issues they could easily use to build a cross-provincial coalition against him in a bid for power.[10] At least, this was the case in the early years of Karimov's rule.

The second force that drove Karimov to respond to mass interests at least to some degree was the fear that a popular uprising could destabilize his republic and threaten his position of power. Uzbekistan, as noted previously, lacked the robust, institutionalized political competition that in Ukraine forced leaders like Kravchuk to cater to public demands or be voted out of office. What Karimov did face, however, was a historically greater threat of bloody mass violence that many believed had the potential to unseat or at least weaken him. Such violence had broken out on several occasions in and around Uzbekistan during the *perestroika* period, including the Ferghana Valley pogroms of summer 1989, the February 1990 rioting against the small minority Meskhetian Turks in Tashkent,[11] the deadly Uzbek-Kyrgyz riots of June–July 1990 in the Kyrgyz city of Osh,[12] and the December 1990 clashes between citizens and police in Namangan.[13] Thus, in one early 1991 interview, Karimov declared that he began each day not with information on politics or economics but with the republic police report on such events.[14] The Uzbek leader surely used these tragedies as justification to crack down on opposition movements (with only a few temporary exceptions), although they also forced him to be at least somewhat attentive to the most critical popular needs and demands so as to prevent domestic instability that could threaten his position or be used by his rivals to weaken him.

To understand why exactly such riots might create an incentive for Karimov actually to respond to at least some mass interests, it is crucial to understand riots less as spontaneous outbursts of mass sentiment and more as a powerful resource that provincial political machines could use to weaken or possibly unseat Karimov. Extensive comparative evidence in countries ranging from India to Russia shows that regionally based political machines quite often foment or otherwise utilize

---

[10] Carlisle, "Islom Karimov," pp. 196, 200.

[11] TASS International Service in Russian 0540 GMT March 6, 1990, FBIS-SOV-90-044, p. 116; *Izvestiia*, February 23, 1990, p. 3, FBIS-SOV-90-041, pp. 114–5.

[12] TASS (English) 1606 GMT, August 13, 1990, FBIS-SOV-90-157, p. 87; Paris APF (English) 0749 GMT, June 5, 1990, FBIS-SOV-90-108, p. 104; Tashkent Domestic Service in Russian 0115 GMT, June 11, 1990, FBIS-SOV-90-112, p. 113.

[13] Moscow Domestic Service in Russian 1311 GMT, December 3, 1990, FBIS-SOV-90-233, p. 44.

[14] *Izvestiia*, January 29, 1991, p. 3, FBIS-SOV-91-037, pp. 103–6.

social unrest as a way of gaining power, maintaining it, or exerting pressure on central governments.[15] Such riots are easier to mobilize (and more effective in discrediting the authority of their target) to the extent that latent grievances among the potentially riotous populations are real. Thus, Karimov's stated fear of public unrest was likely in part a concern that regionally based political machines networks might seek to use or covertly instigate such events to gain power at his expense.

One must also note that Uzbekistan was not completely authoritarian in 1990–1, as Gorbachev pushed for compliance with his liberalizing policies here as in Ukraine. Over 1,100 candidates competed for 500 seats in the 1990 republic parliament and only about a third of these races were uncontested. Most of the uncontested districts, however, did feature leaders of local Communist Party and state organs.[16] Some 59 percent of the victors were high- or midlevel republic officials in party and state structures, and an additional 13 percent were lower-level officials.[17] Karimov did have a credible rival from a major opposition force in the late December 1991 presidential election, although the most potent opposition had been barred from running its candidate.

Overall, we find strong reason in Ukraine and Uzbekistan to believe leaders' and mass material interests were to a significant degree aligned with regard to the specific question of whether their republic should pursue a secessionist or unionist strategy. On one hand, this was because both masses and leaders (be they patronal or predatory) would prefer that their region be more rather than less economically developed. But on the other hand, it was also because leaders in both Ukraine and Uzbekistan had incentive to pay heed to the most acute mass interests so as to maximize their own chances of staying in power and pursue whatever they wanted to pursue as leaders. The previously cited polls show that material welfare was the masses' chief concern in both republics, and evidence presented later will show that people believed their republics' relationships to the union had great importance for their material welfare. Much of the politics of separatism, then, is the process by which leaders explore potential developments in public opinion on the issue of union and then choose the strategy that gains them the most support.

DETERMINING ECONOMIC INTERESTS IN UNION AND SECESSION

The critical difficulty for leaders who want to enrich themselves and/or maximize public support, of course, is how to determine what course of action would in fact be best for the economy and could be perceived as such (with proper framing) by the population. To be sure, there was room for disagreement

---

[15] Brass, *Theft of an Idol*; Wilkinson, *Votes and Violence*; Graeme Robertson, "All They Need Is Someone to Organize It: Protest and Politics in Post-Soviet Russia," Ph.D. dissertation in Political Science, Columbia University, New York, 2004.

[16] *Pravda*, February 16, 1990, p. 1.

[17] Alisher Ilkhamov, "Pervyi Parlament Uzbekistana: Sotsial'nyi Portret," *Komsomolets Uzbekistana*, April 5, 1990, p. 2.

regarding different republics' economic relationships with the union.[18] The disagreement on Ukraine's economic relationship with the USSR provides a good example, though similar issues could be debated regarding Uzbekistan as well. One major problem was how to properly value the flows of goods and services among republics since Soviet prices were not market-based. Most reports incorporating Soviet prices tended to show Ukraine transferred more resources to the union than it got in return, a widespread view in both Ukraine and the West.[19] Yet other calculations based on these same prices reached the opposite conclusion by considering a broader definition of resource flows.[20] Moreover, those who calculated using world market prices instead of Soviet prices reached an even stronger revision of the common wisdom because Ukraine was receiving oil and gas from Russia at prices far below world levels.[21] In fact, Ukraine's leaders were well aware that world prices indicated a Soviet subsidy, treating Russia's threats to move to world market pricing during 1990–1 as a serious danger to the Ukrainian economy.[22] Thus, in the same way that Ukraine's leaders had the opportunity to frame union commitments of nonexploitation in multiple ways and so engineer majority public support for either secession or union, these same leaders could pick and choose from different plausible valuations of transfers to support either breaking or joining with the union. There was much more agreement that the USSR had essentially stripped Ukraine of any control over where its resources would go, depriving it even of power over its own industry.[23] But whether the solution was autonomy within a union or outright independence was open to interpretation. Overall, Ukraine's leaders had significant scope to interpret economic "facts" in ways that could support either a unionist or a separatist argument.

At the same time, leaders could not manipulate all public perceptions of the economy at will – there was in fact a tenaciously evident "reality" to contend with. It is reality in the sense that to contradict it would not have been credible in the eyes of the population or key elites because it would not have sensibly accounted for their own experiences. The most important such reality was these republics' level of economic development relative to the rest of the union. By almost all measures, it is evident that Ukraine enjoyed greater economic development than the Central Asian republics like Uzbekistan, was at roughly the same level as Russia, and was less developed than the Baltic republics. Retail commodity turnover is a particularly good indicator of standards of living in the late USSR, and as of 1988, Ukraine was at 1,210 rubles per capita, behind only the Baltic states, Belarus, and Russia. Uzbekistan was far behind, at just 760 rubles per capita. For some idea of the levels of the other republics, Latvia was at 1,860, Russia at 1,410,

[18] Herrera, *Imagined Economies.*
[19] See Masol, *Upushchennyi Shans*, p. 55; Motyl, *Dilemmas*, pp. 129–30; and Subtelny, *Ukraine*, p. 529.
[20] Masol, *Upushchennyi Shans*, pp. 55–6.
[21] Hogan, "Oil and Gas," p. 19.
[22] Masol, *Upushchennyi Shans*, p. 67.
[23] Kravchuk, *Maemo Te*, pp. 85–6; Krawchenko, "Ukraine," p. 87; Masol, *Upushchennyi Shans*, pp. 12–15.

TABLE 8.1. *Correlates of the Perception that People in One's Own Region Live Better/Worse than in Other Regions: A Multilevel Logistic Regression Analysis of VTsIOM Survey Data from January 1991*

Factors	DV: Life Better in Own Region	DV: Life Worse in Own Region
Republic level		
Republic Economic Development	5.2 (2.61)***	0.1 (−3.73)***
Individual level		
Older	1.0 (−0.60)	1.0 (0.35)
Educated	1.0 (0.72)	1.0 (0.44)
Lives in capital city	1.3 (1.43)	0.7 (−1.51)
Female	1.0 (−0.17)	1.1 (1.13)
Number of republics analyzed	12	12
N	2,263	2,263

Note: Coefficients reported as odds ratios. Figures in parentheses are z statistics, which are an indicator of statistical significance. For readers not familiar with them, the asterisks summarize the most important conclusions to be drawn from them.
***99 percent confidence level.
DV = dependent variable.

Armenia at 1,090, and Tajikistan at 680. These same broad patterns show up in statistic after statistic indicating economic development.[24]

These numbers reflect a reality that was generally obvious to ordinary people who might travel from, say, Ukraine to Uzbekistan. Kyivans visiting Tashkent, for example, might walk into stores and notice that their own establishments had a wider and more consistently available array of finished consumer goods. They would also likely notice that their home city had more such stores. Visiting acquaintances' homes, they would observe that their Ukrainian compatriots had more modern products and services available to them. Traveling around the republic, they would likely observe animals being used more frequently as means of transport. They would have found fairly consistently the opposite while visiting Western Europe. Although not everyone traveled within the union, many did and could be counted on to relate information regarding relative levels of development to their families and friends.[25]

Multilevel logistic regression analysis of survey data collected by the reputable VTsIOM agency in twelve non-Russian union republics during early 1991 confirms the posited connection between actual and perceived levels of republic economic well-being there. As Table 8.1 reports, the odds of someone identifying his or her own republic or region (Transcaucasia, the Baltics, Central Asia)

[24] Oksana Genrikhovna Dmitrieva, *Regional'naia Ekonomicheskaia Diagnostika* (St. Petersburg: Izdatel'stvo Sankt-Peterburgskogo Universiteta Ekonomiki i Finansov, 1992), especially pp. 130–2.
[25] Given that people have such independent sources of information, there is much more scope for divergent perceptions of economic conditions when levels of development are close (e.g., when comparing one Russian region to another, as does Herrera in *Imagined Economies*) than when levels of development are quite different in ways that impact people's perceptions of their own life chances (e.g., comparing Ukraine to Central Asia or Western Europe).

as being a place where people "live better" than in others were more than five times greater for people in the more-developed republics than for people in the less-developed ones. Accordingly, the odds of someone naming his or her republic or region as a place where people "live worse" dropped tenfold as interviewers moved from the less- to the more-developed republics.[26] The null hypothesis that there was no relationship between actual and perceived development levels, as measured here, can be rejected with over 99 percent statistical confidence in both cases.

Ukraine's self-perception as being relatively developed was linked conceptually to its leaders' belief that its public would consider independence "affordable" under certain circumstances, circumstances that came to pass in the fall of 1991 and that did not lead the less-developed Uzbekistan to consider independence affordable. Revealing of this perception is the following passage in former Prime Minister Vitaly Masol's memoirs:

> In the course of multiple discussions on these questions, one could frequently hear the rhetorical question: "Is it really the case that Ukraine could not exist outside the Union?" Of course it could. There exist (and even flourish) many states in various parts of the globe that possess far less potential in resources, production, and science than Ukraine.[27]

Perhaps the most famous piece of evidence linking Ukrainian separatism to economics involves a German report on the relative "ripeness" of Soviet republic economies for cooperation with the West on a market basis. This report gave Ukraine the highest rating among the fifteen union republics, just above the Baltic republics and Russia and far ahead of Central Asia.[28] These summary findings clearly struck a chord in Ukraine and were much discussed in the media during early 1991. Kravchuk himself cited them in late March 1991 as justifying his call for a looser "Union of Sovereign States" instead of the more tightly integrated "renewed federation" that Gorbachev and the Central Asian leaders were advocating.[29]

The Uzbeks tended to see these ties with the union as much more critical to their prospects for economic development and stability. That is, what crucially differentiated Uzbekistan from Ukraine was not any alleged lack of national consciousness but a relative absence of economic development. The economic gap between Russia and Uzbekistan was more than wide enough to make highly plausible an argument that the economy of the former had the potential to "pull up" the economy of the latter. Moreover, while Ukraine could aspire to join such affluent entities as the European Union, Uzbekistan's only foreign neighbor was Afghanistan, not known as a beacon of economic prosperity. Uzbekistan's leaders and masses, therefore, saw themselves as dependent on Russia for economic

---

[26] See Web Appendix to Table 8.1, available on the author's Web site (http://hehale5.googlepages. com) or from the author directly, for technical details of the analysis. The VTsIOM data are described in more detail in Chapter 10.

[27] Masol, *Upushchennyi Shans*, p. 67. See also Moroz, *Kudy Idemo?*, p. 62.

[28] Krawchenko, "Ukraine," p. 88.

[29] *Izvestiia*, March 29, 1991, p. 2.

development, and this "discourse of dependency" drove them to strike a balance among three basic policy directions: keeping subsidies flowing from Russia; retaining as many economic ties with Russia and the other republics as possible; and minimizing their republic's vulnerability to any future Russian attempts at exploitation, hence seeking as much decision-making autonomy as was possible while still preserving access to subsidies and economic links. This involved, in part, firmly establishing the local "native" group's control over "its" republic.

Central to the politics of separatism in ethnofederal systems, therefore, is the process by which leaders, driven by some form of political contestation, explore the potential of public perceptions regarding the collective action problem inherent in political integration and regarding their material interests in this union. Where they face the greatest levels of political contestation, they will tend to be most tightly tied to the framing strategy that would win them the most popular support. Even autocrats, however, face at least some incentive to possess popular support because this lowers the costs of their rule. The rest of this chapter traces such processes in the cases of Ukraine and Uzbekistan during the crucial years 1990–1.

UKRAINE: THE POLITICS OF SECESSION IN A RELATIVELY
DEVELOPED REPUBLIC

The picture of economic development just painted provides the essential backdrop for understanding the process whereby Ukraine came actually to secede in December 1991. This process might be stylized as follows. Ukraine's top leaders faced intense political contestation beginning in late 1989, which led them to seek out a position on the union that would generate the greatest possible support. They thus first competed with their rivals to test and understand public opinion. It soon became evident that most of the public that expressed a view saw the commitment problem in the union but tended not to interpret it as acute and generally viewed some form of autonomy, not actual secession, as the best solution. The 1990 elections made clear that by promoting a nationalist interpretive lens, political leaders could convince significant numbers of people that the commitment problem was severe and that much more autonomy was necessary to counteract it. Thus, Ukraine's elites raced to lead the consciousness-raising effort in this direction lest others do so first and reap the political rewards. When Gorbachev provided for a realistic solution to the commitment problem through the Novo-Ogarevo process in mid-1991, Ukraine's leadership moderated its anti-union rhetoric accordingly. But after the August 1991 coup, and facing elections for the republic presidency in December 1991, Kravchuk astutely realized that he could win a bigger majority through a "moderate secessionist" framing strategy than through a unionist (or radically secessionist) one. Ukraine's masses did not generally want to break economic ties with the union, but their republic's relatively high economic development meant many could be convinced that staying in the union was no longer worth the risk. By staking out a separatist position that did not imply a full economic break with the union, Kravchuk helped ensure his victory in the presidential contest and his continued grip on power in Ukraine. This account is fleshed out in what follows.

As Gorbachev pressured and then forced out longtime republic party boss Shcherbitsky, Ukraine's Communists found themselves facing growing opposition, especially from nationalist forces. As early as 1988, mass demonstrations in support of national issues had taken place in the western city of Lviv and the capital Kyiv.[30] Rukh, growing out of the Ukrainian Writers' Union and containing many famous authors, became the leading nationalist voice after holding its founding congress in September 1989.[31] As fate would have it, the Communist Party official charged with keeping tabs on Rukh was none other than Leonid Kravchuk, then head of the party's republic-level ideology department. Kravchuk, from a western Ukrainian area known for nationalist activity in the 1940s, avers that he became influenced by many of the nationalist ideas that certain Rukh leaders gradually began to advocate.[32] Nationalists also took heart when Shcherbitsky was succeeded by the moderate Ivashko (endorsed by Gorbachev[33]) instead of the more conservative Hurenko. Rukh launched a series of high-profile actions, such as the attempt to form a vast "human chain" stretching from Kyiv to Lviv on the January 1990 anniversary of the 1917 Ukrainian People's Republic's declaration of independence.[34] But despite Rukh's visibility, the Communist Party firmly controlled Ukrainian policy before the March 1990 republic elections.

The 1990 Election Campaign

The general republic elections of March 1990 fundamentally changed the dynamics of Ukrainian politics, and their effects were felt even before they occurred. With Gorbachev enforcing liberalization from Moscow, Ukraine's politicians understood they would have to win at least some popular support at the same time that they had no prior experience with electoral competition. Rukh applied heat, with supporters contesting seats for both local councils and the Rada and appearing regularly in street rallies in major cities.[35] Ivashko, who came to power just months before the elections, almost immediately began stressing the need for Ukraine to gain more autonomy from Moscow and even started work on Ukraine's declaration of sovereignty – all before Rukh members had won any seats in the new parliament. These autonomy calls centered on the need for economic decentralization.[36] Not only would Ukrainian economic autonomy allow for better decisions, he argued, but it would ensure Ukraine a fair share of the

[30] Subtelny, *Ukraine*, p. 576.
[31] On Rukh, see Oleksiy V. Haran, *Ubyty Drakona: Z Istorii Rukhu ta Novykh Partii na Ukraini* (Kyiv: Lybid', 1993); Taras Kuzio and Andrew Wilson, *Ukraine: Perestroika to Independence* (New York: St. Martin's, 1994).
[32] Kravchuk, *Maemo Te*, pp. 13–20, 42–3. He reports his eyes were also opened after Ivashko assigned him to research a report on the Great Famine (p. 44).
[33] Author's interview with Sytnik, 1993.
[34] Motyl, *Dilemmas*, p. 44.
[35] *Izvestiia*, February 12, 1990, p. 2.
[36] Kravchuk, *Maemo Te*, pp. 55–6; *Pravda Ukrainy*, December 31, 1989, p. 1.

return from its economic activity.[37] These demands had broad support among Communists,[38] who also moved during this time to co-opt some of the most powerful themes and symbols involved in Ukrainians' sense of distinctiveness regarding the Russian-dominated USSR. One resolution condemned their own past leadership for the Great Famine of 1932–3, although spun it as a general crime against humanity, not against Ukrainians in particular.[39]

Some Ukrainian Communists, occasionally called "sovereign-communists" (*suveren-komunisty*), courted nationalist sentiments even more strongly than did Ivashko.[40] Kravchuk was among the leaders of this trend, urging greater organizational independence from the central Soviet party organization and cultivating sympathetic relationships with nationalists.[41] A call for "economic self-sufficiency of Ukraine" was also at the center of Kravchuk's efforts.[42] Kravchuk sought support in nationalist circles, although one passage in his memoirs captures the clever manipulation of ambiguity that he had to exercise to pull this off, a skill that Chapter 7 showed proved vital to his later success. This passage refers to an episode occurring right after his speech to the Rukh founding congress in November 1989, a speech made in his capacity as party "overseer" of the nationalist movement:

A woman walked up to me and stuck a little pin on the lapel of my suit jacket – it was a blue-and-yellow streamer with a trident [a Ukrainian nationalist symbol that had been banned by the USSR]. What could I do? A party apparatchik could not permit himself to keep the pin on. To take it off would mean issuing a challenge to the audience. On the spur of the moment, I made a decision: I would walk to my seat, take off my jacket, and hang it on the back of the chair. It all came off naturally – despite the fact that it was autumn outside, it was hot and humid in the hall – perhaps because of political passions. And when I was leaving the congress, I took my jacket in hand and walked out.[43]

When election day finally arrived in March 1990, 85 percent of the republic's citizens turned out to vote, and after a round of runoffs, the results dramatically reflected Ukraine's political cleavages.[44] Rukh managed to capture a quarter of the seats and then led the formation of the important parliamentary fraction[45] *Narodna Rada*[46] ("Popular Council"), whose strength insiders put at between 125 and 139 seats out of the 442 that had been filled through the first round of runoffs. The Communists formed the foundation for what became known as the Group of 239, an informal set of this many deputies who tended to vote together on key

---

[37] *Pravda Ukrainy*, February 24, 1990, p. 2.
[38] TASS (English), 2028 GMT, February 22, 1990, FBIS-SOV-90-037, February 23, 1990, p. 64.
[39] *Pravda Ukrainy*, February 7, 1990, p. 4.
[40] Kuchma, *Ukraiina – Ne Rosiia*, p. 406.
[41] Kravchuk, *Maemo Te*, pp. 43, 47.
[42] Kravchuk, *Maemo Te*, p. 46.
[43] Kravchuk, *Maemo Te*, pp. 22–3.
[44] *Sel'skaia Zhizn'*, March 13, 1990, p. 3.
[45] The standard term used for an officially registered parliamentary delegation.
[46] The term "Rada" used by itself refers to the Ukrainian parliament (Verkhovna Rada) and not the opposition bloc in the parliament known as Narodna Rada. "Rada" means "council" in Ukrainian.

issues.[47] Opposition nationalist candidates enjoyed even more success in city and district council elections since the Communist Party paid little attention to this set of elections.[48]

The Impact of the 1990 Rada Elections

The Rada elections and their results shaped Ukrainian political competition on issues of the union in four crucial ways. First, the campaign and postelection parliamentary sessions increased popular and elite awareness of Ukraine's troubled history with the union, raising the salience of national identification for assessing the risks involved. One Ukrainian general in the Soviet military later called this process "eye-opening" in leading him to support more autonomy for Ukraine.[49]

Second, the elections signaled a major shift of power from the party organization to the Rada. After the March 1990 elections, Ukraine's parliament was no longer a rubber stamp and had a new source of authority: voters. Many new members did not even belong to the party. Almost inevitably, decisions came to be made in the halls of the Rada building itself. The party still retained great influence within the Rada due to its majority. Accordingly, party leader Ivashko was voted in as Rada chairman in May.[50] But the party organization itself ceased to be the locus of decision making, and members began to exit it en masse.[51]

Third, the election results demonstrated that careers were best served if politicians actively cultivated doubts as to Moscow's trustworthiness and if they accordingly stressed the need for increased Ukrainian autonomy, particularly on economic issues. Many observers have interpreted this to mean that Ukrainian leaders, becoming aware of public preferences, merely pandered to this opinion while seeking votes. A more accurate interpretation is that politicians were less driven by public opinion itself than by their newly discovered *ability to shape and manipulate it* along certain lines to their own advantage, primarily by focusing attention on (framing) past and potential problems in Ukraine's relationship with Moscow, often with a national inflection. Politicians were ahead of the popular mood and were largely responsible for influencing it. But, crucially, they did so by first coming to recognize the *potential* for such a development. Leaders were thus simultaneously manipulating and responding to the masses.

The forces of Rukh, suddenly possessing an official parliamentary forum from which to make claims, now pushed separatist ones farthest and stressed economic issues in particular. If the movement had before the election been a cautious voice for increased autonomy, many of its leaders began publicly pushing for outright secession immediately after the election and called Gorbachev's plans for a

---

[47] Dominique Arel, "The Parliamentary Blocs in the Ukrainian Supreme Soviet: Who and What Do They Represent?" *Journal of Soviet Nationalities*, v.1, no.4, winter 1990–1, pp. 108–54, 108–9; Bojcun, "The Ukrainian Parliamentary," p. 229; *Izvestiia*, July 4, 1990, p. 3.

[48] Kravchuk, *Maemo Te*, p. 49.

[49] Morozov, *Above and Beyond*, p. 82.

[50] *Izvestiia*, May 30, 1990, p. 6.

[51] *Izvestiia*, June 19, 1990, p. 1.

"renewed federation" hypocritical.[52] Serhy Odarych, a chief campaign organizer, put it bluntly: "The aim of Rukh is independence for Ukraine."[53] The economic rationale was laid out by Chornovil, the man becoming the most prominent opposition figure and the most important Rukh leader. Ukraine required its own bank and its own currency as a form of protection before Ukraine could move decisively to a market economy, he averred.[54] In his run against Ivashko for leadership of the newly elected Rada in May 1990, Chornovil stated his platform thus: "I stand for the complete state independence of Ukraine as the only way out of the economic and spiritual catastrophe." Ukraine should also prepare, he said, for joining a "common European economic system."[55]

At the same time, Rukh leaders explicitly recognized that they were not *reflecting* public opinion but needed to *shape* it, bring out its *potential*, in order to realize their separatist strategy.[56] The chief editor of Rukh's newspaper *Narodna Hazeta* told a foreign interviewer: "Seriously, the national sentiment of our people is not on the level of, for instance, people in Lithuania. How can we ask for separation?"[57] Thus, Rukh's official platform and charter through much of 1990 reflected the population's own unwillingness to accept secession as a viable strategy for dealing with the risk of exploitation in the union, pursuing instead a sovereign Ukraine under the wing of the Soviet Union.[58]

The 1990 elections also inspired the Ukrainian Communist Party's platform to mobilize nascent nationalist sentiment more vigorously in competition with Rukh, though it saw no potential benefit in advocating actual secession. Communists observed the nationalists' strong election performance, especially in the West where the communists were roundly defeated.[59] They also noted that those communists who had flirted the most with nationalist ideas tended to win by larger margins. Most striking was the comparison between the moderately pro-autonomy Ivashko and Kravchuk, who as party ideologist was more openly courting nationalist sentiment and Rukh supporters. Ivashko required a runoff to gain his Rada seat, yet Kravchuk sailed to victory in a single round despite concerted Rukh efforts to defeat him.[60]

This Communist Party realization generated change in official Ukrainian relations with the union. Ivashko started sounding more like Kravchuk. Facing a

---

[52] *Literaturnaia Gazeta*, no.15, April 11, 1990, p. 3; Paris AFP in English, 1451 GMT, March 12, 1990, FBIS-SOV-90-049, March 13, 1990, p. 104.

[53] Paris AFP in English, 1159 GMT, March 29, 1990, FBIS-SOV-90-056, March 22, 1990, p. 102.

[54] Kyiv International Service in Ukrainian, 1800 GMT, May 28, 1990, FBIS-SOV-90-104, May 30, 1990, p. 103.

[55] Kyiv International Service (English), 2300 GMT, May 30, 1990, FBIS-CHI-90-105, May 31, 1990, p. 93.

[56] For example, Chornovil in *Komsomolskaia Pravda*, May 15, 1990, p. 1.

[57] *Mlada Fronta* (Prague, in Czech), April 5, 1990, p. 5, FBIS-SOV-90-070, pp. 126–7.

[58] *Izvestiia*, October 25, 1990, p. 2.

[59] Arel, "The Parliamentary Blocs," p. 124.

[60] Kravchuk, *Maemo Te*, p. 50; Kyiv in English to Europe, 1900 GMT, March 5, 1990, FBIS-SOV-90-044, March 6, 1990, p. 109; Moscow Domestic Service in Russian, 1900 GMT, March 6, 1990, FBIS-SOV-90-045, March 7, 1990, pp. 112–13.

Rada vote to elect him its chairman, Ivashko now stressed the supremacy of Ukrainian law over union law and the need for Ukraine to be an international actor in its own right.[61] He gave particular emphasis to the economic reasons for autonomy, as in a postelection speech to party leaders where he declared that the chief strategy for "building an effective economy, ensuring high living standards, maximum social and economic protection," was "the republic's transition to economic sovereignty and independence."[62] This context helps frame Chapter 6's description of Ivashko's sharp postelection reaction to unpopular Soviet economic policies.

The realization that pro-autonomy themes could help the communists electorally also facilitated Kravchuk's rise to the chairmanship of the Rada. Thus, in June 1990 when Ivashko ceded his post as Ukrainian Communist Party first secretary to Hurenko, Kravchuk was promoted to Hurenko's old post of second secretary. Then, when Ivashko resigned the Rada chairmanship to become second secretary of the CPSU in July 1990, it was Kravchuk rather than Hurenko who took his place at the Rada helm. Although some mystery remains as to why Hurenko pulled out of the Rada vote on Ivashko's successor, Kravchuk's viability clearly had something to do with the sense in the party that his star was rising, having developed a politically promising combination of communist and nationalist rhetoric. Kravchuk proceeded consciously to build up the Rada's authority at the expense of the party organization.[63]

Now at Ukraine's helm, Kravchuk guided his republic toward ever more skeptical attitudes on Gorbachev's union-saving attempts between July 1990 and April 1991. The new Ukrainian leader later wrote that the 1990 elections not only helped him politically as a vessel of more nationalistic ideas but first awakened in him the dream of an independent Ukraine. He notes, however, that he believed this dream was ahead of its time and did not know when it would have a chance to come about.[64] Indeed, as Chapter 6 showed, he did not come actually to advocate Ukrainian independence until after the August 1991 coup, since prior to that time full independence was seen as an impossible solution to the collective action problem in the union and since Gorbachev was proposing another reasonable solution in the Novo-Ogarevo process of April–August 1991.

The fourth major immediate consequence of the March 1990 elections was to create a new Ukrainian parliament with institutional rules that promoted compromise between Rukh and the Communist-led Group of 239. These rules influenced exactly how Ukraine's official leadership responded to and shaped public opinion in the process of developing policy regarding the republic's relationship with the union between May 1990 (when it first convened) and December 1991, when a directly elected presidency was created. Rada rules gave Rukh and its

[61] Kyiv International Service in English, 2300 GMT May 29, 1990, FBIS-SOV-90-105, May 31, 1990, pp. 92–3.
[62] Kyiv International Service in English, 2330 GMT, March 31, 1990, FBIS-SOV-90-063, April 2, 1990, pp. 107–8.
[63] Kravchuk, *Maemo Te*, p. 66.
[64] Kravchuk, *Maemo Te*, p. 102.

Narodna Rada fraction two main avenues of influence despite their minority status. First, a quorum rule initially allowed Narodna Rada activists to sabotage votes by simply vacating the hall, although by the end of November the Group of 239 had managed to alter the rule.[65] Second, because legislation had to come out of parliamentary commissions and there were no rules restricting deputies from joining any commission they wanted, Narodna Rada could flood its priority commissions with members in order to influence them. They thus streamed into the meeting rooms for the commissions on state sovereignty, foreign policy, education, and the Chernobyl disaster. Rukh's opponents responded in kind, producing some rather unwieldy commissions.[66]

Legislators from the conservative Group of 239 were also at a disadvantage because more of them than of the opposition were not career parliamentarians, instead holding other important jobs along with their Rada seats. Future Ukrainian president Kuchma, for example, was not only a parliamentary deputy but also director of the military-industrial giant Yuzhmash. In fact, half of the full-time deputies (those working on parliamentary committees on a regular basis) were from the opposition.[67]

By virtue of these factors, members of Narodna Rada came to chair a significant share of parliamentary commissions.[68] These institutional features and Narodna Rada's strategies effectively forced the communists and Rukh to compromise and work together in the Rada, as was the case in adopting the republic's sovereignty declaration in July 1990.[69]

This institutionally induced balance of power in the Rada helps explain Ukraine's seeming reluctance to take an unequivocal position on the New Union Treaty, especially during 1990. The chairman of Ukraine's Sovereignty Commission, charged with developing Rada policy on the treaty process, later reported that negotiations on the New Union Treaty simply deadlocked. Yet the deadlock was not the result of a fundamental disagreement over whether Ukraine should sign *any* New Union Treaty but the result of disagreement over *what kind of union* Ukraine should agree to. In fact, both major groupings in the Rada Sovereignty Commission were working on a draft union treaty that Ukraine would present to the union for consideration during the fall of 1990. But the process of compromise was slow, and the commission had not finished its draft treaty before Gorbachev proposed and published his own in late November. Caught flatfooted, the Rada committee put off its own discussion and prioritized the adoption of a new constitution while Kravchuk and the leaders of other republics took the initiative in reacting to Gorbachev's union treaty proposals.[70]

---

[65] *Izvestiia*, November 21, 1990, p. 2; *Vidomosti Verkhovnoi Rady Ukraiins'koi RSR*, 1990, no.28, pp. 554–5.

[66] Author's interview with Shulha.

[67] D'Anieri, Kravchuk, and Kuzio, *Politics and Society in Ukraine*, p. 23.

[68] Kataryna Wolczuk, *The Moulding of Ukraine: The Constitutional Politics of State Formation* (Budapest: Central European University Press, 2001), pp. 69, 97.

[69] Author's interview with Shulha.

[70] Author's interview with Shulha.

This sheds light on many of the positions Kravchuk took in 1990–1. For one thing, he was not being disingenuous in insisting that Ukraine was in support of a union at the same time that he refused to commit himself firmly to any particular version of it. Indeed, this Rada deadlock helps explain Ukraine's policy that it would not commit itself to a union before it hammered out its own new constitution – this was not simply a "stalling tactic" designed to subvert the union.[71] Additionally, Kravchuk's insistence that Ukraine's sovereignty declaration be the basis for any future union decision reflected the fact that the sovereignty declaration was the only major substantive policy on a future union that Ukraine's Rada had been able to agree on. And crucially, the sovereignty declaration was explicitly to be the *basis* for a future and greatly decentralized union, not a rejection of any future union.

Ukraine's forces in the Rada thus agreed on two principles to guide its future relationship with the union. First, Ukraine would be willing to sign onto a union of some kind.[72] Second, this union should involve a great deal of economic decentralization, with the union remaining a "common market space" in terms of economics. Thus, even the communists on the Sovereignty Commission were supporting a system of "single-channel taxation" by which the union government would collect no taxes of its own; republics would gather all taxes and would then designate a certain amount for union structures. This was held necessary to save the Ukrainian economy from poor central policies and the economic radicalism of Yeltsin's Russia.[73] The key disagreement between the Group of 239 and Narodna Rada was primarily over issues of status, such as whether the reformed union should be considered a subject of international law with its own citizenship or whether the union should be considered primarily the sum of its parts with a few necessary central institutions. They also disagreed on what guarantees should be in place to prevent the union from collapsing in a future crisis.[74]

Overall, Ukraine's official reactions to Gorbachev's initiatives between May 1990 and August 1991 can be seen as representing a rough but important aggregation of mass interests through the institution of the Rada. First, a coordination problem (not a roadblock) in the Rada accounts for Ukrainian authorities' failure to present a draft treaty or a fixed position on the union to the working group Gorbachev created to start the New Union Treaty process in summer 1990. Second, the fact that the disagreement in the Rada was not about economic autonomy, on which most agreed, explains how Ukraine's leaders could publicly support a union at the same time that its parliament could easily adopt its own

---

[71] And contrary to a widespread perception, this policy (by which Ukraine made the New Union Treaty conditional on the adoption of its new constitution) was adopted not as a result of massive October 1990 popular protests, but prior to these protests. Rada leaders did somewhat manipulatively present it as a concession to protesters, however. See Moroz, *Kudy Idemo?*, p. 71; Obrashchenie Prezidiuma Verkhovnogo Soveta Ukrainskoi SSR k grazhdanam respubliki, "K soglasiiu i edinstvu deistvii vo imia interesov vsego naroda Ukrainy," *Vedomosti Verkhovnogo Soveta Ukrainskoi SSR*, no.41, 1990, p. 751.

[72] Increasing numbers of Rukh members, however, came to oppose any such signature as time passed.

[73] Author's interview with Shulha.

[74] Author's interview with Shulha.

marketization plan in late 1990.[75] Third, the sovereignty declaration's status as the sole policy statement regarding the union on which Rada agreement had been reached illuminates Ukrainian officials' dogged reference to this document when rejecting or deferring judgment on particular treaty proposals or when crafting their own "Ukrainian question" for the March 1991 referendum. Fourth, the broad agreement that the union involved a danger of exploitation reveals why all major political coalitions in Ukraine increased their skepticism of the union in the face of arbitrary and unpopular central policies like the currency confiscations and crackdowns on the Baltic republics in January 1991. Fifth, all this deepens our understanding of Kravchuk's change in attitude with the April–August 1991 "multilateral stage" of Gorbachev's New Union Treaty negotiations: The version of the union on offer was not only explicitly recognizing Ukraine's sovereignty declaration, but accommodating Ukraine's near-consensus demand for a high degree of economic policy-making autonomy.

Thus, before recessing for its summer 1991 break, both a new Ukrainian constitution and a New Union Treaty appeared not to be far from adoption. The Rada ordered that a draft constitution be presented when its next session began, in early September. Accordingly, it left an official stance on the summer 1991 drafts of the New Union Treaty for the fall. The Rada did, however, order its permanent commissions to study the latest of these drafts. The republic Council of Ministers and Academy of Sciences were called upon to prepare economic calculations and to give legal advice regarding the entrance of Ukraine into the union. A working group, chosen by the Presidium, was then to sum up the proposals and comments of these organs and the people's deputies by September 15, 1991.[76]

Kravchuk's Shift to a Secession-Facilitating Frame

The failed August 1991 coup launched Ukraine into a hotly contested referendum campaign on independence. Union forces, most notably Gorbachev, called on Ukrainians to forego secession, citing the risk of a Yugoslav-style war in the former USSR and the economic benefits of unity. Ukrainian authorities, controlling local media, barraged republic voters with arguments for "independence." But why did Ukrainian authorities opt for the "independence" frame instead of the "unionist" one since Chapter 7 showed that both could likely have won a majority?

The answer lies largely in Ukraine's other campaign of late 1991: the presidential contest. The Rada had previously scheduled Ukraine's first presidential election for December 1, 1991, and so scheduled the independence referendum

---

[75] *Izvestiia*, October 29, 1990, p. 2; *Izvestiia*, November 1, 1990, p. 2; *Izvestiia*, December 26, 1990, p. 7; *Izvestiia*, December 26, 1990, p. 7.

[76] Postanovlenie Verkhovnogo Soveta Ukrainskoi SSR, "O proekte Dogovora o Soiuze Suverennykh Gosudarstv, predstavlennom Prezidentom SSSR," *Vedomosti Verkhovnogo Soveta Ukrainskoi SSR*, 1991, no.28, p. 884; *Vedomosti Verkhovnogo Soveta Ukrainskoi SSR*, 1991, no.28, p. 767.

for the same day. Kravchuk was running hard for the presidency, and his only serious rivals were on the nationalist side of the political spectrum, with Chornovil the
most popular among them. Had Kravchuk not pursued the secessionist framing
strategy, instead promoting a unionist frame, Chornovil would have become the
leading candidate seeking to mobilize the separatist frame. While Chornovil had
limited resources for imposing such a frame, the law did guarantee him television
campaign airtime, and he possessed large and highly motivated volunteer networks of supporters. And crucially, all of the survey results presented in Chapter
7 showed that during fall 1991 *the majority that would have supported "independence"
in a referendum was larger than the majority that would have supported a union.* This
is because the coup had deeply undermined the chances that the union would be
cooperative, not exploitative, and because Ukraine was at a sufficiently high level
of development to warrant avoiding the newly heightened risk of exploitation
that the union now involved. For Kravchuk to have clung to a unionist frame
in such circumstances would have been risky since it would have opened a door
for his rivals to gain control of the potentially most powerful available frame, the
moderate separatist one. Better for Kravchuk, then, to seize control of the most
politically promising frame himself and to ensure his election as Ukraine's first
president.

UZBEKISTAN: THE POLITICS OF UNION IN A LESS-DEVELOPED REPUBLIC

Uzbekistan's leadership also acted according to the economic interests of its population in the union, although in a different way. For one thing, Uzbek interests
were different. Whereas Ukraine was relatively developed economically and thus
its population and leaders were willing to bear less risk of exploitation in a union,
Uzbekistan was less developed and thus its masses and top officials had more to
gain from the union in terms of economic development, making them willing to
accept a greater risk of exploitation in that union. Uzbekistan's political system
was also less contested than Ukraine's, although this itself was not the source of
Uzbek unionism. Even the republic's banned nationalist opposition did not take
so separatist a stand as did Ukraine's main opposition, Rukh. Thus, even though
Karimov was bound less tightly to public opinion in Uzbekistan than Kravchuk
was in Ukraine, public opinion worked in concert with his own personal political
and economic interests to generate consistently more unionism in 1990 and 1991
than Ukraine manifested.

With Gorbachev helping to enforce democratization in the republics, opposition movements were able to express different views on the union in Uzbekistan in 1990–1. Most observers consider Birlik ("unity"), Erk ("freedom"), and
the Islamic Renaissance Party to have been the most important nongovernmen-
tal movements in the republic at the time. Birlik was by far the best known
and enjoyed the strongest following, generally calling for greater democracy
and stronger nationalist policies. Its leaders tended to be more vociferous than
others, including Karimov, in stressing the dangers of political association with

Russia. At the same time, Birlik's leadership believed that an independent Uzbekistan would jeopardize democratic development, another of its stated goals.[77] In early 1990, one faction of Birlik split off to form its own popular movement, Erk.[78] This new movement has often been regarded as a moderate version of Birlik, as it also sought greater economic and political autonomy for Uzbekistan, although less stridently.[79] Erk, like Birlik, also generally forewent demands for actual secession and generally restricted itself to calls for economic and political sovereignty for Uzbekistan within the framework of a renewed Soviet federation.[80] Many observers have cited the Islamic Renaissance Party as a source of potentially powerful fundamentalist opposition, but it appears to have had little support in Uzbekistan, although there were some reports that it was popular in the traditionally more devout Ferghana Valley region of the country.[81] In any case, it seems to have been concerned mostly with the revival of local Islamic culture rather than the establishment of an Iranian-style Islamic republic.[82] Karimov generally allowed these movements little autonomy, although he did not mobilize a great deal of state power to repress them at first. Erk and Birlik both had members who had made it into the republic parliament in the 1990 elections and at times used these posts to voice opposition claims.

One could also find a variety of views on the union, including perspectives that differed from official Uzbek policy, within the intellectual establishment of Uzbekistan. For example, the Uzbek press featured significant debate on the New Union Treaty during 1990–1. In a pair of roundtable discussions printed in a Russian-language newspaper, a senior fellow, Bahtiar Karimov, did not even object when he was accused of favoring the "collapse" of the USSR, although he qualified this to mean that he still supported a "confederation."[83] Other publications, such as an Uzbek-language newspaper from the city of Samarkand, printed criticism of the New Union Treaty that was more measured and hence more in line with official views: Isoqjon Saidahmedov, a USSR parliamentary deputy from Samarkand, for example, stated that a union treaty was necessary like air and water but that the current draft needed to clarify further the division of powers between the center and the republics. It also should be concluded by the republics themselves, not simply handed down to the republics by Moscow, he averred.[84] Some quite radical claims could certainly be found, including that the New Union

---

[77] Shirin Akiner, "The Struggle for Identity," in Jed C. Snyder, ed., *After Empire: The Emerging Geopolitics of Central Asia* (Ft. McNair, Washington, DC: National Defense University Press, October 1995), pp. 3–36, 15.

[78] Some see this split as fostered by Uzbek authorities: Andrew Wilson, *Virtual Politics: Faking Democracy in the Post-Soviet World* (New Haven, CT: Yale University Press, 2005).

[79] TASS (English), 1321 GMT, February 27, 1990, FBIS-SOV-90-040, p. 103.

[80] TASS International Service, 1110 GMT, March 8, 1990, FBIS-SOV-90-090, p. 103.

[81] James Rupert, "Dateline Tashkent: Post-Soviet Central Asia," *Foreign Policy*, no.87, summer 1992, p. 188.

[82] Robin Wright, "Islam, Democracy and the West," *Foreign Affairs*, v.71, no.3, summer 1992, p. 141.

[83] *Molodezh' Uzbekistana*, February 2, 1991, pp. 1–2; *Molodezh' Uzbekistana*, May 4, 1991, p. 2.

[84] *Lenin Yo'li* (Samarkand), January 10, 1991, p. 1.

Treaty should be treated as an international agreement; that the center had deliberately inserted logical inconsistencies into the draft as a divide-and-rule tactic; that Uzbekistan needed its own currency; and that the union presidency should be a rotating one, whereby each republic head would serve for one year.[85] In some ways, then, the popular debate in the Uzbek press was not dissimilar to that found in Ukraine as of the first half of 1991. But Ukraine's debate was much more vigorous, and pro-independence voices were more audible.

With Karimov's personal material interests coinciding in the most general sense with others' expressions of republic interests on the question of the union, he consistently based his reactions to Gorbachev's initiatives on three principal goals: gaining autonomy, obtaining subsidies, and preserving union economic ties. Uzbekistan's pursuit of greater autonomy in response to Soviet policies over the course of 1990–1 was analyzed in detail in Chapter 6 and will not be repeated here. What does bear treatment is the degree to which Uzbekistan's relative underdevelopment informed these autonomy-seeking actions and was used to justify them at the same time that it motivated Uzbek leaders not to carry the pursuit of autonomy too far. Uzbekistan's three principal goals will be briefly discussed in this light before we see how the republic's economic interests converged to lead Karimov toward a unionist rather than separatist framing strategy during the crucial period after the August 1991 coup attempt.

Gaining Autonomy

Uzbekistan's relative underdevelopment was key to informing and justifying republic officials' autonomy-seeking actions in response to Soviet policies during 1990–1. In the leadership's narrative, Uzbekistan had experienced both economic development and economic exploitation in the Soviet regime. On one hand, Uzbekistan had surely gained in terms of economic development, far outpacing neighboring regions that remained outside the union (i.e., Afghanistan). On the other hand, Uzbekistan still remained underdeveloped relative to other republics in the union. Even more crucially, Soviet-style development had produced a serious distortion of the Uzbek economy in the form of the cotton monoculture and the more general focus on raw materials. This was all explicitly recognized by Uzbek leaders at their republic party organization's congress in June 1990.[86]

In these conditions of relative underdevelopment and economic distortion, Uzbek leaders presented autonomy as meaning two essential things. First, it would give republic authorities a chance to reshape their economy, making it more balanced and less focused on natural resource production.[87] The platform of the Uzbek SSR Communist Party, prepared for the 28th Congress of the CPSU in summer 1990, thus came out in strong support of "economic independence."

---

[85] Critchlow, *Nationalism in Uzbekistan*, pp. 21–3.
[86] *Pravda Vostoka*, June 9, 1990, p. 1.
[87] Author's interview with an official of the CIS division of the Ministry of Foreign Affairs of Uzbekistan, September 16, 1993.

This term, it declared, meant fundamentally changing the structure of the Uzbek economy, striving to ensure that its raw material resources were processed inside the republic.[88] Second, Uzbek leaders argued that their low levels of economic development (their disadvantageous "starting position") rendered their republic more vulnerable than other republics to rapid marketization policies, especially those that would sharply raise prices or cripple large state-owned employers.[89] Thus, by the end of 1990, Uzbekistan's parliament had passed a resolution calling for a gradual transition to a market economy, trying to avoid sharp price hikes and mass unemployment. The prime minister concurrently declared it "impossible to carry out" central government proposals that did not consider the peculiarities of socioeconomic development in each republic.[90] The republic even imposed restrictions on goods it exported to other republics in spring 1990, arguing this was necessary to keep products available locally and to prevent shelves from emptying during the transition to the market.[91] Autonomy, then, would allow Uzbekistan to add balance to its economy while shielding it from marketization policies thought capable of generating unrest and desperation in the relatively underdeveloped republic.

Obtaining Subsidies

Uzbek leaders also had strong reason to moderate their autonomy demands lest they find their republic deprived of vital subsidies it enjoyed in the union. According to the International Monetary Fund, Uzbekistan received net union transfers worth 9.4 percent of its GDP in 1989, and this figure grew to 19.4 percent in 1990 and 18.5 percent in 1991.[92] Most of this aid was intended to pay for social protection measures and development needs, two of Uzbek leaders' top concerns given the associated risks of unrest and the prospects of political reward.[93] Thus, when Uzbek experts proposed their own draft New Union Treaty to Gorbachev's working group at the start of the negotiation process in 1990, one clause actually would have obligated the union to "equalize" the levels of socioeconomic development of the different republics. It also would have charged the USSR with environmental protection, effectively making the union as a whole responsible for the ecological disasters that befell Uzbekistan during the Soviet period, such as the decimation of the Aral Sea.[94]

The Uzbek president consistently advocated these concerns over the next year, urging the union to coordinate and direct efforts to solve major regional

---

[88] *Pravda Vostoka*, June 9, 1990, p. 1.

[89] Moscow Television Service 1430 GMT, June 6, 1990 FBIS-SOV-90-118, p. 118.

[90] *Nezavisimaia Gazeta*, November 2, 1990, p. 2.

[91] *Sel'skaia Pravda* (Uzbekistan), May 6, 1990, p. 2; *Pravda Vostoka*, April 28, 1990, p. 1, FBIS-CHI-90-105, p. 103; *Izvestiia* June 1, 1990, p. 6, FBIS-SOV-90-108, p. 103.

[92] International Monetary Fund, *Uzbekistan*, IMF Economic Reviews, v.4 (Washington, DC: International Monetary Fund, March 1994), p. 41.

[93] Ibid., p. 16.

[94] Document, copy in possession of the author.

socioeconomic problems, including demographic and environmental ones.[95] Such language referred to the Aral Sea and the unemployment of Uzbekistan's rapidly growing youth population, which was disproportionately concentrated in the volatile Ferghana Valley. Indeed, the USSR under Brezhnev had planned a "subsidy" of unprecedented scale in the form of a gargantuan project to divert one of Siberia's major rivers southward so as to irrigate the region and replenish the Aral. Ecology experts and Russian nationalists ultimately derailed the project, and even though Central Asian leaders raised the proposal again repeatedly under Gorbachev, he never backed it.[96] Despite this setback, Karimov clearly recognized the benefit of retaining and possibly expanding subsidies and explicit development support in a union.

Preserving Union Ties

Uzbekistan's leadership placed a high priority on maintaining broader economic ties with the union as well, seeing them as crucial for Uzbekistan's long-term development prospects, and this was another important constraint on incentives to claim autonomy. According to Karimov in an interview with a German publication in March 1991:

> After sober analysis of the situation in Uzbekistan . . . we have come to the view that our republic's best prospects lie in a renewed federation. I would like to give you just two figures: The per-capita national income in Uzbekistan is not only three times lower than in the Baltic states, but it is also only half of the union average. The republic has a completely underdeveloped, one-sided economy. We are mainly deliverers of raw material, and even the existing processing industry provides mostly only intermediate products. A total of 92 percent of all Uzbek cotton fibers are not processed in our country. On the other hand, we have to import more than half of the goods needed by the population.[97]

The informally recognized head of Uzbekistan's major Tashkent political machine who later challenged Karimov's leadership, Council of Ministers Chairman Shukurulla Mirsaidov, concurred in June 1990 that the economy was paramount in making decisions on the union:

> The main thing is how we are going to provide for the prosperity of working people. If the prosperity of working people is going to be ensured at an accelerated rate within the framework of a federation, we back a federation; if in the framework of a confederation, we back a confederation; if in the framework of interstate relations, we back interstate relations.[98]

Some of Mirsaidov's other statements show that he in fact believed the best avenue to pursue Uzbek prosperity was to remain in a union, albeit a decentralized

[95] *Izvestiia*, January 28, 1991, p. 3.
[96] Thane Gustafson, *Reform in Soviet Politics: Lessons of Recent Policies on Land and Water* (New York: Cambridge University Press, 1981).
[97] *Berliner Zeitung*, March 5, 1991, p. 3, FBIS-SOV-91-051, pp. 84–6.
[98] Moscow Television Service, 1700 GMT, June 20, 1990, FBIS-SOV-90-120, p. 119.

one.[99] Even though one must take with a grain of salt politicians' stated commitment to the welfare of average people, it remains clear that economic concerns were largely guiding republic strategies on the union issue and that these were prioritized in public rhetoric over purely cultural or ethnic issues.

Denouement: The Coup and the Fall of 1991

These economic and political imperatives converged to lead Karimov to select a "unionist" frame in fall 1991, even though a majority could likely have been manufactured in support of "independence" as in Ukraine. As with Kravchuk, fall 1991 represented a crucial moment at which Karimov had a chance to consolidate his own power. But Karimov's battle was not primarily with opponents in a presidential election, as was Kravchuk's. Instead, Karimov worried most of all about the interrelated threats of popular rioting and the opposition of the republic's major regionally based political machines. These concerns were interrelated because provincial machines can manipulate or even instigate unrest as tactics in political struggle, especially when people can be made to feel they have genuine cause to engage in this unrest. Especially dangerous to the career of a leader like Karimov could be an alliance between leading regional machines and an opposition party capable of articulating a coherent message that would resonate beyond any one region.

Karimov reacted to this vulnerability by cracking down on the opposition while seeking public support, support that could provide him with an important political resource should his crackdown meet serious resistance. It must be recalled that Karimov was initially a weak leader, a novice to republic politics who was installed by Gorbachev from outside to seal a compromise among Uzbekistan's leading provincial machines. The most prominent among these machines was the Tashkent network headed by Mirsaidov, who was made Karimov's prime minister before becoming the Uzbek republic's vice president in late 1990. The August 1991 coup attempt threatened to upset the delicate coalition, sealed by Gorbachev, that had kept Karimov in power. Carlisle reports that Karimov had been in India when the crisis broke, which meant that his deputies formulated the republic's initial reaction to the coup. Thus, while Karimov returned home immediately, the vice president had time to introduce some emergency measures that appeared to support the Moscow coup plotters. The coup's failure undermined Mirsaidov's position, and Karimov stealthily moved to weaken him after that, although Karimov was not confident enough to finish the job until 1992.[100] Karimov also used the failed coup to justify a crackdown on Birlik, which he asserted posed a threat of instability in the republic.[101] A clear victory in Uzbekistan's first direct presidential elections, scheduled for late December 1991, would

---

[99] *Izvestiia*, April 1, 1990, p. 2, FBIS-SOV-90-065, p. 88; Moscow Domestic Service, 1500 GMT, March 27, 1990, FBIS-SOV-90-060, p. 118.
[100] Carlisle, "Islom Karimov."
[101] *Komsomolskaia Pravda*, August 27, 1991, p. 2.

seal his new authority by allowing him to claim a direct popular mandate. Yet he had to be sure that the political machines he depended upon for delivering the vote did not defect to Mirsaidov, Birlik, or some other coalition that could emerge. Making this risky power grab, Karimov saw the benefit of maintaining maximum public support lest Mirsaidov or Birlik gain a resource they could use to attract enough other allies (such as other provincial political machines) to unseat Karimov before he could consolidate his authority.

Given the economic considerations described earlier, Karimov calculated that his best political prospects lay with continuing to support the union and thus chose a unionist rather than a separatist strategy in the crucial fall of 1991. As described in Chapter 7, Uzbekistan's leadership felt compelled to adopt a declaration of independence both to signal the new autonomy it would demand from a new union and to gain bargaining power in negotiations for this new union. But this declaration actually contained promises of a future union, including "a unified economic space in the Union."[102] Indeed, Karimov's team actively emphasized that this form of independence did not mean a sharp or radical break with the union economy, even when it came to promising an eventual Uzbek currency – talk was only about protecting Uzbekistan's economic interests while preserving mutually profitable union ties.[103]

After Uzbekistan had adopted its independence declaration, Gorbachev and his aides scrambled to preserve some kind of union structures that would be acceptable to as many republics as possible in the post-putsch context. True to the economic roots of its unionism, Uzbekistan was enthusiastic about the economic community (EC) that Gorbachev initiated in fall 1991. Even though Karimov stressed that this EC should have only "coordinative–managerial" rather than "executive" institutions, he signed the treaty, declaring: "Time is pressing."[104] Karimov continued to participate in negotiations with Gorbachev and some other republic leaders to salvage some kind of New Union Treaty. Indeed, he made both a free confederation of sovereign states and a uniform economic system central positions of the People's Democratic Party of Uzbekistan, the successor to the republic Communist Party that Karimov founded after the August coup attempt.[105]

Accordingly, Uzbekistan's leadership gave up on the New Union Treaty only after other republics, notably Ukraine, had killed it. Uzbekistan was not invited to the fateful summit outside Minsk where the presidents of Ukraine, Russia, and Belarus conspired to liquidate the USSR in December 1991. Once presented with the fait accompli, Karimov acquiesced and voiced support for the CIS that supplanted the union. By the time Uzbekistan's referendum on "independence"

---

[102] Postanovlenie Verkhovnogo Soveta Respubliki Uzbekistan, "O provozglashenii gosudarstvennoi nezavisimosti Respubliki Uzbekistan," *Vedomosti Verkhovnogo Soveta Uzbekskoi SSR*, 1991, no.11, st.245, pp. 68–9.

[103] *Molodezh' Uzbekistana*, September 17, 1991, p. 1.

[104] Moscow Central Television First Program Network, 1522 GMT, October 18, 1991, FBIS-SOV-91-203, pp. 37–41; *Nezavisimaia Gazeta*, October 2, 1991, p. 1.

[105] Interfax, 1145 GMT, November 1, 1991, pp. 83–4.

and presidential elections took place on December 29, 1991, Gorbachev had already resigned and almost all union institutions had effectively disappeared or been taken over by Russia.

The fall 1991 political situation, therefore, drove Karimov to choose a unionist strategy for Uzbekistan where it led Kravchuk to pursue a separatist one for Ukraine. The primary force tying Karimov to public opinion then was the uncertainty surrounding his risky grab for power in the wake of the bungled coup, which had upset the balance among regional political machines that had previously been the basis of Karimov's power as a compromise leader. A popular mandate would help seal his political victory, a victory that was still uncertain that autumn and that still could have been thwarted by a coalition of regional machines manipulating the republic's poverty to facilitate rioting. The mandate would be stronger if perceived to be genuine, so Karimov did allow the moderate opposition Erk to register as a party and nominate a prominent nationalist poet for president, Mukhammed Solih.[106] Karimov kept for himself the winning side of the most pressing issue, his call for preserving the union with greater economic guarantees for Uzbekistan in the form of autonomy, subsidies, and continued economic ties with the union. These positions were strong because of Uzbekistan's relative underdevelopment, which meant its leaders and masses perceived more to lose from secession than did Ukraine's. Thus, even though media coverage and campaign resources heavily advantaged Karimov, the elections did feature some credible opposition with high name recognition. Solih even held Karimov to just 40 percent of the vote in Solih's home province of Khorezm.[107] But the more powerful nationalist opposition group, Birlik, was denied registration as a party and thus could not nominate its own candidate for president.[108] Karimov thus won the December 29 presidential contest with 86 percent of the vote, leaving only 12 percent for Solih, according to the official count.[109] The referendum on Uzbekistan's unionist version of independence, now moot, passed with over 98 percent of the ballots.

CONCLUSION

We have now reached a satisfactory solution to the puzzle of comparative secessionism in the USSR, one demonstrating the advantages of the relational theory of separatism over ethnicity-as-conflictual and ethnicity-as-epiphenomenal approaches. For one thing, there is clearly a link between ethnic divides and separatism that is hard for ethnicity-as-epiphenomenal theories to explain. Not only did the study of Ukraine find ethnic identification correlated with individuals' support for separatism, but those republics not associated with a major sense of ethnic distinctiveness vis-à-vis Russians were among the least separatist.

---

[106] Interfax, 1415 GMT, August 29, 1991, FBIS-SOV-91-169, p. 130.
[107] *Narodnoe Slovo*, January 1, 1992, no.1, p. 2.
[108] Interfax, 1415 GMT, August 29, 1991, FBIS-SOV-91-169, p. 130.
[109] *Narodnoe Slovo*, January 1, 1992, no.1, p. 2. Erk and Birlik charged that irregularities took place.

Moreover, evidence does not indicate that ethnicity was merely acting as a coordination mechanism for the pursuit and selective distribution of resources. At the same time, evidence confounds the expectation of ethnicity-as-conflictual theory that ethnic divides inherently tend to generate separatism. Nationally conscious groups sometimes advocate unionism, and this is true even when they have the opportunity to push for political independence and even when the union is in growing economic and political dysfunction. Additionally, the present chapter has shown that people actually ranked cultural and national concerns as much lower priorities than material welfare, and that economic considerations lay at the heart of Ukraine's separatism and Uzbekistan's unionism.

The key role of national consciousness was thus not to supply a motive but to provide a psychological uncertainty-reduction mechanism that exacerbated an ethnofederal commitment problem, a problem that could be mitigated either by seceding or by restructuring the union. Even though individual leaders often had the power to frame the commitment problem in ways that could generate a popular referendum mandate either in favor of or against "independence" as a strategy for overcoming the commitment problem, a finding in tension with rival theories, they did not make such decisions in a vacuum. Instead, the present chapter has shown that leaders having at least some interest in responding to important components of popular opinion had incentive to respond to perceived economic interests of their republics' masses. Ukraine's leader reacted largely owing to electoral competition, while Uzbekistan's did so due to its leader's transitional vulnerability to powerful regional political machines. Economic considerations were at the forefront of people's concerns during the period of Soviet reform, so leaders had special incentive to respond to them because their own public support and personal fortunes would benefit from increasing their republics' overall economic standing.

There no doubt was major disagreement as to exactly how the economy should be improved in all republics. This chapter has shown that there was more reason for relatively underdeveloped regions' masses and leaders to have believed they would benefit from a future union than there was for the more-developed ones. This primarily reflects the perception that the most-developed regions of the USSR were less likely to make qualitative leaps in development through association with the union than were the least-developed regions. Thus, as the perceived risks associated with staying in the union spiked and the coercive power of that union collapsed due to the August 1991 coup attempt in Moscow, Uzbekistan's leadership proved more willing than Ukraine's to tolerate the newly assessed risk of union exploitation and less willing to take advantage of the newly lowered expected costs of secession. Leaders' framing strategies matter, but more fundamental are the underlying mass and elite interests (particularly material interests) that work through institutions and lead officials to select from among different potentially winning frames. We thus see one very specific example of how ethnicity is about uncertainty reduction, yet ethnic politics is fundamentally about interests.

9

Ethnicity and International Integration

The CIS 1991–2007

Why have some Soviet successor states been more insistent on preserving their independence, while others have looked more favorably on reintegration proposals? This question touches on a bigger debate in the study of international relations (IR) over how or whether international integration is possible. The theory of separatism developed formally in Chapter 4 suggests that the logic of integrating independent states is not fundamentally different from the logic of integrating regions in an ethnofederal union. In both cases, the core problem is a collective action problem: All units (be they countries or regions) could potentially gain from integration, but once a union is created, the most powerful units within it also face incentives to exploit the others. Just as with regions and separatism, any particular country's attitude to integration with another country is likely to depend on how the collective action problem is understood. These understandings will be influenced in both cases by (1) the degree to which thick ethnic distinctions accentuate perceived risks of exploitation in the collective action problem; (2) the degree to which union institutions provide credible commitments that member countries will not be exploited; (3) the framing strategies that state leaders use when mobilizing any necessary popular support for their initiatives; and (4) those aggregate mass interests on which political support for state leaders is most likely to depend given the particular domestic institutional framework in place to aggregate those interests and to hold politicians accountable to them.

The distinction between the problem of secessionism and the problem of international integration lies primarily in the degree of expected gains to be had from the union in question. For ethnofederal regions, union institutions that are typically capable of using force to thwart unwanted separatist actions already exist, whereas there are no such preexisting union institutions in cases of international integration.[1] Thus, ethnofederal regions bear higher expected costs

---

[1] The exception would be cases of conquest, where a "union" forcibly seeks to incorporate another member. In such cases, the expectation of exploitation in the future union is likely to be perceived as extremely high.

in pursuing independence than do preexisting independent states. Additionally, the transactions costs of transition (including some expected initial dysfunction) must count against the benefits of union for independent states but against the value of independence for regions already in a union. The underlying logic is thus the same, with the primary difference being that the transition of a given set of interregional relations from "domestic politics" to "international relations" is likely to reduce all regions' support for integration, ceteris paribus. In sum, the relational theory of separatism expects patterns in the *relative* degree of separatism across former member regions after independence to remain basically the same as they were before independence but also expects the absolute level of separatism of all of these units to rise.

Rival theories generate alternative expectations for international integration patterns in much the same way as they do for secessionism. Ethnicity-as-conflictual theories all posit that a sense of national distinctiveness itself provides the underlying motive for separatism since national consciousness represents differences in values or a psychological need to assert one's own group's autonomy and self-worth relative to others. Thus, a number of works have explained former republics' attitudes toward reintegration with Russia largely in terms of historically constructed national consciousness,[2] and some prominent theories of more general international relations emphasize identity as a driver of state policies on integration.[3] More unionist (or "integrationist") countries should thus be those with lower levels of national consciousness (National Consciousness theories) or stronger nonethnic interests in a potential union (Countervailing Incentives theories), and changes over time in a given country's policies should derive from changes in these factors.[4] Of course, ethnic differences should also be found to supply the underlying motive for separatism. The vast bulk of the IR literature, however, tends to assume that a state's mere existence as a state is sufficient for explaining its desire to be independent of other states, thus assuming like ethnicity-as-epiphenomenal theory that ethnic divides between states are largely irrelevant for international relations.[5] By these lights, variation in state policies on integration, over both time and space, will depend entirely on nonethnic factors like state interests and state capabilities.

The advantages of the relational theory over these alternatives are established empirically in this chapter. First, an overview of early developments in the

[2] For example, Abdelal, *National Purpose*; Eugene Huskey, "National Identity from Scratch: Defining Kyrgyzstan's Role in World Affairs," *Journal of Communist Studies and Transition Politics*, v.19, no.3, September 2003, pp. 111–38; Ronald Grigor Suny, "Provisional Stabilities: The Politics of Identities in Post-Soviet Eurasia," *International Security*, winter 1999–2000, v.24, no.3, pp. 139–78.

[3] For example, Haas, *The Uniting of Europe*; Wendt, "Collective Identity Formation."

[4] Capabilities theory is not likely to be relevant because representatives of independent nation-states are assumed to have the capacity to voice demands for continued independence.

[5] For example, Joseph M. Grieco, *Cooperation Among Nations: Europe, America, and Non-Tariff Barriers to Trade* (Ithaca, NY: Cornell University Press, 1990); Keohane and Nye, "International Interdependence"; Moravcsik, *The Choice for Europe*; Schelling, *The Strategy of Conflict*. An excellent corrective to this tendency is provided by Andreas Wimmer and Brian Min, "From Empire to Nation-state: Explaining Wars in the Modern World, 1816–2001," *American Sociological Review*, v. 71, December 2006, pp. 867–97.

Commonwealth of Independent States, including a content analysis of treaties signed by the different countries, shows that patterns of *relative* levels of support for the CIS through 2007 have largely reflected the continuation of late Soviet-era patterns of relative levels of support for saving the union. This lends confidence to the claim that we are observing in international relations the same process that was documented extensively in previous chapters to be most consistent with relational theory in the realm of domestic politics. Second, resumption of our case studies of Ukraine and Uzbekistan shows that the transition from domestic to international politics did in fact raise the *absolute* level of separatism in both republics due to the shift in expected gains that the transition caused. Third, tracing the process by which these states forged their first decade-and-a-half of relations with Russia also reveals that the core problem for unionists remained an ethnically charged collective action problem and that a key factor causing Uzbekistan to be more willing than Ukraine to risk CIS integration in the face of this problem continued to be economics – this corroborates the relational theory but not its rivals.

PATTERNS OF SEPARATISM IN THE EMERGING CIS

The CIS was born of disorder, and in disorder it has remained. Unionist republics like Russia, Belarus, and Uzbekistan have been eager to keep as many of the new states as possible in the CIS, but the result has been to bring it down to the level of coherence favored by separatist states like Ukraine, rendering its institutions extremely weak. Even though it has generated seemingly countless agreements, few have actually been both significant and implemented, and the CIS has been widely regarded as doing little more than regulating a "civilized divorce."[6] Nevertheless, careful consideration of state engagement patterns in the CIS, including a content analysis of treaties signed and the conditions attached to signing them, show clearly that some states have been much more supportive of integration projects in the post-Soviet space than have others. With only a few exceptions, these patterns of separatism are almost identical to those observed before these new countries gained their independence.

The accord initiating the CIS was inked on December 8, 1991, by only three of the USSR's fifteen union republics: Russia, Ukraine, and Belarus. This was because none of the others were invited. Russia's leadership had seen the treaty as a last-ditch effort to salvage as much of the union as Ukraine would agree to[7] and did not want to complicate negotiations by inviting other republics.[8] Furthermore, Yeltsin calculated that the risky maneuver of dissolving the USSR, a tactic aimed at facilitating Ukraine's signature on a new union document, could

---

[6] Robert Legvold, "Foreign Policy," in Timothy J. Colton and Legvold, eds., *After the Soviet Union: From Empires to Nations* (New York: W. W. Norton, 1992), pp. 85–112.

[7] Boris Yeltsin, interview in *Argumenty i Fakty*, December 12, 1991. Belarus leader Stanislaw Shushkevich also confirms this interpretation in his interview in *Argumenty i Fakty*, January 8, 1992.

[8] Veber et al., *Soiuz Mozhno Bylo*.

best be legitimized if it came from the three surviving[9] republics that formally founded the USSR in 1922, which meant that Belarus needed to be included as well. Nevertheless, the aim was to invite all republics to join later.

The treaty's text, although vaguely worded, envisioned an organization that would provide for cooperation in politics, economics, culture, education, and other spheres. Borders would be open and recognized by all. Nuclear weapons would remain under a united command. CIS states would act jointly in foreign policy, preservation of a common economic space, customs policy, communications, transport, the environment, migration, the battle with crime, and mitigation of the effects of the Chernobyl nuclear disaster.[10]

It was clear from the beginning, however, that the three leaders had different futures in mind for the new organization. Russia's presidential spokesman declared that CIS structures would effectively supplant the transitional organs that had been set up after the coup to run the Soviet economy. The Belarusian leader said he saw nothing in the agreement that would undercut this transitional Soviet structure. The Ukrainian Rada, however, ratified the CIS treaty only after making Ukraine's membership conditional on the CIS involving only consultations instead of coordination in foreign policy, migration, and the formation of a common economic space, among other things.[11]

This original CIS accord, driven by Russia and attuned most closely to Ukrainian interests, effectively shut the other republics out of the decision-making process on the new entity's fundamental character. Those that had wanted to preserve the USSR in some form now had to work with the CIS or forgo any hope of a future union in place of the Soviet one. Thus, on December 12, 1991, the Central Asian leaders met in Ashkhabad and agreed to join the CIS.[12] Nine days later, the heads of all former republics except the Baltics and Georgia convened in Kazakhstan's capital Alma-Ata to formally join the organization, granting founding member status to all retroactively.[13] As in the treaty founding the CIS, this new protocol promised a series of future documents to regulate cooperation in the framework of the CIS.[14] The meeting also created the first two central organs of the CIS, the Council of Heads of the States and the Council of Heads of the Governments.[15] In addition, it took care of some immediate business, declaring

---

[9] The Transcaucasian republic was broken up into the Armenian, Azerbaijani, and Georgian SSRs in 1936.

[10] Commonwealth of Independent States, *Sodruzhestvo: Informatsionnyi Vestnik Sovetov Glav Gosudarstv i Pravitel'stv SNG* (Minsk: SNG, 1992), v.1, pp. 6–9. This series, which publishes official CIS documents, is hereafter referred to as *Sodruzhestvo*.

[11] James H. Noren and Robin Watson, "Interrepublican Economic Relations after the Disintegration of the USSR," *Soviet Economy*, v.8, no.2, 1992, pp. 89–129, 103.

[12] K. V. Zhigalov and B. K. Sultanov, *Pervyi Prezident Respubliki Kazakhstan, Nursultan Nazarbaev: Khronika Deiatel'nosti (1.12.1991–31.5.1993)* (Almaty: Fond Politicheskikh Issledovanii "Kazakhstan – XXI Vek," 1993), p. 17.

[13] The parliaments of Moldova and Azerbaijan did not ratify this and other agreements until 1993–4.

[14] *Sodruzhestvo*, v.1, p. 11.

[15] *Sodruzhestvo*, v.1, p. 12.

Russia the heir to the USSR's UN Security Council seat and appointing Shaposh-nikov as commander of the united armed forces until their status was decided.[16] The meeting also resolved that the four republics inheriting nuclear weapons on their territories (Belarus, Kazakhstan, Russia, and Ukraine) should jointly decide nuclear policy.[17]

The earliest CIS summits, in December 1991 and January 1992, tended to focus on three types of agreements that were signed by all eleven original CIS states. First, they created and fleshed out the Commonwealth's basic organs, almost all of which were to reach decisions on the basis of consensus.[18] Second, they resolved immediate security concerns, affirming that the newly indepen-dent countries would adhere to USSR treaties, keep strategic forces under a unified command, and be in control of their own military structures.[19] Third, they attempted to mitigate the rupture of some economic ties and divide USSR property in a civilized manner.[20]

The meeting of the Council of Heads of the Governments on February 8, 1992, marked a turning point of sorts as the new states began to create organs and sign agreements that went beyond simple crisis management in the aftermath of the USSR's disappearance. In the security sphere, eight republics (Armenia, Belarus, Kazakhstan, Kyrgyzstan, Russia, Tajikistan, Turkmenistan, and Uzbek-istan) signed onto a CIS "Common Forces," and some others joined this group in supporting a united peacekeeping force and border troop command.[21] On May 15, Armenia, Kazakhstan, Kyrgyzstan, Russia, and Uzbekistan signed the Collective Security Treaty, a mutual defense alliance.[22] In the economic realm, the CIS prime ministers on February 8 created a Customs Council (signed by all but Azerbaijan and Ukraine) and proposed a CIS "interbank organ," supported by all but Azerbaijan and Turkmenistan.[23] In May, CIS leaders created an Eco-nomic Court, backed by Armenia, Belarus, Kazakhstan, Russia, Tajikistan, and Uzbekistan.[24]

The CIS leaders at the time treated the January 1993 summit as a watershed since it adopted the CIS Charter. The Charter, however, essentially just ratified the preexisting weak organs, most of which still made decisions only through con-sensus. Even so, it was signed only by Armenia, Belarus, Kazakhstan, Kyrgyzstan, Russia, Tajikistan, and Uzbekistan. More (all of the original CIS members except Azerbaijan) were willing to sign a mission statement on the CIS, however. The stated mission was largely economic: to find a solution to the economic crisis by forming effective ties between economic actors and removing barriers between states.[25] These same states also agreed to form the Interstate Bank, designed to

[16] *Sodruzhestvo*, v.1, pp. 12–13.
[17] *Sodruzhestvo*, v.1, pp. 13–14.
[18] *Sodruzhestvo*, v.1, pp. 22–4.
[19] *Sodruzhestvo*, v.1, pp. 25–6.
[20] *Sodruzhestvo*, v.2, pp. 20–1, 21–3, 27, 37–40, 41.
[21] *Sodruzhestvo*, v.2, pp. 45–7, 55–6.
[22] *Sodruzhestvo*, v.5, pp. 9–11.
[23] *Sodruzhestvo*, v.3, pp. 10–14, 18.
[24] *Sodruzhestvo*, v.5, pp. 11–12.
[25] *Sodruzhestvo*, v.9, pp. 17–29.

facilitate interstate accounting and coordinate monetary policies.[26] This agreement was seen as involving significant Russian concessions, since Russia would hold only 50 percent of the votes in the proposed bank union, "which deprived it of the opportunity to be a monopolist in credit and emissions policy," according to two Uzbekistan authors.[27] Commonwealth leaders followed up in May 1993 by resolving to create an Economic Union. They produced a list of agreements that were to be reached and implemented over the course of that year to flesh it out.[28] These remained mostly on paper, however.

Overall, at the end of its first year and a half of existence in May 1993, a total of 318 documents had been signed and the overall pattern of signatures gives us an important indicator of the different levels of activity of the different republics in the CIS. A content analysis of these documents is illustrative. Looking first at the overall quantities of treaties signed in the CIS during this period, the most active signers were Russia (315), Kazakhstan (312), Armenia (305), Kyrgyzstan (303), Tajikistan (301), Belarus (298), and Uzbekistan (289). One might dub this group the *CIS Activists*. A significantly less active group included Moldova (232), Ukraine (229), and Turkmenistan (198), whom we collectively refer to as *CIS Skeptics*. A final set of republics might be called *CIS Rejecters*, ranging from Azerbaijan, which signed only seventy-two agreements, to Georgia, which acceded to a mere ten, to the Baltic states, which rejected virtually any association with the CIS. This same spectrum of relative degrees of republic unionism is also reflected in the number of treaties each state signed that envisioned some kind of central organ. Within this set of agreements, the CIS Activists all signed over one hundred, while the CIS Skeptics signed between sixty-two and eighty-three. Among the CIS Rejecters, Azerbaijan inked twenty-six of these documents and Georgia five (and the Baltics none). There appear to have been no significant "issue focuses" among the republics, at least when all signed agreements are examined together. The most active unionists signed both economic and security agreements, whereas the least active tended not to sign either kind.

Because signatory states were permitted to register their own special conditions for signing certain documents, we can also consider how states varied in this regard. In some cases, especially CIS Activists, reservations tended just to clarify certain points. But for Ukraine and Moldova, in particular, reservations often stripped a given treaty of any real meaning. For example, on the May 1993 Decision on Measures for the Creation of an Economic Union, Ukraine registered the following reservation: "with the exception of the concept 'economic union' and the principal sentences flowing from it concerning the content of the future document."[29] Thus, even though the raw numbers count Ukraine as having signed up for an Economic Union, this stipulation shows that this signature did not indicate much support for integration. In general, the states that entered the most numerous and significant special conditions tended to be the

[26] *Sodruzhestvo*, v.9, pp. 29–39.
[27] Anvar Kasymov and Igor Vaskin, *Osnovnye Napravleniia Vneshnei Politiki Respubliki Uzbekistan* (Uzbekistan: Ozbekistan, 1994), p. 34.
[28] *Sodruzhestvo*, v.11, pp. 74–5, 80–6.
[29] *Sodruzhestvo*, v.11, p. 76.

CIS Skeptics, those that signed a medium number of CIS agreements. Thus, at the same time none of the CIS Activists imposed special conditions on more than eleven documents, Turkmenistan included fourteen reservations, Moldova, twenty-seven, and Ukraine, a striking forty, representing over a sixth of all the agreements it signed. Of course, the CIS Rejecters signed few documents upon which to attach special conditions.

These broad patterns of involvement in the CIS remained very nearly the same through 2007, over a decade and a half after the organization's founding. For one thing, the states that were the least engaged in the early 1990s, the CIS Rejecters, generally remained so well into the next decade. The Baltic countries thus continued to reject any association with the CIS. Georgia, which initially refused to join, did finally accede in 1993 after Russian military intervention in support of a separatist region within Georgia (Abkhazia) led to the Georgian army's defeat and a near-collapse of the state. By joining the CIS and partici- pating in a few of its structures, Georgia was able to normalize relations with Russia and reestablish some degree of order at home. Because its membership was largely coerced, however, Georgia consistently avoided the vast majority of CIS commitments that even symbolically promised significant integration. This was true under President Eduard Shevardnadze as well as the man who replaced him in the 2003 "Rose Revolution," Mikheil Saakashvili. Azerbaijan, also an early skeptic of the CIS, remained so as well, opting out of the most important CIS integration projects except for its decision to join the CIS Council of Defense Ministers.

The CIS Activists, with only a couple prominent exceptions, have remained in the vanguard, spearheading a number of efforts that at least on paper promised significant integration. In the security sphere, the most important initiative has been the formation of the Collective Security Treaty Organization in 2003. This formal mutual defense institution, based on the 1992 CIS Collective Security Treaty, included Armenia, Belarus, Kazakhstan, Kyrgyzstan, Russia, Tajikistan, and Uzbekistan as of 2008.[30] These same states also continued to be members of such security-oriented organs as the CIS Council of Ministers of Defense and the Council of Border Troop Commanders. In the realm of economics, as of 2007 all the CIS Activists were members of the CIS Economic Court (along with Moldova) as well as the Eurasian Economic Community, an effort launched in 2000 on the basis of earlier efforts to establish a CIS Customs Union.[31]

Smaller sets of CIS Activists demonstrated willingness to promote even greater degrees of integration, particularly in economics. Thus, Belarus and Russia joined with Kazakhstan, Kyrgyzstan, and Tajikistan to sign a treaty to form an integra- tionist core in the CIS, and the former two republics went even further to declare a "Union State" of Belarus and Russia. A parallel economic formation, known as

---

[30] Collective Security Treaty Organization Web site, *http://www.dkb.gov.ru/start/index.htm*, accessed June 16, 2005.

[31] Olga Serova, "Odin Den' Sodruzhestvo," *RIA Novosti*, *http://sng.rian.ru/688/news251215.html*, April 20, 2004, 10:47. Uzbekistan joined the EEC late, as is described later.

the Single Economic Space, was signed by the presidents of CIS Activists Russia, Belarus, and Kazakhstan as well as the CIS Skeptic Ukraine in 2003.[32] It must be kept in mind, however, that the level of actual integration involved in all of these organs remained very low as of 2008, even with the Russian–Belarusian "Union State."

Nevertheless, we find a clear distinction between what most of the CIS Activists have been willing to sign during the CIS period and what the CIS Rejecters would agree to. The category of CIS Skeptics has also been quite stable, with Moldova, Ukraine, and Turkmenistan signing very few potentially meaningful documents by 2007; even when they did sign them, as before, there were sometimes important special conditions unilaterally attached to their commitments. The overall pattern of activity in the CIS is summarized in Table 9.1, which lists the raw number of CIS agreements that each former Soviet republic was willing to sign between December 1991 and May 1993 and juxtaposes these figures against each republic's willingness to embrace some of the most important CIS initiatives extant as of 2007.[33]

These broad patterns of separatism regarding the CIS are highly consistent with those described in earlier chapters regarding the USSR. Just as Belarus, Russia, and Uzbekistan were shown to have been regularly unionist republics within the Soviet Union, these same states are found to have been among the leading advocates of CIS integration in the time shortly after the USSR's dissolution. A brief statistical exercise provides some rigor to this claim: Among the fifteen union republics, the correlation coefficient between the number of CIS treaties signed during December 1991–May 1993 and the time it took them to declare sovereignty in the USSR (used in Chapter 10 as an indication of separatism) is .91, indicating an extremely strong relationship between the two variables. If we use simple bivariate OLS regression analysis as another method, we find that sovereignty declaration timing is an excellent predictor of the number of CIS treaties signed between December 1991 and May 1993. We can reject the null hypothesis that these numbers are unrelated with over 99.9 percent statistical confidence. Table 9.2 juxtaposes the two sets of figures. Similarly strong relationships (.74 correlation coefficient and 99.8 percent confidence levels) are found when analogous tests are conducted of the relationship between *perestroika*-era sovereignty declaration timing and an index counting the number of memberships/signatures each country had in the CIS as of 2007 among the set of important agreements given in Table 9.1.

This striking continuity in patterns of relative separatism, evident more than fifteen years after the initial transition from USSR to independent statehood, strongly suggests that the factors found to account for secessionism are also crucial for explaining attitudes toward reintegration. This adds additional support to

[32] Ministry of Foreign Affairs, Russian Federation, Web site, *http://www.ln.mid.ru/ns-rsng.nsf/ 559a6afd63bofb02432569ee0048fe70/432569d800221466c3256e22002b5530?OpenDocument*, last accessed June 16, 2005.

[33] Some peculiarities surrounding Uzbekistan will be discussed later.

TABLE 9.1. *Degrees of State Involvement in CIS 1991–1993 Membership/Signatory status in Major CIS Organs/Treaties as of 2007*

State	Number of Agreements Dec. 1991–May 1993	CIS Member	Eurasian Economic Community[a]	Collective Security Treaty Organization[b]	Economic Court[c]	Council of Defense Ministers[d]	Council of Border Troop Commanders[e]	Treaty on Deepening Integration[f]	Union State[g]	Single Economic Space[b]
Russia	315	X	X	X	X	X	X	X	X	X
Kazakhstan	312	X	X	X	X	X	X	X		X
Armenia	305	X		X	X	X	X			
Kyrgyzstan	303	X	X	X	X	X	X	X		
Tajikistan	301	X	X	X	X	X	X	X		
Belarus	298	X	X	X	X	X	X	X	X	X
Uzbekistan	289	X	X	X	X	X			X	
Moldova	232	X			X		X			
Ukraine	229	X					X			X
Turkmenistan	198	X					X			
Azerbaijan	72	X				X				
Georgia	10	X								
Estonia	0									
Latvia	0									
Lithuania	0									

a Olga Serova, "Odin Den' Sodruzhestvo," *RIA Novosti*, *http://sng.rian.ru/688/news25121s.html*, v.10, April 20, 2004, p. 47; Russian Ministry of Foreign Affairs Web site, *http://www.ln.mid.ru/ns-rsng.nsf/oe82a568fbb5b2c043256a65002f56c2f43256gd8002214 66c3256fd5002add83?OpenDocument*, accessed June 16, 2005.

b Collective Security Treaty Organization Web site, *http://www.dkb.gov.ru/start/index.htm*, accessed June 16, 2005, and August 19, 2006. See also Serova, "Odin Den' Sodruzhestvo." while Karimov had signed this treaty by 2007, Uzbekistan's Parliament ratified it only in early 2008.

c According to CIS Web site, *http://www.cis.minsk.by/russian/ustav_organi/estu1.htm*, accessed June 16, 2005.

d According to CIS Web sites, *http://www.cis.minsk.by/russian/ustav_organi/cis_smo.htm*, accessed June 16, 2005; *http://cis.minsk.by/main.aspx?uid=200*, accessed September 6, 2006.

e According to CIS Web site, *http://cis.minsk.by/main.aspx?uid=202*, accessed September 6, 2006.

f This is the treaty "Ob uglublenii integratsii v ekonomicheskoi i gumanitarnoi oblastiakh," described on the CIS Web site, *http://www.cis.minsk.by/russian/cis_reg.htm*, accessed June 16, 2005.

g This is the Treaty on the Formation of the Commonwealth of Belarus and Russia, described on the CIS Web site, *http://www.cis.minsk.by/russian/cis_reg.htm*, accessed June 16, 2005; Russia's Ministry of Foreign Affairs Web site, *http://www.ln.mid.ru/ns-rsng.nsf/*, accessed June 16, 2005.

b Initially signed by presidents in 2003; ratification not indicated here. See Russia's Ministry of Foreign Affairs Web site, *http://www.ln.mid.ru/ns-rsng.nsf/559a6afd63b9f8o2432569ee0048fe70/43256gd800221466c3256e22002b5530?OpenDocument*, accessed June 16, 2005.

TABLE 9.2. *Comparison of Relative Separatism Levels before and after USSR Dissolution*

Rank Order of Republics (1 = most unionist)	Weeks to Declare Sovereignty after November 16, 1988	CIS Treaties Signed December 1991–May 1993
1	Kazakhstan (101)	**Russia (315)**
2	Kyrgyzstan (101)	Kazakhstan (312)
3	Armenia (92)	Armenia (305)
4	Tajikistan (92)	Kyrgyzstan (303)
5	**Turkmenistan (92)**	Tajikistan (301)
6	Belarus (88)	Belarus (298)
7	Ukraine (86)	Uzbekistan (289)
8	Moldova (83)	Moldova (232)
9	Uzbekistan (83)	Ukraine (229)
10	**Russia (81)**	**Turkmenistan (198)**
11	Georgia (52)	Azerbaijan (72)
12	Azerbaijan (44)	Georgia (10)
13	Latvia (36)	Estonia (0)
14	Lithuania (27)	Latvia (0)
15	Estonia (0)	Lithuania (0)

Bolded = more than three ranks different between the two columns.

relational theory, which was shown earlier to best explain patterns of Soviet-era secessionism and which also expects patterns of relative separatism not to be dramatically altered by a transition between the realms of domestic and international politics. We would have greater confidence in the advantages of relational theory, however, if it can be shown that the processes producing the patterns remain the same. Additionally, the relational theory also has concrete expectations for how the union-to-independence transitions will impact absolute levels of separatism: Are these also borne out? To address these expectations, this chapter turns again to a focused process-tracing comparison of Ukraine and Uzbekistan.

UKRAINE: ETHNICITY, ECONOMICS, AND CIS SKEPTICISM

Ukraine's leaders from the beginning avoided ceding any real power to CIS organs, although they remained formally in the organization throughout 1991–2007. In fact, they effectively used the CIS to consolidate Ukraine's political independence. Analysis of Ukraine's leaders' activities and their constituents' views during 1991–2007 demonstrates that the factors influencing Ukraine's policies regarding a Russian-led union in the CIS continued to reflect key variables that had impacted the Ukrainian leadership's attitude toward the possibility of saving the Soviet Union in 1990–1. These variables most notably included ethnicity and economic interests, with leadership framing also playing a significant role – all within the context of a larger commitment problem driving the whole process. Contrary to the expectations of ethnicity-as-conflictual theory, there is scant evidence that national independence was desired for its own sake (by either leaders or populations, even in famously nationalistic western Ukraine). Yet confounding the predictions of ethnicity-as-epiphenomenal theory, ethnicity does play an important role and not just as a coordinating device: Ethnic Ukrainians are found to have seen greater dangers of exploitation at the hands of Russia even as they tended to support the general principle of exploitation-free integration.

Ukrainian Elite and Mass Opinion on the CIS

Although Ukraine was one of the three original CIS co-founders and repeatedly called for purely economic integration after its first year of independence, it staked out a strong antiintegrationist position on nearly every major issue that the CIS faced straight through 2007. The CIS was a top foreign policy priority, but the priority was on using it to divide assets rather than to promote integration.[34] The well-known nationalist leader and parliamentarian Ivan Drach thus accounted for Ukraine's decision to join the CIS:

> Many curse Kravchuk for going into the CIS. But it was not possible not to go into the CIS. We needed to destroy the USSR, to destroy the Soviet Union. But how to do this? We needed only to create another structure to destroy the old structure. It was understood that this was a necessity.[35]

While elite public opinion on Ukraine's position in the CIS was divided, few of the CIS's most influential opponents actually called for reconstituting a strong union with Russia during the first years of independence. Instead, the opposition was mostly from the separatist end of the political spectrum, including within Rukh.[36]

Senior officials in ministries like Foreign Affairs and Finance did voice support for economic integration in interviews but they, too, stressed that Ukraine should not join any union in which Russia refused to share economic decision-making authority, a stand precluding agreement on almost every major issue and reflecting the central importance of the kind of commitment problem described in Chapter 4.[37] Indeed, it was in the early and mid-1990s that Russia was wrapped up in its Western-backed radical "shock therapy" reforms, adamantly rejecting the notion that any other former Soviet republic would disrupt this policy choice. Importantly, even the reputedly pro-integration industrialist and future Ukrainian president Leonid Kuchma, as well as his supporters when he was prime minister in late 1992, were careful to refrain from backing the CIS specifically, preferring to establish ties with Russia on a bilateral basis.[38] Thus, even though

[34] Author's interview with Dmytro Pavlychko, chair of the Ukrainian Rada's Commission on Foreign Affairs, July 8, 1993.

[35] Author's interview with Ivan Drach, Ukrainian Rada member and a top Rukh leader, July 7, 1993.

[36] *Vedomosti Verkhovnogo Soveta Ukrainy*, no.17, 1992, p. 504.

[37] Author's interview with the First Deputy Minister of Finance of Ukraine, July 12, 1993; author's interview with the head of the Russia branch of the Administration of Bilateral Relations in the Ukrainian Foreign Ministry, July 13, 1993; and author's interview with a Ukrainian Foreign Ministry official, June 28, 1993.

[38] *Itogi*, television program, *First Channel* (Russia), December 13, 1992.

most Ukrainian citizens appeared to view integration with Russia as having the potential to benefit Ukraine, and most Russian citizens likewise thought that unification with Ukraine would benefit them, few Ukrainians believed Russia could actually be trusted enough in such a union to make renewed political integration worthwhile given how it had ignored Ukrainian economic interests theretofore.

This collective action problem is also evident at the level of public opinion, which throughout the CIS era has been generally in line with the spectrum of Ukrainian elite opinion. Polling data from the early post-Soviet period, when Ukraine's leadership was making its most fateful decisions, confirms that the public opinion structure with which Kravchuk had to work regarding the CIS was highly similar to that regarding Gorbachev's efforts to save the USSR: an abstract desire for cooperative ties combined with the distrust of actual central intentions (especially in the long run). That is, Ukrainians *preferred* a cooperative union to independence, but chose a separatist *strategy* given that a cooperative union was seen as very unlikely. This specific pattern of public opinion makes sense from the perspective of relational theory, but it is quite puzzling to ethnicity-as-conflictual theory, which posits national independence as the ideal preferred outcome.

Some specific poll numbers help make this clear. Asked in March 1993 whether Ukraine could get out of its current economic crisis while preserving its independence, a majority in every region of Ukraine answered that it could. Yet most people also said that Ukraine could *better* get out of the crisis through a tighter economic union with CIS states, as opposed to a break in ties with them. Majorities in every region of Ukraine except the western Galicia were also found to be supportive of a potential "military–political union" with Russia (66 percent overall), and even in Galicia a solid plurality averred that they backed such a union in principle (37 percent in favor, 29 percent opposed, and 35 percent undecided).[39] Furthermore, a majority in all regions of Ukraine agreed that Russia should act as the guarantor of peace and stability in the territory of the former Soviet Union. The key is this: Ukrainians simply believed that the sort of ideal union they had in mind when answering such questions in the abstract was unrealistic given the kind of Russian behavior they thought most likely. This is additionally clear from another Ukrainian survey taken in early 1993. When asked whether they thought Russia viewed Ukraine "as an equal partner" or whether Russia was "trying to suffocate Ukraine," only 25 percent of respondents agreed Russia viewed Ukraine as an equal partner, while 59 percent thought Russia sought to suffocate Ukraine.[40] People were split on whether Russia could be trusted as an economic partner.[41]

Importantly, these patterns of trusting Russia were linked with ethnic divides in Ukraine, a finding consistent with relational theory's supposition that ethnicity

[39] O. I. Vishniak and M. D. Mishchenko, *Informatsiino-Analitychna Dovidka pro Rezul'taty Sotsiolohichnoho Doslidzhennia 'Ukraiins'ko-rosiis'ki Vidnosyny i Yikh Vplyv na Politychnu Sytuatsiiu v Ukraiini* (Kyiv: Institute of Sociology, 1993).

[40] Institute of Sociology of the Academy of Sciences of Ukraine, results of survey of 1,197 residents of Ukraine taken January 22–February 2, 1993.

[41] Vishniak and Mishchenko, *Informatsiino-Analitychna Dovidka*, pp. 7–8, 14, 24.

tends to exacerbate collective action problems yet is inconsistent with ethnicity-as-epiphenomenal theory's claim that ethnicity is either essentially irrelevant or nothing more than a coordination device. Ethnic Russians in Ukraine, for one thing, tended to be more trusting of Russia than were ethnic Ukrainians.[42] Respondents calling themselves native Russian speakers also tended to be some-what more confident that the former Soviet republics would eventually reunite (with 47 percent allowing that such a turn of events was possible, likely, or certain) than were self-professed native Ukrainian speakers (33 percent).[43] Accordingly, there was also evidence that ethnic Russians in Ukraine were generally more supportive of integration with Russia than were Ukrainians.[44]

These patterns of public opinion in the initial post-Soviet years were still evi-dent well after the Orange Revolution had brought the reputedly pro-Western Viktor Yushchenko to the presidency in 2005. Thus, on one hand, a May 2005 survey reveals that Ukrainians were highly supportive of forms of "integration" that would broaden their personal and economic opportunities but that would not leave them significantly vulnerable to Russian exploitation. To wit, a full 54 percent of respondents agreed Ukraine should allow its own citizens to also hold Russian citizenship, while only 33 percent disagreed. Likewise, 63 percent backed the idea that Ukraine should join the as-yet-unformed CIS Single Eco-nomic Space, against just 22 percent who opposed it. But at the same time, when asked about a concrete preexisting institution associated with Russian attempts at political dominance, the CIS, their responses were decidedly negative. Just 18 percent favored Ukraine's integration into the CIS, while a whole 59 percent opposed it.[45] Additionally, consistent with the claim that different ethnic groups showed differential perceptions of the dangers associated with Russian influence, several studies have found that ethnic Ukrainians (in particular, people who spoke mostly Ukrainian in everyday life as opposed to Russian) were much more likely to vote for the Western-leaning and more Russia-skeptical Yushchenko than for the more Russia-oriented Viktor Yanukovych in the 2004 presidential contest.[46]

Ukrainian public opinion on questions of integration, then, appears much more consistent with the relational approach than with any version of ethnicity-as-conflictual or ethnicity-as-epiphenomenal theory. Indeed, if one assumes that the only choice people have involves a simple dichotomy between union and inde-pendence, or if one conflates *preferences* as to states of the world that maximize life

---

[42] Ibid.

[43] V. S. Nebozhenko, results of survey of 1,200 citizens of Ukraine taken October 12–25, 1992.

[44] Vasilii Kremen', Yevgenii Bazovkin, Mikhail Mishchenko, Viktor Nebozhenko, Petr Sytnik, "Ukraina segodnia: po dannym Natsional'nogo instituta strategicheskikh issledovanii," *Delovaia Gazeta*, October 29, 1993, p. 4. Poll data are from May 1993.

[45] *Ukraïns'ka Pravda*, June 9, 2005, 14:50. Survey taken May 10–23, 2005, by the Kyiv International Institute of Sociology (KMIS) and the Sociological Service of the Ukrainian Center of Economic and Political Research in the name of Oleksandr Razumkov (Razumkov Center).

[46] An engaging discussion is Dominique Arel, "The 'Orange Revolution': Analysis and Impli-cations of the 2004 Presidential Election in Ukraine," Third Annual Stasiuk – Cam-bridge Lecture on Contemporary Ukraine, Cambridge University, UK, February 25, 2005, *http://www.uottawa.ca/academic/grad-etudesup/ukr/pdf/Arel_Cambridge.pdf*.

chances with *strategies* that take into account perceived risks and constraints, public opinion in Ukraine is likely to look quite incoherent, with different polls generating findings that seem to point in radically different directions. Yet as shown here and in the chapters on the late Soviet period, the relational theory makes for a coherent and sensible interpretation of what are otherwise confusing patterns regarding the relationship between ethnicity and separatism. Evidence suggests Ukrainians' ideal first choice was generally for a union with Russia that would maximize their material well-being and general life chances, not for national independence as a paramount value in its own right (as ethnicity-as-conflictual theory generally holds). At the same time, ethnicity's role as a magnifier of collective action problems is revealed in numerous findings that ethnic Ukrainians were less likely to trust Russia to behave nonexploitatively than were ethnic Russians, a finding running counter to the expectations of ethnicity-as-epiphenomenal theory. Ukrainian policy on the CIS, it will now be shown, hewed quite closely to these expectations, as the theory elaborated in Chapter 4 would expect.

Toward a Civilized Divorce

Facing a credible commitment problem that the CIS posed along with the specific pattern of public opinion that it produced, Ukraine's leadership was fairly consistent in seeking primarily to distance itself from the CIS during the first decade and a half of that institution's existence. This stance was evident from the outset: The Rada ratified the CIS Treaty, but did so only after unilaterally attaching twelve special conditions to the document. These reservations included an affirmation of the inviolability of state borders, a provision for the right to a national armed force, and the downgrading of the envisioned joint foreign policy activities from "coordination" to "consultation."[47] Ukrainian delegations regularly participated in major CIS meetings but tended mainly to sign those agreements ratifying divisions of assets or not entailing any kind of formally binding obligation.

President Kravchuk's top policy priority in the early 1990s, as he later confirmed, was state building, or the attempt to free Ukraine from all levers of potential Russian dominance and to insulate Ukraine from the negative side effects of Russia's shock therapy reforms.[48] When Russia ignored Ukrainian pleas and unleashed market prices in early 1992, Ukraine was forced to relax its own price controls on many commodities at the same time in order to avoid massive speculative runs on goods.[49] Without a well-conceived reform plan to deal with the new rupture in ties, the country plunged into a severe economic crisis.[50] According to official measures, Ukraine's economy contracted 15 percent in 1992. In an attempt to regain control, authorities accelerated efforts to introduce a Ukrainian national currency, officially leaving the "ruble zone" in November 1992. In lieu of

[47] Solchanyk, "Russia, Ukraine," p. 355.
[48] Dawisha and Parrott, *Russia and the New States*, p. 177.
[49] Paul J. D'Anieri, *Economic Interdependence in Ukrainian-Russian Relations* (Albany: SUNY Press, 1999), pp. 69–96.
[50] *Demokratychna Ukraiina*, May 22, 1993, p. 1.

a full-fledged currency, the "coupon" became the only legal tender on Ukrainian soil, but soon recorded the highest inflation rate in the CIS.[51]

With the economic crisis deepening, Kravchuk concluded that dependence on the Russian economy was not immediately escapable and had to be accommodated to some degree in the short run.[52] One such accommodation was his fall 1992 appointment of Leonid Kuchma, an industrialist reputed to favor strengthened Ukrainian–Russian economic ties, to the post of prime minister. Ukrainian leaders also lent their signatures to several CIS initiatives aimed at improving interrepublic economic relations, including an agreement on an Interstate Economic Bank and even an "Economic Union."[53] It was to be only an "associate member" of the latter, however, since Ukraine's leadership objected to the term "union."[54] By April 1993, Prime Minister Kuchma was able to claim that Ukraine had signed practically all documents aimed at strengthening economic ties between CIS countries. Few of these agreements, however, took on real meaning, and many observers in part blamed Ukraine's extreme reluctance for this state of affairs. Kravchuk continued to reject any documents smacking of politics, including the 1992 Collective Security Treaty and even the extremely vague 1993 CIS Charter, which he compared to the 1922 Union Treaty that established the USSR.[55] When international pressure ruled out an independent Ukrainian nuclear arsenal, the new state opted to clear its soil of such weapons in the 1994 Trilateral Agreement rather than jointly administer them through a union. Thus, even though Kravchuk was agreeing to some forms of economic cooperation by the end of his tenure, his Ukraine remained a fierce opponent of any political union institutions.

Despite his initial reputation as "pro-Russian," Kuchma largely continued the path beat by Kravchuk after defeating the latter in the 1994 presidential contest. Kuchma's efforts to move closer to Russia were primarily bilateral and economic. For example, he got Russia to lift its value-added tax on Ukrainian goods, restructure Ukraine's gas debt, and assume ownership of all Soviet debts and assets.[56] Seeking Russian backing for his hand-picked successor at the end of his tenure, Kuchma made a few dramatically "pro-Russian" economic moves in 2003–4. These included agreeing to use a Ukrainian oil pipeline to Russian

[51] *Sbornik Postanovlenii Soveta Ministrov*, Ukraine, no.11, 1993, pp. 76–8; *Nezavisimaia Gazeta*, November 13, 1992, pp. 1–2; Dawisha and Parrott, *Russia and the New States*, p. 178.

[52] *Demokratychna Ukraiina*, May 22, 1993, p. 1.

[53] D'Anieri, *Economic Interdependence*, pp. 139–41; Roman Solchanyk, *RFE/RL Daily Reports*, no.15, 1993. The Bank never materialized.

[54] *Demokratychna Ukraiina*, May 18, 1993, no.61, p. 1; Oles M. Smolansky, "Ukraine's Quest for Independence: The Fuel Factor," *Europe-Asia Studies*, v.47, no.1, 1995, pp. 67–90, 84; D'Anieri, *Economic Interdependence*, p. 142.

[55] *Nezavisimaia Gazeta*, December 25, 1992, p. 1.

[56] Sherman W. Garnett, "Like Oil and Water: Ukraine's External Westernization and Internal Stagnation," in Taras Kuzio, Robert S. Kravchuk, and Paul D'Anieri, eds., *State and Institution Building in Ukraine* (New York: St. Martin's, 1999), pp. 107–33, 107; Robert S. Kravchuk, *Ukrainian Political Economy: The First Ten Years* (New York: Pallgrave Macmillan, 2002), pp. 31, 138–9; Arkady Moshes, "Domestic Political Developments and Foreign Policy of Ukraine in 1991–1995," *Institute of Europe Report*, no.27, Moscow, 1996, pp. 39–45, 44.

advantage[57] and inking the CIS Single Economic Space agreement. But true to Kravchukian form, Kuchma attached a "reservation" to the latter agreement that essentially exempted Ukraine from any obligation.[58] As for the political agreements that Kuchma signed with Russia during his time in office, these primarily served not to reintegrate but to divide assets or settle disputes. One of the most prominent examples was the partition of the Black Sea Fleet agreed in the late 1990s.[59] Indeed, Kuchma backed away from virtually all important CIS integration projects, as Table 9.1 makes clear.[60]

Yushchenko, who succeeded Kuchma as president through the Orange Revolution of late 2004, largely continued this Ukrainian policy through 2007. He consistently stressed the need for economic cooperation with Russia, supporting CIS initiatives that "ensure mutual ties in transit, customs, budget, and fiscal relations."[61] At the same time, he sought to reduce Ukrainian vulnerability to Russian policies, vulnerability highlighted by Russia's dramatic cutoff of gas supplies over a pricing dispute in January 2006, suspiciously close to the March 2006 parliamentary elections that Russia was widely assumed to want to influence. This continuity with Kuchma's general policies on Russia was reinforced when Kuchma's chief allies (led by Yushchenko's 2004 presidential rival Yanukovych) gained control of a beefed-up prime ministership through the March 2006 voting.

Ukraine and Europe

Throughout the post-Soviet period, Ukraine's policies did not constitute a knee-jerk rejection of anything that would compromise national independence. In fact, both the Ukrainian leadership and its chief nationalist opposition made the aspiration to join the European Union integration project central to their public appeals throughout the 1990s. Not only was this policy expressed inside government ministries, but it was an integral part of Rukh leader Chornovil's vision for a free Ukraine.[62] Thus, in March 1994, Ukraine became the first CIS state to sign an agreement on partnership and cooperation with the European Union.[63] Even though the agreement mostly promoted economic ties, Ukraine's foreign minister made clear it was Ukraine's goal eventually to join the EU.[64] Only in 2004 did Kuchma, desperate for Russian support in the upcoming presidential election, remove the goal of joining the EU from Ukraine's national security

---

[57] Taras Kuzio, "Ukraine's Multi-Vector Energy Policy," *Eurasian Daily Monitor*, v.1, no.55, July 20, 2004.

[58] Jan Maksymiuk, "Kuchma Signs Accord on CIS Single Economic Space with 'Reservations,'" *RFE/RL Analytical Reports: Poland, Belarus, and Ukraine Report*, v.5, no.35, September 23, 2003.

[59] Garnett, "Like Oil"; Roman Solchanyk, *Ukraine and Russia: The Post-Soviet Transition* (Lanham, MD: Rowman & Littlefield, 2001).

[60] Solchanyk, *Ukraine and Russia*, p. 71.

[61] *RFE/RL Newsline*, May 31, 2005.

[62] Bojcun, "The Ukrainian Parliamentary," p. 235; Author's interview with the Deputy Foreign Minister for Economic Relations, July 1, 1993.

[63] Solchanyk, *Ukraine and Russia*, p. 92.

[64] *RFE/RL Daily Reports*, March 24, 1994.

doctrine. But even this revision still called for a "substantial deepening" of relations with the EU[65] and Yushchenko reasserted joining the EU as Ukraine's
top foreign policy goal immediately after winning office.[66] Survey evidence confirms the popularity of EU aspirations, especially early in Ukraine's independent
statehood. A 1994 poll, for example, found only 3 percent willing to assert that
Ukraine should never become an EU member.[67] Not all Ukrainians fully trusted
the EU[68]; however, the citizenry generally trusted Russian-dominated unions
less. The well-known writer and nationalist politician Dmytro Pavlychko, also
head of the Rada's Foreign Relations Commission until 1994, summed up the
feeling of many Ukrainians in one interview: "Here is our commonwealth – not
in Asia, but here in Europe."[69]

UZBEKISTAN: ECONOMICS, STATE BUILDING, AND CIS ACTIVISM

Uzbekistan resembles Ukraine in demonstrating that the same basic forces drove
its separatist calculus both before and after the USSR's collapse, but with an
important twist. Here we see in clearer relief just how the shifting costs of the
transition to statehood impacted a republic that had been a leading unionist prior
to the collapse of the USSR. Indeed, the predicted increased reluctance of both
Uzbekistan and Russia to incur the costs of political reintegration led both to
demand more of the other, making agreement between them much harder to
reach. Moreover, as a means of compensating for the loss of union benefits and
of defending against potential future Russian coercion, Uzbekistan's leadership
undertook a major project designed to reduce its economic dependence on Russia.
By effectively achieving oil independence, the country was able to back away
from its status as one of the very most unionist republics of the former USSR
and move closer to the more skeptical category of which Ukraine was typical.
Nevertheless, oil is not development; Uzbekistan consistently supported stronger
ties with Russia than did Ukraine, and did so even before its dramatic rejection of
its partnership with the United States in 2005. The dynamics of the Uzbek case,
then, add further evidence that the logic outlined in Chapter 4 lies at the root of
separatism in international relations.

Uzbekistan and the Early CIS: Autonomy, Subsidies, and Economic Ties

Uzbekistan, like the other Central Asian states, found itself independent by
default in December 1991. From this perspective, it is not surprising that it
sought in the CIS a way to avoid or ease this undesired shock and the costs
it entailed. Uzbekistan's President Islom Karimov had good reason to do so
despite his authoritarian proclivities. If he had worried about the possibility of

[65] Vladimir Socor, "Ukraine Rephrases NATO Goal," *Eurasian Daily Monitor*, v.1, no.63, July 30,
2004.
[66] *RFE/RL Newsline*, February 22, 2005; *RFE/RL Newsline*, February 24, 2005.
[67] *RFE/RL Daily Reports*, June 9, 1994.
[68] Solchanyk, *Ukraine and Russia*, p. 94.
[69] Author's interview with Pavlychko, 1993.

popular rioting (potentially manipulated by local political machines) prior to the USSR's demise, he was quickly reminded afterward that this possibility remained real. Less than a month after Gorbachev resigned, Russia unilaterally liberated prices and, because no barriers existed among CIS economies, effectively forced price hikes in Uzbekistan. Students in Tashkent then took to the streets in a major demonstration. There is at least circumstantial evidence that their mobilization against Karimov was "patronized" by Shukurulla Mirsaidov, the powerful Tashkent political machine boss whose government post Karimov had just downgraded.[70] This protest turned bloody, with a number of people meeting their deaths before Karimov regained full control of the situation.

As if this were not enough, in the spring of 1992, unrest in neighboring Tajikistan exploded into a full-scale civil war, toppling the incumbent leader and plunging that new country into virtual anarchy. The Tajik events represented Karimov's worst nightmare, symbolizing his own political vulnerability and threatening actually to spread into Uzbekistan. The deadly chaos lasted until the peace accord of 1997, but even then "Tajikistan" provided extra impetus for him to be wary of any policy that might threaten a sudden deterioration in his people's standards of living and thereby give added mobilizational power to potential rivals atop Uzbekistan's major political machine networks. Indeed, for reasons described in Chapters 4 and 8, Karimov's personal material interests on issues of integration largely coincided with those of the masses regarding questions of integration because both preferred for relations in the CIS to bring their new state's economy greater resources rather than fewer. And Uzbekistan's relative underdevelopment made the country more vulnerable than Ukraine to the break in economic ties with the union. Karimov also found the obvious danger of unrest to be a useful excuse to crack down on opposition movements. Against this background, Uzbekistan was initially one of the leading CIS Activists.

Yet Uzbekistan's unionism has not been as simplistic as some accounts have had it. The union its leadership wanted was imagined not out of love or loyalty but economics. Its top priorities in the CIS were to reap as much as possible the potential gains from union while protecting the republic from any future exploitation at the hands of Russian-dominated central institutions. In this, Uzbekistan's post-independence CIS policy reflected the same basic goals that drove its unionism under Gorbachev. First, it continued to pursue autonomy from Moscow, insulating itself from Russian pressure politics and entrenching ethnic Uzbek control over the local state and economy. Second, it tried to maintain as many subsidies as possible from the former Soviet states, especially Russia, and sought new ones. Third, it endeavored to preserve economic ties more generally with the CIS, minimizing the damage done by the rupture.

After independence, Uzbekistan's leadership remained insistent on autonomy as a guarantee that it would not be exploited by Russia or a Russian-dominated union in the future. Indeed, Uzbek leaders in the 1990s characterized Russia not only as the source of policies, such as shock therapy, that disadvantaged the relatively underdeveloped Uzbekistan, but also as an unstable state whose

---

[70] On Uzbek politics during this era, see Tuncer, "Understanding Violent Conflict."

mood was turning restorationist.[71] As extensive interviews in 1993 confirmed, the Uzbek policy-making elite widely favored as much autonomy as would be possible without sacrificing what economic rewards from integration were still possible. There were two broad views of exactly how much autonomy this meant. One side envisioned the CIS becoming a confederation along the lines of the early United States or the European Economic Community.[72] A second view advocated an economic union without political links.[73] The latter position most closely resembled the public stance of the Uzbek president and actual Uzbek policy.[74] Uzbekistan sought to bolster its autonomy outside the CIS framework as well, notably by diversifying its economy (making it less dependent on high value-added imports[75]) and by pushing for "energy independence" after discovering significant oil reserves on its soil in the early 1990s. The latter endeavor meant not only pumping the oil but building new refining capacity and linking it to Uzbek reserves and markets.[76]

While continuing its pursuit of autonomy, Karimov made very clear that Uzbekistan still placed great value on sustained economic ties in the CIS, which a key foreign policy adviser called of "colossal significance."[77] In a booklet widely circulated in Uzbekistan, Karimov elaborated on just what Uzbekistan hoped to gain from the CIS in economic terms:

1. Coordinated national defense through a Unified Armed Forces
2. "[A]ccess to the achievement of scientific-technical progress, innovations of other states of the Commonwealth, technology, telecommunications, means of space communication, the acquisition of needed raw materials and final production, including consumer goods at prices lower than the world market price, and also the existence of a wide market of realization of our own production"
3. Use of transportation networks and sea ports
4. Joint measures to solve ecological problems[78]

---

[71] Islom Karimov, *Ne Sbivaias', Dvigat'sia k Velikoi Tseli* (Tashkent: Izdatel'stvo Uzbekiston, May 1993), pp. 15–16; Author's interview with an adviser to the president of Uzbekistan on foreign affairs, September 25, 1993.

[72] Author's interview with Karimov's foreign policy adviser, 1993; author's interview with an official of the CIS Department within Uzbekistan's Ministry of Foreign Affairs, September 16, 1993.

[73] Author's interview with an official of the Department of Economic Relations of Uzbekistan's Ministry of Foreign Affairs, September 29, 1993; Author's interview with an economist in the staff of the president of Uzbekistan, September 30, 1993.

[74] M. Faiziev, *Sodruzhestvo Nezavisimykh Gosudarstv (SNG)* (Tashkent: Nauchno-Prosvetitel'skaia Assotsiatsiia Intelligentsii Uzbekistana, 1993), p. 17; *First Channel* (Russia), 1904 GMT, May 14, 1992, FBIS-SOV-92-095, pp. 7–8; Interfax (Russia), 1913 GMT, December 30, 1992, FBIS-SOV-92-252, p. 65.

[75] Islom Karimov, *Uzbekistan: Sobstvennyi Model' Perekhoda na Rynochnye Otnosheniia* (Tashkent: Izdatel'stvo Uzbekiston, 1993), p. 108.

[76] Henry E. Hale, "Integration and Independence in the Caspian Basin," *SAIS Review*, winter–spring 1999, pp. 163–89.

[77] Author's interview with Karimov's foreign policy advisor, 1993.

[78] Islom Karimov, *Uzbekistan: Svoi Put' Obnovleniia i Progressa* (Tashkent: Izdatel'stvo Uzbekiston, 1992), pp. 27–8.

Karimov's points 2 and 4 highlight the importance of subsidies as a factor continuing to pull Uzbekistan into Russian-led integration projects even after the USSR collapsed. Indeed, Russia continued to provide massive transfers to Uzbekistan during 1992 and 1993. For one thing, Russia did not switch to world prices in supplying Uzbekistan with energy. Less well-known but at least as important was another source of subsidy: Uzbekistan's continued use of the Russian ruble. Using rubles to purchase Russian goods cost former republics less than using precious reserves of hard currency.[79] But the ruble zone was much more than this. It was also a massive source of direct financial aid. In the form of printed rubles, Uzbekistan effectively received subsidies equal to an astounding 69 percent of its GDP in 1992. Most of this money went to pay Uzbek wages, covering nearly the entire salary fund of the republic.[80] The "ruble zone subsidy" was of far greater scale for the less-developed Uzbekistan than for the more-developed Ukraine.[81]

The Russian government, feeling both international and domestic pressures to balance its reformist budget, soon decided these subsidies needed to end. Russia first sought to impose ever stricter conditions for using its ruble. States would be required to contribute hard assets to help back the ruble; abide by Russia's credit, emissions, and banking policies; and synchronize their overall economic, budget, trade, and customs policies with those of Russia. Strikingly, newly "independent" Uzbekistan's leadership agreed to these conditions, signing the "Ruble Zone of a New Type" agreement and the associated bilateral treaty with Russia in September 1993.[82] Uzbekistan thus expressed formal willingness to cede virtually all control over its own economy to Russia in order to maintain access to these subsidies. Only after Russia made absolutely clear that the new ruble zone would not involve any subsidies whatsoever did Uzbek leaders finally (and bitterly) pull out, realizing that the rubles they would receive would no longer constitute subsidies but, essentially, credits for which a down payment would first have to be made.[83] Uzbekistan thus introduced its new national currency, the *som*, in November 1993.

Uzbekistan's Shifts in 1996 and 2005

Table 9.1 shows Uzbekistan was consistently more willing than Ukraine to engage major CIS initiatives throughout the first sixteen years of the CIS's existence, sustaining its position as a staunch CIS Activist, but a closer look at Uzbekistan's history during this period reveals two significant shifts.

[79] Author's interview with an economist and deputy of the Uzbekistan parliament, September 22, 1993.
[80] Internal report circulating in the Russian government, dated October 15, 1993. Copy in possession of author.
[81] The same report shows that Ukraine, which was in the ruble zone for 11 months of 1992, got financial aid worth 24 percent of its GDP.
[82] Author's interview with Karimov economics advisor, 1993.
[83] *Nezavisimaia Gazeta*, November 6, 1993, p. 1.

First, Uzbekistan drifted toward a more separatist stance after it finally achieved a high degree of energy independence. Uzbekistan had been a natural gas exporter before the USSR fell apart, but it depended heavily on Russian oil even after local reserves were discovered.[84] By building two new refineries to go along with the one it previously had in the 1990s, Uzbekistan was able to claim oil self-sufficiency by 1996.[85] This facilitated a shift in policy on the CIS. At the October 1997 CIS summit, Karimov flatly warned that Russia and Belarus wanted to restore the Soviet regime, and that the concept of "Eurasia" was simply a cover for revanchism.[86] During that same year, Uzbekistan showed new resistance even to economic integration measures, including a blueprint for a CIS Economic Union and more technical multilateral agreements, proposing instead to conclude bilateral agreements.[87] It subsequently declined to join the tightest subunions in the CIS, including the Russian–Belorussian Union State, the Eurasian Economic Community, and the Single Economic Space.[88] In 1999, it even withdrew from the CIS Collective Security Treaty, which had originally been concluded in Tashkent. While the rise of the Taliban in neighboring Afghanistan did prompt closer security relations with Russia, Uzbekistan preferred these to be formalized not in the CIS but on a bilateral basis.[89] And this need for Russian security help was largely obviated after the United States established a military base in Uzbekistan as it invaded Afghanistan in the wake of the September 11 attacks. Thus, Uzbekistan remained party to most of the CIS agreements it had previously signed and never approached Ukraine's degree of separatism, but it was no longer counted among the very most ardent CIS unionists between 1997 and 2005.

Uzbekistan's second shift, a return to full-fledged CIS Activist status, was catalyzed by a mass uprising in the Ferghana Valley city of Andijon, an uprising that had been preceded by a series of violent incidents in Uzbekistan. Karimov reacted brutally, by his own estimate killing nearly two hundred people and by many foreign accounts murdering close to one thousand. This uprising strongly appeared to be inspired by mass mobilization in neighboring Kyrgyzstan that had earlier that year toppled President Askar Akaev, the third leader to go down in a wave of "colored revolutions" in CIS countries during 2003–5.[90] The Andijon uprising should not be interpreted as purely a spontaneous reaction of ordinary people. Instead, it is better understood as an effort by an important regional political network (led by a group of wealthy Muslim businessmen) to mobilize

---

[84] Stanislav Zhukov, "Economic Development in the States of Central Asia," in Boris Rumer, ed., *Central Asia in Transition* (Armonk, NY: M. E. Sharpe, 1996), p. 121.

[85] *OMRI Daily Digest*, Part I, August 1, 1995.

[86] *Narodnoe Slovo*, October 25, 1997, p. 1.

[87] *Narodnoe Slovo*, October 25, 1997, p. 1; *Nezavisimaia Gazeta*, January 18, 1997, pp. 1, 3.

[88] See Table 9.1; *Narodnoe Slovo*, October 23, 1997, p. 1; *Narodnoe Slovo*, October 25, 1997, p. 1.

[89] Roger N. McDermott, "Karimov Moves Closer to Russian Fold," *Eurasian Daily Monitor*, v.1, no.24, June 4, 2004; Eric A. Miller and Arkady Toritsyn, "Bringing the Leader Back In: Internal Threats and Alignment Theory in the Commonwealth of Independent States," *Security Studies*, v.14, no.2, winter 2004–5, pp. 325–63.

[90] Henry E. Hale, "Regime Cycles: Democracy, Autocracy, and Revolution in Post-Soviet Eurasia," *World Politics*, v.58, no.1, October 2005, pp. 133–65.

discontent against Karimov after the Uzbek leader sought to break the network's control over the provincial political machine by firing the *khokim* (governor) and prosecuting the businessmen.[91]

Along with his massacre of the protesters, Karimov reacted by realigning Uzbekistan more closely with Russia and thereby shoring up his regime in two ways: realizing economic opportunities that closer relations would bring himself and the population and gaining as an ally the most determined and powerful opponent of colored revolutions more generally.[92] This was formalized by Uzbekistan's rejoining the Collective Security Treaty in 2006–2008, acceding to the Eurasian Economic Community in 2005, and expelling the United States from the military base it had been using for the war in Afghanistan.[93]

Thus, Uzbekistan wavered more than others during the first fifteen years of the CIS, yet its relative underdevelopment and its lack of a neighboring EU-like alternative led its policy makers to consistently opt for less separatist solutions to the CIS commitment problem than were chosen by Ukraine. This analysis also confirms that that the transition to independence itself raised the costs and uncertainties involved in integration and thereby led not only Uzbekistan but also Russia to demand a greater promise of economic gain in return for actually pursuing integration. In fact, as negotiations over the Ruble Zone of a New Type show, an opportunity for significant reintegration was fully realizable in 1993, but both sides forewent it, calculating that the benefits were no longer great enough once so many of the costs of independence had been sunk.

These findings also add weight to the relational theory of separatism relative to ethnicity-as-conflictual theory. For one thing, in those two instances when Uzbekistan made significant shifts in policy on the CIS, these corresponded not to changes in national consciousness but to the realization of oil self-sufficiency and a political crisis accentuating Karimov's vulnerability to popular unrest. Moreover, given the high risks and small tangible material benefits for which Uzbekistan was ready to cede significant sovereignty during the 1993 Ruble Zone of a New Type negotiations, any absolute preference for national independence would seem to have been quite weak indeed.

CONCLUSION

The relational theory of ethnicity proves to be a sound basis upon which to understand the role of ethnicity in the politics of international integration. For

[91] Eric McGlinchey, "Regeneration or Degeneration? Youth Mobilization and the Future of Uzbek Politics," paper prepared for the NBR conference on "Generational Change and Leadership Succession in Uzbekistan," Washington, DC, March 2, 2006, pp. 4–5.

[92] Pavel K. Baev, "Russia's Counterrevolutionary Offensive in Central Asia," PONARS Policy Memo No.399, *http://www.csis.org/media/csis/pubs/pm_0399.pdf*.

[93] Eric McGlinchey, "Avoiding the Great Game and Domestic Unrest in Eurasia," PONARS Policy Memo No.402; Kimberly Marten, "Understanding the Impact of the K2 Closure," PONARS Policy Memo No.401; Alexander Cooley, "Difficult Engagements: Political Lessons from the K2 Experience," PONARS Policy Memo No.400. These memos are available at *http://www.csis.org/ruseura/ponars/pm*. While Karimov moved to enter the CSTO in 2006, Uzbekistan's parliament ratified this only in early 2008. See *RFE/RL Newsline*, March 31, 2008.

one thing, as expected, we find that separatism in international relations is generally driven by the same sorts of factors that influence it when a union is already in existence. At a minimum, we can conclude this is the case for new states a decade and a half after acquiring independence, although the logic is not restricted to this condition. The core problem is one of credible commitment, the difficulty involved in guaranteeing to a potential union's would-be member states that they will not later be exploited in that union but will instead partake in a share of the benefits. States at higher levels of development (or with greater access to alternative sources of that development like the European Union) are less likely to accept higher levels of such risk because they stand to gain the least. Thus, Ukraine, despite much cultural commonality with Russia, was shown to be consistently oriented more to Europe than to the Russian-led CIS, even under the reputedly "pro-Russian" President Kuchma. States at lower levels of development, on the other hand, are likely to prize the potential gains from integration more greatly and thus to be willing to accept more risk of exploitation in return.[94] Thus, even though Uzbekistan's discovery and utilization of oil led to significantly more separatist behavior in the mid-1990s, this change was relatively moderate and was later effectively reversed after the Andijon uprising. This indicates that levels of economic development (readily visible and tangibly beneficial to the population) remained more important in driving separatism than the possession of energy resources (which only hold out the promise of future economic development).

Leaders retained the ability to manipulate the great ambiguity involved in such abstract concepts as "union" and "integration," in part by emphasizing the dangers over the possible gains or vice versa, but they also had incentive to adopt those frames that had the potential to win them the greatest degrees of popular support. This was true even in autocratic Uzbekistan, whose leaders feared not electoral competition (virtually nonexistent) but popular unrest fueled by economic discontent and strategic manipulation by regionally based political machines or networks. Examples of such unrest include the Tashkent events of early 1992 and the Andijon tragedy of spring 2005.

The cases of Ukraine and Uzbekistan also show how the transition from being in a union to entering the near-anarchy of international relations tends to raise the level of separatism of all states, even core ones like Russia. The costs of transition, including the initial dysfunction to be expected from any major institutional change, no longer weigh against the option of political independence (since these costs have already been borne) but instead against the option of reintegration with all its associated uncertainties. Every state can be expected to require more in return for supporting the integration option. This, in turn, reduces the set of possible deals. Where the transition costs of reunification are seen to be high, as they were by Russian leaders undertaking radical market reform, a state may have an extremely narrow set of conditions under which it would accept reintegration even where it would have been much less choosey before the union collapsed.

---

[94] At least when, as with the EU and the CIS, the unions in question do not have a demonstrated history of making poor nations systematically poorer than they were upon joining.

Thus, we saw Russia in the early 1990s seeking reintegration in the CIS at the same time that it sought to impose extremely strict conditions on those with whom it sought to reintegrate, effectively demanding all of the gains from union for itself. Uzbekistan, standing to benefit more than Ukraine from reintegration due to its relative underdevelopment, quite consistently agreed to Russia's ever-tightening strictures in order to remain in the ruble zone. But once it became clear that Uzbekistan would not reap any short-term gains and would bear a substantial risk of future exploitation, it pulled out.

This chapter's detailed process-tracing analysis also weighs against ethnicity-as-epiphenomenal and ethnicity-as-conflictual approaches to understanding ethnicity's role in international relations. For one thing, the case study of Ukraine found that popular pluralities in even the most separatist regions actually preferred some sort of integration with Russia in the abstract. Ukrainians were not value-rational pursuers of independence for its own sake during 1991–2007. Instead, they tended to recognize the benefits of integration but favored separatism as a strategy for improving their life chances primarily because they did not believe they could trust a union dominated by Russia. We also find, however, that we cannot stop after simply identifying that we are dealing with a commitment problem, as ethnicity-as-epiphenomenal theories would have it. The commitment problem does operate in international relations even where no ethnic distinctions are present (just as such problems generally do not require ethnic divides), but the wide variety of polling data available in Ukraine makes clear that ethnic Ukrainians have been much less likely to trust Russia than have ethnic Russians when it comes to integration. As relational theory suggests, the presence of thick ethnic divides can exacerbate the commitment problems that the anarchy of international politics tends to generate. Thus, even though a strong consciousness of national distinctiveness does not provide a motive for seeking independence, it colors the degree to which people see maintaining national independence as a good strategy for maximizing their life chances.

The patterns described in this chapter also nicely account for the behavior of the other former Soviet republics since the USSR's disintegration. A detailed account of all the complexities involved is beyond the scope of this volume; however, a brief note is suggestive. The Baltics, by far the most developed new states of the lot with undoubtedly strong senses of national distinctiveness vis-à-vis Russia, remained by far the leading separatists throughout 1991–2007, with Ukraine just behind. Belarus and Russia, lacking a clear sense of ethnic distinctiveness vis-à-vis the union as shown in Chapter 5, remained the strongest unionists, even declaring the creation of a Union State between them.[95] Among the other states, the most impoverished Central Asian countries have demonstrated the most pro-integration sentiment, especially the poorest of the group, Kyrgyzstan and Tajikistan. Even Turkmenistan, which pushed a relatively separatist

---

[95] There is some evidence that a sense of distinctiveness was gradually developing in Belarus after 1991, however. See Natalia Leshchenko, "A Fine Instrument: Two Nation-Building Strategies in Post-Soviet Belarus," *Nations and Nationalism*, v.10, no.3, 2004, pp. 333–52.

strategy during the life of its longtime ruler Turkmenbashi, appears to be return-
ing to the pattern set by other Central Asian states under the leadership of its
new president.[96]

Indeed, the Uzbek case highlights the interesting role of natural resource
wealth: Natural resource wealth is not itself economic development, which is
what is actually desired most at the mass level. But natural resource wealth can be
used under certain circumstances to acquire development and to avoid vulnerability to economic disruption at the hands of other states (notably, in the former
USSR, oil-rich Russia). These "certain circumstances" are the means to process
and market the resources domestically and internationally. Azerbaijan and Turkmenistan, essentially energy-independent of Russia early on, have thus tended to
be less willing to accept the levels of danger implied in the CIS than have Kyrgyzstan and Tajikistan.[97] Kazakhstan, while oil-rich, has faced an infrastructural
problem in that its oil reserves have been distant from and unconnected to its
refining capacity (which is additionally geared for a different quality of oil), meaning that Kazakhstan's own oil has had to be shipped to Russia for processing and
that Kazakhstan's refineries have depended on Russian oil for their business.[98]

The remaining states, Moldova, Armenia, and Georgia face special conditions
in that all three (at middle levels of development in the CIS) are involved in local
conflicts that have sometimes been manipulated by Russia. Landlocked Armenia's
war with Azerbaijan over Nagorno-Karabakh has left it politically and economically isolated and hence dependent on Russia. Georgia, which Azerbaijan is using
as a major pipeline route for its oil, has suffered Russian military intervention
in two of its ethnic enclaves and has thus been driven to fear Russian-led integration at the same time it is coerced into accommodating it to some degree.
Moldova is essentially a Romanian irredenta whose territorial integrity has been
threatened by Russian-backed separatists in Transdniestria. Oil-rich Azerbaijan
is also impacted by these special conditions due to the conflict over its Nagorno-
Karabakh region, in which Russia has effectively backed Armenia.[99]

All this suggests that theories of secessionism and international integration
would do well to engage each other more actively than they have thus far, and
that relational theory can contribute significantly to the subfield of IR theory
that seeks to explain the foreign policy behavior of states.[100] This is an important

---

[96] *RFE/RL Newsline*, May 29, 2007.
[97] Azerbaijan and Turkmenistan have not been able freely to export their energy products, however,
     depending heavily on Russia for this. They are, though, capable of supplying their own markets
     without Russian interference, for the most part.
[98] Hale, "Cause Without a Rebel."
[99] Hale, "Integration and Independence."
[100] Prominent works in this direction on former Soviet states include Jeffrey T. Checkel, *Ideas and
      International Change* (New Haven, CT: Yale University Press, 1997); D'Anieri, *Economic Inter-
      dependence*; Matthew Evangelista, *Unarmed Forces: The Transnational Movement to End the Cold
      War* (Ithaca, NY: Cornell University Press, 1999); Hopf, *Social Construction*; Celeste Wallander,
      Mortal Friends, Best Enemies: German Russian Cooperation After the Cold War (Ithaca, NY: Cornell
      University Press, 1999); William Zimmerman, *The Russian People and Foreign Policy: Russian Elite
      and Mass Perspectives, 1993–2000* (Princeton, NJ: Princeton University Press, 2002).

subfield to develop since it is relatively neglected, with most theory-driven IR research concentrating instead on explaining patterns of interstate relations rather than variation in how individual states respond to similar systemic stimuli.[101] The primary exceptions are those works that focus on the influence of particular independent variables, notably the psychology of leaders vis-à-vis war[102] or economic actors vis-à-vis trade policy.[103] Thus, more research into the ethnic factor in international relations would appear quite appropriate. There is a significant literature that at least implies explanations for variation in state policies regarding integration projects, but it primarily focuses on the European Union and is strikingly eclectic, citing an enormous array of factors in a largely unsystematic way.[104] This chapter thus provides a framework by which we might begin to systematize our understanding of this type of foreign policy behavior in Europe as well as the part of the world to which this volume pays closest attention, Eurasia.

[101] Seminal works include Kenneth N. Waltz, *Theory of International Politics* (New York: McGraw-Hill, 1979); Peter J. Katzenstein, *Small States in World Markets: Industrial Policy in Europe* (Ithaca, NY: Cornell University Press, 1985).

[102] For example, Deborah Larson, *The Origins of Containment* (Princeton, NJ: Princeton University Press, 1989); Yuen Foong Khong, *Analogies at War* (Princeton, NJ: Princeton University Press, 1992).

[103] For example, Helen V. Milner, *Resisting Protectionism* (Princeton, NJ: Princeton University Press, 1988); Peter A. Gourevitch, *Politics in Hard Times: Comparative Responses to International Economic Crises* (Ithaca, NY: Cornell University Press, 1986).

[104] Some prominent works collectively identifying dozens of causal factors include: Moravcsik, *The Choice for Europe*; Andrew Moravcsik, "Negotiating the Single European Act: National Interests and Conventional Statecraft in the European Community," *International Organization*, v.45, no.1, winter 1991, pp. 19–56; Geoffrey Garrett, "International Cooperation and Institutional Choice: The European Community's Internal Market," *International Organization*, v.46, no.2, spring 1992, pp. 533–60; Richard C. Eichenberg and Russell J. Dalton, "Europeans and the European Community: The Dynamics of Public Support for European Integration," *International Organization*, v.47, no.4, autumn 1993, pp. 507–34; Robert Rohrschneider, "The Democracy Deficit and Mass Support for an EU-Wide Government," *American Journal of Political Science*, v.46, no.2, April 2002, pp. 463–75; Wayne Sandholtz, "Choosing Union: Monetary Politics and Maastricht," *International Organization*, v.47, no.1, winter 1993, pp. 1–39.

10

Quantitative Evidence

Micro-, Macro-, and Multilevel

The preceding five chapters have employed a carefully chosen set of qualitative methods, including illustrative focused comparisons involving Ukraine and Uzbekistan, to demonstrate how a relational approach to ethnicity can improve our understanding of the totality of events related to former Soviet republics' separatist behavior. One might still wonder: Would a systematic study of more ethnic regions confirm the patterns that seem evident when the focus is on Ukraine and Uzbekistan? And even though earlier chapters have discussed public opinion survey findings, readers may yet ask: Would a more rigorous analysis of such figures – one introducing relevant control variables – still support the theory in comparison with its rivals? Ideally, the answers would be linked: Would appropriate quantitative techniques bear out this volume's claim that there actually was a connection between what was happening at the level of the republics and what was going on at the level of individual opinion?

There is good news and bad news here. First, the bad news: Because the events of primary interest took place in 1990–1, we cannot go back in time to collect the ideal data that would allow us to dismiss these concerns with complete confidence. The good news, though, is that there are at least some data available. And even though many of these data were not collected specifically for this purpose and are often far from ideal, they are of sufficient quality to weigh significantly toward or against accepting the rival theories under discussion here. This is especially true when the weight of their cumulative findings is considered, and even more so in conjunction with the wealth of systematically generated qualitative findings presented in the earlier chapters.

This chapter devotes one section to each of three types of available data on patterns of separatism. One examines patterns at the "macrolevel," patterns in the official behavior of Soviet ethnic regions' governments. We consider forty-five – nearly all of them. The subsequent section presents evidence from 1991 opinion data available from twelve minority Soviet ethnic regions that macrolevel variation in economic development significantly influenced *individuals'* views on separatism. The section after that concentrates more directly on expected patterns at the microlevel, using particularly high-quality survey data from Ukraine and Lithuania both to confirm the importance of nonethnic interests and to demonstrate that ethnicity's role is more consistent with relational theory than with its rivals. First, though, we revisit the main rival theories so as to lay out the differences in precisely what patterns each would expect us to find in the data.

THEORIES OF ETHNICITY AND PATTERNS OF SEPARATISM

Each broad conceptualization of ethnicity studied in this volume generates distinct expectations as to *whether* ethnicity matters for separatism, *how* it matters, and *what else* is likely to matter in the post-Soviet context. Readers should refer back to Chapters 2–4 for more detailed explications of these theories, but it is important to specify their different predictions here so as to facilitate proper interpretation of the findings.

Ethnicity-as-Conflictual Theory

The core proposition of ethnicity-as-conflictual theories is that national consciousness inherently provides an important motive for pursuing political independence. This generates the following expectations:

- *Whether ethnicity matters.* Ethnic distinctions will be strongly correlated with separatism.
- *How ethnicity matters.* Different versions attribute the ethnic motive for separatism to one of three sources, as described in Chapter 2. *Hard* theories link it to a desire for group-based self-esteem and would expect correlations between ethnic divides and separatism to reflect, at root, a dislike for other groups, pride in one's own group, or resentment of perceived subordinate group status. *Soft* theories see separatism as the pursuit of ethnically defined values and would, accordingly, predict the strongest ethnic effects on separatism to involve differences in ethnically defined interests or values. *Ultrasoft* theories treat separatism as an expression of historically or institutionally constructed national identity, expecting the correlation between ethnicity and separatism to be grounded in either ethnic pride or antipathies toward other groups.
- *What else is likely to matter.* Regardless of how ethnicity comes to matter, *National Consciousness* theories generally expect the only significant influences on separatism to be ethnic, not material, in nature. *Capabilities* arguments posit that minority regions with the greatest resources should demonstrate the most separatist policies since their native groups are the most able to mobilize in favor of their separatist policy preferences, but that variation in individuals' attitudes to secession will hinge on ethnic factors, not material or other concerns. *Countervailing Incentives* theories acknowledge that other considerations

weigh into the separatist calculus at both the regional and individual levels. Most such accounts hold that group advantages in the union's economy, society, or polity tend to lead otherwise separatist individuals and governments to oppose secession.

Ethnicity-as-Epiphenomenal Theory

These accounts' central tenet is that national consciousness provides no motive for pursuing political independence. Such pursuits are instead motivated by desires for goods like power or wealth. This has the following implications:

- *Whether ethnicity matters.* Ethnic factors will generally not be correlated with separatist behavior or attitudes.
- *How ethnicity matters.* If one does find a correlation between ethnicity and separatism, this likely reflects only the usefulness of ethnic divides' visibility and relative unchangeability in facilitating individuals' attempts to coordinate their self-interested pursuits of wealth or power and to distribute such goods selectively. Bargaining theories would allow for ethnicity to correlate with official regional government separatism if leaders believe their regions' ethnic distinctiveness gives them more credibility in threatening to secede as a way to gain better treatment from the union government. These theories would not expect ethnic distinctions to correlate with individuals' attitudes to separatism.
- *What else is likely to matter.* Variation in secessionism depends on who has the most to gain from independence or the greatest credibility in threatening secession in center–periphery bargaining. Most such theories hold that the wealthiest regions have the most to gain and that powerful and ethnically distinct regions have the most bargaining power.

The Relational Theory of Ethnicity and Separatism

The relational theory posits that political integration is generally desirable and that separatism is the product of an ethnically charged commitment problem. Predictive implications include:

- *Whether ethnicity matters.* Ethnic divides will generally be correlated with separatist behavior and attitudes.
- *How ethnicity matters.* Ethnicity does not supply a motive for separatism; thus, what specifically correlates with secessionism will not be pride or intrinsic worth attached to one's ethnicity. Instead, ethnicity serves as an uncertainty-reducing device that introduces a sense of separation from control of the union that accordingly exacerbates minority groups' perceived risks of exploitation at the hands of a union-dominant group. What correlates most strongly with both micro- and macrolevel separatism, then, will be senses of ethnic distinctiveness itself, lower intergroup trust, and beliefs that the dominant group is disproportionately benefiting from union policies.

- *What else is likely to matter.* People are motivated not by ethnic concerns but by "ordinary" interests, especially economic and security concerns impacting life chances. Thus, people in and governments of those minority regions with the most to gain materially from a union will be willing to bear the highest levels of exploitation risk to stay in that union. Chapter 8 argued that the regions with the most to gain from the union in the Soviet context were those with the lowest levels of economic development.

A MACROLEVEL ANALYSIS: FORTY-FIVE ETHNIC REGIONS IN THE LATE USSR

To launch the quantitative study, let us first consider patterns at the macro level, variation in ethnic regions' official policies regarding integration in the USSR.[1]

Measuring Secessionism

The closest thing to a generally accepted measure of Soviet-era official regional secessionism that exists in the literature is the date that each republic declared its sovereignty in relation to the USSR's central government.[2] The assumption is that the most eager secessionists declared sovereignty the earliest. This makes good sense because, in the Soviet case, true separatists generally pushed for immediate declarations of sovereignty so as to seize the moment offered by Gorbachev's political liberalization. Importantly, a sovereignty declaration did not necessarily mean that an ethnic region valued secession above all other strategies, but it was a declaration that the region would remain in the union only on its own terms, if at all. This was practically always the first step taken on the road to independence by those that did aim for it. Thus, the most ardent secessionists like the Baltic republics tended to declare sovereignty the earliest, while the more unionist republics like Kazakhstan did so only after becoming convinced it was necessary for bargaining position in negotiations to reconstruct the union. Since nearly all ethnic regions eventually declared sovereignty in some form, the dates they did so give us a measure that applies to nearly every case and the remaining few can be included in the analysis as "censored" observations.[3]

The primary alternative measure with precedent in the literature would be an index counting the number of "separatist acts" that each regional government undertook. Although reasonable, this approach lacks some of the advantages of sovereignty declaration timing.[4] For one thing, it assumes an arbitrary equality

---

[1] A similar macrolevel analysis is reported in Henry E. Hale, "The Parade of Sovereignties: Testing Theories of Secession in the Soviet Setting," *British Journal of Political Science*, v.30, no.1, January 2000, pp. 31–56. On the differences, see Web Appendix 10A, available from the author or at http://hehale5.googlepages.com.

[2] This was first proposed by Kisangani N. Emizet and Vicki L. Hesli, "The Disposition to Secede: An Analysis of the Soviet Case," *Comparative Political Studies*, v.27, no.4, January 1995, pp. 492–536.

[3] A "sovereignty declaration" is defined for this analysis as the adoption of any official republic policy that a republic's own laws took precedence over union laws on its own territory.

[4] Chapter 11 shows the index approach still tends to support the relational theory, even on the reduced number of cases for which indices are available.

in the weight of different sorts of separatist acts, a source of "noise" mitigated by considering a single "natural" measure like sovereignty declaration timing. And even though count-based indices have proven useful in studying post–Soviet Russia,[5] we lack confidence that enough information on the Soviet period is available to construct such an index reliably for the lowest-status or most remote ethnic regions. Perhaps most importantly, though, the sovereignty declaration measure involves timing, allowing us to test and control for demonstration effects and other time-related variables that are held to be important by major works.[6]

Sovereignty declaration timing is measured in weeks, scoring the first region to declare (Estonia) a zero so that it serves as a baseline. The dependent variable, therefore, is the number of weeks after Estonia that a given region declared sovereignty. The observation period ends with the USSR's August 1991 coup attempt in week 144, by which time only six ethnic regions had not asserted sovereignty.[7]

The Statistical Model and Interpretation

This dependent variable is thus a duration, and since a duration cannot have a negative value, results will be most reliable with a nonlinear statistical technique that does not assume negative values.[8] We also want a method that can test for time-related effects, so a Weibull statistical model, which estimates a time-dependence parameter, is used.[9] Essentially, the model assumes there is a baseline probability that a sovereignty declaration might occur for random reasons (e.g., the mere whim of a leader), considers whether the events are becoming more or less likely as time passes, and estimates the degree to which various factors make the event likely to happen sooner or later. If the coefficient on an independent variable has a positive value, we know that greater values on this factor are associated with longer periods of time before sovereignty is declared (*lower* levels of separatism). We can also calculate the level of confidence with which we can reject the null hypothesis that there is no relationship between the dependent variable and a given factor.

Just to say that wealth has an effect, however, does not tell us how *large* this effect is. Determining the magnitude of an effect is, unfortunately, not straightforward with Weibull because it is not a linear model. To gauge the effect of a given factor, therefore, we undertake a series of mock social experiments by artificially changing particular republics' values on that factor and observing the difference in sovereignty declaration timing that our Weibull model predicts would result.

---

[5] Giuliano, "Secessionism," Treisman, "Russia's 'Ethnic Revival.'"

[6] Beissinger, *Nationalist Mobilization*; Gurr, *Minorities at Risk*.

[7] The Ust-Orda Buriat AO, the Jewish AO, Khakassiia, Mordviniia, Evenkiia, and Khantii-Mansiisk.

[8] Gary King, "Statistical Models for Political Science Event Counts: Bias in Conventional Procedures and Evidence for the Exponential Poisson Regression Model," *American Journal of Political Science*, v.32, 1988, pp. 838–63, 851.

[9] For technical information on Weibull models, see Hale, "The Parade," and works cited therein.

TABLE 10.1. *Correlates of the Timing of Sovereignty Declarations Issued by Ethnic Regions in the USSR 1988–91: Results of a Weibull Regression Analysis*

Factors	Weibull Coefficient (Standard Error)	Interpretation
Ethnic group distinctiveness	−.014 (.006)**	Increases separatism
Regional economic development	−.592 (.188)***	Increases separatism
Consumer goods production	−.282 (.121)**	Positively correlated with separatism
Group education	.021 (.019)	Not significant
Elite upward mobility	−.037 (.074)	Not significant
History of independence	−.145 (.187)	Not significant
Past grievous victimization	−.101 (.131)	Not significant
ASSR status	.296 (.131)**	Decreases separatism relative to union republics
AO status	.599 (.188)***	Decreases separatism relative to union republics
Russian sovereignty declaration	−.635 (.318)**	Separatism greater after Russian declaration
Time-dependence parameter	$p = 3.73$	Declarations become more likely as time passes
Constant	6.81	
Number of ethnic regions analyzed	45	

** We can reject the null hypothesis with at least 95 percent confidence.
*** We can reject the null hypothesis with at least 99 percent confidence.

The sample of ethnic regions studied here is restricted to forty-five for four technical reasons. First, Estonia is left out because it serves as the baseline for measuring separatism; this also controls for any demonstration effect that this first sovereignty declaration is likely to have had. Second, the Ajar and Nakhichevan ASSRs and the Gorno-Badakhshan AO are excluded because they were no longer ethnically designated according to Soviet census criteria as of 1989. Third, three more cases are dropped because measures of key economic variables could not be found for the appropriate years: Abkhazia, South Ossetia, and Nagorno-Karabakh. Finally, the Aga-Buriat AO is omitted because the right measure of its degree of separatism has remained elusive.

Findings: Correlates of Macrolevel Secessionism

Table 10.1 presents a list of the factors analyzed in the statistical analysis (including control variables) and the findings as to the strength and quality of their correlation with the timing of Soviet ethnic regions' sovereignty declarations. Most fundamentally, there is strong evidence that ethnic distinctiveness is associated with greater secessionism, a finding consistent with relational and ethnicity-as-conflictual theories but in tension with ethnicity-as-epiphenomenal theories. Ethnic distinctiveness is measured as the share of a region's titular group's union-wide population (as assessed in 1989 census responses) that claimed the titular language as their native language in that same census. This measure captures the importance that the Soviet state placed on language as a marker of identity, as shown in Chapter 5. The Weibull analysis gives us over 95 percent confidence in rejecting the null hypothesis that there is no relationship between ethnic distinctiveness and sovereignty declaration timing. Moreover, the estimated magnitude of the relationship is substantial and in the predicted direction. A counterfactual exercise illustrates. Let us take Georgia, whose titular group members claimed Georgian as their native language over 98 percent of the time, and create a national nightmare scenario in the computer realm. That is, we enter all of Georgia's true values on the regression's variables back into the statistical model *except* that we report Georgians' level of native language retention at a mere 30 percent, the level of the Evenk AO. The model then estimates that the new "Assimilated Georgia" would take nearly three times longer to declare sovereignty than it estimates the real Georgia would (71 weeks instead of 28).[10] Similar exercises on other ethnic regions produce similar estimates. This strongly reinforces the comparative process-tracing evidence from Chapter 5, which showed how low senses of national distinctiveness led Belarus and Russia to refrain from secessionism.

   This macrolevel analysis is unable to tell us precisely how and why ethnic distinctiveness mattered, but we gain considerable information on the question of what else the rival theories expect will have an impact on separatism. One crucial finding is a strong positive relationship between economic development and separatism.[11] Here we must keep in mind that we cannot mechanically use measures having the same name as economic development indicators commonly used in the West, such as GDP. The USSR was a command economy, meaning that many familiar-sounding quantities are in fact seriously distorted as indicators of economic development and the key related concept of standard of living. The present analysis thus employs a measure more appropriate to this context: retail commodity turnover per capita as of 1988. An exhaustive study by economist Oksana Dmitrieva singles out this measure as an accurate and sensitive indicator of late Soviet-era territorial standards of living because it reflects levels of production and demand for consumer goods.[12] This variable is measured for 1988, when the examined durations all begin, so as to eliminate a potential source of endogeneity in the analysis.[13] The Weibull analysis allows us to reject the null hypothesis, that this variable is unrelated to sovereignty declaration timing, with over 99 percent confidence. It also estimates the effects to be quite large. If we do in our quantitative world what Stalin may have yearned to do, radically impoverishing the economically developed Latvia so that it is on the level of Tajikistan, the

---

[10] These and other estimates of effect magnitude are conservative because, due to a software limitation, they assume that Russia's sovereignty declaration was accelerating the declaration process from the very start, thereby compressing a given republic's estimated time-to-sovereignty.

[11] The negative sign on the estimated coefficient indicates that more regional development corresponds with shorter periods of time before sovereignty is declared.

[12] Dmitrieva, *Regional'naia*, pp. 116–17, 130–2. For further discussion, see Hale, "The Parade."

[13] The other independent variables are also measured for this year, or for the closest possible year to this point, for the same reason.

model estimates that "Poor Latvia" takes more than twice as long to declare sovereignty as the real Latvia (45 weeks as opposed to 22). Analogous exercises with other regions produce similar findings. Notably, economic development remains significantly correlated with separatism even when we control for 1989 consumer goods production per capita, which one prominent study has linked to circumstantial budgetary pressures toward separatism.[14] All this reinforces Chapter 8's extensive qualitative evidence that economic development (or, more broadly, material interest) is an important determinant of secessionism.

The development–separatism link is straightforwardly in line with the expectations of the relational and ethnicity-as-epiphenomenal approaches, but it has more complex ramifications for ethnicity-as-conflictual theories. The finding is most damaging for the pure National Consciousness version, which either tends to deny any role for economic factors or expects economic differentials to matter only as sources of relative group status or self-esteem. Yet we do not find relatively disadvantaged groups and regions moving most quickly to escape their lowly status in the union; instead, those that are best off economically in the union take the separatist lead. Indeed, even beyond purely economic measures, there is no evidence that groups in position of low status drive any more separatism in their republics than their more-advantaged peers. No significant relationship is detected between separatism and any of the following indicators of disadvantage: lower average group education levels, lower upward mobility into the union's political elite, and particularly grievous victimization under Stalin.[15] Nor does the negation of past status seem to have mattered systematically: Republics that were independent states for more than a fleeting period before being conquered by the USSR were, as a categorys no more separatist than others once one controls for other factors.[16] Moreover, we find that the highest-status republics in the union (the union republics as opposed to ASSRs and the lowest-ranked AOs) were the quickest to declare sovereignty. Countervailing Incentives versions of ethnicity-as-conflictual theory also locate the source of separatism in an ethnic desire to escape positions of group disadvantage in terms of status and self-esteem, so these theories are also seriously challenged by the findings. The trappings of

---

[14] Bahry, "The Union Republics."

[15] The indicator for group education levels is the share of the ethnic group's unionwide population over 15 years of age with a higher education as determined in the 1989 USSR census. For Stalinist victimization, a dummy variable is coded "1" for regions whose dominant ethnic groups suffered wholesale national deportation (Chechen-Ingushetia, Kalmykiia, and Karachaevo-Cherkessiia) or were forcibly invaded as independent states (the Baltic countries) in the USSR. See Aleksandr Nekrich, *The Punished Peoples* (New York: W. W. Norton, 1978) and Simon, *Nationalism.* The measure for elite upward mobility is the degree to which each nationality group was under- or overrepresented in the Communist Party of the Soviet Union as of 1989. Membership in the CPSU was generally considered necessary for advancement to elite Soviet posts, and the Party was explicitly meant to be an institution containing the economic and political elite. In *Ethnic Groups in Conflict*, Horowitz presents the most prominent argument that such factors should matter. The finding that these variables are insignificant also weighs against ethnicity-as-epiphenomenal theories that suggest such variables should be important but in different ways, including Rogowski, "Causes and Varieties," and Laitin, "The National Uprisings."

[16] This category includes the Baltic states and Tuva.

group advantage in the union, trappings that these theories expect will encourage a group to *forego* its posited "ethnic interest" in political independence, are in fact correlated with *greater* degrees of separatism if they are correlated with it at all.

Capabilities theory fares best among the different versions of ethnicity-as-conflictual theory. Capabilities theory is quite consistent with an argument that actual desires for secession matter less than the ability of a group to act collectively to pursue it, and capabilities tend to come from positions of advantage rather than disadvantage in the union. Indeed, as noted in Chapter 4, Capabilities theorists have frequently given pride of place to differences in economic development and institutional capacity among union republics, ASSRs, and AOs in their arguments on the Soviet cases, and the Weibull analysis confirms that the lower-level units were much slower to declare sovereignty than were the higher-level ones.[17] Turning again to a counterfactual exercise, if we reduce the union republic of Latvia to a Latvian AO, this is estimated to nearly double the time it takes Latvia to declare sovereignty, delaying its declaration from the twenty-second week to the forty-first. The analysis is also consistent with the argument that capabilities can involve perception and consciousness, and in particular that earlier declarations of sovereignty rendered national independence more conceivable and that later ethnic regions learned by watching processes in those whose sovereignty declarations preceded theirs. Such "demonstration effects" are captured by the statistical analysis in two ways. First, the Weibull model estimates a time-dependence parameter (p) that is greater than 1, indicating that sovereignty declarations became more likely to occur at any given moment as time passed ($p = 3.73$). Second, Russia is widely theorized to have had the greatest demonstrative impact on other republics in declaring sovereignty by virtue of its size and centrality,[18] so a variable that varies over time is included. It is coded '1' for the period after which Russia declared sovereignty and '0' before that. As expected, we find that Russia's declaration of sovereignty is strongly correlated with accelerated subsequent sovereignty declarations by other ethnic regions: We can reject the null hypothesis of no relationship with over 95 percent confidence.

The macrolevel statistical story, then, would appear to be strongly in line with both the relational theory and the Capabilities version of ethnicity-as-conflictual theory. It raises serious doubts, though, about the National Consciousness and Countervailing Incentives versions of ethnicity-as-conflictual theory. The finding of ethnicity's importance is consistent with these latter accounts, but the way in which other factors matter appears to be nearly the opposite of what they would expect. The macrolevel analysis is also problematic for ethnicity-as-epiphenomenal theories: They generally appear right in expecting the most economically developed ethnic regions to be the most separatist, but the finding that ethnic distinctions correlate strongly with republic separatist behavior is unexpected for this approach. Ethnicity-as-epiphenomenal theory still retains

---

[17] Beissinger, *Nationalist Mobilization*; Gorenburg, *Minority Ethnic Mobilization*; Roeder, "Soviet Federalism."

[18] Lapidus, "From Democratization," p. 59.

a couple plausible defenses, however: Perhaps ethnic distinctions simply give regional elites greater bargaining power, or perhaps ethnicity mattered as a set of lines along which people coordinated their "nonethnic" activities or selectively distributed resources. The latter possibility is unlikely. As noted earlier, the USSR already possessed ample and more cost-effective lines that elites could have used to coordinate their resource-seeking activities and selectively distribute the spoils: The subrepublic territorial-administrative divisions that had long been institutionalized precisely for resource distribution. Thus, it is unclear why elites would have needed to mobilize ethnicity for this purpose if this were truly the only reason ethnicity mattered. To be sure, however, we need to move beyond macrolevel analysis to examining patterns in individual support for separatism, a task the following two sections take up.

INDIVIDUAL ATTITUDES TO SEPARATISM: A MULTILEVEL ANALYSIS

It is fortunate that some mass surveys touching on ethnic politics were conducted during 1990–1 in the countries of interest, and datasets from a few of them are publicly available. The present author thus searched the holdings of the Interuniversity Consortium for Political and Social Research (ICPSR), the main repository of such data that are publicly available, looking for relevant data from the post-Soviet region. Only a handful of survey datasets turned up, and after examining their questionnaires, only three were found with even a minimum set of questions necessary for testing our rival theories' core hypotheses for the crucial period of 1990–1: the New Soviet Citizen surveys of 1990 and 1991, designed by Arthur Miller and his University of Iowa collective, and the 1991 General Social Survey of the European USSR, conducted by Michael Swafford and a Russian team including Polina Kozyreva and Mikhail Kosolapov – all through the high-quality Institute of Sociology of the Soviet Academy of Sciences. Of these, the General Social Survey was least useful because it did not focus on political questions, and among the minority republics, it contained a plausibly representative sample only for Ukraine.[19] The New Soviet Citizen surveys harvested some very useful information that will be considered later, but among the minority republics, it covered only Ukraine and Lithuania.

The New Soviet Citizen surveys will thus provide reasonable opportunity to examine the microlevel correlates of individuals' inclinations toward or away from separatism; however, it is important to note the following: Our theories' predictions involving regional levels of economic development, unlike those involving national consciousness, imply a *cross-level* effect. That is, whereas national consciousness works primarily within the individual (an individual's ethnic identification influences his or her perceptions of the union), economic development

---

[19] Data were sufficient to test whether ethnic divides were correlated with variation in trusting the central relative to the republic leadership, which they were, as predicted by the relational theory. See Web Table 10.5 and the associated appendix available on the author's Web site (http://hehale5.googlepages.com) or directly from the author.

works by linking the regional (macro) level to the individual (micro) level. A given *region's* degree of economic development relative to other regions' is posited to be generally recognized by individuals in a minority ethnic region and to influence *individuals'* willingness to accept a given amount of risk that their region will be exploited in a union that it does not dominate. The fact that the New Soviet Citizen surveys cover only two minority republics thus means that they provide insufficient republic-level variation to facilitate meaningful efforts to investigate the cross-level effects of regional economic development on individual attitudes.

To test for the expected cross-level effects during the late Soviet period, then, the present study was left only with a partial dataset obtained for personal scholarly use from the Russian survey agency VTsIOM not long before state officials asserted control over the organization, leading to the departure of its highly reputable longtime director, Yury Levada. The package did not include precise information on data collection and sampling, so no judgment about proper weighting could be made. Despite this major drawback, the dataset has some important strengths. For one thing, the survey was conducted in January 1991 – when separatist politicking was in full flower and a wide range of popular views on it likely – and included multiple questions on relations between the republics and the central government that facilitate testing key propositions of interest. Answers from all respondents to these and other requested questions were supplied to the author. Even more importantly for present purposes, the survey includes respondents from twelve of the fourteen minority union republics of the USSR. Specifically, 4,849 respondents throughout the USSR were queried, with 2,263 being from the minority union republics. Of the latter respondents, 1,078 were from the largest, Ukraine. It must be kept in mind that the survey was meant to be representative of the entire USSR, not of the individual republics.

For the reasons just given, it would be inappropriate to attach too much weight to findings based on the sample from the non-Russian republics. Yet these data from VTsIOM provide the only opportunity obtained by the author to conduct even a rough test of the proposition that the republic-level variable of economic development influenced individuals' attitudes regarding the union back in 1991. Because there is no reason to expect that the aforementioned deficiencies in the data should produce bias toward reporting a correlation between these key variables of interest, and because any such findings could be corroborated by other quantitative and qualitative evidence presented in this volume, it is at a minimum suggestive to see what these data have to tell us while keeping in mind the important caveats just mentioned.

The Variables: Dependent and Independent

Although the survey did not directly ask people if they would support the secession of their republic, it did inquire: "Do you agree that now the economic and political unity of the USSR should not be violated?" It is, of course, theoretically possible to disagree with this statement and not be a separatist; for example, someone in, say, Uzbekistan could favor keeping Uzbekistan in the union but think that it would be OK for the Baltic countries to leave.[20] It is reasonable to expect, however, that the disagree responses will have captured much more strongly the sentiments of those who favored separation for their own republic, especially since the question was asked right after respondents were queried on whether they believed their *own* republic entered the USSR illegally and against the will of its own people. For want of a better indicator, then, a "dummy" (binary) variable labeled "secessionist" is created, coded "1" for those who disagree and "0" otherwise. This is the main dependent variable. The extent to which this choice of indicator matters can be tested by running the same analysis using an alternative specification: a dummy variable coded "1" for respondents who agreed with the statement that "it is better to conclude not a new union treaty, but instead direct treaties on cooperation among republics without the participation of the center." This is also likely to capture attitudes toward actual secession, but it is a bit further from the concept because it does not actually talk about parts of the union breaking away – the alternative to the union treaty does not necessarily imply no union would result.

The rest of the equation is as follows. To maximize consistency with the macrolevel study, regional-level economic development is measured the exact same way as it was there, as retail commodity turnover per capita in 1988. Unfortunately, the dataset does not include indicators of individuals' nationality or native language, although we can partially compensate for this: A dummy variable is created that codes as "1" people who, when asked "who should be considered citizens of your republic," selected "only residents of the native nationality" – the only ethnic criterion given. Because members of the titular ethnic group are the only ones likely to answer in this "chauvinist" way in a given minority republic, this variable serves as a crude indicator of nationality, albeit combined with extreme ethnic views. A series of individual-level control variables are also included in each version of the regression for age, education levels, gender, and residence in the republic capital city.

The Statistical Model and How to Interpret It

To assess whether republic economic development has a cross-level effect on the separatism of individuals, we must employ a statistical technique that does not assume observations within a given republic are completely independent of each other. Likewise, because the dependent variable is binary, linear methods are likely to be inefficient. We thus use a multilevel ("mixed effects") logistic model, which is designed for datasets sharing these two important features.[21] The estimated coefficients for each independent variable are reported as odds ratios, which in the case of a dummy variable reflect "the odds that someone with

---

[20] Even this, though, captures a weak commitment to the union's territorial integrity.
[21] Andrew Gelman and Jennifer Hill, *Data Analysis Using Regression and Multilevel/Hierarchical Models* (New York: Cambridge University Press, 2007), Chapter 14, and Stata Corporation, *Longitudinal/Panel Data* (College Station, TX: Stata Press, 2007).

TABLE 10.2. *Correlates of Individual Separatist Attitudes: A Multilevel Logistic Regression Analysis of VTsIOM Survey Data from January 1991*[a]

Factors	DV: Secessionism	DV: No Union Treaty
Republic level		
Republic economic development	13.5 (3.7)***	3.8 (2.7)***
Individual level		
Chauvinist	2.0 (3.1)***	1.0 (0.3)
Older	0.9 (−3.6)***	0.9 (−3.5)***
Higher education level	1.2 (4.5)***	1.1 (2.6)***
Lives in capital city	1.2 (0.9)	1.3 (1.6)
Female	0.7 (−3.7)***	1.1 (1.1)
Number of republics analyzed	12	12
N	2,263	2,263

***Null hypothesis rejected with at least 99 percent confidence.

DV = dependent variable

[a]Coefficients are reported as odds ratios. Figures in parentheses are Z statistics. Z statistics are an indicator of statistical significance. For readers not familiar with them, the asterisks summarize the most important conclusions to be drawn from them.

a value of 1 on that factor is a separatist" divided by "the odds that someone with a value of 0 on that factor is a separatist." An odds ratio greater than 1, therefore, indicates that an increase in a given factor raises the odds of someone being a separatist while a value of less than 1 indicates that the factor tends to reduce these odds.

Findings

The primary findings, presented in Table 10.2, bear out the expectations of the relational theory. Most importantly, being located in a republic at the highest levels of economic development raises the odds of an individual being a secessionist more than tenfold, and we can reject the null hypothesis with over 99 percent confidence.[22] The detected correlation between economic development and separatism remains above that same threshold of statistical confidence with the alternative measure of separatism ("no union treaty"). The odds ratio estimate of development's effect drops from 13.5 to about 4 with the alternative measure, but this still means that a one-unit increase in economic development (which would make up about two-thirds of the difference between the least- and the most developed republics) raises the odds of an individual within a given republic giving a separatist answer to the survey question at hand fourfold.

This finding is most supportive of the relational and ethnicity-as-epiphenomenal theories, both of which posit an unambiguously positive relationship between the economic development level of an ethnic region and separatism among individuals within that region. It weighs strongly against most National Consciousness and Countervailing Incentives theories. These accounts expect

[22] Recall also Table 8.1, which presents survey evidence establishing a link between real and perceived minority republic economic standing.

development and separatism to be either uncorrelated or related in the opposite way, with separatism either feeding off positions of inferiority or being overridden by the prospect of doing relatively well in the union. The multilevel analysis also starts to call some versions of Capabilities theory into question. Specifically, it runs counter to any notion that economic development matters only as a resource enhancing individuals' *ability* to collectively mobilize: We have found here that greater economic development also influences people's *views*, making them more likely to favor separatism, not just to act. Capabilities theory still retains a viable defense, however: Economic development may supply nationalist elites with greater resources for *raising national consciousness* among the masses, which then provides the motive for the individual-level separatism we observe in the survey and explains the greater separatism observed in the more-developed regions. Since a rough indicator of strong national consciousness is included in the equation, however, the analysis does control at least partially for such a consciousness-raising effect.

Turning to this crude indicator of national consciousness, the analysis described in Table 10.2 reports over 99 percent statistical confidence that it is related to our primary measure of secessionism. Being an ethnic chauvinist is estimated nearly to double one's odds of being a separatist. This, as with the finding on ethnic distinctiveness in the macrolevel analysis, tends to support the relational and ethnicity-as-conflictual theories and to raise concerns about the accuracy of ethnicity-as-epiphenomenal assumptions. When the alternative measure of separatism ("no union treaty") is used, however, the direction of the estimated effect is as predicted, but our confidence in rejecting the null hypothesis drops below even the forgiving 90 percent threshold. Because the sense of national distinctness is expected to have its causal effects at the individual level, however, this is not the end of our ability to evaluate its role.

ETHNICITY, INTERESTS, AND SEPARATIST ATTITUDES: A MICROLEVEL
ANALYSIS

The finer instrument of the 1990–1 New Soviet Citizen surveys of Ukraine and Lithuania enable us to take one more crucial step for which the VTsIOM data were inadequate, exploring precisely *how* ethnicity influences attitudes toward separatism. Careful analysis not only reiterates that nonethnic interests are important, as the relational theory expects, but confirms that ethnicity's effects arise from the exacerbation of a union commitment problem rather than from self-esteem- or pride-based motives (as per hard and ultrasoft ethnicity-as-conflictual theory), culturally specific values (as per soft ethnicity-as-conflictual theory), or a desire for favoritism in patronage distribution (as per ethnicity-as-epiphenomenal theories).[23]

---

[23] The survey authors also analyzed the implications of these data for understanding secessionism, although not to test the specific theories under the microscope here. See Vicki L. Hesli, William M. Reisinger, and Arthur H. Miller, "The Sources of Support for Separatism: Public Opinion in Three Soviet Republics," *Nations and Nationalism*, v.3, no.2, 1997, pp. 201–29.

Important Features of the Surveys

The 1990 and 1991 versions are not identical. The 1990 iteration surveyed about 600 people per republic, while the 1991 number was expanded to about 1,000 for Ukraine (keeping Lithuania at 600). The samples were designed to be reasonably representative for each republic in both years.[24] The questionnaires were also not the same. Some useful questions were asked in 1990 but not 1991 and others in 1991 but not 1990, so certain topics can be investigated best with reference to only one round of the survey.

The Dependent Variable and Statistical Model

Neither of the New Soviet Citizen surveys asked respondents explicitly whether they favored the secession of their republic from the USSR, although they both contained questions that would clearly capture such preferences. The 1990 questionnaire included only one such item, asking people to choose from among four different balances of center–republic authority as the one that would "work best" in "representing the interests of people like you." To construct the 1990 dependent variable, then, respondents who selected "all decisions rest with the republic leadership" instead of the other options, each of which involved delegating some significant authority to the central government, are coded as "1" and others "0."

   This same question was again asked in 1991, in addition to a new one that is likely to have more precisely captured attitudes to secession: People were presented with a five-point scale, ranging from a view that "all political power should remain with the central leadership" to one that all power should "be located at the republic level." This new question also left out the decision criterion specified by the 1990 edition ("in representing the interests of people like you"). A binary dependent variable for separatism based on this new question was thus created that codes people "1" if they thought all power should go to the republic. The 1991 survey also included a third reasonable measure of separatism: When asking people what measures they thought the union should take to preserve itself, unprompted responses of "I do not consider it essential to preserve the union" were also recorded as a category. Those responding in this way were coded "1" in a third binary indicator of separatism. As it turns out, it makes almost no difference for the rival theories which of the three 1991 measures of separatism are used in the analysis.[25] This chapter thus reports results from the most precise indicator, the second one described in this paragraph.

   Because all dependent variables are binary and we are no longer exploring cross-level effects, a standard logit model is used for the statistical analysis. Each analysis includes several control variables.[26]

---

[24] Variables indicating weights and territorial clustering provided by the survey designers were incorporated in the following analysis.

[25] See Web Appendix to Table 10.3, available from the author directly or on his Web site (http://hehale5.googlepages.com).

[26] Indicators of gender, age, education, residence in the capital city, and being a student are available and included in each of the regressions. Also included in each are dummy variables indicating sociotropic and pocketbook economic assessments: "USSR Economy Worse" codes as 1 those

Findings: Correlates of Microlevel Separatism

The first step in exploring how ethnicity matters is to verify that the macrolevel correlation between ethnic distinctiveness and separatism (see Table 10.1) holds when it comes to individual people. To maximize consistency, it is desirable to use the same measure of ethnic distinctiveness that was used in that earlier analysis. Thus is created a dummy variable that codes as "1" people who said they belonged to the titular nationality of their republic and also claimed the titular language as their native tongue. Unfortunately, the survey included the necessary question on native language only in Ukraine and only in 1991. For Lithuania in both years and Ukraine in 1990, then, we operationalize ethnic distinctiveness with a slightly less perfect indicator, the nationality claimed by respondents in the survey.[27]

As expected, we find that individuals' ethnic distinctiveness is strongly correlated with separatist attitudes and that this relationship is robust to different specifications of both ethnic distinctiveness and secessionism.[28] Table 10.3 reports that the magnitude of the effects is also significant: Ethnic Ukrainians were nearly twice as likely to voice separatist views in spring 1990 as were others, and those Ukrainians claiming to be native Ukrainian speakers were even more likely to do so in 1991. The effects in Lithuania appear even stronger: The odds of a Lithuanian advocating the transfer of power to Lithuania in 1990 were nearly seven times as great as the odds of someone else doing so, and by 1991 the odds ratio had risen to nearly 10. This weighs strongly against ethnicity-as-epiphenomenal theories treating ethnic divides as nothing more than a bargaining resource used by elites; they appear to affect not only elite behavior but also mass attitudes.

Because many of the theories under consideration are consistent with at least some role for ethnicity in separatism, we can distinguish among them only by exploring precisely what this role is. To do this, we replace the simple indicator of ethnic distinctiveness with a set of variables intended to capture different specific mechanisms by which the various theories expect ethnicity to have its effects. We thus essentially test them head-to-head, as summarized in Table 10.3.

The relational theory holds that ethnicity's effects derive chiefly from its tendency to exacerbate commitment problems in the union, with thick ethnic divides creating an added sense of separation from control that raises the risk that minority groups attach to staying in the union. If true, we would expect to find a strong relationship between separatism and the degree to which titular group members

---

people who reported that the Soviet economy had gotten worse over the prior year as opposed to getting better or staying the same, while "Pocketbook Worse" is the analogous variable for how people's own families' economic situations had reportedly changed over the previous year. The 1991 survey facilitates one additional control, a dummy variable coded 1 if the respondent lived on a collective or state farm.

[27] It is less perfect because it is more likely to include assimilated Ukrainians and Lithuanians, people with a lower sense of ethnic distinctiveness vis-à-vis Russians.

[28] The only exception is that self-professed Lithuanian nationality was not significantly correlated with the third 1991 measure of secessionism (the volunteering of a view that the USSR should not be saved).

TABLE 10.3. *Individual-Level Correlates of Secessionism in Ukraine and Lithuania: Estimated Effects, Given as Odds Ratios (t-statistics in parentheses), Resulting from Logit Analysis of New Soviet Citizen Survey Data from 1990 and 1991*

Factors	Ukraine					Lithuania				
	1990: All Decisions by Republic	1990: All Decisions by Republic	1991: All Power to Republic	1991: All Power to Republic	1991: All Power to Republic	1990: All Decisions by Republic	1990: All Decisions by Republic	1991: All Power to Republic	1991: All Power to Republic	1991: All Power to Republic
Testing ethnicity										
Ethnic distinctiveness (nationality)	1.8 (3.8)***		2.4 (3.7)***		2.1 (3.7)***	6.8 (8.4)***		9.8 (5.7)**		8.4 (4.6)**
Ethnic pride		0.9 (−0.3)					1.1 (0.6)			
Ethnic mistrust		1.3 (3.0)**		1.4 (4.6)***			1.7 (4.9)**		1.8 (3.7)**	
Russophobic (commonality w/Russians)		1.2 (2.3)*		0.9 (−1.2)			1.3 (3.7)**		0.6 (−2.0)	
Ethnic patronage				1.9 (1.3)					1.9 (1.0)	
Russians benefit				2.3 (3.4)***						
Testing nonethnic interests										
Interest representation	2.2 (8.1)***	2.3 (8.7)***	2.8 (5.9)***	2.6 (5.5)***	2.4 (5.2)***	12.4 (12.8)***	11.3 (14.2)***	4.6 (7.5)***	3.9 (5.9)***	5.5 (12.0)***
Ethnic interest representation					1.6 (1.5)					0.5 (−1.5)
Ethnicity is primary ID					1.3 (0.9)					2.1 (1.7)
Controls										
USSR economy worse	2.2 (2.4)**	2.1 (2.4)**	1.0 (−0.2)	0.9 (−0.6)	0.9 (−0.4)	0.7 (−0.5)	0.6 (−0.9)	2.1 (1.8)	1.8 (1.6)	1.9 (1.5)
Pocketbook worse	1.2 (0.8)	1.1 (0.6)	1.7 (2.6)**	1.7 (2.7)***	1.7 (2.7)**	0.8 (−0.9)	0.8 (−0.9)	0.7 (−1.3)	0.7 (−1.0)	0.7 (−1.2)
Female	0.8 (−1.4)	0.8 (−1.3)	0.8 (−1.3)	0.8 (−1.4)	0.8 (−1.3)	1.1 (0.3)	1.0 (0.1)	0.7 (−3.8)**	0.7 (−4.1)**	0.7 (−4.1)**
Older	1.0 (−1.1)	1.0 (−0.7)	1.0 (−0.8)	1.0 (−1.0)	1.0 (−1.0)	1.0 (−1.3)	1.0 (−0.9)	1.0 (−0.8)	1.0 (−1.8)	1.0 (−0.3)
Education	0.8 (−3.5)***	0.8 (−2.9)**	1.0 (0.4)	1.0 (0.3)	1.0 (0.1)	0.8 (−7.0)***	0.8 (−7.5)***	1.0 (−0.1)	1.0 (−0.02)	1.0 (−0.1)
Capital city	1.4 (1.7)	1.4 (1.7)	1.8 (4.2)***	1.7 (4.0)***	1.8 (3.9)***	1.4 (1.1)	1.4 (1.2)	1.4 (1.7)	1.5 (1.4)	1.5 (1.8)
Student	1.5 (2.0)*	1.4 (1.6)	1.3 (0.7)	1.7 (0.5)	1.2 (0.6)	1.1 (0.2)	1.0 (0.02)	0.7 (−1.2)	0.7 (−1.3)	0.8 (−0.9)
Collective/state farm			0.5 (−1.6)	0.5 (−1.8)*	0.5 (−1.7)*			0.8 (−0.6)	0.9 (−0.2)	0.8 (−0.7)
N	592	592	986	986	986	599	599	600	600	600

* We can reject the null hypothesis of no relationship with at least 90 percent confidence.

** We can reject the null hypothesis of no relationship with at least 95 percent confidence.

*** We can reject the null hypothesis of no relationship with at least 99 percent confidence.

Note: Variable names in parentheses indicate that the variable was used as a substitute because the one listed above it was not available for that particular regression.

"trust the All-Union leadership to do what is right," in the words of a New Soviet Citizen query posed in both the 1990 and 1991 surveys. The relational theory would also predict greater separatism among those who, when asked "does the economic policy of the center benefit some groups more than others," replied "yes" and then named the dominant group in the union (Russians) as the disproportionately benefiting group – this set of questions was asked of Ukrainians in the 1991 survey. As Table 10.3 shows, for each of these two variables, we have at least 95 percent confidence in rejecting the null hypothesis. Moreover, the estimated magnitude of the effect for each variable is larger than for any of the rival theories' indicators. The odds of being a separatist were between one-and-one-quarter and two times greater for titular group members who mistrusted union leaders than for others, and people who believed central economic policies disproportionately benefited ethnic Russians were over twice as likely to express separatist views compared to others.

If ethnicity's mass-level importance instead derives primarily from its usefulness as a set of hard and bright lines around which individuals coordinate their pursuits of patronage resources, as important ethnicity-as-epiphenomenal theories posit, we would expect significantly greater separatism to be found among titular group members who believed that "in terms of getting a job . . . public officials of your nationality give preference to members of your nationality" at least "sometimes" or "often." This question was asked of both Ukrainians and Lithuanians in the 1991 survey. The statistical analysis, however, finds that Ukrainians and Lithuanians who believed that their coethnics distributed jobs along ethnic lines in their respective republics were generally no more separatist than anyone else there, controlling for other factors.

Ethnicity-as-conflictual theory sees ethnic divides as embodying natural desires for political independence rooted in ethnic antipathies, distinct cultural values, or ethnic pride. The data analysis, however, provides no evidence that separatism is primarily an expression of pride in one's ethnic identity: Lithuanians in Lithuania who reported having a "very positive view of" Lithuanians (i.e., a 5 on a five-point scale of "feelings"), as well as the analogous Ukrainians, were no more likely than others to advocate separatist policies in 1990, the only year in which the survey included the relevant question. There is some significant evidence, though, that separatism is associated with ethnic antipathies: Respondents who reported having "very negative" views of ethnic Russians in 1990 (also on a five-point scale of feelings) were between one-and-one-fifth and one-and-one-third times more likely to favor separatism than were others. The null hypothesis of no relationship could be rejected at the 90 percent level in Ukraine and at the 95 percent level in Lithuania. Even though the survey included this direct measure of Russophobia only in 1990, the 1991 version did ask a question that we would expect to at least partially capture the same antipathies: Respondents were asked how much they "have in common (share their ideas, interests, their outlook on different events) with" ethnic Russians. Feelings of low commonality with Russians were not significantly correlated with separatism in either Ukraine or Lithuania, although a significant correlation did appear in some of the robustness checks.[29] The possibility that ethnic divides reflect culturally distinct values will be treated later because it relates strongly to the concept of "interests" that is separately discussed.

In weighing results, it is important to note that the tested predictions are not all mutually exclusive, although some are. Ethnicity-as-epiphenomenal theory is consistent with the finding that separatism is correlated with a perception that Russians are unduly advantaged in the union and with a lack of trust in the union leadership, but it is in great tension with the importance of ethnic antipathy and with the insignificance of ethnic patronage politics. Hard ethnicity-as-conflictual theorists would not be surprised to find separatism associated with perceptions of Russians disproportionately benefiting in the union and with ethnic mistrust, although they would also have generally expected a significant positive relationship between separatism and expressions of ethnic pride, which was not detected. Ultrasoft ethnicity-as-conflictual theory is likewise compatible with the finding that separatism is positively related to ethnic mistrust and Russophobia, but its association with Russian *economic* advantages in the union and, especially, the insignificance of positive ingroup feelings stretches the theory's ability to account fully for observed patterns.

The relational theory is highly consistent with all of these findings, however. For one thing, its indicators were more strongly correlated with separatism in terms of both statistical significance and the magnitude of effects than were the indicators of each rival theory. Moreover, the expression of Russophobia was the only ethnic variable from a rival theory found to be significantly correlated with separatism, and this does not necessarily contradict the relational theory. This Russophobia could very well reflect antipathy for members of a group that is the ethnic source of the posited commitment problem. That is, it may be that this antipathy is not driving separatism, as is often assumed, but is instead a by-product of the core process that produces separatism. Chapter 3 in fact explained the passion and emotion accompanying ethnic conflict in essentially this way. The relational theory also accounts better than ethnicity-as-epiphenomenal theory for how the ethnic and the economic interact: Separatism is associated not with the proactive pursuit of disproportionate gains in ethnic patronage, as ethnicity-as-epiphenomenal theory tends to posit, but rather with an essentially defensive perception that another group is disproportionately benefiting materially.

The relational theory finds even more support when we turn more directly to interests not derived from ethnicity. The 1990–1 New Soviet Citizen surveys asked each year: "On the whole, which political leaders do a better job of representing the interests of people like you, the All-Union political leaders or those of your Republic?" Table 10.3 shows that people who indicated "republic leaders" were consistently between two and three times more likely than others

---

[29] Feelings of commonality with Russians in 1991 were correlated with the first measure of separatism (that included in both the 1990 and 1991 surveys) in Ukraine and with the third measure of separatism in both republics using at least a 90 percent confidence level. The significance of the other tested "ethnic effects" variables did not depend noticeably on which measure of separatism was used.

to favor secession in Ukraine and as much as twelve times more likely to do so in Lithuania, although the estimated odds ratio for the latter had fallen by 1991 to the still large figure of 4.6 in the simple regression. Very consistently, we can reject the null hypothesis with at least 99 percent confidence.

There is strong reason to believe that respondents, when hearing interviewers say "the interests of people like you," did in fact have nonethnic sources of interest in mind and that the "interest representation" variable in the analysis is capturing this more than ethnic interests. For one thing, other variables in the first four reported regressions for each republic are included explicitly so as to capture (and thus control for) the most important ethnic effects. Moreover, the 1991 survey included an item that presented respondents with a list of identity categories and asked them to name "the one with which you have the most in common." Even though the list of categories did not include anything close to a full set of major nonethnic identity categories,[30] the list did include the categories "Ukrainians" and "Lithuanians." We would certainly expect Ukrainians and Lithuanians who saw their ethnic identity as their primary source of interests to have selected their ethnic category here. As it turns out, only 31 and 42 percent of respondents selected "Ukrainians" and "Lithuanians" in each respective republic.[31] This adds confidence that the results for interest representation in Table 10.3 are not primarily reflecting "ethnic" interests.

We test this more rigorously by creating an interaction variable designed to distinguish the effects of interest representation among those people who are likely to have had *ethnic* interests in mind from the effects of interest representation among those who are likely to have had *other, nonethnic interests* in mind. That is, we create a variable capturing ethnic interest representation that is coded "1" for people who both claim titular ethnic identity as their primary identitification and say that republic leaders do a better job of representing the interests of people like them. This is an interaction term – anticipating that the combination of the ethnicity and interest variables has an effect that is not simply additive – so we also include the two variables of which this one is composed in the equation (general interest representation and the indicator of whether people say they have the most in common with the ethnic over other given categories).[32]

The results are striking. For one thing, we note that there is no significant correlation between separatism and specifically "ethnic interest representation" in either Ukraine or Lithuania in 1991, the only year for which the necessary questions were asked. This strongly indicates, contrary to soft ethnicity-as-conflictual theory, that what matters about ethnicity is not culturally specific values from which interests might be derived. Even more importantly, the inclusion of this interaction term means that the odds ratio reported for the variable labeled simply "interest representation" in Table 10.3 must be interpreted not as the estimated

---

[30] Professional categories were limited to pensioners, workers, housewives, businessmen, and miners.
[31] Cross tabulations given by Miller et al.
[32] On the proper use and interpretation of interaction terms, see Bear Braumoeller, "Hypothesis Testing and Multiplicative Interaction Terms," *International Organization*, v.58, fall 2004, pp. 807–20.

effect of interest representation generally but as the estimated effect of interest representation *among people who do not claim ethnicity as their primary source of identification*. And crucially, we see not only that the estimated effect is as statistically significant as ever, but that it is almost exactly as large (even a bit larger in Lithuania) as was estimated when we did not explicitly attempt to separate out any ethnic component.

This finding supports the relational and ethnicity-as-epiphenomenal theories, both of which posit that nonethnic interests are highly important influences on secessionism. It is also consistent with the Countervailing Incentives version of ethnicity-as-conflictual theory, which also allows for the possibility of other concerns weighing alongside ethnically rooted ones. Conversely, it casts doubt on the National Consciousness version of ethnicity-as-conflictual theory, which leaves little room for nonethnic concerns to play a significant role in shaping individual attitudes regarding secession. The results also sit uneasily with the Capabilities version of ethnicity-as-conflictual theory: This theory posits that economic development is correlated with separatism primarily because it gives nationalist elites additional resources to raise national consciousness (seen as the true underlying motive for separatism), not because economic interests supply motives in their own right. The results indicate otherwise.

CONCLUSION

Overall, rigorous statistical analysis of patterns in Soviet ethnic regions' official policies and public opinion adds a great deal of confidence to the conclusions drawn from the previous, less quantitatively oriented chapters. As we would expect if separatism derives primarily from an ethnically charged commitment problem in the pursuit of "ordinary" interests, the most separatist government behavior among forty-five ethnic regions was found in the set with the least-assimilated titular ethnic groups and the weakest economic incentives to remain in the union. Survey evidence from twelve of these ethnic regions in 1991 confirms that individuals living in the most economically developed republics were significantly more likely to voice separatist views than those residing in the least economically developed ones. More elaborate survey data available from Ukraine and Lithuania in 1990–1 strongly corroborate the claim that individuals' perceptions of their "nonethnic" interests are a crucial consideration in forming attitudes toward secession. These latter surveys also confirm the important link between ethnic distinctiveness and separatism and supply evidence that the link is ethnicity's accentuation of the difficulty union governments face in credibly committing not to exploit minority groups for the dominant group's benefit: Separatism was significantly more common among people who believed ethnic Russians were benefiting disproportionately from central economic policies and among titular group members who trusted republic leaders over central ones.

All rival theories can find at least some results to point to in isolation, which helps explain their continuing ability to appear in peer-reviewed publications, but the overall pattern calls into doubt their suppositions as to the nature of ethnicity and its role in separatist politics. The robust findings that higher levels of development and considerations of nonethnic interests correlate with separatism are decidedly in line with the expectations of ethnicity-as-epiphenomenal theory, but the striking influence of ethnic distinctiveness is not. Bargaining theories can explain the macrolevel importance of ethnic divides as a resource that enables regional elites to push separatist claims further for bargaining purposes, but they cannot explain why ethnic traits influence the attitudes of individuals within these republics. Other ethnicity-as-epiphenomenal theories account for both the macro- and microlevel importance of ethnic markers by treating them as particularly efficient lines along which elites and masses can coordinate their pursuits of material and political gain. These accounts are weakened both by the observation that other lines are likely to have obviated any such need for ethnicity in the Soviet context and by the finding of no significant relationship between the perception of ethnic patronage and separatism in two of the most separatist republics, Ukraine and Lithuania. This is not to deny that ethnicity and patronage are often linked elsewhere both in reality and in people's minds, and that this often has to do with ethnicity's usefulness as a marker, but it is to say that we cannot characterize this link as somehow constituting the fundamental essence of ethnicity and its relationship to separatism.

Similarly, each version of ethnicity-as-conflictual theory seems to explain some patterns very well, but none is satisfactorily consistent with the bigger pattern of events and public opinion in the late USSR. The biggest boost for ethnicity-as-conflictual theory in general is the strong, consistent, and positive correlation between ethnic difference and separatism. The approach is seriously challenged, though, by the equally robust finding that other factors matter at least as much and in ways that contradict the logic of the theory. National Consciousness theory expects nonethnic factors to matter only insofar as they impact national consciousness, generating senses of group inferiority or grievance that accentuate a national desire to escape the union. Yet the greatest minority secessionism is found among groups in positions of economic and political superiority, not inferiority. Similarly, Countervailing Incentives theory holds that ethnicity is but one of many sources of peoples' interests and that the natural national desire for independence can be outweighed by any economic or political benefits expected from integration. Yet the strongest separatism was consistently found in those minority regions that enjoyed the most economic development and the highest institutional status within the union.

The version of ethnicity-as-conflictual theory that emerges strongest from the quantitative findings is the Capabilities argument: Economic and political advantage may correlate with separatism by providing greater resources to nationalist leaders in their quest to raise and mobilize nationalist sentiment. Yet the pattern of public opinion that we see in two of the most important republics that actually seceded, Ukraine and Lithuania, indicates neither that separatism is only about nationalist sentiment nor that other factors matter only in heightening or mobilizing it. Instead, we find that people's perceptions of nonethnic interests are central influences on their attitudes to separatism.

In fact, when we test the various ethnicity-as-conflictual assumptions as to the nature of ethnicity's effects against the assumptions on which the relational theory is built, the relational theory strikingly outperforms all versions of ethnicity-as-conflictual theory. We find no evidence that the ethnicity–separatism link derives from feelings of ethnic pride or distinct ethnic values, the assumptions on which ultrasoft and soft ethnicity-as-conflictual theories tend to rest. And even though we do find a significant connection between separatism and ethnic antipathies, which is consistent with hard and ultrasoft ethnicity-as-conflictual theory, this can equally well be explained as a by-product of the ethnically charged commitment problem that lies at the heart of the relational theory. This interpretation is sturdily reinforced by the fact that the relational theory's concepts of ethnic mistrust, nonethnic interests, and undue benefits accruing to the dominant group are *each* more strongly related to separatism than are ethnic antipathies in both Lithuania and Ukraine, in both years in which the survey was taken, and in terms of both substantive and statistical significance. The quantitative findings thus return us to this book's central thesis: Ethnicity is about uncertainty reduction, whereas separatist politics is about interests.

It is striking that this basic proposition is borne out so consistently despite the motley and imperfect nature of the available data. Although data imperfections would certainly be grounds to question a given finding taken by itself, the pattern that emerges in combination starts to become compelling. And when this evidence is compiled with the findings from previous chapters' process-tracing analyses and focused comparisons, the appeal of the relational approach to understanding separatism becomes quite strong indeed. The concluding chapter starts to explore how well it can account for patterns beyond Eurasia and ventures a sketch of what a more general relational theory of ethnic conflict (not just separatism) might look like.

PART III

CONCLUSION

11

Toward a General Theory of Ethnic Conflict and Solutions

This book has made two core arguments. First, it has contended that social science will best advance with a new fundamental theory of what ethnicity is and why it is what it is, a theory grounded solidly on psychological research into human behavior. Second, it has proposed a candidate for such a theory, a relational theory that is based on the following premise: Ethnicity is driven by uncertainty reduction, whereas ethnic politics are driven by interests. This approach was shown to be capable of underpinning a new theory of national separatism that has logical and empirical advantages over existing theories. In fact, Part II of this volume demonstrated it was capable of significantly revising standard understandings of one of modern history's most momentous sets of events: the breakup of the USSR, the continued failure of reintegration efforts in the CIS, and the separatism that lies behind such developments. Separatism arguably follows similar patterns elsewhere in the world.

The implications of the relational theory of ethnicity are not limited to national separatism, however. After summing up the conclusions of the preceding chapters and relating them to worldwide patterns of separatism, this concluding chapter distills a core logic from the analysis of separatism to posit what a general relational theory of ethnic conflict might look like. Such a theory is shown to have promise for illuminating prospects for multiethnic state collapse, international integration failures, and various forms of deadly ethnic violence, drawing on suggestive examples from across the world. Finally, we discuss some implications as to how policy makers might best seek to end and avoid ethnic conflict.[1]

THE BALANCE OF EVIDENCE

The first core argument of this book has been that social science is more likely to make headway in understanding ethnic politics if we can develop a more solidly grounded understanding of what ethnicity is in the first place. It is striking how

---

[1] Additional implications for theory building can be found in Hale, "Explaining Ethnicity."

fundamental the disagreement currently is about the nature of ethnicity. Chapter 2 broke the literature down into two broad categories, one treating ethnicity as inherently conflictual (even if historically contingent) and the other viewing it as essentially epiphenomenal, merely a convenient set of lines along which self-interested individuals can exclude others from spoils, foment conflict, or coordinate their actions and expectations. These two broad approaches tend to structure current debates on ethnic politics, leading experts to dramatically different views as to the causes of and solutions to ethnic conflict. Surely both sets of theories capture important truths. A great deal of conflict in the world involves ethnic divides, which frequently are associated with distinct values and aspirations. It is also true that ethnic lines are useful for elites wishing to distribute spoils, provoke violence, or coordinate activities and expectations. But neither of the broad theoretical traditions adequately captures why these important observations are true, and evidence presented by each side frequently stumps the other side. Some of the most promising recent work in each camp has started to deeply engage psychological research. But the leading ethnicity-as-conflictual theorists rely too heavily on an increasingly discredited interpretation of certain findings, whereas those few ethnicity-as-epiphenomenal theorists who do engage this research cannot account for some crucial evidence suggesting ethnicity is not epiphenomenal. If we can develop a theory that is better grounded in research on human behavior, we may be able to recast earlier findings in a way that reconciles key insights from the two camps while generating new ones, facilitating more robust advancement in our efforts to understand and resolve ethnic conflicts.

The second core argument of this book has been that ethnicity is the realm of uncertainty reduction, whereas ethnic politics is the domain of interests. Ethnic identification itself does not inherently supply people with particular values, senses of self-esteem, or even dignity. Ethnic consciousness is also not simply a by-product or manifestation of material or political interests. Instead, ethnicity derives from the inherent human need to reduce uncertainty in the world, a need well established in psychological research and consistent with evolutionary theory. If identity is the set of personal points of reference on which people rely to navigate the social world, then ethnicity is a set of these points that possesses special properties for uncertainty reduction. Ethnicity, therefore, is most fundamentally relational, availing individuals of information on how the social world relates to them. This argument is more consistent with research into human psychology than are alternative perspectives.

While many others have noted that ethnicity serves an uncertainty-reducing function, they have usually not expanded upon this insight, overlooking its far-reaching implications. Perhaps most important is the fact that those markers usually falling into the category "ethnic" share a strong capacity for serving as highly meaningful rules of thumb in interpreting important aspects of the world of human relations. First, ethnic symbols "thickly" connote a sense of common fate due largely to the myths of common origin and history they typically imply. Second, ethnic divides frequently involve communications barriers that are inherently noticeable and important because they involve significant transactions costs in social interaction. Third, ethnicity frequently features highly visible physical differences that are hard to change or disguise. And fourth, ethnic differences frequently coincide with other important determinants of humans' life chances (e.g., socioeconomic status, value systems, ways of life), meaning that ethnic markers can become convenient cognitive shorthand for rapidly inferring a wide range of information about a person one has never actually met before. Thus, ethnicity is important to people primarily because of the crucial role it plays in navigating the social world, in uncertainty reduction.

What people *do* in their less uncertain worlds, on the other hand, depends on the same banal interests that drive the rest of human behavior, most notably the interest in maximizing their life chances. Ethnicity can involve great emotion when people view their life chances as being significantly constrained along the lines of an ethnic divide. All this was shown to be consistent with a wide range of psychological research, and more so than the most developed alternatives. Ethnicity, then, is neither an inherently conflictual motive nor epiphenomenal. Instead, it is a cognitive device for uncertainty reduction that precedes and enables interest-oriented behavior.

How this general logic can facilitate theory building on major political phenomena was shown through the particular subject of separatism, both in ethnofederal countries and among already-independent states. The object of explanation was the strategies chosen by official representatives of ethnic regions/states regarding their regions'/states' relationship to a given (potential) union. Since the relational theory posits there is no inherent ethnically inspired value attached to independent national statehood, and since political integration generally involves at least potential gain for all due to reduced transactions costs and economies of scale, we gain a starting assumption: Ethnic regions will generally *prefer* union to independence, ceteris paribus. This statement does not mean that ethnic regions will always opt for independence as a *strategy* for maximizing life chances, however. This is because union governments typically have the power not only to distribute gains for the benefit of all but to exploit individual member regions, making them worse off than they would be as independent countries. Moreover, governments sometimes have incentives to exploit, as when they have reason to prioritize short-term over long-run gains. This collective action problem, not the expression of national consciousness, is the driving force behind separatism in both ethnofederal countries and international relations. That is, separatism is one strategy for escaping exploitation in a union. The fact that some governments exploit while others cooperate, along with the facts that exploitative governments typically disguise their intentions in cooperative promises and that governments can change their collective minds later, creates a situation of uncertainty. Regions have to decide whether to choose a separatist strategy not knowing for sure whether a future union will be exploitative or cooperative.

Ethnicity comes into play because it is an uncertainty-reduction device. Crucially, it does not necessarily convert uncertainty into certainty, but more often converts uncertainty into *risk*, establishing expectations as to the likelihood of each possible outcome occurring.[2] Ethnicity is not neutral in assessing risk, however. Ethnic distinctions lead people to attach higher probabilities to the danger of exploitation for at least one of two reasons: (a) Symbols associated with them frequently connote interpretations of exploitative or cooperative mutual histories; and (b) they create a sense of separation from control over outcomes in the union, and research on risk management finds that people generally tend to overestimate the likelihood of bad outcomes over which they have less control. Ethnicity thus exacerbates the collective action problem of union without actually causing it, increasing the chances that separatism will be seen as a necessary strategy without actually motivating it.

Separatism is not the only strategy for managing this collective action problem, however, since solutions such as consociationalism and decentralization can also be seen as viable under certain conditions. Whether an ethnically distinct region chooses a secessionist or unionist strategy, therefore, is likely to depend on how regions perceive the collective action problem as it exists in the particular union at hand. These perceptions can be influenced by central state policies, the framing strategies of leaders, and different regional interests as aggregated and expressed through regional institutions. Due to their strong implications for life chances, material interests are expected to be especially important. Unless certain central policies create different expectations, we would posit that the most developed regions would have the least to gain economically from a particular union and would therefore be the first to resort to separatist strategies as the risk of exploitation in a union rises. Whether a region is already an independent state or is already in a union also matters: Preexisting independence means that integration involves transactions costs that would not have to be borne by a region that is already integrated in a union. Conversely, when it comes to opting for independence, the transactions costs of change must be borne by a seceding region but not by an already-independent state. Plus, a strategy of independence undertaken by an independent state, as opposed to a seceding region, is less likely to bring about a military reaction from the jilted union partners.

The power of this relational theory of separatism was demonstrated in a thorough, multimethod study of developments in Eurasia. Not only does the theory explain a series of very important events better than do existing alternatives, but it also helps spawn new insights into the events themselves that differ from those reached even by area specialists. For one thing, contrary to the expectations of ethnicity-as-epiphenomenal theory, senses of national distinctiveness were found to be crucial in heightening the risk of exploitation that regions' leaders and populations attach to a given union project. This helps explain why both Belarus and Russia, the two republics whose titular populations had the least "ethnic material" distinguishing them from the (former) union central government, sought to save

---

[2] Recall the distinction between uncertainty and risk from earlier in this volume: Under *uncertainty*, people cannot attach probabilities to various possible outcomes, whereas they can attach probabilities to outcomes under *risk*.

the USSR during the crucial fall of 1991 and became the two leading champions of reintegration after the Soviet Union's breakup.[3] Belarusian unionism is especially puzzling for ethnicity-as-epiphenomenal theories, which posit no reason why Belarus should have behaved differently from other republics, including its highly separatist neighbors Ukraine and Lithuania. The importance of ethnic divides was confirmed in statistical analyses of forty-five ethnic regions as well as of public opinion in Ukraine and Lithuania. Not only were the most ethnically distinct regions systematically the most separatist, but ethnic divides were strong predictors of individuals' levels of trust in the union government and of support for separatism. Some ethnicity-as-epiphenomenal theories might posit that ethnicity correlates with separatism because the pursuit and distribution of resources were expected to be coordinated along ethnicity's highly visible and relatively hard lines. But territorial-administrative lines were available, previously used, and potentially far more efficient for such coordination and resource distribution, leaving us to wonder why ethnic divides would have been used instead of territorial-administrative ones for such purposes. Accordingly, mass survey analysis in Ukraine and Lithuania, two highly separatist republics, found separatism to be unrelated to whether individuals believed their republic leaderships engaged in such ethnic patronage.

At the same time, evidence is strong that ethnic divides are not themselves the key source of separatist impulses, as virtually all major versions of ethnicity-as-conflictual theory posit. Survey data from 1990–1 in Ukraine and Lithuania provide evidence that ethnicity had its separatist effects precisely by accentuating the commitment problem at the heart of the union, as relational theory expects, not by producing feelings of ethnically inspired pride, hostility to outgroups, or ethnically derived interests. Nonethnic interests were also found to have weighed heavily on the separatism of ethnic regions and individuals within those regions. And crucially, survey evidence showed that people were far more concerned with their own economic well-being than with ethnic concerns like preserving culture or reviving the nation, even in highly separatist Lithuania and western Ukraine. Accordingly, accounts that explain separatism primarily by explaining national consciousness can have a strong whiff of tautology about them. Thus, the received wisdom prior to the Soviet breakup had been that the Central Asian republics posed a greater ethnic threat to the union than did Ukraine, but the prevailing assessment of relative national consciousness reversed itself after it was observed that Ukraine actually seceded in 1991 while Uzbekistan and other Central Asian republics did not. In reality, as Chapter 5 showed, both Ukrainians and Uzbeks had developed a strong sense of national distinctiveness vis-à-vis the dominant Russians, and both groups associated these ethnic divides with grievous wrongs committed by the union government in the past. Thus, it would have been possible to construct a national consciousness narrative "explaining" separatism in either republic, but separatism had only developed strongly in one by 1991.

---

[3] The perception that some hold of Russia being antiunion before the USSR's breakup was shown to be a misinterpretation.

Some versions of ethnicity-as-conflictual theory do attempt to account for variation that can occur if one assumes national consciousness and holds it constant: Capabilities theory argues that groups can vary in their ability to mobilize separatism, whereas Countervailing Incentives theory posits that the supposed ethnically rooted desire for political independence can be outweighed by other incentives that might point toward unionism. But the balance of evidence is still more consistent with relational theory. For one thing, despite the fact that Soviet state capacity was deteriorating and its economy was falling into chaos during mid-1991, Ukraine as well as Uzbekistan began to converge with the central government on saving the union once Gorbachev found a more credible solution to its central collective action problem. This convergence was disrupted only when the August coup attempt undermined Gorbachev's strategy. Additionally, Ukrainian and Uzbek separatism was powerfully influenced by how leaders framed the union's collective action problem for their masses, yet this should not have mattered if the absence of separatism reflected only a group's inability to mobilize it. So strong was this framing effect that Ukrainian separatism and Uzbek unionism could actually have been reversed had republic leaders adopted different framing strategies, even during the fateful fall of 1991. And leaders chose these frames not in a vacuum but largely in response to mundane economic interests and in a way distinguishing relational theory from its rivals. Most versions of ethnicity-as-conflictual theory see economic advantage in a union as a source of status and countervailing incentives that can pull otherwise separatist regions into the union fold. Yet analysis of official republic policy as well as public opinion consistently found the opposite, that economic advantage correlated with greater separatism because the least developed republics had the most to gain from the union. More generally, almost everywhere a significant relationship was found, what was correlated with separatism was not lower positioning in union hierarchies, as ethnicity-as-conflictual theories typically posit, but higher positioning in terms of wealth and territorial-administrative status. Importantly, these patterns endured with only slight fluctuation straight through the transition to independence until the time of this writing, although as expected this transition created sunk costs in independence that raised levels of separatism across all republics.

All this does not necessarily negate seminal findings on separatism that appear in earlier works, but it does suggest some modest but significant reinterpretations that place them on firmer theoretical ground. For example, higher levels of regional autonomy were indeed correlated with higher levels of Soviet-era secessionism, and the usual interpretations are either that autonomy provides nationalists with greater opportunity to pursue their separatist goals or that autonomy gives political entrepreneurs greater resources to grab power and/or promote national consciousness. More consistent with overall findings, though, is a slightly different interpretation: Elites can use the resources of ethnofederal autonomy to cultivate awareness of commitment problems in the union at the same time that these resources enable more aggressive strategies to insulate oneself against the dangers of union exploitation that flow from such commitment problems.

Similarly, the "tidal" patterns in the spread of nationalism that Beissinger documents do not so much *produce* national consciousness and *enable* it to take a natural course toward political independence, but instead act more to *heighten the situational availability of ethnicity* as a means of understanding highly uncertain situations and thereby *heighten fears of exploitation that arise due to the collective action problem inherent in political integration projects*. This formulation accounts for Beissinger's impressive findings while still being able to explain the reversal in separatist trends that took place during April–August 1991.[4]

More generally, by providing a sounder foundation for theories of national separatism and shedding unwarranted assumptions about the nature of ethnicity and nationalism, the relational approach has helped significantly reinterpret one of the twentieth century's most important developments. The USSR's breakup turns out to have been a far more contingent event than is commonly recognized. Its dissolution was not simply the denouement in a process of inexorably rising separatism produced by national identity and the growing failure to restrain or counteract it. Nor did the union's incentive structure guarantee it would be torn asunder by avaricious political entrepreneurs hiding behind ethnic masks. Instead, the central problem was the challenge Gorbachev faced in finding a way to guarantee (to the satisfaction of local populations and leaders) that union institutions would not one day exploit minority republics. And while such guarantees were difficult to find and sustain in the presence of thick ethnic divides and institutional flux, they were not impossible in the union framework, as Ukraine's change in behavior before the August 1991 coup demonstrates. The Soviet Union may have been delicate, but it was certainly not doomed.

WORLDWIDE PATTERNS OF SEPARATISM

There is at least prima facie evidence that the relational theory of separatism gives us purchase in understanding separatism in contexts other than the USSR. For one thing, the USSR provided what is arguably the best opportunity available for social scientists to study patterns of relative separatism because it contained more ethnic regions than any ethnofederation in history at the same time that many useful data are available on each of these regions. This evidence adds special comparative validity to the findings for two reasons. First, few dispute the fact that separatism can involve multiple considerations, so it is important to consider multiple cases so as to include necessary controls and to rule out alternative theories. Second, one of the central claims of the relational theory of separatism is that central state policy is among the most crucial determinants of secessionism. In fact, the driving force behind separatism is the collective action problem inherent in political integration, a collective action problem whose central referent is a given union state. This has major implications for how theories of secession should be tested: The central state referent cannot be ignored when evaluating theories. To illustrate, let us take two other variables found in this study to

[4] Beissinger, *Nationalist Mobilization*.

be important determinants of separatism: ethnic distinctiveness and economic development. The claim that these factors are important is not falsified by a failure to find a correlation between absolute measures of wealth among ethnic regions of the world and their degrees of separatism. Instead, *regions must be measured relative to other regions in the same country* because this holds constant the variety of other country-specific factors (e.g., countrywide institutions, central policies on ethnic minorities, or histories shaping expectations of future union payoffs) that are highly likely to influence the levels of secessionism in all ethnic regions of a given country.

The failure to use adequate controls may be one reason why leading theorists seem to reach very different conclusions, for example, regarding whether "wealth" or "poverty" causes secessionism. A very poor region, for example, may be driven to a secessionist strategy despite prospects for gain in the union if its representatives calculate that the union is almost 100 percent certain to be exploitative. Thus, despite the overwhelming pattern of "economically developed separatists" in the USSR, as documented in Chapter 10, we find that impoverished Chechnya is generally regarded as the Russian Federation's most avidly separatist republic. This was not always the case. During the Gorbachev era, it was among the more moderate ethnic regions of the USSR; for example, it declared sovereignty only after more than two-thirds of the other ethnic regions had done so. But due to a series of contingent events (including a local coup), it became singled out for intervention on the part of Russia's central government starting in late 1991, an intervention that was botched and then spiraled into armed conflict as Russia resorted to imposing greater and greater levels of destruction on the tiny republic without exercising the level of competence necessary for successfully quashing the separatists. This experience, more than anything else, turned Chechnya into a die-hard secessionist region in the 1990s by fueling the local belief that Chechnya would likely reap exploitation rather than cooperation in any future union with Russia. Likewise, a highly developed ethnic minority region might opt to stay in a union if that union has very credible guarantees in place that the union will be cooperative, allowing all to benefit from the gains of union. Ethnofederal Switzerland, for example, has experienced few serious separatist movements among its various cantons, all more prosperous than the highly separatist Baltic republics of the USSR. Just to count the numbers of secessionists that are rich or poor will thus not tell us very much by itself.

These methodological considerations point out the great strength of the statistical studies of the Soviet cases: the existence there of enough ethnic regions to bring out important large-scale patterns of separatism by comparing regions in the same country, thereby largely controlling for central state policies. When we seek to study patterns of separatism extending beyond a single country, we start to encounter all kinds of difficulties controlling for these important central state policies and contextual factors.

In fact, we have good reason to suspect that different histories of center–periphery relations can produce different expectations as to whether economically less-developed regions will be able to benefit from a given union. One instance of the importance of historical context may be the distinction between postcolonial and postcommunist countries. European colonialism typically brought and/or reinforced theories of racial and ethnic superiority by which some groups were seen as good managers of wealth, for example, and others were thought more suited for menial labor. Given that colonial rule was entrenched for decades in many countries, one might very reasonably posit that the "natural" expectation would become that central governments tend to make the rich richer and the poor poorer. Indeed, this may help reconcile Horowitz's landmark observation based on African and Asian cases that "backward" groups tend to be the leading seceders with Chapter 4's contention that, in general, less-developed regions have more to gain from a given union than do more-developed regions.[5] Because expectations of central state policies are the primary determinant of separatist tendencies, powerful colonial legacies may well override what would otherwise be a "naturally" stronger attraction of poorer regions to a union.

All this must remain in the realm of hypothesis until better tests are possible; however, there is at least suggestive evidence that economic considerations may be systematically related to separatism in cases other than the Soviet Union, although in a context-sensitive way. Some limited data are readily available for four of the world's ethnofederal countries that have contained the most nondominant ethnic regions: the Russian Federation (thirty-one nondominant ethnic regions), India (eighteen), Ethiopia (seven), and the former Yugoslavia (five). This gives us a total of sixty-one ethnic regions with which to work.[6] Through readily available media reports and specialists' accounts, it is possible to determine which of these regions are most inclined to secessionism and to compile indices of separatism to reflect this during different points during the 1990s. The Russian data come from Treisman's index of regional ethnic activism, which counts the various kinds of separatist acts observed in a given region. Analogous indices were constructed by the author for the other ethnofederations studied here based on secondary accounts and newspaper reports.

Importantly, because we are interested in what explains variation in separatism across regions in the same country, each region is measured on all these factors only in relation to other nondominant ethnic minority regions in the same country, and then these measures (when not simply dichotomous variables) are made comparable by expressing them as in-country percentiles or as the number of standard deviations they are away from a country's mean. For example, for the percentile measure of relative secessionism, the most separatist region of Yugoslavia (Slovenia) represents the country's 100th percentile of separatism and is given a score of 100, whereas the least separatist (Montenegro) is considered to be in the "naughth" percentile and hence scored 0. Using the standard deviation measure, Slovenia's level of separatism is 1.3 standard deviations above

---

[5] Horowitz, *Ethnic Groups in Conflict.*

[6] The Russian figure does not count Ingushetia, created only in 1992 and for which key data are missing. Yugoslavia's Kosovo and Vojvodina are not counted because their autonomy was revoked by the federal government between 1989 and the country's disintegration.

Yugoslavia's mean, and Montenegro's is 1.3 below it. Importantly, therefore, what we are measuring is not degrees of separatism relative to some absolute standard but the degrees to which different regions are separatist *relative to other regions in their own country*.[7] Linear statistical techniques are appropriate for analyzing patterns in the continuous standard deviation measure of separatism, and the percentile measure is better suited to a Tobit model because it is strictly limited to the range of 0–100.

A highly preliminary statistical analysis of these data, summarized in Table 11.1, does indicate both that material considerations impact separatism beyond the USSR (temporally as well as geographically) and that context strongly influences how they matter. Thus, if we use standard indicators of ethnic regions' economic development and create a measure comparing them to their country's mean,[8] we find no direct relationship between relative "wealth" and relative separatism across our four ethnofederations. Yet if we include an interaction term in the equation, which considers the possibility that relative wealth might have a unique relationship to separatism in postcolonial contexts, we find that this is indeed the case. The wealthiest regions in a given postcolonial country (India or Ethiopia) tend to display less separatist activism than the poorest regions in that country, as is indicated by the negative sign on the coefficients. This finding, though, should be treated as suggestive only because it is quite sensitive to measurement techniques: The relationship is extremely strong when relative measures are gauged using percentiles, but when standard deviations are used we can no longer reject the null hypothesis of no relationship with even the minimal 90 percent statistical confidence. The sign on the coefficient remains negative though, in both cases. Outside the postcolonial realm, in Russia and Yugoslavia, it is relative wealth that is correlated with separatism, just as in the USSR. One fruitful area of future research, then, is likely to be how context impacts the economic considerations germane to separatism.

Testing the cross-national importance of cultural variables is extraordinarily difficult, though, because the situational nature of identity and the variety of ethnic attributes that can become significant markers can change radically from environment to environment. Thus, even though the USSR's policies and other factors helped make language an extremely thick identity category in those parts of the world it dominated, different markers can thicken in other contexts. It was thus beyond the scope of this book project to create a reliable index of ethnic distinctiveness that could capture such contextual variation in what people see as the key markers of ethnic distinction. In order to suggest the promise of this line of research, though, the quantitative analysis reported in Table 11.1 included measures of two ways in which ethnic groups might see themselves as distinct from the group perceived to control the central government. Of these, there was

---

[7] See Web Appendix 11–1, available from the author directly or on his Web site (http://hehale5. googlepages.com), for technical details on these regressions.
[8] Using the standard deviation technique where the dependent variable is measured in standard deviations and the percentile technique where the dependent variable is measured in percentiles.

TABLE 11.1. *Correlates of Regional Secessionism Relative to Own Country's Mean in Complex Ethnofederations (Ethiopia, India, Russia, and Yugoslavia)*

Factors	Technique of Measuring a Region's Secessionism Relative to Other Regions in Same Country			
	Standard Deviations[a]	Percentiles[b]	Standard Deviations[a]	Percentiles[b]
Relative wealth[c]	0.13 (0.10)	0.02 (0.21)	0.25 (0.08)**	0.39 (0.07)***
Relative wealth in postcolonial countries[c]	0.80 (0.17)**	37.34 (27.96)	−0.22 (0.28)	−0.72 (0.21)***
Different religion than dominant group	0.05 (0.16)	−0.15 (0.36)	0.83 (0.10)***	39.72 (24.68)[d]
Relative local dominance of native group[c]	−1.12 (0.19)***	−38.44 (7.70)***	0.05 (0.20)	−0.12 (0.39)
Subordinate administrative status (Russia only)			−1.45 (0.29)**	−64.93 (15.61)***
Postcolonial country			−0.50 (0.27)	−5.15 (17.29)
Constant	−0.11	44.43	0.17	46.07
N	61	61	61	61

* Null hypothesis rejected with at least 90 percent confidence.
** Null hypothesis rejected with at least 95 percent confidence.
*** Null hypothesis rejected with at least 99 percent confidence.
[a] OLS statistical model used.
[b] Tobit statistical model used.
[c] Measured in standard deviations from the country mean when relative secessionism is measured in standard deviations from the country mean, but measured in country percentiles when relative secessionism is measured in country percentiles.
[d] Null hypothesis can be rejected with 89 percent confidence.

no evidence that separatism was consistently linked to the degree to which an ethnofederal region's officially native group (or groups) dominates the demography of that region. There was strong evidence, though, that religious differences captured an important sense of distinctiveness that tended to promote separatism across a variety of contexts. Whereas the null hypothesis could be rejected with just under the commonly used 90 percent threshold when the percentile measure of relative separatism was employed, the equation using the standard deviation measure would lead us to reject the null with well over 99 percent statistical confidence. The interpretation ventured here is that religious differences in and of themselves did not *cause* separatist conflicts in places like Chechnya and Kashmir, but that the sense of distinctiveness these religious lines connoted helped intensify these conflicts, exacerbating the commitment problem at the heart of the union.[9] Clearly, future studies will do well to find and construct better indicators and to conduct more rigorous analyses, but the limited central objective here has been met: to demonstrate the empirical plausibility of a claim that both material considerations and ethnic distinctiveness correlate with separatism beyond the USSR in a way anticipated by relational theory.[10]

Indeed, this analysis helps us sort out the many studies that conclude the economy impacts separatism but contradict each other on what the patterns are. The most thorough studies linking separatism to underdevelopment generally focus on the postcolonial "developing" world of Africa and Asia.[11] Those based on other parts of the world (mostly Western Europe and the postcommunist world) have been the ones tending to conclude economic development promotes greater separatism.[12] Natural resource wealth is likely to have somewhat more complicated dynamics because countries' masses tend to value oil wealth not in its own right but because it holds out the *promise* of bringing economic development. Its effect on separatism is thus likely to be less clear than for actual economic development. Even though vast hydrocarbon reserves seem clearly correlated with separatist activity in Nigeria's Ogoni region and with Norway's rejection of the EU, they were not a clean predictor of separatism in the USSR,[13] although they did take on more importance after the union broke apart.[14]

---

[9] Georgi Derlugian, "Che Guevaras in Turbans: Chechens versus Globalization," *New Left Review*, v.237, 1999, pp. 3–27; Ganguly, *The Crisis in Kashmir*.

[10] The result on subordinate administrative status depends entirely on the Russian cases, where some ethnic regions (AOs) were officially lower in rank than the other ethnic regions.

[11] For example, Horowitz, *Ethnic Groups in Conflict*; Mitra, "The Rational Politics"; Rudolph and Thompson, "Ethnoterritorial Movements."

[12] Emizet and Hesli, "The Disposition to Secede"; Timothy M. Frye, "Ethnicity, Sovereignty and Transitions from Non-Democratic Rule," *Journal of International Affairs*, v.45, no.2, winter 1992, pp. 599–623; Jason Sorens, "The Cross-Sectional Determinants of Secessionism in Advanced Democracies," *Comparative Political Studies*, v.38, no.3, 2005, pp. 304–26; Woodward, *Balkan Tragedy*.

[13] Three of the four most resource-rich states were generally unionist during 1990 and 1991: Kazakhstan, Turkmenistan, and Russia.

[14] Hale, "Integration and Independence."

EXTRACTING A THIRD CORE ARGUMENT: A GENERAL THEORY OF ETHNIC CONFLICT?

Can the relational theory of separatism from Chapter 4 be generalized to produce a broader relational theory of ethnic conflict? The two core arguments of this book have been that we need a fundamental theory of ethnicity and that ethnicity is about uncertainty reduction, whereas ethnic politics is about interests. The power of this relational theory was illustrated by showing it could undergird a strong, concrete theory of separatism that has advantages over existing alternatives in explaining major, concrete events. It may thus be possible to extract the core of this theory of separatism to produce a more general relational theory of ethnic conflict. The relational approach to ethnicity might be operationalized in a variety of ways, however, so no claim is made that what follows is the only specific theory of ethnic conflict that can arise from or be consistent with the broader approach.

The driving force behind conflict in Chapter 4's relational theory of separatism is a collective action problem, and this is a proposition that can surely be generalized. If the relational theory is correct that ethnicity is about uncertainty reduction and does not inherently imbue intergroup noncooperation with any greater value than intergroup cooperation, then it is quite reasonable to assume that any given set of people can collectively be best off in terms of life chances when they cooperate regardless of ethnic distinctions. That is, moving from a state of conflict to cooperation generally produces a greater social good and the "surplus" that comes from cooperation can at least in principle be distributed such that no individual is worse off than before.[15] One might also reasonably posit that the chief problem is that individuals can often gain at the expense of the greater good by "cheating" or, in the language of the game theorist, by "defecting." This is the heart of the collective action problem. Individuals contemplating cooperative strategies thus face a crucial element of uncertainty: Will their potential partners actually cooperate or will they take advantage of opportunities to cheat?

Ethnicity can come to serve as a means for reducing this uncertainty depending on its levels of cognitive accessibility (situational or chronic) and fit with the structure of the collective action problem at issue. Because ethnicity is an imperfect uncertainty-reducing mechanism, one implication is that some individuals can become involved solely due to their relationship to the ethnic categories that are invoked, even though these individuals may have not originally had anything to do with the particular collective action problem at hand. Moreover, if accessible and sufficiently fitting ethnic divides are thick with symbols of past noncooperation, they can render the collective action problem more difficult to overcome as individuals assess greater risks of future defection from cooperative endeavors.

---

[15] One reason is that conflict usually involves the destructive or nonproductive expenditure of resources, as Chapter 4 noted. Cooperation also arguably facilitates the production of public goods and the taking advantage of economies of scale.

Even without such negative symbolism, though, thick ethnic divides invoked as uncertainty-reduction devices can introduce a sense of separation from control when "another group" potentially holds positions of control, as in typical credible commitment problems. And one of the core findings of risk management research has been that people are more likely to exaggerate the likelihood of bad outcomes to the extent that they perceive they lack control over the situations leading to them.[16] By implication, ethnic divides have the potential to intensify and broaden the number of people affected by collective action problems when people understand these problems in terms of ethnicity. Thus, the impetus for ethnic conflict comes from collective action problems that ethnicity itself does not create. A great deal of ethnic conflict, it is ventured, can be explained as the result of just such ethnically inflected collective action problems.

Crucially, this does *not* predict that ethnic divides always or even often lead to choices of conflictual strategies. For one thing, no claim is made that ethnic divides make people *certain* that a potential partner will defect, at least not always. Furthermore, not all situations involve collective action problems and not all collective action problems have the potential to impact individuals' life chances to the same extent. So long as there is no perceived *certainty* of defection given a collective action problem, there is always a possibility that the expected gains from cooperation could be "worth the risk" for would-be cooperators even when thick ethnic divides greatly exacerbate perceptions of the danger involved. And since ethnicity does not motivate conflict, it is at least potentially possible to resolve a given conflict by addressing the core collective action problem at the heart of it.[17]

Thus, whether conflict occurs will depend on the actual quality of the particular collective action problem, the thickness of any ethnic distinctions involved, other factors influencing how people perceive the collective action problem and available strategies (especially elites' framing strategies), and the actual value of the gains and losses in life chances that are involved. It is worth noting here that elites often have tremendous potential to create, raise the stakes in, and influence perceptions of collective action problems; thus, they are frequently found instigating various forms of ethnic conflict when it can work to their advantage. This logic arguably underlies variation in the occurrence and nonoccurrence of many important forms of ethnic conflict, as is discussed briefly in what follows.

Multiethnic State Failure

States with many ethnic minorities that are thickly distinguished from the centrally dominant group face the collective action problem of union writ large: It is harder for such countries to stay together because their ethnic minority populations are more likely to see themselves as being somehow separated from

---

[16] Slovic, "Perception of Risk."
[17] For example, through in-group policing: Fearon and Laitin, "Explaining Interethnic Cooperation."

control over their fate in the union than would populations perceiving no eth-nic distinctions between themselves and those in power. If we turn to federal states as a well-defined example and require an element of democracy and the universal application of federal principles across state territory for a country to be counted as truly and fully federal, we see that the only federations to disin-tegrate or devolve into massive civil war since at least World War II have been *ethno*federations, federations where at least one region is intentionally associated with a minority ethnic group.[18] The subverted federations include Czechoslo-vakia, the Mali Federation, the Nigerian First Republic, Pakistan (1970–1), the USSR, Yugoslavia, and, depending on one's criteria for "state," Senegambia.

Yet ethnicity does not cause the collective action problem at the heart of these instances of state collapse, meaning that ethnofederal states have multiple means by which they can minimize the collective action problem and survive despite strong internal ethnic divides.[19] One strategy is to establish policies of resource redistribution such that all regions see it as economically beneficial to remain in the union.[20] Another is to decentralize, giving regional group representatives a greater sense of control over their own fates in the union and resources with which future exploitation attempts can be resisted.[21] Ethnofederalism is also compati-ble with consociational solutions.[22] The present author has shown elsewhere how these strategies can be more difficult when the ethnofederation contains a core ethnic region, a single ethnic region that overshadows others in terms of popu-lation and hence perceived potential influence in the union. Core ethnic regions constrain central government autonomy to make collective-action-problem-defusing concessions to minority regions (such as financial redistribution) while simultaneously heightening minority-region fears of domination by the larger group. Hence, all the ethnofederations that have collapsed have had core ethnic regions.[23] At the same time, Chapter 6's discussion of the USSR showed that central leaders like Gorbachev can be capable of negotiating creatively to over-come even these challenges. Thus, the USSR nearly survived, and several other ethnofederations (such as Belgium) have held together despite containing core ethnic regions.

To be sure, nonethnofederal but multiethnic states can fail. And states can collapse in ways that do not involve ethnicity at all. But to the extent ethnicity is involved in state collapse, the logic sketched here suggests that this involve-ment is likely to be through exacerbating the commitment problem of political integration. This approach also expects, however, that this exacerbation can be

---

[18] See Hale, "Divided We Stand" for more precise definitions of "federal," "ethnofederal," and "ethnofederal state collapse." Island microstates are not included in this claim.

[19] This recasts somewhat Riker's claim that local identities, including ethnic ones, are a typical source of tension in federal systems. The problem is not the identification itself, although ethnic divides can exacerbate collective action problems that federalism can involve. See William H. Riker, *Federalism: Origin, Operation, Significance* (Boston: Little, Brown, 1964).

[20] Treisman, *After the Deluge.*

[21] Horowitz, *Ethnic Groups in Conflict*; Amoretti and Bermeo, *Federalism and Territorial Cleavages.*

[22] Lijphart, *Democracy in Plural Societies.*

[23] Hale, "Divided We Stand."

successfully counteracted through central state policies and institutions that build on regional interests in cooperation and provide assurance that cooperation, not exploitation, will be the norm.

The Failure or Nonoccurrence of International Integration Projects

These same considerations generate expectations as to when we are likely to see international integration efforts succeed, fail, or begin in the first place. For one thing, we might expect them to be easier to pull off when the groups that are dominant in the relevant states perceive no significant ethnic divides between them. Hence the swift integration of East and West Germany after the Soviet collapse and the merger of North and South Yemen in the same year. Likewise, while Rector and Ziblatt convincingly demonstrate that economic and political considerations rather than "identity motives" drove statelets originally to form the Australian and German federations, respectively, surely the absence of thick interstate ethnic cleavages dividing these statelets from each other facilitated the integration process in that it meant the absence of one important tendency to exaggerate perceived risks of exploitation involved in integration.[24] Nevertheless, given all the uncertainties and transactions costs involved in integration as well as the exaggeration of dangers that thick ethnic distinctions can bring, international integration has been extremely rare and, where it has advanced, frequently tenuous and limited.

The most promising projects among significantly ethnically differentiated states are likely to be those where integrating countries face significant possible gains and go to extraordinary lengths to tackle the collective action problem, making highly credible commitments that the union will not be exploitative. This attitude has long been seen as the strength of the European Union project, which began with highly technical forms of cooperation that could be presented as extremely low risk but potentially beneficial to the economies of the countries involved. After years of establishing the credibility of the EU's nonexploitative promise, and indeed after making good on promises to support the development of its less-well-off member states, it came to take on momentum.[25] This achievement is particularly remarkable given the long and tragic history of warfare among the nations involved. Indeed, even ethnic regions whose leaders had loudly refused to cede even an ounce of sovereignty when it came to the USSR wasted no time in joining the EU when they gained the opportunity, as was the case with all three Baltic states.

Credibility is also influenced by the same kind of institutional features that are important for ethnofederations: Just as core ethnic regions tend to destabilize ethnofederal states, so can the presence of a single, overly large, and potentially dominating country undermine international integration efforts. Thus, Russia,

---

[24] Rector, *Federations*; Daniel Ziblatt, *Structuring the State: The Formation of Italy and Germany and the Puzzle of Federalism* (Princeton, NJ: Princeton University Press, 2006).
[25] Haas, *The Uniting of Europe*; Moravcsik, *The Choice for Europe*.

which as a republic in the USSR raised minority region fears of its dominance in that union, continues to inspire wariness even among the most pro-integration states in the CIS. Russia's size is also the primary reason why few in the EU have even conceived of the possibility that Russia might join this initiative. Indeed, the EU is likely facilitated by the fact that no single country is so large that it clearly dominates the rest. Thus, even though a hegemon might be important for promoting international cooperation through the disproportionate underwriting of collective institutions,[26] a hegemon may well have a reverse effect when it comes to prospects for actual state integration.

The relational theory also implies that sets of countries that expect particularly large benefits from integration will be more likely to take on the risks of integration. These gains might be economic, as early theorists of the European Union posited would be derived from high levels of economic development.[27] They might also come in the security realm, when state leaders calculate that integration is worth the risk of internal exploitation because the risks of conquest or other forms of exploitation coming from an outside source are seen to be greater. Indeed, a common interest in resisting British rule helped bring together the original United States, and the Baltic countries' decision to join the EU was surely partly influenced by a popular desire to secure these countries against Russian revanche. The Soviet threat also undoubtedly facilitated the initiation of the European Union project.

Deadly Violence within and between States

It would be consistent with the relational theory to posit that ethnic violence results from one of two sources: ethnically charged collective action problems where the stakes in terms of life chances are extraordinarily great or situations in which individuals can benefit (as by gaining power or wealth) by intensifying these collective action problems. That is, conflict is not an expression of ethnicity. It is more likely to be a strategy influenced by an ethnic interpretation of a situation. And when some people in a society believe they can benefit if more people interpret situations in terms of ethnicity, conflict has proven to be an extraordinarily effective way to thicken ethnic categories, making them meaningful and accessible for people in interpreting how the world will affect them.

Due to their properties as convenient and meaningful rules of thumb for interpreting situations, ethnic divides tend to be resorted to as uncertainty rises in situations where the actions of others can have great importance for people's life chances. Unfortunately, thick ethnic divides that cut between a set of people and power holders can also accentuate these people's sense that they lack control over events, thereby leading them to attach greater likelihood to the dangers involved in a given situation of uncertainty. When the sense of danger is acute, people can come to see violence as a strategy for regaining some control and mitigating the

[26] Keohane, *After Hegemony.*
[27] Haas, *The Uniting of Europe.*

collective action problem. This may mean attempting to solve a perceived local manifestation of the problem (assaulting a neighbor) or attempting to "send a message" that one's group will not be pushed around. Periods of massive economic upheaval and war can generate the kind of intensely felt uncertainty where people see major implications for their life chances. Even though violence might well sometimes erupt spontaneously, either out of emotion[28] or local considerations,[29] elites frequently play roles in promoting violent as opposed to more peaceful strategies in reaction to the collective action problems involved.[30]

This meddling helps explain why some researchers have found that ethnic violence tends to flare up during periods of transition, even transition to institutions that are meant to improve individuals' actual control over their own lives, such as democracy.[31] This is because these transitions can create uncertainty as to ultimate outcomes – indeed, Przeworski writes that stable democracy's essential feature is in fact "institutionalized uncertainty."[32] Especially when the "institutionalized" part is also uncertain, existing ethnic divides can become attractive as rules of thumb for converting this aversive uncertainty into more manageable risk. And sometimes this risk assessment leads to choices of conflictual strategies. Even decentralization, granting more power to a regionally dominant ethnic group, can create conflict-inducing uncertainty when local minorities fear that the regionally dominant group might radically curtail their life chances. The most intractable violent conflicts that broke out as the USSR decentralized, therefore, have involved the dominant Russians in only two cases (Transdniestria and Chechnya) and have pitted regionally dominant groups against regional minorities in three (the Abkhaz and South Ossetians in Georgia and the Armenians in Azerbaijan).

When levels of uncertainty are great and the perceived implications for life chances immense, ethnicity is sometimes invoked and thickened as an uncertainty-reducing device even when it might seem to rational outsiders not to fit a given situation at all. This can happen when there is no other simple, immediately accessible explanation that serves this uncertainty-reducing function in a better way given the perceived pressing need for immediate guidance in such dire circumstances.[33] Dominated groups facing, for example, economic catastrophe can find it tempting to reduce their plight's uncertainty by seeing domination as the source of all their ills, even when members of the dominant group are also hit hard by and clearly did not intend to promote a given catastrophe. Some nationalist rhetoric in the Soviet republics had such a ring at times. Dominant

---

[28] Petersen, *Understanding Ethnic Violence.*

[29] Stathis N. Kalyvas, *The Logic of Violence in Civil War* (New York: Cambridge University Press, 2006).

[30] Brass, *Theft of an Idol.* Kaufman, *Modern Hatreds,* also nicely discusses important interplay between elites and masses in expressing and manipulating the "ethnic" concerns that he characterizes.

[31] Snyder, *From Voting to Violence.*

[32] Adam Przeworski, *Democracy and the Market* (New York: Cambridge University Press, 1991).

[33] Recall the findings of Kurzban, Tooby, and Cosmides, "Can Race Be Erased?"

groups suffering from the same economic catastrophe might explain their plight as a result of ethnic conspiracy or see a solution in gaining firmer control over their lives through ethnic cleansing. This latter sort of thinking seems to have characterized interwar Germany, for example. Indeed, much research in psychology as well as in other fields of social science has found that situations of great social uncertainty can generate rises in ethnic thinking, replete with conspiracy theories and other myths of rival groups' cohesiveness and threatening intent. Consequently, people both think and act more cohesively in preparation for potential threats that the rise of uncertainty has rendered less predictable. One very good example is hostility toward immigrants, which Alexseev demonstrates is highly correlated with precisely such factors in countries ranging from Russia to the United States.[34]

Indeed, ethnicity's power and attractiveness as an uncertainty-reducing device (and not an unbiased one) helps explain a kind of vicious cycle that massive upheavals can set in motion. A situation of uncertainty that greatly threatens life chances can lead people to interpret these situations through perceptible ethnic divides when simple, obvious alternatives are not immediately accessible. Yet as psychological research shows, the perception of a threat based upon group categorization tends to make these groups much more robust. In particular, such threats tend to produce a rise in group cohesion, ingroup favoritism, a greater willingness of individuals to accept centralized leadership of the group, reduced communication between groups, an increase in distrust, and a greater emphasis on winning over considering the merits of the particular issue at stake.[35] This effect is particularly well documented in wartime, when uncertainty runs rampant and people's very lives and livelihoods are unambiguously at stake.[36] Indeed, wars frequently lead to the "ethnicization" of the other, as has been seen many times in the United States, from the rise in anti-German stereotypes during World War I, anti-Japanese sentiment during World War II, and prejudices against Arabs and Muslims during the "war on terror." Thus, even though many see conflict primarily as a *result* of group solidarity, psychological research finds strikingly little evidence this is true.[37] Instead, although thicker ethnic divides may be more likely to be invoked to interpret a given collective action problem in a way that makes conflictual responses seem like viable strategies, conflict itself can play an extremely important role in thickening ethnic identification as a rule of thumb for navigating the conflict. At their thickest, these identifications can essentially be seen as schemas that virtually dictate conflictual strategies. These sorts of situations can also trigger emotional responses, which can reinforce the

[34] Mikhail Alexseev, *Immigration Phobia and the Security Dilemma: Russia, Europe, and the United States* (New York: Cambridge University Press, 2006).

[35] Forsyth, *Group Dynamics*, p. 388; Tajfel, "Social Psychology," p. 15; Van der Dennen, "Ethnocentrism," pp. 35–6.

[36] Shils, "Primordial, Personal"; Tajfel, "Social Psychology," p. 15.

[37] Some research even finds that more cohesive groups are more likely to employ cooperative strategies in prisoners' dilemma situations. See Brown, *Group Processes*, 1st edition, pp. 200–5.

conflictual strategies by even further reducing the range of considerations people bring to bear in choosing among available courses of action.[38]

At the same time, ethnic divides do not actually motivate conflict and ethnic identification is rarely so thick as to turn uncertainty into actual certainty (as opposed to risk), so there usually remains a very important sense in which ordinary material or political incentives can influence whether people resort to violent strategies. Indeed, the role of *mass* economic interests is often neglected in studies of ethnic conflict.[39]

A comparison of Russian irredentas in the former USSR illustrates how people's material interests might factor into an explanation. There are four cases where ethnic Russians outside Russia are concentrated in territories that would be plausibly separable from their host Soviet successor state. These are the Russians in and around the Estonian city of Narva, those in Ukraine's Crimean peninsula, those in the Transdniestria region of Moldova, and those in northern Kazakhstan. Only one of these irredentas, Transdniestria, has turned violent. Why? The answer is not simply emotional resentment or general cultural antipathy[40]: The author conducted extensive interviews among ethnic Russian leaders in northern Kazakhstan in 1994 and can attest that resentment against Kazakhs there was extremely high, yet no sustained violence broke out.[41] Nor is the possession of institutional resources the explanation[42]: Crimea was the only one of these four territories to be granted autonomy, yet it has also remained peaceful. Some have also noted that the Russian military openly backed up the Transdniestrian separatists, giving them the capacity for rebellion that others lacked,[43] but this still leaves us wondering why the Russians gave these particular irredentists and not others this capacity to rebel. Plus surely at least some Russian elites in other republics, elites with the capacity to spark violence, might have expected Russian Federation aid in their time of need should violence have broken out in this region. This expectation would be especially reasonable as Russia came to adopt protecting ethnic Russians in its "near abroad" as one of its top public foreign policy priorities.

The best explanation, one might venture, should incorporate economic considerations along with the tendency for people in these states to assess their life chances through the uncertainty-reducing mechanism of ethnicity. Russians in Estonia perceived and continue to perceive Estonia as more economically

---

[38] Petersen, *Understanding Ethnic Violence*.

[39] Petersen (*Understanding Ethnic Violence*) is something of an exception since material considerations factor into his "resentment" narrative.

[40] As Petersen's *Understanding Ethnic Violence* and Horowitz's *Ethnic Groups in Conflict* would variously seem to hold.

[41] Laitin, "Secessionist Rebellion," provides a systematic analysis of survey evidence in these countries that bolsters the argument that cultural hostilities were not the cause of violence in the set of cases considered here.

[42] As is the implication of arguments such as Cornell, "Autonomy." There is also nothing peculiar about Moldova by which Toft's theory of geographical symbolic indivisibility would seem to explain the outcome: Toft, *The Geography*.

[43] Laitin, "Secessionist Rebellion"; Kaufman, *Modern Hatreds*.

developed than Russia and themselves as better off materially than the average Russian in Russia, dampening support for irredentist strategies. Ukraine was seen as being roughly at the same level of development as Russia, reducing the intensity with which Crimeans reacted to Ukrainian independence. In Kazakhstan and Moldova, ethnic Russians reacted with alarm to the USSR's breakup because they suddenly found themselves in significantly less-developed countries. Moldova was even considering joining Romania in the early 1990s, and Romania was seen by many Russians as being yet another step down the ladder of economic status. Additionally, the ethnic Russian territories were the most economically developed parts of both Kazakhstan and Moldova. Yet in the face of ethnic Russian alarm, Kazakhstan went to great lengths to accommodate its ethnic Russians, in part by pursuing reintegrationist policies vis-à-vis Russia and only gradually breaking institutional ties with it (e.g., leaving the ruble zone as late as autumn 1993). Ukraine also provided concessions to its Crimean Russians, not in the form of reintegrationist policies but in the form of granting Crimea formal status as Ukraine's only autonomous ethnic region.

But Moldova reacted very differently: It pursued a strongly separatist course, granted few concessions to its Russian minority, and even allowed local Moldovans to arm themselves, all while initially considering bringing the entire country under the control of a state seen by many Russians as not only ethnically alien but also less prosperous.[44] One must keep in mind that economic considerations are not merely a few extra dollars when the question of political integration is involved but reflect long-term expectations of one's own life chances. Thus, such considerations, combined with the tendency to judge one's prospects (reduce uncertainty) through the lens of ethnic difference, arguably played an important role in why Moldova became the only country in which sustained ethnic violence involved an ethnic Russian minority.

All this puts leaders in good position to impact whether violence occurs since they frequently have the power to directly minimize or exacerbate collective action problems (as through outright attacks, warmongering, or deliberately incendiary activity), to manipulate how people interpret these collective action problems (including whether they are framed in ethnic terms), and to influence how individuals understand their range of options. They can also attempt to thicken ethnic categories in ways that facilitate desired outcomes or to increase the situational accessibility of these categories, making them more likely to be invoked by people as means of uncertainty reduction. Sometimes this can be done through media manipulation[45] or, as was illustrated in Chapter 7, by wording referenda. Several studies provide evidence that another effective strategy can be to deliberately provoke violence so as to set in motion the kind of vicious cycle of ethnic identity thickening described earlier. Wilkinson's study of Hindu–Muslim riots in India, for example, documents how hardline Hindu nationalist politicians

---

[44] One interesting discussion of these developments is an MA thesis by Timothy Buchen, Russian and East European Studies program, Indiana University.
[45] Snyder and Ballantine, "Nationalism and the Marketplace."

sometimes defeat moderates and win office by provoking ethnic polarization, a pattern he also detects regarding lynchings in the American South and Catholic–Protestant riots in Ireland.[46]

Indeed, by one count, a discourse of ethnic divide has been used in close to two-thirds of all sustained armed conflicts.[47] This pattern testifies not that ethnicity caused these conflicts but that ethnicity has unusually strong potential both to exacerbate preexisting collective action problems and to supply a plausible "master narrative" that can tie together civil wars' disparate elements[48] in publics' eyes, even where ethnicity was not involved in the initiation of violence.

IMPLICATIONS FOR POLICY: FINDING SOLUTIONS TO ETHNIC CONFLICT

In some ways, the relational theory of ethnic politics suggests optimism in the endeavor to end and ultimately prevent ethnic conflict. Many theories posit that ethnicity inherently sows the seeds of conflict wherever it appears, but this book has argued that there is no inherently conflictual urge associated with ethnicity. Instead, ethnicity mainly serves as a way of interpreting the social world, with ethnic politics (actual human behavior) being driven by a variety of other motives that might make the realm of interethnic relations positive-sum rather than zero-sum as the most pessimistic accounts would have it. This possibility may hold out the hope that we can go beyond just containing ethnic conflict to actually preventing or eradicating it.

At the same time, this book does not agree that ethnicity is epiphenomenal, an argument that might tempt some to ignore ethnicity as nothing more than post hoc spin put on events for the sake of hiding or legitimating all and sundry dirty deeds. We cannot ignore ethnicity because it is not a perfect or even unbiased reducer of uncertainty. Instead, there is evidence that ethnic interpretations of collective action problems can unnecessarily involve innocent people in conflicts and lead many to exaggerate the perceived likelihood of maltreatment at the hands of members of other groups. Ethnicity does not inherently produce conflict, but under some circumstances, it may magnify the fear or mistrust that can lead some to consider conflictual strategies to be among their most promising options.

This position suggests that solutions to ethnic conflict, in the most general sense, may do best to take one of two forms once the nature of a given problem is sufficiently studied. In some cases, it may be possible to somehow supplant, diminish, or remove ethnicity as a shorthand for assessing likely outcomes in collective action problems. This would serve to avoid drawing innocents into conflicts merely on the basis of their belonging to an ethnic category. It may also reduce the degree to which people exaggerate the chances of noncooperative outcomes and thus seriously consider conflictual strategies. In principle, at least, it may be

[46] Wilkinson, *Votes and Violence*.
[47] Toft, *The Geography*, p. 3.
[48] Kalyvas, *The Logic*.

good to avoid structuring political systems along ethnic lines or otherwise insti-
tutionalizing "ethnic thinking" in the state.

Of course, ethnic thinking is frequently embedded in society even when the
state does not formally recognize it. Whole systems of interaction and ways
of life can be structured around ethnic differences without state support. The
state may be able to counteract some of the worst manifestations of this phenomenon. For example, it is surely a good thing for states actively to combat
racism or other forms of ethnic chauvinism through education and the promotion of norms through legal sanctions and campaigns. While people may well
have a natural tendency to resort to ethnic stereotypes to navigate the social
world, these are always lazy and imperfect strategies that can frequently lead to
folly or tragedy. People sometimes need to be challenged to become aware of
their unconscious tendencies so as to actively combat them and ultimately overcome them. But given how complex society is and how established much of this
ethnic thinking is (including as coordination equilibria[49]), such state endeavors
to change social thinking about ethnicity may take decades, perhaps even gener-
ations, to succeed. And one has to be very careful not to turn the battle against
stereotyping and discrimination into a battle for assimilation, which can impose
disproportionate costs on minority groups and can accordingly backfire, heightening a sense that a group's life chances are under attack. Thus, we cannot expect
instant success in reducing, preventing, or ending ethnic conflict when ethnic
divides are already deeply ingrained as ways in which average people navigate the
social world (including the world of politics). In any case, scholars should surely
invest great energy into better understanding exactly how and when ethnicity is
invoked as an uncertainty-reducing rule of thumb, when it can be supplanted by
other rules of thumb, and how societies can best take advantage of ethnic diversity while eliminating the kind of ethnic thinking that fosters mistrust and makes
conflictual behavior more likely.[50]

Unfortunately, some instances of ethnic conflict simply cannot wait for a study
or for intergenerational change. Ongoing violence requires immediate solutions,
as do any forms of behavior that injure or denigrate people. Given how deeply
and how quickly ethnic thinking can become embedded in society, it is likely to
be impossible to eradicate it or alter it quickly enough to solve any given ongoing
conflict. Removing reference to communal divides from state institutions will
not, at this point, end sectarian violence in Iraq. Nor will removing any mention
of ethnicity in Rwandan law instantly heal society and prevent renewed violence
there.

In such situations, where conflicts are ongoing and ethnic differences entrenched, the best solutions are likely to be those that find some way to accommodate the particular differences that have become implicated in the conflicts.
This is the second general form that solutions to ethnic conflict might take. In

---

[49] Hardin, *One For All*; Laitin, *Nations, States, and Violence.*
[50] One pioneering study is Kurzban, Tooby, and Cosmides, "Can Race Be Erased?"

some cases this may mean adopting ethnofederalism.[51] In different situations consociationalism may be more desirable.[52] In still other instances, gerrymandering to produce minority–majority districts may be appropriate.[53] Perhaps all three and more may be called for in some places.

Naturally, all such solutions must be crafted very cautiously in at least two senses. First, they must be carefully constructed so as actually to solve the problem. For example, the present author has argued that ethnofederalism tends to work reasonably well unless it is structured in a way that produces a core ethnic region, in which case there is a good chance that the ethnofederal state will collapse.[54] Second, they must be designed in ways that can both diminish the number and intensity of collective action problems with major implications for people's life chances and promote a long-run de-ethnification of any remaining collective action problems of importance. Finding a workable solution is likely to be quite difficult, although not impossible.

The European Union may be an example of an emerging workable solution. There is at least preliminary evidence that this gradual integration process, not overtly challenging any member nation-state's sovereignty, is creating a sense of European commonality that is grounded in a hard economic and increasingly political community. That is, individual Europeans' life chances are coming to depend more and more heavily on their belonging to the European Union, giving people a greater stake in cooperation and making them more willing to accept the risk of exploitation that has not been fully escaped but that has been minimized. Of course, the EU itself may yet fail. But its successes to date, especially remarkable given that its core members were at full-scale war with each other within living memory, are testimony to the hope that ethnic conflict is not inevitable or unsolvable. If ethnicity is about uncertainty reduction rather than conflict, and if ethnic politics is about interests, then there is hope for aligning interests and managing uncertainty in ways that promote cooperation.

---

[51] Amoretti and Bermeo, *Federalism and Territorial Cleavages*; Horowitz, *Ethnic Groups in Conflict*.

[52] Lijphart, *Democracy in Plural Societies*.

[53] Jane Mansbridge, "Should Blacks Represent Blacks and Women Represent Women? A Contingent 'Yes,'" *The Journal of Politics*, v.61, no.3, August 1999, pp. 628–57.

[54] Hale, "Divided We Stand."

Index

history
  discipline of, 2
  role in ethnicity, 22–4, 42–3, 46
    in Eurasia, 94–117
Hogg, Michael, 38, 49
Horowitz, Donald, 41, 53–4, 249
Hroch, Miroslav, 71
Hrushevsky, Mykhailo, 101
Hurenko, Stanislav, 146, 166, 173,
    177
Hutu. *See* Rwanda

identification with social group. *See*
    identity; ethnicity
  motivations for. *See*
    ethnicity-as-conflictual theories;
    ethnicity-as-epiphenomenal
    theories; relational theory;
    belonging; comfort of home;
    dignity; identity; material interests;
    self-esteem; status;
    uncertainty-reduction
identity. *See also* ethnicity
  debate on whether to discard the term,
    25
  definition of, 34
  expression of as source of separatism, 6
  identity repertoires, 28
  personal identity, 29, 40
  as pursued for its own sake, 17, 29, 32
  relational theory of, 34–40
  social identity. *See* age; class; ethnicity;
    gender
  Social Identity Theory (SIT). *See also*
    Social Identity Theory (SIT)
  switching of identities, 28
Igbo, 1, 57, 67
immigrants, hostility to, 259
India, 64, 81, 159, 167, 249–52
  Hindu-Muslim riots in, 1, 25–6,
    261
industrialization, 22–3, 28
instinct, 51–2, 54
institutions. *See also* consociationalism,
    democracy; federalism;
    ethnofederalism
  as aggregators of interests in separatism,
    57, 78, 84–7, 89, 92
  as cause of ethnic identification, 58, 91
  as cause of state collapse, 8, 30
  change in

as cause of ethnic conflict, 258
as cause of separatism, 82, 88, 92
how process of change can avoid
    separatism, 82, 126
as culturally distinctive public good, 20
ethnic symbols embedded in, 54
as link between mass and elite interests,
    162, 165–8
of patronage distribution, 30
as solutions to commitment problem in
    union, 81
as source of group-oriented behavior
    (groupness), 24
as source of identity repertoires, 27–8
interests, of ethnic region, definition of,
    65, 162
internal colonialism, 46
international integration, 3, 23, 31, 57–90,
    92, 190–215, 244, 256–7
international relations. *See also*
    international integration;
    separatism; war; Commonwealth of
    Independent States; European
    Union
  theory of, 61, 190
  hegemonic stability theory, 257
  promise of relational theory for,
    214–15
Iraq, 1, 263
Ireland, 67, 262
irredentas, and ethnic conflict, 260–1
Islam, 5, 105, 182. *See also* Islamic
    Renaissance Party
Islamic Renaissance Party, 181–2
Ivashko, Volodymyr, 123–4, 160, 165,
    166, 173, 175–7

Kalyvas, Stathis, 26
Kanazawa, Satoshi, 49
Karimov, Bahtiar, 131, 182
Karimov, Islom, 124
  and August 1991 coup attempt, 136
  and CIS, 206, 208–9
  and deadly riots in Uzbekistan, 167–8
  motivations of, 160
  and New Union Treaty, 128
  and presidential election of 1991, 188
  and regional political machines, 167
  rise to power of, 167, 186–7, 207
  and Soviet subsidies to Uzbekistan,
    184–5

Wolfgang C. Müller and Kaare Strøm, *Policy, Office, or Votes?*

Maria Victoria Murillo, *Labor Unions, Partisan Coalitions, and Market Reforms in Latin America*

Ton Notermans, *Money, Markets, and the State: Social Democratic Economic Policies since 1918*

Aníbal Pérez-Liñán, *Presidential Impeachment and the New Political Instability in Latin America*

Roger Petersen, *Understanding Ethnic Violence: Fear, Hatred, and Resentment in Twentieth-Century Eastern Europe*

Simona Piattoni, ed., *Clientelism, Interests, and Democratic Representation*

Paul Pierson, *Dismantling the Welfare State? Reagan, Thatcher, and the Politics of Retrenchment*

Marino Regini, *Uncertain Boundaries: The Social and Political Construction of European Economies*

Jonathan Rodden, *Hamilton's Paradox: The Promise and Peril of Fiscal Federalism*

Marc Howard Ross, *Cultural Contestation in Ethnic Conflict*

Lyle Scruggs, *Sustaining Abundance: Environmental Performance in Industrial Democracies*

Jefferey M. Sellers, *Governing from Below: Urban Regions and the Global Economy*

Yossi Shain and Juan Linz, eds., *Interim Governments and Democratic Transitions*

Beverly Silver, *Forces of Labor: Workers' Movements and Globalization since 1870*

Theda Skocpol, *Social Revolutions in the Modern World*

Regina Smyth, *Candidate Strategies and Electoral Competition in the Russian Federation: Democracy without Foundation*

Richard Snyder, *Politics after Neoliberalism: Reregulation in Mexico*

David Stark and László Bruszt, *Postsocialist Pathways: Transforming Politics and Property in East Central Europe*

Sven Steinmo, Kathleen Thelen, and Frank Longstreth, eds., *Structuring Politics: Historical Institutionalism in Comparative Analysis*

Susan C. Stokes, *Mandates and Democracy: Neoliberalism by Surprise in Latin America*

Susan C. Stokes, ed., *Public Support for Market Reforms in New Democracies*

Duane Swank, *Global Capital, Political Institutions, and Policy Change in Developed Welfare States*

Sidney Tarrow, *Power in Movement: Social Movements and Contentious Politics*

Kathleen Thelen, *How Institutions Evolve: The Political Economy of Skills in Germany, Britain, the United States, and Japan*

Charles Tilly, *Trust and Rule*

Daniel Treisman, *The Architecture of Government: Rethinking Political Decentralization*

Lily Lee Tsai, *Accountability without Democracy: How Solidary Groups Provide Public Goods in Rural China*